State Crime in the

*In memory of all the victims of state crime,
and with hope for a future where human needs
truly take precedence over state power.*

State Crime in the Global Age

Edited by
**William J. Chambliss,
Raymond Michalowski and
Ronald C. Kramer**

WILLAN
PUBLISHING

Published by

Willan Publishing
Culmcott House
Mill Street, Uffculme
Cullompton, Devon
EX15 3AT, UK
Tel: +44(0)1884 840337
Fax: +44(0)1884 840251
e-mail: info@willanpublishing.co.uk
Website: www.willanpublishing.co.uk

Published simultaneously in the USA and Canada by

Willan Publishing
c/o ISBS, 920 NE 58th Ave, Suite 300,
Portland, Oregon 97213-3786, USA
Tel: +1(0)503 287 3093
Fax: +1(0)503 280 8832
e-mail: info@isbs.com
Website: www.isbs.com

First published 2010

ISBN 978-1-84392-703-7 paperback
      978-1-84392-704-4 hardback

British Library Cataloguing-in-Publication Data

A catalogue record for this book is available from the British Library

FSC
Mixed Sources
Product group from well-managed
forests and other controlled sources
Cert no. SGS-COC-2482
www.fsc.org
© 1996 Forest Stewardship Council

Project managed by Deer Park Productions, Tavistock, Devon
Typeset by TW Typesetting, Plymouth, Devon
Printed and bound by T J International Ltd, Trecerus Industrial Estate, Padstow, Cornwall

Contents

Figures and tables   *vii*

Abbreviations   *viii*

Notes on contributors   *ix*

Preface   *xiii*

1   Introduction   1
    Raymond Michalowski, William J. Chambliss and Ronald C. Kramer

Part One: Framing State Crime

2   In search of 'state and crime' in state crime studies   13
    Raymond Michalowski

3   The centrality of empire in the study of state crime and
    violence   31
    Peter Iadicola

4   Obligatory sacrifice and Imperial projects   45
    Frank Pearce

5   Toward a prospective criminology of state crime   67
    David O. Friedrichs

Part Two: The Brutal Realities of State Crime

6   Modern institutionalized torture as state-organized crime   83
    Martha K. Huggins

7   War as corporate crime   103
    Vincenzo Ruggiero

8   From Guernica to Hiroshima to Baghdad: the normalization
    of the terror bombing of civilians   118
    Ronald C. Kramer

9   The neo-liberal state of exception in occupied Iraq   134
    David Whyte

10 China's aid policy toward economically weakened states: a case of state criminality?   152
Dawn L. Rothe

11 Framing innocents: the wrongly convicted as victims of state harm   170
Saundra D. Westervelt and Kimberly J. Cook

12 Prosecutorial overcharging as state crime?   187
Lauren N. Lang

Part Three: Responding to State Crime

13 The politics of harm reduction policies   199
William J. Chambliss, Jonathan William Anderson and Tanya Whittle

14 The globalization of transitional justice   215
Elizabeth Stanley

15 The reason of state: theoretical inquiries and consequences for the criminology of state crime   232
Athanasios Chouliaras

16 Epilogue: toward a public criminology of state crime   247
Ronald C. Kramer, Raymond Michalowski and William J. Chambliss

References   262

Index   294

Figures and tables

Figures

2.1	The state crime wedding cake	23
4.1	Schema for human sacrifice – all moments ritualizable	50
4.2	Dominant discourses of sacrifice in the contemporary United States	53
4.3	Aztec sacrifices	61
4.4	US society, sacrifice and repression	65
10.1	Growth of Africa's exports to China since 1992	163
10.2	Share of regions in China's export, per cent	164

Tables

2.1	State crime: definitional variants	17
2.2	Models for defining state crime: strengths and weaknesses	20
2.3	State theories and state types	28
10.1	Quotas and voting power of selected industrial countries in 2000	158

Abbreviations

CCSA	Canadian Centre on Substance Abuse
CIA	Central Intelligence Agency
CPA	Coalition Provisional Authority
DFI	Development Fund for Iraq
DRC	Democratic Republic of Congo
ESAF	Enhanced structural adjustment facility
FBI	Federal Bureau of Investigation
FDHA	Federal Department of Home Affairs
HIG	High-Value Detainee Interrogation Group
HRDAG	Human Rights Data Analysis Group
IAMB	International Advisory and Monitoring Board
IBRD	International Bank for Reconstruction and Development
ICC	International Criminal Court
ICRC	International Committee of the Red Cross
ICSID	International Centre for Settlement of Investment Disputes
ICTJ	International Center for Transitional Justice
ICTR	International Criminal Tribunal for Rwanda
ICTY	International Criminal Tribunal for the former Yugoslavia
IDA	International Development Association
IFC	International Finance Corporation
IFI	International financial institution
IMF	International Monetary Fund
INCB	International Narcotics Control Board
MHRA	Medicines and Healthcare products Regulatory Agency
MIGA	Multilateral Investment Guarantee Agency
NAFTA	North American Free Trade Agreement
NAOMI	North American Opiate Maintenance Initiative
NGO	Non-governmental organization
NSA	National Security Archive
NSC	National Security Council
PSA	Production Sharing Agreement
PSD	Private sector development
SAP	Structural adjustment policy
SIGIR	Special Inspector General for Iraq Reconstruction
TNC	Transnational corporation
UDHR	Universal Declaration of Human Rights
UNODC	United Nations Office on Drugs and Crime
UNSCR	United Nations Security Council Resolution
WB	World Bank
WHO	World Health Organization
WTO	World Trade Organization

Notes on contributors

Jonathan William Anderson holds a BA degree in Criminal Justice from the George Washington University and a JD from New York University School of Law. Since 2001, he has been a staff attorney with the Public Defender Service for the District of Columbia representing indigent clients facing trial, collateral proceedings, or appeals. He is also part of the Public Defender Service's Appellate Division and a Professorial Lecturer in the Sociology Department of George Washington University.

William J. Chambliss is Professor of Sociology at the George Washington University and past President of the American Society of Criminology and the Society for the Study of Social Problems. He has published over 25 books, including *Law, Order and Power* (with Robert Seidman) (1971), *On the Take* (1988), and *Power, Politics and Crime* (2000), as well as numerous scholarly articles in sociology, criminology and law. His awards include a Doctorate of Laws, University of Guelph, Guelph, Ontario, Canada, 1999, the 2009 Lifetime Achievement Award from the American Sociological Association Division on Law, the 2009 Lifetime Achievement Award of the Society for the Study of Social Problems Division on Law and Society, the 2001 Edwin H. Sutherland Award from the American Society of Criminology, the 1995 Major Achievement Award from the American Society of Criminology, the 1986 Distinguished Leadership in Criminal Justice, Bruce Smith, Sr Award from the Academy of Criminal Justice Sciences, and the 1985 Lifetime Achievement Award from the American Sociological Association Division on Criminology.

Athanasios Chouliaras is an attorney at law in Greece. In addition, he holds an LLM in Criminology from the University of Barcelona, and LLM degrees in Philosophy of Law and the Sociology of Law from the National and Kapodistrian University of Athens. He is currently completing his PhD thesis on state crime, international criminal law and human rights protection at Democritus University of Thrace. He is awarded a research grant from Alexander S. Onassis Public Benefit Foundation.

Kimberly J. Cook is Professor of Sociology and Criminology and Chair of the Department of Sociology and Criminology at the University of North Carolina-Wilmington. Her research interests include the death penalty, abortion rights, violence against women, and restorative justice. She is the author of *Divided Passions: Public Opinions on Abortion and the Death Penalty* (1998), and past Vice President of the Society for the Study of Social Problems. She is a recipient of a Senior Scholar Award from the

Australian-American Fulbright Commission in 2001 where she studied restorative justice.

David O. Friedrichs is Professor of Sociology/Criminal Justice and Distinguished University Fellow at the University of Scranton (Pennsylvania, USA). He is author of *Trusted Criminals* (4th edn 2010) and *Law in Our Lives: An Introduction* (2006), as well as editor of *State Crime*, Volumes I and II (1998). He has authored over 100 scholarly publications, as well as 300 book reviews. He is also former Editor of *Legal Studies Forum* (1985–89), past President of the White Collar Crime Research Consortium (2002–04), and a recipient of the 2005 Lifetime Achievement Award from the Division on Critical Criminology of the American Society of Criminology.

Martha K. Huggins holds the Charles A. and Leo M. Favrot Professor of Human Relations in Sociology at Tulane University, and is a faculty member of Tulane's Roger Thayer Stone Center for Latin American Studies. She is the author of seven books, two of which, *Political Policing: The United States and Latin America* (1998) and *Violence Workers: Torturers and Murderers Reconstruct Brazilian Atrocities* (with Haritos-Fatouros and Zimbardo) (2002) have each received two distinguished book awards. Her most recent book is *Women Fielding Danger: Negotiating Ethnographic Identities in Field Research* (2008).

Peter Iadicola is a Professor and Chair of the Sociology Department at Indiana University – Purdue University in Fort Wayne, Indiana. He has authored more than 35 publications including *Violence, Inequality, and Human Freedom* (2003). His work has focused on crime and violence and most recently the nature of empire and its relationship to forms of violence in the world.

Ronald C. Kramer is Professor of Sociology and Director of the Criminal Justice Program at Western Michigan University. He is the author of a wide range of articles on white collar and corporate crime, and co-author with Dave Kauzlarich of *Crimes of the American Nuclear State* (1998) and with Raymond Michalowski of *State-Corporate Crime: Wrongdoing at the Intersection of Business and Government* (2006). He is also the 2006 recipient of the Lifetime Achievement Award from the American Society of Criminology Division on Critical Criminology.

Lauren N. Lang is a sociology graduate of the University of California – Santa Barbara.

Raymond Michalowski is Regents Professor of Criminology at Northern Arizona University. His publications include *Order, Law and Crime* (1985),

Radikale Kriminologie (1991), *Run for the Wall: Remembering Vietnam on a Motorcycle Pilgrimage* (with Jill Dubisch) (2001), *Crime, Power and Identity: The New Primer in Radical Criminology* (with Michael Lynch) (2004), and *State-Corporate Crime* (with Ron Kramer) (2006), as well as numerous articles on the political economy of crime and punishment, corporate crime, globalization, and law and justice in socialist Cuba. A recipient of the Lifetime Achievement Award of the American Society of Criminology Division on Critical Criminology, his current work focuses on the intersection of moral panic, state crime, and immigration policy.

Frank Pearce is a Professor of Sociology at Queen's University, Kingston and Ontario, Canada. His publications include *Critical Realism and the Social Sciences: Heterodox Elaborations* (with Jon Frauley) (2007), *The Radical Durkheim* (2nd edn 2001), *Toxic Capitalism* (with Steve Tombs) (1998), *Corporate Crime: Contemporary Debates* (with Laureen Snider) (1995), *Global Crime Connections* (with Mike Woodiwiss) (1993), and *Crimes of the Powerful* (1976). He is also the author of numerous articles on crimes of the powerful and the sociology of law, crime and justice. His major current interest is in developing Sociology of Sacrifice.

Dawn L. Rothe is Assistant Professor at Old Dominion University, Department of Sociology and Criminal Justice; Director of the ODU International State Crime Research Consortium; and Chair of the American Society of Criminology Division of Critical Criminology. She is the author of four books including *State Criminality: The Crime of All Crimes* (2009) and *Blood, Power, and Bedlam: Violations of International Criminal Law in Post Colonial Africa* (with Christopher Mullins) (2008) and the author of over three dozen articles and book chapters.

Vincenzo Ruggiero is Professor of Sociology at Middlesex University in London (UK). He has conducted research for the European Commission and the United Nations. His major publications include *Eurodrugs* (1995), *Organized and Corporate Crime in Europe* (1996), *The New European Criminology* (1998), *Crime and Markets* (2000), *Movements in the City* (2001), *Crime in Literature* (2003), *Understanding Political Violence* (2006), and *Penal Abolitionism* (2010).

Elizabeth Stanley is Senior Lecturer in Criminology at Victoria University of Wellington, New Zealand where she teaches and researches on issues of state crimes, human rights, transitional justice and social justice. Her published works include *Torture, Truth and Justice: The Case of Timor-Leste* (2009) and a number of articles on human rights in post-conflict situations.

Saundra D. Westervelt is Associate Professor of Sociology at the University of North Carolina at Greensboro. Her areas of interest include miscarriages of justice and the sociology of law. She is author of *Shifting the Blame: How Victimization Became a Criminal Defense* (1998) and co-editor of *Wrongly Convicted: Perspectives on Failed Justice* (2002).

Tanya Whittle graduated from the University of West Florida in 2006 with a Bachelor of Arts in interdisciplinary social sciences focusing on sociology, criminal justice and psychology. She is currently an MA candidate at the George Washington University studying sociology with a specialization in criminology.

David Whyte is Reader in Sociology at the University of Liverpool. He is co-author of *Safety Crimes* (2007) and co-editor of *Unmasking the Crimes of the Powerful* (2003) and *State, Crime, Power* (2009). His most recent book is *Crimes of the Powerful: A Reader* (2009). His research interests include corporate crime, state crime and the social impacts of counter-terrorism. He has recently completed studies on the social construction and criminalization of deaths and injuries at work, and on the role of corporations in the occupation and reconstruction of Iraq. He is currently a board member of the Centre for Corporate Accountability and an advisor to UK Corporate Watch.

Preface

William J. Chambliss, Raymond Michalowski and Ronald C. Kramer

Were the eye not attuned to the Sun
The Sun could never be seen by it.
                                    Goethe

On 29–30 May 2008, in response to an invitation by the International Institute for the Sociology of Law, we organized and held a workshop on 'State Crime in the Global Age' at the Institute's beautiful facility in Onati, Basque Country, Spain. Each participant presented a paper followed by a lively, often critical, discussion. The papers presented at the workshop, now substantially revised in response to the discussions that took place, constitute the core of the book you hold in your hands.

The papers presented at the conference embody what the philosopher of science T. S. Kuhn referred to as a 'paradigm revolution' currently taking place in criminology. The essence of this revolution is a dramatic break from the traditional criminological paradigm that blindly adopted the state definition of what constitutes a crime and as a consequence focused on 'nuts, sluts, perverts and drug addicts'. Contemporary criminology is replacing the state definition of what constitutes a crime with a more humanistically focused definition of 'social harms'. One important implication of moving from state definitions of crime to a paradigm that incorporates a much broader perspective of 'social harms' is to bring 'state crimes' into sharp relief. The fact that state crimes are rarely exposed or punished in the criminal justice system makes it all the more imperative that social scientists take an active role in exposing, describing and analyzing the social harms of the state.

As will be clear as you read the chapters in this book, many of the crimes discussed are in fact a violation of the criminal law and as such fall under the purview of traditional criminological study. Other crimes dissected and analyzed in this volume, however, are not contained in the criminal law statutes but nonetheless cause serious injuries that cry out for systematic analysis. By co-joining state crimes that are incorporated in the criminal law, including international criminal law, with social harms that have been excluded from the statutes, we open a new and exciting area of inquiry that promises not only to call attention to the importance of shedding the limitations imposed by state and government definitions of reality, but promises also to open significant new areas of research and theory in criminology.

Like all books, this one is the product of the work of many individuals to whom we owe a debt of thanks. We extend our thanks to the International Institute for the Sociology of Law in Onati, Spain for the invitation to organize a state crime workshop, and to all of the Institute staff who worked so diligently to make the workshop a resounding professional and experiential success. We also want to thank all of the workshop participants and contributors to this book who have given the best of their knowledge to advancing our understanding of state crime. And finally, we thank our families, who, as always, have had to endure our long hours of work and obsession that are always part of assembling any book. *Mil esker* to all.

Chapter I

Introduction

*Raymond Michalowski, William J. Chambliss and
Ronald C. Kramer*

> Criminology has managed the astonishing feat of separating the study of
> crime from the contemplation of the state.
>
> Stanley Cohen, *Against Criminology*

Since its inception, the discipline of criminology has served as an
extension of state power. While this is obviously true for applied
criminological research undertaken directly by or in service to government agencies, it is equally true for most basic research in criminology
done in university settings or private research firms. Although, in liberal
democratic societies, these organizations are presumably part of civil
society, the line that separates civil society from the state is often much
thinner than it is presumed to be. To the extent that criminological inquiry
defines its primary subject matter as the causes and control of behaviors
that states have selected for criminalization, it becomes part of the
'ideological apparatuses' whose functions are to promote and preserve the
legitimacy of state power (Althusser 1971). Or, as Foucault (1977) would
have it, criminological knowledge, like all state-approved knowledge, is
an artifact of power.

As part of the power-knowledge apparatus of modern states, criminology has always had a difficult time addressing harmful actions that fall
outside the narrow range of wrongdoings selected by states' condemnation. This is particularly evident when the wrongful acts in question are
committed by states themselves.

Wrongdoing in the state arena can be divided, most broadly, into crimes
against the state and crimes by the state. Crimes in the first category, such
as treason, sedition, theft of government property or terrorism, are
soundly condemned and severely punished. Equally or more injurious
actions such as torture, aggressive war or political repression committed

in the service of state goals are typically either not criminalized by the offender state, or if criminalized, typically investigated and/or prosecuted only after they have served their purpose or failed to advance state interests. A case in point would be the 2009 decision by the Obama Department of Justice (Johnson 2009) to establish a special prosecutor to investigate potential criminal acts of torture committed during the CIA interrogation of suspected terrorists, more than five years after evidence of these crimes had become widespread (Welch 2009).

Even if we limit the definition of state crime to the less problematic category of legally designated crimes against the state, criminological inattention to state crime is notable. Legacy criminology journals in the United States such as *Criminology, Justice Quarterly* and *Journal of Research in Crime and Delinquency* are dense with articles about juvenile delinquents, drug users, murderers and thieves, or about the policies and systems designed to control them. Articles addressing prosecutable state crimes, by contrast, are rare, and criminological inquiry into wrongful but legal acts in service of state interests are almost totally absent. In those instances where wrongful state actions have received attention from US orthodox criminologists, the focus has typically been on crimes of foreign governments, such as the current criminological interest in the crime of genocide (Hagan *et al.* 2005).

Even though criminology emerged as a separate discipline, with its own professional associations such as the American Society of Criminology and the British Society of Criminology, in the decade after the Nuremberg trials ended, and as we detail in the epilogue an important American criminologist played a central role in these prosecutions, there are no canonical works in criminology focusing on war crimes. This is clear testimony that states and their crimes were not part of the founding consciousness of the discipline. Simply put, the criminological canon excludes from its catalogue of concerns most harms against human, animal and environmental well-being committed by states.

Whether democratic or authoritarian, capitalist or communist, every modern state has generated criminological practices whose core theories and research 'findings' validate the vision of social reality favored by political-economic elites (Chambliss 1969; Michalowski 1985; Quinney 1970, 1977). Such practices legitimate the foundational consciousness of the political order in which it operates, dividing injurious actions and actors into the 'dangerous' and the acceptable (Renee 1978).

This reproduction of dominant consciousness frequently occurs even in cases where criminological inquiry calls into question specific governmental practices. In recent years, for instance, many criminologists have questioned government claims that long, mandatory prison sentences are an effective tool in the longstanding US 'war on drugs' (Austin and Irwin 2001). Few of these critical inquiries, however, question the origin or broader implications of the claim that the state has, and ought to have, the right to determine what substances humans can willingly allow into their bodies. Yet this assumption is a prime example of what Foucault (1998: 140) calls 'biopower', that is, 'numerous and diverse techniques for achieving the subjugations of bodies and the control of populations' (1998: 140). Developed as an essential part of the eighteenth-century formation of capitalist political-economies, the right of states to designate legitimate and illegitimate consumption remains dimly and safely lodged in the past, beyond the consciousness of criminologists concerned primarily with whether or not contemporary drug policies are good or bad. Nor do most criminologists concerned with excessively punitive drug laws directly question the right of the state to inflict pain on some people to avoid law violation by others. This right was born with the emergence of utilitarian-ism as core justification for the state in market society, and like the public health authority of the state, operates as a typically unquestioned background assumption of modern state policy (Polanyi 1944/2001: 124–6). Thus, the state's right to discipline our bodies in the most intimate ways by controlling what we eat, smoke or inject, along with the deterrent logic of the penal state, remains unquestioned, even as those seeking a more sensible drug policy chip away at a particular application of state power.

Questioning whether a particular use of state power is effective is far less troubling to an established order than inquiring into the nature of that power in the first instance. Inquiry into the assumptions underlying state power often reveal that which state managers would prefer to remain in the shadows – that the benefits derived from the application of state power typically advance specific group interests and harm others, rather than serving the 'public good' that is the presumed basis of state legitimacy. For instance, while many orthodox criminologists study why people willingly consume drugs defined as illegal by the state, few study how state law facilitates and in some cases even promotes corporate actions that subject tens of millions of people in the United States and around the world to unwanted daily doses of cancer-causing chemicals and other environ-mental pollutants (Burns and Lynch 2004; Lynch and Stretesky 2001).

Criminology's near exclusive attention to state-defined crimes is not the result of intellectual or moral failings on the part of criminologists. The problem is much deeper. It resides in the contradiction inherent in joining the terms 'social' and 'science' into the concept of 'social science'. The dominant idea of 'science', as constructed during the period between 1500 and 1800 CE known as the Enlightenment, holds that analytic inquiry must separate itself from religious beliefs and moral preferences in order to clearly recognize the underlying laws of nature that explain the natural world (Gray 1996). For late medieval and early Renaissance scientists, there was no notion that this scientific model could or should be applied to the world of human behavior. Human actions remained rooted in the theological struggle between good and evil, between moral and immoral action, even if those roots were beginning to weaken. By the early 1700s the rise of the mercantile, capitalist state and the death of rule by divine right required a new justification for state power. The solution was found in the emergent philosophy of utilitarianism, which located both morality and the motivations for human behavior in the natural rather than the metaphysical world – in what Bentham (1780/1973) called 'the twin principles of pleasure and pain'.

A powerful blow to the understanding of human inquiry as moral inquiry came with the 1859 publication of Darwin's *On the Origin of Species*. Darwin and other evolutionary theorists lodged human beings firmly in the world of animals, not the world of angels and devils. As animals responding to laws of nature, humans could be studied with the epistemological tools heretofore reserved primarily for the study of the natural world (Morrison 1995). Thus emerged a new epistemology of social inquiry that saw the human world as governed by social laws of nature just as the physical world was governed by material laws.

One important prescription resulting from the application of the epistemology of natural science to social inquiry is that to be 'scientific', social inquiry must be devoid of moral judgments. This became a potent barrier to criminological inquiry into state crime. The laws made by government are not the consequence of natural forces. They are, at their historical root, statements of the moral preferences of some versus those of others.[1] Consider the laws governing illegal drug use or the laws of theft. In both cases these laws displaced a set of previous cultural and political practices that in the first instance left what people consumed entirely up to them, and in the second instance left the problem of theft in the realm of personal matters to be resolved by individuals not the state (Duster 1970; Hall 1952). Moreover, these changes reflected specific political goals rather than some interest-neutral pursuit of social order (Diamond 1979). Nevertheless, because the passage of time rather quickly buries these interests beneath the weight of established practices, most state law takes on qualities of naturalness and neutrality. To question why state laws are what they are unavoidably locates the researcher in an arena of moral considerations where it is impossible to avoid moral preference. Despite claims to scientific neutrality, inquiry into the nature of state law reveals that any criminological orientation that accepts only those acts that states have decided to criminalize as appropriate topics of inquiry is itself the expression of moral preference.

An epistemology of social science that requires moral detachment from the subject matter being studied is an illusion. Humans studying rocks, plants, fish or quarks inhabit a moral space that differs from that of humans studying other humans. Human beings, as the twentieth-century philosopher and economist Robert Heilbroner (1974) points out, always occupy a moral standpoint relative to other humans, including those they approach as research subjects. Criminologists studying methamphetamine users, for instance, occupy a moral space in which the behavior of the drug users in question is accepted as problematic and therefore eligible for discipline by the state. This is no less a moral preference than a criminologist who elects to study the US invasion and occupation of Iraq in 2003 as a state crime. The only difference is that the drug use in question is condemned by the state, while the war and all its grave harms are not. In short, states and their harmful actions, whether or not those harmful actions are legally defined as crimes, are legitimate and important topics of criminological inquiry.

Beyond normal science

In contrast to orthodox criminology's almost exclusive focus on working-class crime, this volume foregrounds inquiries into crimes and social injuries of state power regardless of their status under law. In doing so it seeks not only to provide analyses of specific state crimes, but also to fracture the normal science, state-oriented consciousness that has rendered criminology a politically captive enterprise since its emergence in the early twentieth century. This book is certainly not the first effort to do so. Since the late 1960s, in Britain, Europe and the United States various schools of thought within criminology have challenged the field's routine acceptance of state definitions of crime. The 'new criminology', 'radical criminology', 'critical criminology', 'feminist criminology', 'cultural criminology' and 'anarchist criminology' have all sought to challenge the dominant state-centric paradigm, and in various ways have contributed to the contemporary critique of states and their crimes (Ross 2009).

The roots of this intellectual movement reach back to the general social upheavals of the 1960s and the early application of symbolic interaction and its offspring, labeling theory and social constructionism, to the problems of law, crime and justice (Becker 1963; Chambliss 1964, 1969; Lemert 1972; Platt 1969; Quinney 1970; Schur 1971; Taylor et al. 1974). Although not specifically concerned with state crime, these early critical analysts challenged the apparent ontology of crime, revealing crime as a social product of political choice and human interaction, not an immutable fact. This opening, fueled by the growing struggles for civil rights and against the US war in Vietnam, prompted a growing recognition that any meaningful analysis of law, crime and justice required analytic attention to be given to the nature and use of power, particularly the political power of the state (Chambliss 1974; Michalowski and Bohlander 1976; Pearce 1976; Platt 1978; Quinney 1974, 1977; Schwendinger and Schwendinger 1970; Takagi 1981; Tifft and Sullivan 1980).

Informed by a new wave of post-McCarthy Marxism in the academy, these inquiries analyzed the role of political-economic arrangements in creating the definitions of crime, framing the practice of justice, and facilitating the social conditions that generated the working-class crimes and urban social unrest that threatened to embarrass the capitalist state's promise that it could deliver social peace.

To use Cohen's (1988) term, each of these 'anti-criminologies' offered valuable insights into the relationship between power, knowledge and the definition of what is crime and who is the criminal. However, to some extent these critical approaches constituted a type of counterculture within criminology. Like other countercultures, much of what came to fit under the broad umbrella of critical criminology was shaped by the culture it sought to counter (Roszak 1969). As a result, the bulk of critical inquiry in criminology continues to focus on the same subsets of crime that hold the attention of more orthodox inquiries – street crimes against property or persons, drug use, domestic violence, and youth deviance involving gangs, graffiti and guns. The result has been a kind of critical orthodoxy devoted to building critiques of and offering alternatives to orthodox approaches to the causes and control of crimes characteristic of less advantaged rather than more advantaged sectors of society. Crimes committed by powerful actors in the world of governments and corporations have played very much a secondary role in critical criminology, just as they have been a secondary concern of orthodox criminology. The result is that even though orthodox and critical criminology frequently ask different questions, they tend to ask them about the same people and the same crimes.

While ordinary criminal law and the routine practices of criminal justice systems have been examined by critical criminologists, the state *qua* state has received relatively little theoretical attention. In some instances critiques of state practices are part of a framework of thought that sees the state as the solution as well as the cause of problems. The goal is often to 'correct' the state by creating better laws and more humane enforcement strategies. Thus, more punishment for domestic abusers and less for marijuana users; more punishment for those who use 'hate' speech and less for juvenile lawbreakers; these are common themes in contemporary critical criminology (Bohm 1993). While pursuing more humane and just state policies is a worthwhile endeavor, doing so needs to be more closely coupled with theoretical analysis of the state that is supposed to serve as the vehicle for rectifying harms for which the state, either through commission or omission, is often responsible.

As long as critical criminology remains largely focused on whether the state is governing the masses through appropriate definitions and prosecutions of interpersonal crimes against individuals or their property, the powerful who operate in a sphere largely separate from the controlled multitude disappear from view, except on those rare occasions when they too commit some ordinary crime.

Because of its focus on expanding the critique of class, race and gender inequities embedded in the capitalist justice systems, critical inquiry in criminology did not initially generate an explicit model of state crime. It did, however, drop a number of breadcrumbs leading in that direction. The intersection of the early insights of radical and critical criminology, together with the cumulative weight of the Vietnam war, the revelations of Watergate, and US support for terrorist 'national security states' in Latin America and Africa, ultimately spurred a small but vibrant new concern with the criminal state among some critical criminologists (Frappier 1985; Huggins 1987; Michalowski and Kramer 1987; Pearce 1976; Quinney 1977; Tifft and Sullivan 1980). In this context of a new concern with governmental wrongdoing, Bill Chambliss (1989), in his American Society of Criminology presidential address, called for the study of 'state-organized crime', which he defined as 'acts defined by law as criminal and committed by state officials in the pursuit of their jobs as representatives of the state'. Chambliss' address became a touchstone for criminologists concerned with either individuals who used state power illegally in service of state interests or the state itself as an organizational deviant. The understanding of state crime began to reach beyond state law to acts that violated international but not national laws, and those that did not specifically violate either, but were so grievous as to be necessarily part of any serious study of state criminality.[2] By the late twentieth century, the study of state crime had grown into a recognizable branch of critical criminological inquiry. Friedrichs (2010), Green and Ward (2004) and Rothe (2009) provide useful overviews of this process. This growth in interest in state crime has been fueled by four external forces: (1) the collapse of the Soviet bloc of nations and the emergence of the United States as the dominant force in a 'new world order'; (2) a growth in the political significance of the international human rights regime first envisioned by the UN Charter and the Universal Declaration of Human Rights; (3) the spread of neo-liberal globalization; and (4) the seeming return of empire as a key element of international politics as symbolized most prominently by the US-UK invasion and occupation of Iraq.

Each of these arenas focused attention on a distinct yet interconnected set of problems. The creation of a 'uni-polar' new world order in which the capitalist states of the Atlantic alliance were able to impose their will on the collapsed economies and governments of the former bloc of both socialist and non-aligned nations, created a new era of global economic exploitation and new relational dynamics between foreign investors and local elites, to the detriment of the working-classes in many developing nations (Bales 2000; Falk 1999; Farmer 2005). Meanwhile, the growth of the international human rights regime focused attention on states as criminal actors in the areas of genocide, discrimination against women and minorities, and crimes against humanity, such as wartime atrocities (Falk 2000; Lyons and Mayall 2003). Neo-liberalism revealed the close linkages between governments and the corporate sector in maximizing profit through the manipulation of politics in subordinate states (Falk 2004b;

Garrison 2004; Goff 2004; Harvey 2003; Perkins 2004). Finally, the invasion and occupation of Iraq based on unilateral decisions by the US and UK governments, in contradistinction to international law and mass popular will, seemed to signal a new era of imperial power where states openly declare the equivalence of might and right (Kramer and Michalowski 2005). Many of the chapters that follow examine these new potentials for state crimes in the contemporary era of global neo-liberalism.

What follows

The chapters that follow examine the contemporary problems of state crime in the wake of nearly three decades of neo-liberalism as both a domestic and an international model for the relationship between state and economy. The goal of these chapters is to provide not just a catalogue of domestic and international state crimes but also both a framework for the study of state crime, and a feel for the potential of controlling state crime. Toward these ends the chapters are divided into three sections: Framing State Crime, The Brutal Realities of State Crime, and Responding to State Crime.

Part One brings together four chapters that each in a different way addresses the question of how we might theorize state crime. As a set of chapters, the goal here is not to establish a singular model for the study of state crime, but to raise questions about the possibility of expanding the study of state crime in the contemporary global age beyond the more common focus on relatively small-scale depredations of corrupt politicians and their associates to larger-scale state crimes. Toward this end, the authors in this section suggest that we bring legal state harms under the umbrella of criminology (Michalowski), consider the ways in which the pursuit of empire so characteristic of twenty-first century United States is a criminal enterprise (Iadicola), ask whether political states are fundamentally dependent on the spectacle of sacrifice as a well-spring of their power (Pearce), and imagine how to create a criminology of state crime that is prospective rather than just retrospective (Friedrichs).

Part Two explores five international and two domestic varieties of state crime. Three of the internationally focused articles concern war: Kramer's examination of the aerial bombing of civilians as normalized deviance, Ruggiero's contemplation of war as corporate crime, and Whyte's close-grained analysis of efforts to use US and UK military power to convert the post-invasion Iraqi economy into a cash-machine for international business. These chapters offer an important perspective on state crime since as we write, in 2009, US and UK troops (but increasingly few others) remain garrisoned in Iraq, and US and NATO forces are further away from an exit strategy in Afghanistan than when the US first invaded the country eight years earlier. Huggins' examination of torture as state crime offers a broad perspective on this particular form of state brutalization of human bodies at the very moment when the US government finds itself dealing with the consequences of torture as part of the Bush administration's 'war on terror', and facing the political and practical challenges of forging alternative policies for the interrogation of suspected domestic and international terrorists. In the final internationally oriented chapter, Rothe considers the ways in which one state's foreign policy, in this case China's, can either facilitate or restrain state crimes by dependent client states. Turning to domestic state crimes, Westervelt and Cook examine the ways in which wrongful conviction constitutes a state crime, particularly in view of continued state commitment to ignore actual innocence in favor of juridical processes as the basis for determining what will happen to those erroneously convicted of murder. Finally, Lang examines the (mis)use of prosecutorial power to maximize organizational goals of prosecutorial success, rather than societal goals of genuine justice.

Part Three presents four chapters that address strategies for confronting state crime. In two of these, the chapters by Stanley and by Chouliaras, the focus is on the potential for emergent supra-national bodies and their attendant international legal processes to confront heinous political crimes through prosecution and/or strategies of truth commissions and national reconciliation. The two other chapters in this section, Chambliss and colleagues' examination of the potential for harm reduction policies to replace crime suppression models as the basis for domestic and international justice, and our Epilogue, which calls for the creation of a public criminology of state crime, suggest that we need to open doors into new ways of thinking about harm, crime, power and criminology. It is our hope that by combining compelling research with public engagement, critical criminologists of state crime can make common cause with all those who seek to confront what Farmer (2005) calls the 'pathologies of power', and in doing so help restrain the devastation to human lives and social bonds that is so often, and so casually, committed by the contemporary neo-liberal state.

Notes

1 A good example of morality masquerading as evidence-based legislation is the construction of the Poor Laws in England. These laws effectively defined the problem as the 'pauper' rather than a system that pauperized former agrarians. See for instance, Bentham (1812) and Boyer (1990).
2 See Friedrichs' assessment of the impact of the Chambliss presidential address in Chapter 5 of this volume.

Part One
Framing State Crime

Chapter 2

In search of 'state and crime' in state crime studies

Raymond Michalowski

For most orthodox criminologists the operative meaning of the word 'crime' is relatively straightforward: crime is murder, rape, robbery, burglary, theft, drug offenses and maybe fraud. While most criminologists might subscribe to a somewhat broader definition of crime as 'an act in violation of law', in practice few offenses appear in the criminological literature other than routine street crimes.

For critical criminologists who study state crime (and these are the majority of criminologists who study state crime) the meaning of crime is somewhat more complicated. For some, the modal form of state crimes are atrocities such as war crimes, genocide and terrorism. For others it is any state action that has been prosecuted at a national or international level, including relatively prosaic violations of regulatory laws and bi- and multilateral treaties, or any state acts that can be argued to have violated national or international law, even if no legal response was made. Finally, some argue that state crime encompasses all of the harms and social injuries that result from the intersecting processes of governance and capital accumulation, regardless of their standing under law.[1]

This chapter offers a preliminary and partial answer to this question: as an epistemological proposition, how do we understand the meanings of 'state' and 'crime' in the compound 'state crime'?

Despite different foci, most analysts of state crimes tend to focus on wrongful acts committed to serve the organizational interests rather than on what Friedrichs (2010: 147–55) terms 'political white collar crime', that is, acts designed to serve the personal interests of the offender. It is also true, however, that personal motivations and organizational goals frequently intersect. Many individuals who conform to deviant organizational practices do so for personal reasons such as retaining or advancing their position in the organization, garnering other personal benefits such as salary increases, perks or accumulating reputational power. Despite these personal motivations, however, most acts of corporate or political wrongdoing are structured and elicited by organizational procedures that have made the harmful actions in question normal, tolerated, and in some instances expected and rewarded (Vaughan 1983).

A number of critical criminologists have considered what it might mean to approach state crime as an organizational problem rather than a simple consequence of the personal motivations of government actors (Barak 1991; Chambliss 1989; Chambliss and Zatz 1993; Kramer and Michalowski 2005; Michalowski and Kramer 1987; Mullins and Rothe 2008; Pearce 1976; Ruggiero 2006). Nevertheless, 'the state' in state crime studies is often indexed to 'government', that is, the state as 'the governmental and administrative institutions of a society' (Alvarez 2001: 57). This focus on state as government has two drawbacks. One is that the idea of 'government' tends to direct attention to 'leaders', and in doing so shifts it away from organizations as deviant actors. The other is that treating government as organizationally distinct from economic institutions and civil society is more a statement of how free-market societies are *supposed* to operate than a description of how they actually operate. Thus, one of the goals of this chapter is to examine the different uses of the term 'state' in state crime studies, and to suggest that expanding the theoretical lens through which we view the state beyond government may help deepen our understanding of the intersection of political, economic and cultural practices that can be deeply injurious to human life and planetary survival.

The meaning of crime has also come under scrutiny within critical criminology. The foundations of today's critical criminology reach back to an earlier 'radical criminology' that was founded on analyses of how the criminalization process – that is, making and enforcing laws – is fundamentally shaped by power, money and class conflict, rather than straightforward codification of universal social norms (Chambliss and Seidman 1971; Diamond 1974; Michalowski 1985; Quinney 1977; Schwendinger and Schwendinger 1970). While this recognition of the role of power in constructing the definition of crime is well established in critical criminology, there are two areas where I think greater attention to the link between law and power might be useful for state crime studies.

First, if laws reflect the will of the powerful, to what extent can we consider the development of humanitarian and human rights law under the post-World War Two human rights regime a victory over state power?

Second, insofar as they represent increased centralization of power, what are the risks of promoting an expansion of supra-state entities to control state crime?

I begin my inquiry with the concept of crime.

Crime

Within criminological writing, the concept of crime typically takes on one of three meanings. The first, and most common, is a juridical meaning which treats crime as an ontological reality encompassing those acts, and only those acts, designated as crime by law (Morrison 1995). Among criminologists, this is by far the most widely accepted understanding of crime, and can be found prominently in the opening chapters of popular criminology textbooks (Schmalleger 2008; Siegel 2005).

The second model reflects Sellin's (1938) observation that the subject matter of criminology ought not to be defined as a violation of law, but as a violation of 'conduct norms'. From this perspective, acts that violate rules of behavior shared among culturally bounded groups, i.e. their conduct norms, are as sociologically meaningful as acts designated as criminal by law, particularly because the distinction between violations of conduct norms that are designated as crimes and those that are not is the outcome of political processes that should not determine the nature of scientific inquiry. Consequently, in order to heighten our sociological understanding of how actions come to acquire the status of acceptable, deviant, or criminal, criminology should study the range of behaviors that violate the conduct norms of identifiable social groups, rather than just those defined as criminal by law.[2] For Sellin (1938: 30) this did not represent a break with a normal science, but rather 'a necessity imposed by the logic of science' because it enabled criminology to operate as a source of knowledge uncoupled from political power. From Foucault's (1981) perspective on 'power-knowledge', Sellin's image of a criminology wholly separate from the operations of power is an Enlightenment-era fantasy that ignores or fails to recognize that power is always immanent in knowledge, and that accepted knowledge always constructs and (re)produces relations of power. Foucault's caution notwithstanding, Sellin's recognition that there is an intellectual and moral difference between a criminology reliant on state definitions of crime and one based on its own vision of sociological processes is an important one. While the study of 'conduct norms' may never be free from the circulation of power inherent in any academic discipline, it may matter whether the power in play is integral to the operation of the discipline or imported from the practice of government.

Many analysts of state crime, without directly invoking Sellin's theory of conduct norms, embrace his approach when they study acts that have not been expressly prohibited by law, but that are sufficiently similar to designated criminal acts that they are viewed by social movements or identifiable sub-segments of national or global populations as so wrongful that they should be prosecuted as crimes (Green and Ward 2004).

The third approach focuses on 'social injury' or 'social harm'. (While the term 'social harm' is more common, I prefer, and will use, 'social injury'.

Harm has a passive quality. It refers to something that happened to someone. Injury seems, at least in my mind, to imply something more active. It suggests that whatever was suffered was caused by some person or process.) From a social injury perspective, the content of criminology's portfolio should be determined by the substantive outcome of actions rather than their legal status. The social injury approach calls for a matrix of outcomes that enables us to identify actions that are analogous in their consequences to acts defined as illegal or deviant, including those that are not (yet) the target of either legal control or widespread social approbation.

This last element, bringing acts that are condemned neither by a government nor some broad social sentiment under the umbrella of criminology renders the criminologist a claims-maker in the social movement sense of the term (Spector and Kitsuse 1977). The criminologist becomes a social activist seeking to create public condemnation and possibly legal prohibition of injurious outcomes where little or none presently exists. Criminologists who do so transform themselves from purely academic researchers into 'public criminologists', as we discuss in the Epilogue to this volume. The position of public criminologist is both at odds with criminology's commitment to normal science because it appears to involve moral choice, and yet closely linked to the foundation of criminology as a form of engaged social inquiry that represented distinct moral choices about what social problems should be ameliorated and how governments should go about doing so (Beirne 2006: vii–ix).

Juridical, conduct norm and social injury approaches to the meaning of crime remain operative in criminology today. Table 2.1 sets forth the epistemological assumptions characteristic of each of these models. It also points to the key benefits and liabilities offered by each. The ways in which each of these definitional approaches facilitate and hinder the study of state crime and the communicability of that research to wider audiences is set forth in Table 2.2.

The definitional framework that informs any study of state crime will influence, and in some cases determine, the suite of harms that can be studied. A juridical framework directs attention to high-profile instances of state crime that have attracted the enforcement attention of national or supra-national bodies. The prosecution of officials or elected representatives for fraudulent schemes, such as the 2008 prosecution of Alaskan senator Ted Stevens for kickbacks and graft, are emblematic of high-profile national enforcement (Lewis 2008). The Nuremberg prosecution of Nazi officials for war crimes and the various prosecutions under the International Criminal Tribunal for Yugoslavia after the Bosnian war are characteristic of high-profile prosecutions of state criminals under international law (Conot 1993; Hazan 2004).

While offering methodological clarity, the juridical framework poses a potential straitjacket for the study of state crime since states rarely

Table 2.1 State crime: definitional variants

Juridical
- State crime is an act in violation of *law*, including:
  - national laws
  - proscriptive international law
  - other multilateral treaty obligations
  - prescriptive human rights law.
                                    (Chambliss 1989; Kauzlarich and Kramer 1998)

Deviance
- State crime as *organizational deviance*, requiring:
  - a harmful act,
  - in pursuit of organizational (typically governmental) goals
  - that violates established conducts norms, and
  - generates an audience willing to sanction the offender.
                                          (Friedrichs 2010; Green and Ward 2004)

Social injury
- State crime as analogous *social injury/harm* refers to:
  - intentional human actions
  - in pursuit of political and/or economic goals
  - that result in harms equally grave as acts defined as crimes.
                                          (Michalowski 1985; Pemberton 2004)

---

criminalize or prosecute wrongful acts undertaken to facilitate their own interests. Meanwhile, supra-national efforts to control state crime through international law have been largely limited to either victor's justice or the prosecution of leaders or ex-leaders of weak or failed states.

There are several ways of escaping this straitjacket. One is to utilize a 'social definition' of wrong to label harmful but legal acts as crime (Kramer 1982). Another is to identify acts that are arguably sufficiently similar to acts prohibited by law, that even if no action is taken against them they warrant being labeled as criminal (Michalowski 1985). This opens the field to a wider array of topics. From a theoretical standpoint, however, applying the juridical term 'crime' to acts, however wrongful, that have not been defined as crimes by law-making bodies or treated as crimes by law-enforcing bodies, may create an undesirable narrowing of our vision. This is particularly true when we are considering violations of human rights and international laws by political states. Defining putative violations of human rights that states or international bodies have chosen to not criminalize or have chosen to not prosecute as crimes tends to direct our attention away from these actions as contested political terrain where offender states and their allies argue that no violations of international law have been committed, and attempts by social movements of victims, their allies and interested third-party states to gain support for their belief that the behavior in question is criminal and its perpetrators ought to be punished. I suggest that it is theoretically more useful, factually more accurate, and politically more effective to treat wrongful state actions that have not (yet) been targeted for control by authoritative national or international bodies as arenas of conflict rather than as crimes, for several reasons.

First, many foundational elements of both international human rights law and humanitarian law (laws of war) tend to be proscriptive, rather than prescriptive. For instance, most of the 30 provisions of the Universal Declaration of Human Rights (UDHR) specify desired relations between states, and between individuals and states, in language that leaves wide latitude for interpretation as to what might be a violation.

For instance, Article 11(1) of the UDHR states, 'Everyone charged with a penal offence has the right to be presumed innocent until proved guilty according to law in a public trial at which he has had all the guarantees necessary for his defence.' Based on this provision, Amnesty International (AI) argued that 'The rules and procedures governing military commission trials at Guantánamo are at odds with international law' (Amnesty International 2009). At the same time US government under George W. Bush, and now under Barack Obama, claimed that holding individuals found on the battlefields of Iraq and Afghanistan indefinitely and without trial does not violate the nation's obligations under either US law or the UDHR (Greenwald 2009b).

Similarly, a number of sources have criticized the apparent depredations of human rights committed by US and British forces operating in Iraq during the 2003 invasion and subsequent occupation as violations of human rights (Ali 2003; Grey 2007; Johnson 2004; Kramer and Michalowski 2005; Parenti 2005). However, no international tribunal has declared the torture, economic exploitation and civilian slaughter associated with that war to be a violation of the contemporary international rights regime. The few prosecutions that have occurred have targeted a handful of low-ranking soldiers brought to trial under US law for the abuses at the Abu Ghraib prison or several other egregious instances of civilian murder or rape (Cloud 2005; Taguba 2004). These prosecutions aside, most of the likely violations of human rights and international law resulting from the invasion and occupation of Iraq have not (at least at the time of writing in 2009) been subject to indictment and prosecution by either national or international tribunals.

It would, I think, be more sociologically and politically informative to analyze why the different positions in these two examples have strong support, rather than to begin with the assumption that the acts in question are crimes, and then move directly to explaining their causes.

While important and useful, particularly from a social movement, claims-making standpoint, beginning from the 'it's a crime' standpoint tends to minimize the analytic attention given to the political and sociological questions of why the act(s) in question have avoided legal consequences, what arguments have been successfully mounted to establish the claim that they are not crimes, and who finds these arguments persuasive and why.

Approaching uncriminalized state wrongs as crimes is even more problematic for violations of broad human rights provision. Consider Section XX(1) of the Universal Declaration of Human Rights, which holds that 'Everyone has the right to a standard of living adequate for the health and well-being of himself and of his family, including food, clothing, housing and medical care and necessary social services, and the right to security in the event of unemployment, sickness, disability, widowhood, old age or other lack of livelihood in circumstances beyond his control.' There are certainly many situations around the world that would seem to represent clear violations of both the letter and the spirit of this provision. However, because what is specified by international human rights law is an ideal outcome rather than a prohibited set of behaviors, it would be substantially more difficult to index these situations to crime than the violations of civil liberties and human rights in a wartime context. In this case, and many others, focusing on the legal status of acts risks directing us away from the broad structural arrangements that deprive people of 'a standard of living adequate for . . . health and well-being'. Yet these are precisely the conditions, I would argue, that state crime analysts should give the greatest attention, because they victimize the greatest number of people. My standpoint here is unapologetically radical. That is, I think that state crime analysis is freer to take a more oppositional stance toward the brutalities of twenty-first century political economy when it moves beyond a juridical or quasi-juridical framework.

For many critical analysts of state crime, the deviance model is less attractive than a juridical one because the word 'deviance' does not communicate the sense of outrage that attends the term 'crime'. By calling unprosecuted acts 'crimes', researchers add moral punch to their claims that state actions are criminal even when no legal action is directed against them. However, by focusing on these acts as deviance rather than crime directs attention to the social movement processes whereby claims-makers have transformed these actions from acceptable to problematic, at least for certain populations (Best 1993; Spector and Kitsuse 1977). It also directs attention to why those claims-makers have been unable to see their understanding reflected in legal action, while those who wish to have these harms remain outside of national and international courts have succeeded in doing so. Criminologists who seek to understand the structure of claims-making within the contested terrain of wrongful state actions who are themselves partisan to one side of the claims-making struggle or other, ought to bring a degree of reflexive analysis to bear on their own partisanship. I mean this not in the sense of 'full disclosure', as media pundits sometimes say, nor in the sense of simple personal revelation. Rather,

Table 2.2 Models for defining state crime: strengths and weaknesses

Definitional model	Strengths	Weaknesses
Juridical	Based on politically validated systems of laws.	Limits scope because:
	Seems to minimize the preferences of researcher in determining subject matter.	Nation-states rarely criminalize their own political and economic wrongdoing.
	Best fit with normal science.	Criminalization of state offenses by international bodies is significantly shaped by interests of powerful political and economic entities.
	Most defensible to funding bodies.	
Organizational deviance	Broadens scope by transcending laws and rules created by politically animated entities.	Requires informed, troubled audience willing to impose penalty.
	Based on established sociological theories of deviance and organizations.	Limits role of state crime analysis as change agent.
	Potential fit with normal science.	More difficult to explain to lay audience than straightforward law violation.
Social injury/harm	Broadest analytic scope.	Poor fit with normal science.
	Analytic choices made by researcher.	Analytic choices made by researcher.
	Best able to address political-economic intersections.	Concepts of social injury and 'harm' are culturally variable.
	Best potential for participatory research.	

I am referring to an inquiry into one's own partisanship in the sense of reflexive ethnography, interrogating one's own experience with the phenomenon at hand as a form of 'data' that reveals complexities of the wider phenomenon, and that destabilizes dominant narratives by revealing the author to be more than the absent cause of words on a page (Davies 2007; de Vries 1992).

When it comes to the study of state crime, approaching legal state wrongs as deviance in general, and organizational deviance in particular, offers the most promise (Perrow 1986; Vaughan 1983). The organizational deviance perspective provides an institutionally focused framework for analyses of harms that have not risen to the level of law violations, but which have attracted the approbation of significant audiences who would define these acts as deviant, and would be willing to impose sanctions on the offenders if they were able (Green and Ward 2004). More than this, however, it directs us to unravel the ways that complex, multi-faceted and multi-purposed entities – and few organizations are more complex or multi-purposed than contemporary liberal and neo-liberal states – can produce great wrong, but do so through analyses that avoid falling into the *mens rea* straitjacket that requires individual blame be assigned to deliberate miscreants. Avoiding this individualized line of thinking is particularly important for the study of state crime because there is often no 'smoking gun', or more correctly no smoking memo, pointing to specific guilty political actors. Because, like corporations, states have 'no pants to kick and no soul to damn', the vast majority of state crimes fall outside the juridical framework of both most liberal democracies and international criminal law frameworks. This remains true even where there may be political will to take action. Without guilty individuals to put in the dock, both national and international justice systems remain stalled.

An important practical drawback to research from an organizational deviance perspective, however, is that it requires close-grained, detailed, and usually time-consuming research of often difficult-to-access institutions and actors (Vaughan 1996). This is, of course, one of the reasons why criminological research has most often focused on crimes more typical among poor and subaltern classes: the members of these classes are powerless to avoid being subjects of the criminological gaze. The organizational processes and practices that lead to the normalization of deviance in the institutions that constitute the political state are shielded from scrutiny in ways that tend to dissuade all but the most persistent (and probably tenured) researchers from making them a focus of study.

The final approach, the social injury model, is the least definitive of the three insofar as it offers neither the clear boundaries of a juridical approach defined by statutes, nor the developed theoretical framework of the organizational deviance model. What it offers, instead, is a standpoint from which to search out that which both law and deviance models obscure: that is, the structural and operational harms brought about by state practices that have become either normalized routines in the pursuit of what Foucault (2007) terms 'security', or have been rendered non-criminal and acceptable, even if odious, during those times when governments convincingly establish that they must operate according to a 'state of exception' (Agamben 2005b; Schmidt 1922/1985).

By targeting acts whose consequences, rather than intentions, are as bad as crime regardless of the juridical or public approval, the social injury model casts a wide net. In doing so, it makes several significant demands on those who would use it. First, it requires the analyst to clearly establish that actions and outcomes selected for scrutiny are indeed equivalent in gravity to juridical crimes. Attending to the victimology of state crime facilitates this process by directing us to recognize that regardless of intention or legal status, many state actions produce injured victims who are important subjects for criminological inquiry (Kauzlarich *et al.* 2001).

Second, any analysis based on a social injury model must be able to offer a persuasive counter-factual narrative that shows how the events in question could realistically have happened otherwise. For instance, to label as deviant a nation's trade policy that impoverishes millions in a less developed country, offers little analytic understanding without demonstrating that the relations between the nations could have been otherwise.

Despite these requirements, the social injury model offers the substantial benefit of a standpoint from which to pierce, however partially, the perceptual scrim that liberal thought and practice, since the late seventeenth century, has placed between our perceptions of how social life operates and what is actually happening to the human bodies that constitute that social life. It is this scrim that enables us to view eighteenth and nineteenth century expropriation and wanton killing of indigenous populations in North America, India, Africa and China as the 'march of progress', to see the emiseration of families, the disruption of social life and the accumulation of immense private fortunes that accompanied capitalist industrialization as 'development' (Polanyi 1944/2001), and that today allows us to embrace a growing wealth gap between highly developed and less developed nations as a desirable 'new world order'. Only by recognizing the everyday human victims of state actions can we begin to see clearly what it is that states are about when they pursue political-economic strategies in accordance with the proposition that human progress is measured by the life conditions of the most well-off, rather than those of the least well-off.

These different three approaches – juridical, organizational deviance, and social injury – represent an increasing scope of harm, from the least to the most prevalent. With apologies to Sam Walker (2005), I have arranged these in a state crime wedding cake. While I do not wish to minimize the horror and gravity of atrocities, it is worth noting that atrocities injure smaller numbers than the normalized organizational deviance of many nation-states (and sometimes even of international enforcement bodies). These, in turn, affect fewer individuals than does structural violence embedded in the deep fiber of the neo-liberal, corporate state (Hedges 2009; Miller 1975; Nader 2002). By no means should this be read as an argument for focusing state crime analysis exclusively on the widest level of this array. There are victims deserving of attention at all levels of state crime. Rather it is meant to establish how different definitions of crime direct us to different levels of the problem.

While we can speak about different levels of analysis in the study of state crime, and different types of crimes and social injuries occurring at these different levels, it is also important to recognize the high degree of interconnectedness among these levels and types. Wars and their brutal-

High profile
- Genocide
- War crimes
- Terrorism

Semi-tolerated violence
- War-related death, injury and illness to combatants and civilians
- Torture
- Human consequences of embargos
- Juridogenic crimes
- Brutal punishments

Structural violence
- Injury, illness or death due to preventable, state-facilitated forms of:
  - Poverty and inequality
  - Workplace hazards
  - Consumer risks
  - Environmental pollution
  - Sexism, racism and ethnic 'othering'
- Loss of life, health, economic resources and autonomy due to:
  - Neo-colonialism
  - Neo-imperialism
  - Neo-liberal globalization

Figure 2.1 The state crime wedding cake

ities, for instance, often derive support from citizens who, having suffered economic hardship or difficulties as a consequence of state-supported political-economic arrangements, can be convinced to displace their frustrations onto an external enemy (Mack 1988). Similarly, state atrocities have often arisen in the mutual desire by governments to sell and corporations to exploit the domestic resources of developing nations (Sriram 2005). Thus, it becomes critical whenever we consider any state crime to always remain alert to the layered dynamics that often lie behind or well underneath the more obvious crime.

State

Like the meaning of crime, the meaning of 'state' in the compound 'state crime' may benefit from some explicit theoretical attention. In some studies of state crime, 'the state' refers to the activities of actors in institutions of government. In others, it refers to a loosely defined linkage between economic and political institutions. Less common are analyses of state crime that approach the state in a manner similar to what is typical of contemporary thought in sociological and political science. In these fields the state is increasingly understood as a set of dynamic processes through which capital accumulation, political governance and ideological construction intersect to produce what might loosely be termed a socio-political order, but do so in such a fluid and interpenetrating manner that it becomes difficult to draw absolute boundary lines between state, economy and culture (Block 1977; Foucault 1977; Jessop 1991; Poulantzas 1968).

A good example in the state crime literature of approaching the 'state' as an assemblage of governmental institutions can be found in Green and Ward's *State Crime*, a well-reasoned effort at developing a general framework for the study of state crime. As part of their introduction, Green and Ward (2004: 3), quoting Engels, define the state as institutions of governance:

> When we discuss the 'state', therefore, we shall be using the term in the traditional Marxist sense to refer to a 'public power' comprising personnel organized and equipped for the use of force, 'material adjuncts, prisons and institutions of coercion of all kinds' and agencies which levy taxes.

What Green and Ward refer to as the 'traditional' Marxist sense of the state is rooted in Marx and Engels' instrumentalist vision of government in capitalist society as the 'executive committee of the ruling class' (Marx and Engels 1848/1969). However, beginning with Gramsci's (1935/1971) work on ideology in the early decades of the twentieth century, many Marxian theorists came to recognize that governmental institutions and actors both enjoyed at least some degree of 'relative autonomy' from the ruling class (Althusser 1971), and are also at times constrained from openly facilitating the interests of the capitalist class by the risk of jeopardizing state legitimacy in public consciousness (O'Connor 1973; Poulantzas 1968).

By the latter part of the twentieth century, building on Polanyi's insights various western analysts, such as Block (1977), Jessop (1982), Foucault (1997), Poulantzas (1968) and Wonders and Solop (1993), began theorizing the state not as a *thing* – that is, an ensemble of geographically bound institutions and institutionally empowered individuals – but rather as a set of intersecting processes that both reproduce and alter the social order as articulations of interdependent economic, political and cultural practices. These approaches highlighted three characteristics of the modern state: its internal complexity, its ubiquity, and its role in generating independent reaction.

As Jessop (1979: 16) observed, the various apparatuses of the modern states are so complex and so often operate in conflict with one another that state analysis must begin from a view of the state 'as a set of institutions that cannot, *qua* structural ensemble, exercise power'. That is, any analysis of state actions must be attentive to what parts of the 'structural ensemble' we often casually group under the linguistic umbrella of 'state' were effectively responsible for the outcomes under scrutiny, and what other parts of the ensemble opposed, canalized or shaped the outcome. In addition to being complex and internally conflictual, the 'state', or what might be termed the effects of the state, appear in many arenas of social life well beyond the boundaries of state institutions.

The dynamics of 'governmentality', to use Foucault's (2003) terminology, point to societies in which state effects penetrate and discipline human societies in ways that individuals both self-align their interests to those of the state and become part of the state by reproducing its ideology and its practices as part of their daily lives. Thus, for instance, it is difficult if not impossible for a nation to have a 'war front' without having a 'home front' in which citizens 'rally around the troops' and engage in rituals of sacrifice (see Pearce, this volume) that circulate and normalize the state's call for people to die or otherwise be damaged on behalf of the 'nation'.

Finally, states 'unintentionally influence the formation of groups and the political capacities, ideas and demands of various sectors of society' (Skocpol 1985: 21). From this standpoint, we need to be attentive not just to the formal goals of states as expressed by state agents, but all of the other social formations that exist in either supportive or oppositional reaction to the state. This is particularly important in nominally democratic, free-market societies that rely very much on civil society to undertake much of the heavy lifting involved in creating social order and social peace.

In an effort to erase, or at least minimize, the conceptual bright line that often separates researchers who examine state crime from those who study economic crime, in the 1990s Ron Kramer and I offered the concept of state-corporate crime as a focus for criminological inquiry (Michalowski and Kramer 2006). Our goal was to create a framework to facilitate examinations of how institutions of governance and institutions of accumulation interact to produce violations of positive law and/or regulation, or social injuries that fall outside legal strictures, but are nevertheless significant sources of human suffering.

In our writings, as well as those of others who have applied the state-corporate model to a variety of crimes and social injuries, the primary focus is on how businesses and governments intersect in ways that produce injurious actions that may or may not be held criminal under law (Ainsley and Israel 2004; Bruce and Becker 2006; Matthews and Kauzlarich 2000; Reifert and Carlson 2007; Rothe and Mullins 2006; Rothe and Ross 2008). The concept of state-corporate crime has proved to be a useful heuristic device for revealing the way linkages between the interests and/or the operations of government and business can generate crime and social injury.

By focusing on social injuries or violations of law arising when one or more governmental entities operating in concert with one or more economic entities, the state-corporate crime model tacitly accepts the idea that the state is an ensemble of governmental institutions that, *sui generis*, are capable of wielding political power, and that this ensemble is distinct from those corporate institutions that wield economic power (Kramer and Michalowski 2006). This approach, like many other models of state crime analysis, may benefit from giving greater attention to how in liberal – i.e. free-market – states (1) economies are 'embedded' in governance as the central source of state revenue and the labor pool from which primary state actors are drawn (Offe and Ronge 1982); (2) governance is embedded in the corporate economy as the primary purchaser of goods and services, including the increasing tendency for neo-liberal states such as the US and Britain to purchase services involving what had been distinctly state functions such as public education and war-making; and (3) both are embedded in civil society through the construction and conflation of liberal/neo-liberal concepts such as 'free markets' with 'free people' or 'equality' with 'equal opportunity', and circulating these through face-to-face and mass-mediated forms of communication, from public education, to entertainment, to news, to religious practices. As Polanyi (1944/2001: 143–5) observed over 50 years ago, *laissez faire* was planned, and planned by those in positions to wield the political power that could produce and reproduce first liberal, capitalist, and later neo-liberal capitalist economies. In short, while we can, from an organizational perspective, identify institutions of government, of economy, and of civil society, it is probably theoretically wise to remain aware that these elements of contemporary society are so tightly woven that it is risky to consider one without examining their intersection with the others.

From this standpoint, state crime arises not out of the singular actions of institutional actors or particular organizational goals, but out of the relational processes through which institutions of governance and accumulation, aided by ideological processes, ensure that individuals will embrace the goals of accumulation and governance as their own (Barrow 1993). State crime research can make significant steps forward, I suggest, if it gives greater attention to how crimes seemingly originating within the halls of governance are actually consequences of an economics-politics-culture nexus that produces a normalized exercise of bio-power that is frequently deeply injurious to particular segments of the society, or even the society as a whole.

Drawing on Foucault's work in *The State Must be Defended*, Achille Mbembe offers what might be a third vision of the state – necropolitics. In this approach the central processes of sovereign states, and here the state appears to mean the mutually reinforcing relational practices of accumulation and governmentality, are determining 'who may live and who must die' (Mbembe 2003: 11). I include Mbembe's formulation here because it has a particular resonance with state violence, both intentional and structural.

When it comes to analyzing state crime, any consideration of 'the state', as my historian friends remind me, must answer the question, which state? This is not merely a matter of naming the state in question. It is a matter of locating the particular practices of that state as they bear on human life within the global matrix of state processes. The relations between accumulation and governance have changed in significant ways over the six centuries of market domination of human social organization, and likewise vary geographically today. This variation is perhaps being replaced by a greater degree of convergence today as the forces of neo-liberal globalization increasingly homogenize the globe by promoting regimes based on a US vision of what it means to have open markets and electoral democracy, while demonizing and undermining all other systems. Nevertheless, notable differences still remain in how neo-liberal states are configured, and those differences have significant consequences for the production of state violence and structural harms.

Sweden and the United States, for instance, are both modern market democracies, but market democracies with distinct histories and significant differences in social welfare policies (Flora and Heidenheimer 1982; Wilensky 1975). Those differences have meant that Sweden is notably less of a necrotist state than the United States, whether the measures are infant mortality, interpersonal violence or state violence (Esping-Andersen 1990). This comparison, or many others that can be made between more and less harmful states, suggests two things. First, that less harmful states can serve as at least a partial model for constructing plausible counter-narratives of actually occurring state harms. Second, there is significant need for more explicitly comparative work in the area of state crime. To date, most state crime analyses have focused on single incidences of state crime within single states.

Table 2.3 provides examples of how the theoretical implications of instrumentalism, structuralism and necropolitics differ depending on the type of state under scrutiny. It also attempts to visualize the implications of each of these theoretical models for the current age of emerging transnational governmentality as manifest in the processes of global finance and US military hegemony (Johnson 2006; Stiglitz 2003).

Conclusion: Does it matter?

I have suggested that state crime analysis can benefit from more explicit theorizing about the nature of the state. The question I have not addressed

Table 2.3 State theories and state types

State theory	Mercantile	Corporate	Finance
Instrumentalist (state as instrument of ruling class)	Rulers are members of capitalist class. Military colonialism. Direct government dispossession of citizen property and repression of working-class interests.	National capitalist class dominates but does not control selection of political leaders. Neo-colonialism. Leaders facilitate interests of capitalist by laws and ideological apparatuses. Political leaders avert rebellion by 'carrot and stick' policies.	International capitalist class influences selection of national and supra-national leaders. Leaders seek to facilitate international capital accumulation via neo-liberal globalization. Some states are allowed to fail to facilitate accumulation in others.
Structuralist (state as network of accumulation, political and ideology relations)	Hereditary rulers facilitate accumulation by pursuing their own interests in military expansion and other projects. Church–state relations are a formal, mutually reinforcing ideological framework.	Political leadership somewhat broader than capitalist class. Functions of state apparatus have 'relative autonomy' from accumulation function. Organizational tensions reflect tension between accumulation and legitimation.	Global ruling class drawn significantly from international investor class. State apparatus must increasingly manage tensions among nation-state legitimacy, national capital, and international capital.
Necrotist (state as organization of power to determine who may live and who to let die)	Accumulative territorial expansion through violence. Geography becomes racialized in pursuit of wealth/power. Racialization validates dispossession and exterminations of colonized people.	Emergence of patriotism as justification for expansionist killings. War making re-defined as 'national defense' War expenditures become central to capital accumulation.	Neo-liberalism dispossesses and impoverishes many in developing world. Developed societies rooted in destructive culture of limitlessness. Legitimacy in developed states depends on affirming limitlessness.

is, does it matter? My answer is that it depends on the purpose of the inquiry. If, as Mullins and Rothe (2008: 4) suggest, 'crimes that states commit [are] not generally relevant to expanding the contours of criminology', is there any particular reason to link state crime research closer to the academic theories of the state? Or should state crime analyses be designed primarily to support social change by providing conscience-troubling narratives about the ways that governments and wider social systems can harm human beings? If 'public criminology' (see the Epilogue, this volume) is the primary goal, then it probably matters little whether state crime analysts deepen their theorization of the state. Political mobilization alone may be sufficient justification for descriptive narratives and taxonomic analyses of whatever governmental wrongdoing happens to be the latest headline, regardless of whether or not these analyses are informed by academic theorization of the state.

I suspect that most state crime researchers, including myself, recognize that orthodox criminology's focus on street crime to the near total exclusion of crimes of the powerful is the perceptual equivalent of watching a ping-pong match while bowling balls are being rolled beneath the table. This recognition further suggests that any movement toward true human justice requires significantly constraining, if not dismantling, social systems that allow the exercise of bio-power to harm millions in search for accumulation and/or dominance.

This recognition is all to the good, and if all we ever do as critical criminologists is produce powerful quasi-sociological, or perhaps quasi-journalistic reframings of press, NGO and court reports on crimes by the powerful, that may be enough. If, however, our goal is to develop sociological analyses of state crime that move beyond debunking the image of the sovereign states as a beneficent provider of social well-being, we may need some additional theoretical tools.

Examining the crimes and social injuries committed by governmental leaders and their corporate allies in both developed and developing states has the potential of calling attention to, and stimulating action against, such governmental wrongdoing. However, examinations of state wrongs in the absence of a developed theory of the state are, I suggest, somewhat akin to studying patterns of rape in the absence of a theory of gender and patriarchy. Much can be learned from revealing the patterns, but understanding their wider implications requires a broader and more sociological framework.

My goal here in problematizing unearthing the meaning of the state in state crime study is to determine if and how more explicit framings of the state might be useful for expanding our analyses of state crime. I am not suggesting that we need a single definition of crime or a single theory of the state. I am suggesting, however, that we more clearly theorize what we mean by state and crime in order to make the various state crimes studied reveal more than just who did what to whom. That is, to make them reveal the deeper structures through which political power over people and corporate dominance over production and distribution, which is itself power over people, not only generate crimes and social injuries but also have become so normalized that only in the most egregious instances are they viewed as social problems, let alone as crime.

Notes

1 Capital accumulation is not unique to capitalist societies. All modern industrial states, including those who call or had called themselves 'socialist' or 'communist', actively pursue the generation of financial profit as the source of investment for future growth.

2 It should be noted that Sellin was particularly concerned with the obverse: actions such as honor killing that were designated as criminal by law but were acceptable within a given cultural grouping.

Chapter 3

The centrality of empire in the study of state crime and violence

Peter Iadicola

The largest, most powerful, violent, and rarely defined 'criminal' organization in the world today is the empire of the United States of America. The criminological story of empire is the story of stealing resources and killing those who resist. Although the crimes of empire are legion, they are rarely part of the empire's history, which often becomes part of the grand narrative of world history.

Today the barbarism of the American empire has become too transparent for criminologists to continue to ignore. So much of the story of crime in general is linked to the nature of empire. This is certainly the case for conventional crimes that are disproportionately committed by the minority groups that are creations of imperial conquest and experience systems of disadvantage relative to those from the center. It is also a result of the militarization of the imperial society that requires a population ever ready for war. Violence is an important instrument of the imperial state, one that is learned by the citizenry in their relations with each other. The story of crime is also directly related to the state and economic offenses that governments and multinational corporations commit throughout the world. But these linkages of conventional crime and the international crimes of empire are not a focus of most of what criminologists study because, for the most part, criminologists pretend empire doesn't exist.

We are certainly not alone; the vast majority of those who reside in the center of the most powerful empire in human history don't recognize the existence of their empire. Ferguson (2004) refers to this peculiar American syndrome as the 'empire in denial'. As a celebrator of the British and now the American empire, he claims that this is one of the principal weaknesses of the US as the successor to the British empire. On the other hand, it may be one of its greatest strengths. For when the state acts to conquer and occupy a foreign land, it is always interpreted for the American people as an act of liberation of these peoples – even if the people we are liberating are actively resisting that 'liberation', as is most recently the case in Iraq and Afghanistan. The narrative of our political leaders and mass media that defines the reality of international affairs to the citizen is that we are a nation that is bringing freedom to the world, freedom from the tyranny of evil dictators or evil empires. As Johnson (2006: 76) notes, all empires 'require myths of divine right, racial preeminence, manifest destiny, or a "civilizing mission" to cover their often barbarous behavior in other people's countries'. In the case of the United States, it's the myth of a non-empire liberating people around the world from the tyranny of evil empires and dictators.

Defining empire and state crime

Maier (2005: xii) defines empire as 'a major actor in the international system based on the subordination of diverse national elites who, whether under compulsion or from shared convictions, accept the values of those who govern the dominant center or metropole'. The idea that empire may be consensual is an important part of Maier's definition. He sees the American empire as in part an empire by invitation. Of course, who is being invited is left unstated, yet it certainly is an important question and reveals much about who benefits and who pays the cost of inclusion in the empire. This is the class basis for empire, for it is organized by and principally for those who own and control production. And even in this case, not all members of the owning class within the conquered nation will benefit from inclusion. Even for those who become part of a comprador class, I'm not sure how much shared conviction there would be if not for the conquest and the economic, political and cultural penetration. Nevertheless, Maier recognizes the hierarchical nature of empires whereby a center establishes and enforces the rules of the system.

It is only recently that the field of criminology has generated a significant amount of scholarly interest in the study of state crime. Chambliss' 1988 presidential address to the American Society of Criminology, calling on criminologists to increase their research in this area, was a particularly important historical landmark in the field's development. Chambliss (1989: 184) defined state crime as 'acts defined by law as criminal and committed by state officials in pursuit of their jobs as representatives of the state'. Michalowski and Kramer (2006) provided further specification to the definition by including activities of the state that fail to constrain criminal and dangerous acts of corporations.

The limitation of the legal code in the definition of state crime has been an important area of scholarly debate. It is beyond the purpose of this chapter to summarize this debate and it has been done elsewhere (Rothe and Friedrichs 2006). But alternative definitions have been advanced, from international legal codes to basic human rights precepts, and the perceptions of the state's citizens. In Chapter 2 Michalowski described the strengths and weaknesses of three approaches to defining state crime: juridical, organizational deviance, and social injury/harm. He notes that the juridical framework will tend to direct attention to high-profile instances of state crime that have attracted the enforcement efforts of supra-national bodies. The organizational deviance perspective, best represented by Green and Ward (2004), enables analysis of notable harms that have not risen to the level of law violations, but which have attracted the approbation of significant audiences who would define these acts as deviant, and would be willing to impose sanctions on the offenders. Lastly, a social injury model opens the door to considering the kinds of structural violence (Iadicola and Shupe 2003; Scheper-Hughes and Bourgois 2004) and harm that often is so normalized as a consequence of 'governmentality'. Michalowski claims that these different foci represent an increasing scope of harm – from the least to the most prevalent. Iadicola and Shupe (2003) make a similar point in describing the different scale of violence as we move from interpersonal to institutional to structural forms of violence. Whether we define state crime in a more restrictive, juridical framework, or the more expansive, organizational deviance or social/harm framework, the crimes of empires are in the forefront.

Crimes and violence of empire versus empire's crimes and violence

It is important before we proceed with the discussion of the crimes of the US empire to conceptually distinguish empire's crimes from the crimes of empire. Those who dominate the governing circles of the empire define empire's crimes. These crimes are acts of violence and theft that threaten the empire, while acts of violence and theft of the empire are defined as normative, if not heroic, in imperial history. The terrorist today is defined from the perspective of the imperial center, not from the people whose country is occupied and resisting imperial control.

The story of empire is the story of crime and violence. Empires are, criminologically speaking, criminal organizations. They are organized to conquer and control the resources and markets of other territories and people. From the perspective of the conquered, all empires are criminal. On the other hand, from the perspective of the conqueror, empires are civilizers, liberators, and in the most recent justification, democratizers of the world's peoples, at least that part of the world that they can dominate. However, the process of domination begins with conquest or wars of aggression, which in most cases also involves genocide or ethnic cleansing. After conquest there are the crimes of empire of theft in acquisition of the valued resources, and then crimes of empire to maintain control of the vanquished such as assassinations, torture and illegal imprisonment.

Wars of aggression

Wars of aggression are crimes that are a violation of Article 2, Section 4 of the United Nations Charter that states that all members shall refrain in their international relations from the threat or use of force against the territorial integrity or political independence of any state, or in any other manner inconsistent with the Purposes of the United Nations. As a ratified treaty, the UN Charter is binding law in the United States. Under Article 6, Clause 2 of the US Constitution, treaties are considered the supreme law of the land. Article 103 of the UN Charter makes clear that the charter supersedes all other conflicting treaties. The Nuremberg Tribunal defined wars of aggression as the 'supreme International crime' (Bartholomew 2006).

The United States has a long history of wars that violate the territorial integrity or political independence of other states (Blum 1995; Kinzer 2006; Pearce 1981). Or in today's language, it has a long history of 'regime change' including regime changes throughout the Caribbean, South and Central America under the Monroe Doctrine and Roosevelt Corollary, and throughout the rest of the world when the United States extended this prerogative after World War Two to all those areas it was allowed to police under the Yalta Agreement. With the collapse of the Soviet Union this prerogative is being extended throughout new areas of the world that were within this former power's imperial sphere. It is 'the New World' order, as President George H. W. Bush declared. This most recent chapter in the extension of the US empire includes the wars in Central Asia and the Middle East and the military, political, economic and cultural penetration of Eastern Europe and the former 'republics' of the USSR in Central Asia.

It is important to recognize that complicity in war is also a violation of international law. The United States' sponsorship of war is unsurpassed in modern history. The death toll of the proxy wars sponsored by the United States fought throughout Central America, Asia, the Middle East and Africa is extensive. The United States' sponsorship and participation in the Ethiopian invasion of Somalia is a recent example of complicity in this type of state criminal behavior.

Rarely is the United States charged with violations of international law for the wars it conducts or sponsors. The case of Nicaragua in the 1980s is one that illustrates the difficulty in prosecuting an empire for committing war. In this case, the United States government refused to participate in the trial before the World Court, claiming that the Court did not have jurisdiction over the case. Nevertheless, the World Court decided that the US government was essentially guilty of state terrorism (International Court of Justice 1986). The United States has made sure that this situation is not repeated by excluding itself from the jurisdiction of the new International Criminal Court.

Genocide and ethnic cleansing

The Genocide Convention (Article 2) defines genocide as any of the following acts committed with intent to destroy, in whole or in part, a national, ethnical, racial or religious group, as such: (a) Killing members of the group; (b) Causing serious bodily or mental harm to members of the group; (c) Deliberately inflicting on the group conditions of life calculated to bring about its physical destruction in whole or in part; (d) Imposing measures intended to prevent births within the group; (e) Forcibly transferring children of the group to another group (United Nations 1948). The crimes of genocide and ethnic cleansing occurred at the beginning of the history of the empire of the United States. The continental conquest targeted more than 300 distinct societies for genocide and ethnic cleansing (Brown 2001; Churchill 1997). The crime of genocide is also a part of customary law and there is no statute of limitations (Glauner 2001). In addition to the outright killing of large portions of the indigenous population, Glauner notes that the other acts committed by the US against Native Americans, such as the forced relocation (Indian Removal Act and legacy of treaty violations including the Northwest Ordinance), forced sterilization (70,000 native American women between 1930 and 1976), and the transfer of children into boarding schools, are all acts of genocide that are punishable under current international law.

Assassinations

Another area of state crime and violence that has recently increased as part of the 'war on terrorism' is the use of assassinations, or what the United Nations and Amnesty International define as 'extra-judicial executions'. The United States has a long history of participation in assassination programs such as Operations Phoenix and Condor, and the sponsorship of death squads in Central America from the 1960s through to the 1980s (Iadicola and Shupe 2003; United States 1975).

The executive order ban on assassinations, which began with the Ford administration in the wake of the Church Committee hearings that uncovered US participation in planning and carrying out executions, has not stopped US presidents from lifting the ban at times to carry out these crimes. In 1985 the CIA under Reagan attempted to kill Sheikh Mohammed Hussein Fadlallah using a car bomb that killed 80 innocent persons in Beirut. In 1986 the US military dropped bombs on Libyan leader Muammer Gaddafi's home, killing his daughter. President George H. W. Bush issued a 'memorandum of law' that would, according to Blum (2000), allow for 'accidental killings'. Blum lists 36 individuals whose assassination had been planned by the United States government during the period of 1949 to 1999.

According to CNN, sometime between 11 and 14 September 2001, President Bush signed a secret intelligence order revoking Ford's executive order, and instructing the CIA to engage in 'lethal covert operations' to destroy Osama bin Laden and his Al-Qaida organization. CNN also reported that on 3 November 2002, an unmanned CIA Predator drone fired at a convoy traveling in Yemen, killing a man believed to be Al-Qaida's district manager for Yemen. Unknown to the CIA was the fact that there were five other people traveling with the target who were killed in the attack, one American and four other Yemenis. President Bush alluded to the assassinations in his 2003 State of the Union Address when he stated that 'more than 3,000 suspected terrorists have been arrested in many countries, many others have met a different fate. Let's put it this way – they are no longer a problem to the United States and our friends and allies' (CNN 2002). White House and CIA lawyers believe that the ban on political assassination does not apply during wartime. They also contend that the prohibition does not preclude the United States government from taking action against terrorists (CNN 2002).

The operations of the military against what is referred to by the US government as enemy combatants involve the assassinations of suspected terrorists. These executions occur without the messiness of a trial to determine guilt or innocence. The use of high-altitude bombings and the use of missiles to strike homes and communities where suspected terrorists or supporters reside also have resulted in the collateral damage of civilian lives that goes uncounted, a collateral damage that would be called terrorism if it were not perpetrated by imperial military forces. In 2005 there was a report that the United States was considering organizing death squads similar to the ones used in Central America to conduct assassinations or kidnappings. Referred to as the 'Salvador Option' after the US sponsorship of death squads during the Reagan administration in El Salvador, the 'Pentagon proposal would send Special Forces teams to advise, support and possibly train Iraqi squads, most likely hand-picked Kurdish Peshmerga fighters and Shiite militiamen, to target Sunni insurgents and their sympathizers, even across the border into Syria, according to military insiders familiar with the discussion' (Hirsh and Barry 2005).

In 2005 the United States, France and Great Britain sponsored a resolution passed by the United Nations Security Council to threaten Syria with sanctions if it did not allow for an investigation of the assassination of former Lebanese Prime Minister Rafiq Hariri. The goal of the three nations was to create conditions for regime change in Syria. This is one assassination that was deemed to be criminal by those who have the power to define it as such.

Torture, kidnapping and imprisonment

Another example of the violence that is associated with empire is the use of torture. The use of torture is not exclusive to an empire. However, the current empire is flagrantly using torture and spreading the practice of torture throughout the world as a means of imperial control and intimidation. Harbury (2005) notes that the current techniques of torture used by US personnel are similar to the techniques used in Central America by US-trained El Salvadoran, Guatemalan and Honduran military or police personnel during the 1970s and 1980s in US-funded civil wars. She points out that many of these techniques were used directly under CIA supervision. Lesley (2004) has described the training in torture techniques at the US military's School for the Americas. McCoy (2006) traces the use of torture techniques by US personnel to the origins of the CIA program of mind control from 1950 to 1962. He notes that after experiments with hallucinogenic drugs, electric shocks and sensory deprivation there developed what he referred to as a revelation in 'the cruel science of pain'. McCoy notes that the CIA's new torture paradigm fused sensory deprivation with 'self-inflicted' pain, the combination of which causes the victim to feel responsible for their own suffering and thus capitulate more readily to the torturers' demands.

These same torture strategies have been used by the United States, or under the direction or supervision of US government personnel, at Abu Ghraib, Guantánamo and 24 additional sites including sites that were part of the Central Intelligence Agency's Rendering Program where suspects are kidnapped and then sent to countries that are known to use torture during interrogation (Center for Cooperative Research 2005; Priest 2005). The acts of torture committed by US military and civilian personnel are part of a strategy of interrogation and terror that has been often used against those who threaten imperial rule.

Empire's law or law's empire

The central problem with identifying the crimes of empire is that the power of empires is the power to control the definition of crime, especially in a unipolar world. Empires essentially choose if the law is to be applied, who is to be charged, and who will prosecute the case. This is essentially the United States' position regarding international law today. This is the era of what Bartholomew defines as 'Empire's law'. Empire's law is 'an attempt unilaterally to constitute and impose an illegitimate and unaccountable form of rule by a global power that seeks to arrogate to itself the role of global sovereign by declaring it to be the exception' (Bartholomew 2006: 163). Swan (2006) describes the US as engaging in a form of legal exceptionalism as it relates to the functioning of international tribunals for war crimes and the International Criminal Court.

Empire's law is fundamentally based on a system of unequal justice that violates a central principle of law. In describing this exceptionalism Panitch and Gindin (2006: 30) contend that:

> Only the American state could arrogate to itself the right to intervene against the sovereignty of other states (which it repeatedly did around the world) and only the American state reserved for itself the 'sovereign' right to reject international rules and norms when necessary. It is in this sense that only the American state was actively 'imperialist'.

Preuss (2006) notes that in accordance with the laws of empire, it is entirely legitimate to force regime change in a country falling within the empire's sphere of interest and influence. The United States is following this logic of empire when it declares that it does not need UN authorization for war, and can ignore at its will international law and a nation's sovereignty as it relates to acts of war for regime change, kidnapping, torture or assassinations. According to Purvis (2006), the events of 9/11 ushered in a dramatic and ominous shift in the Bush administration's approach to international law. He contends that 'with the advent of the Bush Doctrine the Administration has unilaterally pronounced a death sentence on those features of international law that marked the specificity of the post-World War II International order and that had underpinned the fragile emergence of an international rule of law sui generis' (Purvis 2006: 122).

However, the US strategy has gone beyond exceptionalism to giving the United States power over the International Criminal Court whose jurisdiction it has excluded itself from. Mamdani (2008) notes that the end of the Cold War has led to an international humanitarian order that had promise to hold state sovereignty accountable to an international human rights standard. This new humanitarian order was officially adopted at the UN's 2005 World Summit and claims responsibility for the protection of vulnerable populations. However, Mamdani notes that responsibility for this protection is said to belong to 'the international community', to be exercised in practice by the Security Council in which the United States has the greatest influence given that the majority of its member states are considered to be within the US 'sphere of influence'. Mamdani also notes that the transition from the old system of sovereignty to a new humanitarian order is confined to those states defined as 'failed' or 'rogue' states. Again, defined as failed or rogue states by the United States and the Security Council.

This era of the international humanitarian order is not really new. Mamdani (2008) notes that it draws on the legacy of modern western colonialism. At the outset of colonial expansion in the eighteenth and nineteenth centuries, leading western powers – Britain, France, Russia – claimed to protect 'vulnerable groups'. He notes that these two systems – one defined by sovereignty and citizenship, the other by trusteeship and wardship, worked in a complementary fashion in the context of a world of empires or global empire, under the regime of empire's law. They are essentially two parts of a bifurcated international system.

Mamdani (2008) claims that this strategy is part of the eventual accommodation between the world's only superpower and the struggling ICC. He notes that what is essentially prosecuted by the ICC are governments that are US adversaries and that violent actions that the United States doesn't oppose or commits itself are ignored, effectively conferring impunity on them. Mamdani also notes that the absence of formal political accountability has led to the informal politicization of the ICC and it is not surprising that the United States used its position as the leading power on the Security Council to advance its bid to capture the ICC.

Empire's law is opposed to a system of international law that rules the relations between all states and requires equality before the law for its legitimation. Bartholomew (2006) contends that the promotion of the universalism of international law, 'law's empire', is recognized as a threat to the prerogative of empire to disregard it. She notes that the National Defense Strategy Doctrine of the United States of America released in 2005 explicitly identifies law's empire as posing a threat to the United States. The doctrine asserts that the need for the US to possess 'global freedom of action' to promote and secure its security and interests is a response to the changing security environment. The doctrine states: 'our strength as a nation will continue to be challenged by those who employ a strategy of the weak using international fora, judicial processes, and terrorism' (p. 5). Undersecretary of Defense Douglas Feith's example of a strategy of the weak was the International Criminal Court (Bartholomew 2006).

Bartholomew (2006: 182) argues that 'supporting and reforming law's empire is a crucial move against imperialism, the extent to which it will be resisted, undermined and instrumentalized, and the extent to which empire will attempt to install another "law", can only be addressed with a more developed analysis of American imperium'. However, throughout the history of international law, law's empire has been much weaker than empire's law. The *ad hoc* tribunals established by the imperial powers and the International Court of Justice, created prior to the International Criminal Court, have been relatively ineffective in prosecuting the crimes of empire. They most often operate to confirm and legitimate victor's justice and the will of empires (Cryer 2005a).

Empire's criminology and the criminology of empire

Following the distinctions of law and crimes both defined by and committed on behalf of empires, we can also distinguish between empire's criminology and the criminology of empire. In the former area of inquiry, the concept of empire does not exist. Empire's criminology focuses on the crimes that threaten the empire's functioning and control. This includes the common crimes that threaten the distribution of resources that come about as a result of the economic and political mechanisms of empire, acts of theft, drug crimes enforced to maintain the hierarchical relationships within and between societies, and common forms of interpersonal violence that plague the cities and communities of the center and periphery of the empire.

The theoretical and conceptual tools that are available within empire's criminology are developed to principally explain the crimes of those who are relatively powerless within the imperial society and the dominated world system. Furthermore, empire's criminology is weak in the study of the crimes of organizations that are structured, not as criminal organizations, but as legal entities that have been organized by and function in the interest of powerful actors who are attempting to maintain the imperial order. When 'legitimate' organizations are the 'deviant' actors, questions of etiology are often reduced to the pathology of individuals within them or to defects in the organizational structure, not in the intended function of the organization itself. The disciplinary preoccupation with the question of the legal status of the act, instead of the harm, leads to the problem of focusing on those acts that are defined by the powerful as criminal, and ignoring those acts which may be more harmful in general, but not specifically to those in the power structure.

The most severe crimes in empire's criminology are those that threaten imperial control. The crimes of 'rogue or failed states', those outside of imperial control, and the crimes of non-state actors who threaten the empire with acts of violence or 'terrorism', will be increasingly important within empire's criminology as the empire expands and struggles to maintain control over new territories it occupies or seeks to dominate. These also include the crimes of the proliferation of nuclear weapons – except in those areas that have imperial blessing, for example, India and Israel. The empire increasingly attempts to stem this proliferation of weapons in those areas that are not within its control at the same time that the empire violates and abrogates treaties that block its own development of weapons of mass destruction.

For empire's criminology, the few discussions of state violence it engages in will focus on those states, and state leaders, who have been prosecuted in the international tribunals it has sponsored. Even cases that come before the International Criminal Court may also be included since crimes of the empire will be excluded for consideration by the preroga- tives and exceptionalism defined by the empire. As Rothe and Mullins (2006: 76) point out regarding the US position toward the ICC, 'the US wanted a court for the rest of the world, but insisted the jurisdiction could not impinge on the US, its policies, or its own state actors'.

On the other hand, for the criminology of empire, the empire itself is central to understanding the nature of crime in the imperial center and its periphery. In many respects, like the empire itself, the relationships between crime and empire are most visible in the periphery. The crimes resulting from conquest, and then the transformation of the systems of stratification within these populations as the territories are incorporated into the empire, are of central importance for the criminology of empire. Crimes become rampant as part of the chaos that occurs in the aftermath of conquest and incorporation. The illegal wars for regime change (Blum 1995), the promotion and use of torture and assassinations to control suspect resisters to empire defined as terrorists, the confiscation of resources through privatization and the market dominance of multina- tional corporations sponsored by imperial states, and the outright expul- sion of populations from incorporated territories are all crimes of empire that would be central to the criminology of empire.

Furthermore, the harms of empire that are rarely criminalized, the structural violence (Scheper-Hughes and Bourgois 2004; Iadicola and Shupe 2003) that stems from the creation and extension of ethnic and class stratification systems especially in the newly incorporated or conquered territory into the empire would be an important focus for a criminology of empire. The cultural and physical genocide of conquered populations and the creation of their minority status is an area of harms that would be included. The transformation of the class system resulting from the integration of the territory into the world market dominated by the empire leads to the harmful effects of economic displacement and the increasing class inequality, and the resultant increasing size of the world population that is experiencing the violent consequences of famine would also be a focus of a criminology of empire (Iadicola and Shupe 2003; Bello 2009).

Another area of crime within a criminology of empire would be crimes resulting from the environmental destruction and resultant ecocide of indigenous populations in Africa, South America and Asia. This environ- mental destruction occurs in the imperial center (Grinde and Johansen 1998) as well as throughout the periphery of the empire. The cases of Texaco in Ecuador (Jochnick 1995), Shell in the Niger Delta (Okonta and Douglas 2001), and Stepan Chemical and the ecological destruction in Matamoros, Mexico (Iadicola and Shupe 2003) illustrate environmental crimes that result from growth of empire in these regions of the world.

A criminology of empire would also focus on the sponsorship of crimes by political elites that are part of a comprador class acting in the interest of the imperial center. The sponsorship and active support by a comprador class and the imperial state of crimes committed by military and police forces of states and territories within the empire would also be a focus of study of a criminology of empire. This would include the history of death squad activity organized and supported by the United States' government throughout Latin America since the Kennedy administration (Iadicola and Shupe 2003; Pearce 1981) and most recently in Iraq as part of the counter-insurgency warfare. A criminology of empire would also focus on the efforts of crime control by the empire and its ability to deflect prosecution for its own harmful and criminal behavior and thus be able to commit crime with impunity (Andersson *et al.* 2008). The expansion and co-ordination of control systems throughout the empire including the rendition program and the collaboration of policing agencies across the empire and in the US efforts to combat terrorism would be an important focus of research in a criminology of empire.

In addition to the crimes that are committed in the furtherance of the imperial mission, the crimes that empire's criminology focuses on are also better understood if they are analyzed in the context of empire. For example, the increasing pressure on consumption in the center, coupled with the economic displacement that results from more opportunities for the movement of capital to cheaper labor markets in the imperial periphery, are certainly related to the forces that promote acts of theft. The crimes of violence that disproportionately occur in lower income and ethnic minority communities are not unrelated to the changes in levels of poverty and inequality that are a result of the erosion of income and government services that are due to the increasing costs of empire. Furthermore, there are increasing levels of violence in the imperial center as the population becomes more militarized as it is ever prepared for new wars of conquest and control. The pattern of violent crime that occurs in the wake of warfare is important to take note of considering how frequently the empire conducts wars (Gurr 1979, 1990). The drug trade has also been connected to imperial goals. The Opium Wars between the British empire and China, whereby the British were promoting the sale and distribution of opium to extend their economic power into China, in conflict with Chinese efforts to enforce its drug laws, is an example of the role of drugs in imperial expansion. The imperial goals of the United States have also been linked to the distribution and control of illicit drugs (Cockburn and St Clair 1998; McCoy 1972; Sharpe 2006; Youngers and Rosin 2005).

However, the supreme crimes of empire previously mentioned, the crimes of the state in extending and managing empire and the crimes of economic violence resulting from the exploitation of resources, are the central focus of the criminology of empire (Chambliss 1989; Iadicola and

Shupe 2003; Kramer and Michalowski 2005). In Chapter 2 Michalowski describes the 'state crime wedding cake' which includes the high-profile state crimes of genocide, war crimes and terrorism, the semi-tolerated policy violence of torture, civilian war deaths and the injury and death of civilians from embargos, and the structural violence that results from poverty and systems of stratification created or maintained. In all these areas of state violence, the role of empire is often the context of the action. The concept of empire is central to understanding the nature of state crimes that are most devastating to people throughout the empire. The crimes of aggressive war, genocide and ethnic cleansing, assassinations, torture and repression, state-corporate crimes that devastate the environ-ment and economic crimes of exploitation of labor that result in death and injury, are all part of the process of empire, especially the empire of the United States of America from its beginning through to the twenty-first century. The criminology of empire prefers to use the standard of international law as a basis for defining these crimes, since given the regime of empire's law in the unipolar world of today, the definition of crime is often restricted to only the domain of cases that have been actually prosecuted by the imperial state. For empire's law generally serves to exclude most of the crimes of empire.

Conclusion

The concept of empire is central to the study of state crime and violence and, I would argue, to the study of violence as a whole (Iadicola and Shupe 2003). In Chapter 5 Friedrichs asks, where does a criminology of state crime go? He calls for the creation of a 'prospective criminology' as opposed to the retrospective approach that characterizes much of the research on state crime. He goes on to say that 'A prospective criminology of state crime not only has to be rooted in a retrospective criminology of state crime, but also must adopt a coherent framework of a rapidly evolving world, including the present character of globalization and post-modernity in the world, and the significance of a post-9/11 world.' Friedrichs asks if the notion of an 'American empire' is also a key part of this evolving world. In reviewing those state crimes that are most heinous – genocide, wars of aggression, torture and assassinations – empire is central to this evolving world within which these crimes occur.

However, in empire's criminology and under the regime of empire's law, the concept of empire is missing from the analysis of state crime and violence, and crime and violence in general. In order to understand the nature of state crime and violence we need to further develop a criminology of empire, especially given the current crimes of empire being committed with impunity (Andersson et al. 2008), and the fact that these crimes are likely to continue to occur in the future as the empire expands

43

and acts to maintain its control. To begin this important project, we need to better understand the nature of empires and how they influence state officials to commit acts of violence and crime. We need to look at the different ways in which empires extend their power and influence and to analyze the nature of conquest and control as acts of state crime and violence. Acts of genocide are not reserved for countries like Rwanda, but they are more likely the result of the functioning of empires whether we are discussing the genocide of Jews throughout Europe, the genocide of Armenians by the Ottoman Turks, genocide throughout Africa that was part of British, German or Belgian imperial conquests, the genocides of the 'New World' in both North and South America by the Spanish, French, Dutch, British and American empires, or the ethnic cleansings that are occurring today in the Middle East as a result of the conquests and extension of the current American empire (Kiernan 2007; Petras 2007). Furthermore, how can we understand the acts of torture, kidnapping and assassinations throughout the world today without understanding the role of empire, and in particular the empire of the United States of America?

A criminology of empire will automatically include the promotion of law's empire as a means of control, for without the universalism of law there is no law or justice, and there is no way to control the imperial state's crimes and violence. Furthermore, a criminology of empire may help to force the 'empire in denial' to recognize its own existence and its criminal and violent actions. To continue empire's criminology, rather than develop a criminology of empire, only serves to maintain the façade and perpetuate the criminal regime of the US empire.

Chapter 4

Obligatory sacrifice and Imperial projects

Frank Pearce

This chapter focuses on the role played by sacrificial discourses and sacrificial practices in the organization of states and in the pursuit of their goals. In it, as an aid in the understanding of the contemporary American Imperium I examine the role played by such discourses and practices in the social organization of the Aztec empire, which dominated Meso-America in the sixteenth century. This is not to deny that there are important and significant differences between the Aztec and American systems. And yet, it is instructive that both systems show evidence of instabilities and contradictions; in both the military controlled an extraordinary amount of social resources; both were born from conquest; both developed a combination of territorial and hegemonic empires; and, surprisingly, in both there has been an occlusion of human sacrificial processes.

Successful imperialistic societies always impose great sacrifices, including death and physical injury, on the members of the societies that they dominate, but in the process they also sacrifice the lives and well-being of many of their own members. In this dual sense, then, human sacrifice is routine in imperialistic societies although it is only sometimes ritualized. I begin by theorizing sacrifice. Next, I turn to the United States of America and briefly consider some of the discourses on sacrifice to be found in the speeches of recent American presidents. I then explore the role of human sacrifice in Aztec societies, and finally I revisit American society in light of the discussion of the Aztecs.

Theorizing sacrifice

A major resource for this article is the work of Emile Durkheim, which in emphasizing its radical possibilities, I take in somewhat unexpected directions. Durkheim argues, both explicitly and implicitly, that sacrifice is integral to all human societies. In his earliest work he notes that children are 'forced to take into consideration interests other than their own, to make sacrifices and dedicate themselves to the good of the family'; through the appropriate conditioning and development of children's personalities they are equipped to enter the adult world as free and responsible grown-ups where 'society demands an enormous amount of disinterestedness and reciprocal sacrifice' (Durkheim 1883–84/2004: 255). The normal personality is developed through targeted behavioral conditioning. In societies manifesting mechanical solidarity all make sacrifices, because in order for social order to be possible all must equally submit to the uniform conscience collective. What matters is more that values are learned than that they have specific content (Durkheim 1893/1984: 34–9). To refuse the demands of the collective is to risk severe sanctions, which might include death or expulsion.

Organic solidarity is more complex. While all social members still need to learn rules, the social world is more differentiated, thereby increasing individuation and rendering the consciousness of actors more complex and diverse. It also involves reciprocal interdependence, providing a possible basis for a different kind of solidarity. The rules are less unified and more flexible, designed to regulate often changing social interactions. Indeed, many rules are meta-rules, determining how rules should be established, how the harm occasioned by transgressions should be ameliorated, and how criteria should be established to judge whether rules and social arrangements are compatible with equity and justice. These developments in collective social organization and social thought have produced a new social morality found in the ethical and political movements inspired by the thought of Kant and Rousseau. While here, one finds a 'religion of which man is, at the same time, both believer and god', what is valorized is not egoism, but the capacity of all humans to develop 'that wise and pure reason which, dissociated from all personal motives, would make laws in the abstract concerning its own conduct' (Durkheim 1898/1994: 62–3, 72–3).

Nevertheless, social organization and values are moving beyond an abstract and ontologically individualistic Kantianism. The modern family gives will and effort 'an end going beyond egoistic and momentary enjoyment' but it also nourishes and strengthens the child insofar as it is 'a refuge where the wounds of life may find their consolation and errors their pardon'; 'the family is a source (*foyer*) of morality, energy and kindness' (Davy 1925 cited in Lukes 1975: 185–6). True, the child needs to develop a taste for discipline and order in his or her conduct, and to learn to value reason as well as feelings (Durkheim 1925/1961: 149). But the goal is not only to produce autonomous reflective individuals who can think beyond their immediate circumstances and their particular interests, and who can be morally aware, but to produce ones who are sensitive to the value of humanity *per se* and aware of their society's specific rules. They should be able to recognize their obligation to 'alleviate the functioning of the social machine' so that all individuals in fact have 'the means to develop their faculties', which means finding 'new means of organizing social life and introducing more justice in contractual relations' (Durkheim 1898/1994: 71). Durkheim identifies one such means – redistributing wealth that is not earned but merely inherited. If this were to occur, there would no longer be extremely wealthy parents who can install their offspring as managers of industries, and purchase exclusive private schooling and access to the professions, including the military (Durkheim 1893/1984: 319–22). In the United States such practices as using the privileges of wealth to join the National Guard, rather than combat units, would also no longer occur.

In his discussion of altruistic suicide, Durkheim argues that because war increases nationalism and hence altruism it tends to reduce the suicide rate. He also argued that militarism *per se* tends to increase the suicide rate; soldiers' excessive identification with their army units often leads them to prioritize its interests, attenuating their cognizance and pursuit of their own. For the purposes of his research, Durkheim used a restrictive and legalistic definition of suicide – the term 'applied to all cases of death resulting directly or indirectly from a positive or negative act of the victim himself, which he knows will produce this result' (Durkheim 1897/1951: 44). Soldiers do not know, even in the most fraught battle situation, that they rather than others will die. By definition, then, they do not commit suicide. But Durkheim also notes that 'a man exposing himself knowingly for another's sake, but without the certainty of a fatal result' is acting in a way that 'is not radically distinct from true suicide', an action that results from a 'similar state of mind' since it also entails 'mortal risks not unknown to the agent ... and the prospect of these is no deterrent; the sole difference is a lesser chance of death' (Durkheim 1897/1951: 45). This implies that the willingness of soldiers to risk their lives in typical battle situations is both suicidal and self-sacrificial. This raises the question, can the state legitimately ask for such sacrifices? A democratic state operating in a truly egalitarian democratic society might have a right to so. One that is autocratic, separated from the rest of society, not expressing a 'General Will' but captured by sectional interests, would have no such right. Under these circumstances soldiers are more sacrificed than self-sacrificing. Durkheim focuses on Germany during World War One (Durkheim 1915), but, as Elwin Powell (1988) has shown, there is no reason to restrict Durkheim's theorizing to that war, and nor shall we. Overall, in an unequal and undemocratic society, the interests of the mass of the population will often be sacrificed to those of the privileged, intent on holding on to their wealth and power. Further, in any unjust order the privileged are over-compensated for any sacrifices they make and those with little or no resources are under-compensated for their (often large) sacrifices. While all social life requires some sacrifice (Durkheim 1914/1960: 328), not all sacrifices are necessary and just.

In his writings on religious phenomena Durkheim discusses sacrifice in the context of more ritualized forms. In all societies, he argues, an absolute distinction is made between those beliefs, rituals and activities that are seen as sacred and those seen as profane. The sacred realm is produced through the collective activity of society, which is 'infinitely superior to each individual, since it is a synthesis of individuals' and since we are always in a state of 'perpetual dependence' upon society it 'inspires in us a feeling of religious awe' (Durkheim 1899/1994: 93). The profane realm is more the everyday world, of routine activities and contingent beliefs, as experienced individually. Society needs both realms but it is essential that they are kept separate (Durkheim 1912/1995: 313). Yet at the same time there must be mechanisms by which the realms are connected; one such mechanism is ritual sacrifice. Durkheim's colleagues Henri Hubert and Marcel Mauss define this as a procedure *'establishing a means of communication between the sacred and the profane worlds through the mediation of a victim, that is, of a thing that in the course of the ceremony is destroyed'* (Hubert and Mauss 1898/1964: 97, original italics). 'The purpose of the cult', Durkheim remarks, 'is not only to bring the profane into communion with sacred beings but also to keep the sacred beings alive, to remake and regenerate them perpetually' (Durkheim 1912/1995: 350). Sacrificial consecrations generate a religious power that passes both to the sacred sphere, to the gods, who then 'have received their share', and to the profane sphere where the sacrifier is 'raised above . . . his ordinary and normal nature' (Hubert and Mauss 1898/1964: 44).

In most religious systems, a deity or deities create the cosmos, and deities play some role in its continuity and development. In 'Brahmanic' systems, a major focus is on continuity and development, usually seen as dependent upon the desires and activities of one or more divine beings. However, these in turn often require nourishment from 'effective sacrifices' made by humanity, who thereby also control and maintain the order of the universe. In other religions the focus is on the deity who has created the universe and who is willing to sustain it for the benefit of a chosen people and for the rest of humanity providing that this people honor a contract made between them and the deity. In such systems sacrificial acts and ceremonies seem to have no effectivity; they merely demonstrate respect for the deity and memorialize and reassert the contract (Herrenschmidt 1982). This argument will be revisited.

Religious and ritual sacrifice articulate different forms and levels of the cosmic and human world. But as Durkheim makes clear, the sacred and profane and, by implication, sacrificial systems are not only associated with formal religions but can also be found in what religions define as the secular realm. For example, insofar as humanity is worshipped for the intrinsic human capacity to develop a sophisticated reflective consciousness, this requires that we treat humanity as a whole and the particular societies in which we live as equally sacred. Thus national and international collective assemblies and patriotic rituals are sacralizing mechanisms (Durkheim 1950/1957: 74–5).

At this point it is useful to clarify and elaborate somewhat on the way the term sacrifice has been used thus far. A *sacrifier* is a person or collectivity whose desire motivates a sacrifice. A *sacrificer* (who may also be the sacrifier) is a person or collectivity who arranges and possibly presides at a sacrifice (it could be a parent, an army officer, or priest). Some sacrifices, but by no means all, involve ceremonial rituals. A sacrifice will honor a *superior other*; this can be human or divine, and an individual, collectivity or ideal. In that all of these are connected with collective values and aspirations, which are foundational of the sacred, the superior other is always sacred. The beneficiary of a sacrifice may be the sacrifier and/or some designated individual or collective other. While sacrifice is always altruistic it does not preclude self-interest, but if there is self-interest it usually involves self-transformation.

The term sacrifice refers to an act or acts by which a sacrifier gives up something it values to a *superior sacred other*, sometimes through a ritual officiated by a sacrificer, in the hope of creating for itself and sometimes for designated others a right relation with the superior other and possibly to receive other benefits that the latter can bestow. Sacrifice implies both the hope of some positive outcome and a lack of certainty that this will occur. In summary, from these analyses, an analysis of sacrifice requires the deployment of the following terms and categories: sacred/profane; sacrifier(s); sacrificer(s); victim(s); community; recipient(s), beneficiary(ies); hierarchy; effective; covenantal; cosmic order; divinities.

While this schema applies to all sacrifices made by humans, the concern in this chapter is to apply it primarily to situations where humans sacrifice other humans, i.e. human sacrifice. For the United States, when one of its military personnel dies in battle, this has long been described as the ultimate self-sacrifice, undertaken in the interests of the nation and American values. Many other instances of sacrifice, while not so final, also refer to physical harms and other deprivations that Americans suffer. For the Aztecs, the major form of sacrifice was the ritual slaughter of captive warriors in honor of their gods and to keep the sun moving in the sky.

Sacrifice in the United States

There is a long tradition in America of presidents making explicit reference to sacrifice in their public addresses. Here I look at some sacrificial themes in such speeches by a number of presidents. For example, in his second inaugural address President Eisenhower portrays the world of 1957 as caught in a struggle between the 'Free World' and

---

Sacrifier: Individual/collectivity seeks 'right relation' to superior being and other benefits. Sacrifier's worth relates to frequency/quality of their sacrifices.

Societally superior sacrifier: Elite individual or institution that can in part appropriate the sacrifice.

Victim: Person of value donated by sacrifier(s) and destroyed: high-status persons often most desirable.

Sacrificer: Agent of the sacrifice: if ceremonial usually already sacralized.

Ceremony: A set of rituals sacralizing participants, and spatio-temporally separating them from and returning them to mundane life.

Beneficiary(ies): Designated individual(s) or collectivity(ies).

Recipient: Superior other – sacred/mundane individual, collective, being or ideal.

Cosmic order: Articulated, hierarchical.

Community: Inclusionary and exclusionary.

Other societal effects: Complex effects that may differ for different groups.

Figure 4.1   Schema for human sacrifice – all moments ritualizable

'International Communism'. Peace could only be maintained if an equal or superior force confronts the latter; but he cautions: 'Splendid as can be the blessings of such a peace, high will be its cost: in toil patiently sustained, in help honorably given, in sacrifice calmly borne. We are called to meet the price of this peace' (Eisenhower, 21 January 1957).

In his first inaugural address, George H. W. Bush broadened the discourse of sacrifice by reminding Americans of the danger of being too 'enthralled with material things, less appreciative of the nobility of work and sacrifice'. There is a need to help:

> [T]he homeless ... children who have nothing ... those who cannot free themselves of enslavement to whatever addiction – drugs, welfare, the demoralization that rules the slums ... crime to be conquered, the rough crime of the streets ... young women ... about to become mothers of children they can't care for and might not love ... The old solution, the old way, was to think that public money alone could end these problems. But we have learned that is not so ... We will turn to the only resource we have that in time of need always grows – the goodness and the courage of the American people ... (George H. W. Bush, 20 January 1989)

While the explicit focus is on those who give up their leisure time for unpaid volunteer work in the community, implicit is reference to other kinds of sacrifice. For example, there are the good parents who give up their time and comfort in the interests of their children. Many of these will have worked hard to build businesses or to gain qualifications that means they receive a good income that helps them provide well for their families. He is also suggesting that welfare is an 'addiction', crime is the province of the poor, children 'born to single mothers' are unloved. As a wealthy patrician, Bush sees the American political, economic and social system as a valid and moral order and that its distribution of wealth and advantage, poverty and disadvantage, are merited (Phillips 2004). While charity might be a moral imperative, there would be no legal requirement for the wealthy to help the poor through the redistributive effects of taxation. Indeed, in his election campaign, Bush had promised not only to impose 'no new taxes', but to cut corporate taxes.

Even though the Soviet Union was clearly unraveling and the Berlin Wall had fallen, in this speech Bush retained the same belligerent emphasis on combat readiness. He promised the world that 'We will stay strong to protect the peace ... The "offered hand" is a reluctant fist; but once made, strong, and can be used with great effect' (George H. W. Bush, 20 January 1989). Within the year, the US had invaded Panama, toppling its former ally Manuel Noriega, allegedly in order to protect American service personnel, defend democracy and human rights, safeguard the neutrality of the Canal and because he was a major drug trafficker. In his State of the Union Address on 31 January 1990, Bush quoted a letter written by Private 1st Class James Markwell, a 20-year-old Army medic to his mother, prior to his death during the invasion:

> I've been trained to kill and to save, and so has everyone else. I am frightened of what lays beyond the fog, and yet ... do not mourn for me. Revel in the life that I have died to give you ... But most of all, don't forget that the Army was my choice. Something that I wanted to do. Remember I joined the Army to serve my country and ensure that you are free to do what you want and to live your lives freely. (George H. W. Bush, 31 January 1990)

Among Bush's justifications for the invasion of Iraq in January 1991 was that, Saddam Hussein, a leader, in fact, supported by the US as an ally while, as they knew, he was using poisonous gas against Iranians and Kurdish dissidents, had suddenly been revealed as a cruel and murderous dictator: 'Saddam Hussein systematically raped, pillaged, and plundered a tiny nation, no threat to his own. He subjected the people of Kuwait to unspeakable atrocities – and among those maimed and murdered, innocent children' (George H. W. Bush, 16 January 1991).

If we turn to the (post-9/11) speeches of George W. Bush we find he links different sacrifices with a besieged community unified in its warlike resistance:

We see our national character in rescuers working past exhaustion, in long lines of blood donors, in thousands of citizens who have asked to work and serve in any way possible. And we have seen our national character in eloquent acts of sacrifice. Inside the World Trade Center, one man who could have saved himself stayed until the end and at the side of his quadriplegic friend. A beloved priest died giving the last rites to a firefighter. Two office workers, finding a disabled stranger, carried her down 68 floors to safety . . . Today, we feel what Franklin Roosevelt called, 'the warm courage of prevail against our enemies. And this unity against terror is national unity.' . . . Our unity is a kinship of grief and a steadfast resolve to now extending across the world . . . God bless America. (George W. Bush, 13 September 2001)

The imagery in these examples, and others, present a Manichean vision. This produces the conditions for an 'othering' that permits ruthless treatment of the enemy. The use of the term evil is also significant here because it often means not only that human beings do evil things, but that doing evil things means that they are doing the work of the devil. God is not only on the side of the United States, but the devil is with its opponents. In this schema I am also drawing upon some of my previous work (Pearce 1976, 2007; Pearce and Tombs 1998).

The Tenochca and the Aztecs

I now turn to the Aztecs. This may seem a surprising choice; after all, the Aztecs are notorious for their practice of ritual human sacrifice and aggressive warfare. Further, their religion was a mixture of shamanism, animism and polytheism, and it was all-embracing; their political leader was also their military and spiritual leader; their technology was minimal and their economy was based on peasant farming and on wealth redistributed to hereditary classes by tributes raised both from their own peasants and from the societies they conquered. Americans may often talk about sacrifice but by this is meant self-sacrifice, which is not ritualized; their government is formally democratic; there is a separation of church and state; the main religions are monotheistic and claim to be based upon compassion; science and technology are both well developed; America claims to be a meritocracy and its economy is capitalist; and, finally, America has no colonies. But while the role of sacrifice in Aztec societies superficially is very different from that in the US, I hope to show that on a deeper level there are significant similarities between them.

The term Aztec is used to refer to the twenty or so northern Nahua-speaking peoples who in the eleventh, twelfth and thirteenth

A: Sacrifice and evil

Sacrifiers and sacrificers: (a) Undemocratic, statist, fanatical, atheistic or Islamic fundamentalist nations or terrorists; (b) Disloyal Americans favoring foreign interests and ideologies over America's; (c) The venal, envious, lazy, cowardly and self-indulgent welfare/criminal classes.

Societally superior sacrifier: At different times, Moscow and Beijing.

Victims: (a1) American youth in the military; (a2) Entrepreneurs throughout the world but particularly American companies denied essential materials and markets; (a/b/c) The loyal, hard-working American people as a whole bearing the cost of keeping world peace and the cost of the justice and welfare systems.

Human recipients: (a/b) Dictatorial rulers of unfree nations; (c) Different 'mafias'.

Cosmic order: God has created human beings who have been able to build social orders, such as the US, based on the worship of the one true God, freedom, property rights and democracy. Others have built inefficient and oppressive systems, often through ignorance but at times malevolently. In practice, they align themselves with the devil, the evil power that plots against God.

Community: The lives of the devout, productive and deserving are constricted and disrupted.

Societal effects: Great harm throughout the world, but as a God-fearing nation America is basically unassailable

B: Noble self-sacrifice in contemporary United States

Sacrifiers/sacrificers: (a) The military and other useful public servants; (b) Capitalist wealth creators; (c) Wage earners; (d) Parents; (e) The charitable.

Societally superior sacrifiers: Monotheistic American nation including (a) The President and Congress; (b/c) Free market economy; (d) Network of families; (e) Charities.

Victims: (a) Youth in military; (b) Capitalists deferring gratification; (c) Wage workers accepting discomfort to earn money for their family; (d) Housewife depriving herself of luxuries for family; (e) Those giving up time and pleasure for the unfortunate.

Ceremonies: Memorializations marking individual and collective self-sacrifices under the aegis of the state.

Human recipients: (a/b) Democratic nation/free world; (c/d) Family; (e) Deserving poor.

Cosmic order: God created and sustains human ability to build a social order based on worship, freedom, property rights and democracy. Through skill, effort and thrift individuals determine the kind of life they live. They have a manifest destiny to spread this way of life to others and to oppose the fanatical, irreligious, envious, cowardly, self-indulgent, collectivists.

Community: The devout, productive and deserving.

Societal effects: As a god-fearing nation America is basically unassailable.

Figure 4.2 Dominant discourses of sacrifice in the contemporary United States

centuries (CE) arrived in the Valley of Mexico and the surrounding valleys (Gibson 1964). The Aztecs included the Culhua, Alcolhua, Tepaneca, Tlaxcala, Huexotzinca and the Mexica peoples. They shared the legend that they had left a northern homeland called Aztlan in order to journey south. They subscribed to similar cosmologies, and pantheons of gods, and practiced similar rituals including human sacrifice. Their forms of political, economic and social organization were similar. When settled, they did so in autonomous tribal units called *altepetls*, each of which controlled a territory, consisted of a number of clans or *calpolli*, and had an overall leader, called their *tlatoani*. If they became more populous and urbanized they evolved into one of many hierarchical city-states.

The Mexica founded a settlement in a swampy part of Lake Texcoco, which became the city-state of Tenochtitlan. At first, the Tenochca Mexica were in a subordinate relationship to the powerful Tepanec city-state of Atzcapotzalco, but along with the Alcolhua of Texcoco and the tacit support of the Tepanecs of Tlacopan they were able to defeat their former rulers. The three victorious city-states formed a 'triple alliance' and created a huge empire. In 1519 this empire controlled an area of some 77,000 square miles (Fagan and Beck 1996: 81) and consisted of three provinces in the Valley of Mexico and another 36 or so provinces from which the triple alliance demanded tributes, plus another 23 provincial regions with which it had an asymmetrical client-like relation. The empire as a whole was sustained by a combination of alliances, including the intermarriage of women of the Mexican nobility with ruling-class men of the city-states; the appropriation of land and serfs; the offer of protection and relative prosperity; and the threat of force. Economically it was tied together through a series of circuits of tribute and trade involving goods, labor and, indeed, lives (Berdan 2004: 264).

The Valley of Mexico was home to between one and two million Aztecs living in 50 or so city-states in three provinces with a relatively high degree of social, political and economic integration. Up to another two million Aztecs lived in the surrounding valleys. Ideologically, this heartland was unified, at least to some extent, by appeals to the superior Toltec/Culhua heritage, by the shared Meso-American pantheon of gods, and by the Tenochca's claim to a unique role in world-making, world-centering, and world-renewing (Carrasco 1999: 36–40). However, the Aztec city-states of Tlaxcala, Huexotzinco and Cholula were neither conquered by nor allied with the triple alliance. Tenochtitlan was the largest city-state in the Americas, organized in 20 *calpolli*, each numbering about 8,000 residents, and each mustering about 400 warriors for the Tenoch army (Hassig 1988: 65–7). It was the political, economic and ritual center of the empire, clearly dominating the other members of the triple alliance.

Human sacrifice

While all the Aztec peoples made many different kinds of offerings to their gods it was human beings and human blood that were deemed the most important offerings. People of all ranks used maguey spines on their own bodies, drawing blood from these lacerations, but they also sacrificed male and female children, criminals and other wrongdoers, slaves and captives, and particularly male warriors. The victims were put to death in a variety of rituals involving drowning, burial while alive, bludgeoning, stoning, impaling, being thrown into fires, having their throats cut, being shot with arrows, flaying, being decapitated and through excision of the heart, with the last often combined with one or more of the former (Graulich 2005: 19). They were sacrificed on feasts to celebrate the gods and on calendar dates relating to the seasons and the passing of years and to memorialize important events in history. Of all the Aztec peoples the Tenochca Mexica engaged in human sacrifice with particular frequency and with the largest number of victims. While some estimates of the number sacrificed annually are implausible – 250,000 (Harner 1977) – human sacrifice was certainly widespread. Throughout the empire 5,000 people were probably sacrificed each year (Davies 1981: 239). Many slaves and captive warriors were provided as tributes by the provinces both creating a general fear of the Tenoch and providing grounds for revolt – what more could be taken from a subaltern people than their lives (Conrad and Demarest 1984: 44–71)? Nevertheless, captives were of particular significance during most major festivals and celebrations of great victories. Below I focus on the great warrior festival, of Tlacaxipeualitzi, the feast of the flaying of men, celebrated at the time of the spring equinox and dedicated to Xipe Totec, Our Lord the Flayed One, god of spring, fertility and success in war.

Many authors have shown that a major rationale proposed for these sacrifices was the need to sustain the movement of the fifth sun. The Tenoch believed that the cosmos was permeated and shaped by *teotl*, a dynamic, vivifying, sacred and impersonal power, energy or force (Maffie 2002). Its movement was in and through dualities, endless opposition of mutually arising, mutually interdependent and mutually complementary forces, sometimes in equilibrium but more usually with one temporarily dominant. Some of these forces manifested themselves as gods, the sacrifice of which played a key role in the workings of the cosmos. In order to keep the sun moving in its course there was a need to replicate the sacrificial actions of the gods by human sacrifice; the human body was a container of divine energy and the blood, the head, the heart and the liver all contained important regenerative powers.

Sacrifice was a sacred duty towards the sun and a necessity for the welfare of the people; without it the very life of the world would stop.

Every time a priest on the top of the pyramid held up the bleeding heart of a man and then placed it in the *quahxicalli* the disaster that perpetually threatened to fall upon the world was postponed once more. Human sacrifice was an alchemy by which life was made out of death; and the gods themselves had given the example on the first day of creation.

As for man, his very first duty was to provide nourishment *intonan intota tlaltecuhltli tonatiuh*, 'for our mother and our father, the earth and the sun'. To shirk this was to betray the gods and at the same time all humankind, for what was true of the sun was also true of the earth, the rain, growth and the forces of nature. Nothing was born, nothing would endure, except by the blood of sacrifice (Soustelle 1955/1970: 96–7).

Humanity has always relied on the gods for their very existence and for their well-being and in exchange the gods required sacrifices to sustain them in turn (Clendinnen 1993: 74; Sahagun 1981: 199).

This system of exchange with the gods, however, was not necessarily symmetrical and there were no guarantees that appropriate conduct would produce positive outcomes. Events and the trajectory of individual lives were, after all, the outcome of conflictual superhuman forces, but also Tezcatlipoca, in particular, was feared for his quixotic interventions in human affairs (Clendinnen 1993: 80). True, divination and priestly sleight of hand allowed people to circumvent aspects of their fate (Sahagun 1981: 39), but the universe was essentially an unsafe, insecure and largely unknown place. So, despite all these human sacrifices, a day would come when the sun would be no more and earthquakes would destroy the world (Soustelle 1955/1970: 96).

Tlacaxipehualitzli

The festival of Tlacaxipehualitzli was a payment to the gods for the favors they had shown humankind and to beg for more favors. It was particularly addressed to Xipe Totec, who had flayed himself in an act of self-torture just as the sprouting maize seed separates into multiple shoots. Flaying a victim's skin represented the maize seeds' own self-sacrifice when they shed their outer covering; wearing the victim's skin represented the regeneration of the plant. The ceremonies were intimately connected with other annual events; for example the war season that began in the November of the previous year and which lasted for 120 days. Ideally, major military campaigns were started and completed during this period, which ended just before Tlacaxipehualitzli. During these months new territories were sought and existing provinces secured in bloody and often fatal warfare and ideally a large number of enemy warriors would be captured and be available for sacrifice. Sometimes the numbers of captured warriors would be supplemented with warriors captured in a *xochiyatl*, 'flower war', a ritual combat usually between the triple alliance and the unconquered 'Enemies-of-the-House', the cities of Tlaxcala, Huexotzinco and Cholula. In such wars, warriors on both sides sought to capture as many enemy warriors as possible so that they could be ritually sacrificed. 'Sacred war was a cosmic duty' (Soustelle 1955/ 1970: 203).

At the beginning of January, Tenoch warriors would begin to display the warriors they had captured in their *calpolli*. At the beginning of March these captives were transformed into *xipeme*, living images of Xipe Totec. The next day, when Tlacaxipehualitzli officially began, the priests, in accord with the royal prerogative of controlling ritual human sacrifice, took the captives to the Great Temple. This was believed to be the *axis mundi* and the Tenoch saw it as their responsibility to maintain its essential role in sustaining the universe. The priests told the captive warriors to climb to the shrine of Huitzilopochtli (Carrasco 1999: 142). Some captives displayed reluctance while others embraced their fate, but in each case:

[T]hey stretched them out on the sacrificial stone. Then they delivered them into the hands of six offering priests; they stretched them out upon their backs; they cut open their hearts with a wide bladed knife.

And they named the hearts of the captives 'precious eagle-cactus fruit'. They raised them in dedication to the sun, Xipilli, Quauh-tleunatil . . .

And these captives who had died they called eagle men. (Sahagun 1981: 48)

The priests flayed each victim and the old men of the captor's *calpulli* took the body to their temple and then to the captor's house. The corpse was cut into pieces, the thighbone going to the *tlatoani*, the rest to members of the *calpulli*. The captor distributed bowls containing pieces of the victim's flesh to his family; he himself ate none of the flesh. He was decorated with 'bird down', covered with 'chalk' and named the 'sun', because he 'had not died there in war, or else because he would yet go to die, to pay the debt [in war or by sacrifice]' (Sahagun 1981: 48).

On the second day, young Aztec warriors wearing the skins of the sacrificed warriors travelled from door to door collecting food but also harassing other captive warriors in mock battles. Elite aristocratic warriors then led some of these captives to the place of gladiatorial sacrifice. Each captor tied his captive to the hub of the Temalacatl, a round flat stone about nine feet in diameter, and then provided him with defanged weaponry. He was attacked in sequence by elite warriors until overcome and sacrificed. Watching these ceremonies, but hidden from the crowds of the Tenoch, were foreign dignitaries, some from friendly states but others from the very states whose warriors were being sacrificed. Each warrior who had provided a captive walked around the city placing the captive's blood on the images of the gods and the captive's body was taken to his *calpolli*. There it was flayed, cut up and distributed. Again, this captor ate none of it. He said: 'Shall I perchance eat my very self?' For when he took [the captive], he had said: 'He is my beloved son.' And the captive had said: 'He is my beloved father' (Sahagun 1981: 54). But he did take the flayed skin, at first wearing it himself, and then lending it out to poverty-stricken Tenochca.

On the third day there were more sacrifices but also many ceremonial dances. The *tlatoani* of each of Tenochtitlan, Texcoco and Tlacopan danced together, wearing the skins of the most important flayed victims, and accompanied by many of the greater nobility. The Tenochca *tlatoani* then distributed presents of cloaks and food to the warriors for their accomplishments (Sahagun 1981: 56). And then variations of the ceremonies went on and on until the end of the month. In the next month maize seeds and other seed were planted.

David Carrasco provides an incisive analysis of the overall significance of the event.

> The gorgeous and terrible displays of warriors draped in the skins of sacrificial victims and the cuauhxicalli filled with blood moving throughout the city show that the Tlacaxipehualitzli was a story the Aztecs told to themselves about their triumphant wars, in the way they wanted it known . . .
>
> [For] the observer, deity impersonator, mother carrying child, teenager in the street, or novice in training, the ceremony is a perfect battle, is a middle place, their pivotal place in a process of production and completion. It is both the end point and the starting point. It is a perfect battle after the war and a magic display to the citizens of how things should go in the next war. It is a public victory within the city, and a preparation for a future battle. It is an ideal recollection and an anticipatory ceremonial practice because it provides a clear cognitive and experiential system or map . . . [P]ower in the Aztec world was perceived as much in ceremonies of sacrifice and their charismatic transformations as in the stomping, moving hoards who blazed like a sacred fire in the lands beyond the capital city. (Carrasco 1999: 163)

Rereading the sacrificial discourse and practices of the Tenochca

Such accounts of the complexus of mythological discourses and ritual practices associated with human sacrifice underline much that is of significance. However, while useful in describing the practice of human sacrifice and in helping to understand the workings of Tenochca society as a whole, as explanations such accounts are underdeveloped, need clarification, elaboration, retheorizing and articulation with other theoretical positions. Soustelle and Carrasco in particular are culturalist in that they start and remain constrained by the discourses of the Tenoch about both everyday activities and more formal ritualized ones, paying almost exclusive attention to what the Tenoch said that they did and also the explanations they provided for their conduct. They do not, however, pay sufficient attention to all that was taking place, that which was underemphasized, and much of that which while neither seen nor spoken can be theorized.

The Tenochca ceremonial machine was part of a social formation based upon a tax-rent system whereby 'the surplus product' was 'appropriated in the form of a tax ... paid in labor ... or in kind' (Hindess and Hirst 1975; Knight 2002: 183). This came from various sources; of great significance were tributes from other states, going to the royal treasury, some of which was distributed to the 6 per cent of the population who constituted the nobility. These also owned large estates, farmed by serfs, outside of Tenochtitlan in conquered territories. Within Tenochtitlan itself, produce and communal labor, including military service, were provided by its twenty *calpolli*. Social order was sustained by a complex combination of an economic order, which usually guaranteed an adequate subsistence living, a very ordered and regulated life and a combination of ideology and repression (cf. Padden 1962; Wolf 1999).

While there is no doubt that part of the purpose of Tenochca sacrificial rituals was to show their might to themselves, to their allies and their opponents, it was also to make clear to the citizens that war was necessary and good, that they benefited from war, and that their contribution was essential. Carrasco (1999: 163) is accurate that the whole festival 'is a perfect battle after the war and a magic display to the citizens of how things should go in the next war . . . and preparation for a future battle'. But inherent in the mythologies, the ceremonies and the discourses of the Tenoch warriors themselves was the inherent reversibility for them of the role of sacrifier and victim. This was why the captor ate none of the flesh of his sacrificed captive, saying: 'Shall I perchance eat my very self?' It was also why on another occasion after the sacrifice of his captive, he was decorated and named the 'sun', because although he 'had not died . . . he . . . would yet go to die'.

The root sacrifice of the Tenochca was the sacrifice of their own young warriors. At the same moment that the massive ceremonial machine of Tenochtitlan centripetally pulled in enemy warriors to be ritually sacrificed it centrifugally pushed out its own warriors to be sacrificed – on the battlefield or, if captured, ritually. This was a society dedicated to war. Its resources, social organization, ideologies, socialization practices, schooling, reward structures all promoted militarism (Clendinnen 1993). It was also allegedly meritocratic in that the nobles were seen as the best warriors and exceptional commoners could receive special honors. In fact, the nobles were better trained, better armed and better protected. The *tlatoani* rulers represented their wars as defensive, arising from incipient danger, disobedience or their being treated with contemptuous disrespect. But there were always sanctions against those who resisted military discipline or proved cowardly or inept on the battlefield; warriors were meant to fight to the death to avoid capture, and to return home after being a *bona fide* captive was dishonorable (Hassig 1988: 115). Even when the Tenochca were successful in their campaigns, nearly 20 per cent of their warriors were probably killed, maimed or missing (Hassig 1988: 117). When they were badly defeated, for example, as in the wars against the Tarascans, the triple alliance lost over 20,000 warriors, 90 per cent of their army. It is necessary to modify Carrasco's words: sacrifice in the Tenochca empire was first, of the Tenoch warriors who died when as 'stomping, moving hoards' they 'blazed like a sacred fire in the lands beyond the capital city' and the peoples thereby ravaged, and only second, of those ceremonially sacrificed in Tenochtitlan.

All societies that routinely engage in warfare have been willing to sacrifice their own people on the battlefield, and they are unlikely to have more compunction about killing other people on the battlefield than in risking the lives of their own warriors. The same holds true for the treatment of prisoners. From the point of view of captors, but not that of the captives, there is little difference between slaughtering enemies on the battlefield, capturing them and then massacring them, torturing them to death, or ritually sacrificing them. There are, of course, other ways of dealing with prisoners: ransom; prisoner exchange; temporary imprisonment; serfdom or slavery; impressment in the victor's army; colonization; and simple release (Patterson 1982: 106). Each and every way of dealing with prisoners has costs and benefits, and choices made between them are likely to be determined by pragmatic responses to situational exigencies rather than by moral considerations. But these exigencies are also determined in part by the goals of any particular state.

In Meso-America warfare was common, but the enslavement of captives was minimal, in part because production was so organized that they were unlikely to be a useful addition to the labor force. On the other hand, the sacrifice of some captives was common, although not on a mass level. Yet not all powerful city-states dedicated themselves to war. Teotihuacan, for example, possessed significant military capacity, and a warrior elite was of great significance to the city (Sugiyama 2005; Headrick 2007), but its internal growth and the external expansion of its influence were not primarily dependent upon the use of force; trade, albeit on often unequal terms, was much more significant (Pasztory 1997). Cholula, during much of its existence and including during the post-classic period, which was the centre of the Quetzelcoatl cult, generally avoided offensive actions (McCafferty 2000). Even the more warlike and equally powerful city-states of Atzcapotzalco and Chalco, intense and often belligerent rivals, avoided war for a long period of time. Instead, the two city-states engaged in ritual confrontations, the goal of which was not to physically harm their opponents, who were mainly nobles, but to take them captive and then release them unharmed back to their home city. These were one kind of flower wars, *xochiyatls*. However, after eight years or so of this, and in the context of a continuing stalemate, Atzcopatzalco brought the Tenoch Mexica into the conflict. This coincided with a shift whereby while captured nobles were still released, captured commoners were now killed, presumably as human sacrifices (Hassig 1988: 128–30). Chalco remained unconquered but in about 1420 it precipitated another flower war with the Tenochca; and now both sides captured and sacrificed the other's nobles as well as their commoners. Conflict with Chalco continued, although the latter was finally defeated in 1450. But this victory was followed by four years of famine, and Tenochtitlan then instituted flower wars with the independent Aztec states of Tlaxcala, Huexotzinco, Atlixco and a reluctant Cholula (Duran 1994: 231–6).

Tenochtitlan was above all an imperialist power, claiming a 'manifest destiny' to sustain the cosmos. In most of their campaigns, including those against other Aztec peoples, the Tenochca's main goal was to defeat their

---

Sacrifier: Aztec warrior kills on the battlefield or captures enemy Aztec warrior; seeks position in competitive hierarchical society.

Superior sacrifier: Each *tlatoani* controls all ritual human sacrifice, but also decides whether or not to send warriors to secure and expand imperium and keep the sun moving in the sky. Sacralizes the Aztec hierarchy.

Victims: Aztec warriors embrace death, whether on the battlefield or in ritual sacrifice. Their souls rise with the sun and later become a butterfly or hummingbird.

Sacrificer: On the battlefield another warrior; in the temple the *tlatoani*'s priests.

Ceremony: In battle somewhat ritualized fighting; in the temple rituals including heart excision.

Recipient: Huitzilopochtli, and the other gods.

Cosmic order: Order of the fifth sun is sustained, particularly in Tenochtitlan, the 'city of sacrifice', where the great temple is the cosmogonic axis.

Community: Collective involvement in the many rituals encompassing the sacrifice: nobility and some ordinary community members eat victim's remains.

Social effects: Sustains military hierarchy and warlike spirit; victories required to sustain leader's charisma/sacral credentials otherwise possible instability. Rituals stable but mythology often changes in line with interests: violence usually externalized creating internal solidarity and terror in subaltern people but it may also create resistance in the latter.

Figure 4.3 Aztec sacrifices

opponents, ruthlessly killing them on the battlefield, sometimes massacring prisoners after the battle, but usually saving some for sacrifice. The major sacrifices were on the battlefield, and the ritual sacrifice of prisoners was as impelled as much by pragmatism as religious ideology. The Tenochca were very successful, but their success had within it crucial dangers; it created problems of control and their methods of control created further problems (Conrad and Demarest 1984). Then the Spanish arrived.

Conclusion: back to the USA

Let us turn again to the United States. Probably nothing has exposed the dubious claims of the US to be an ethical power and one always forced to go to war by malevolent opponents than its relation with Iraq. George H. W. Bush's address on the eve of the first Gulf War was effective both because it is not a complete misrepresentation of the world – it includes reference to uncontestable facts – and because it subjects these to rhetorical strategies which decontextualize them and then recontextualize them within a motivated ideological and self-interested discourse, which in this case uses a sacrificial trope (Pearce and Fadely 1992). But the manipulations engaged in by George W. Bush are too well known to need detailing here, as is much of the mayhem and unnecessary deaths for which he is responsible. Yet one issue is of particular relevance here, namely torture. It is not coincidental that at the same time that many of the American elite were boasting that the United States was the only superpower, and, in fact, imperial power, the Bush administration publicly redefined who they might hold as prisoners, and how, in violation of Geneva Conventions. Further, the interrogation of prisoners would now take place in a way that was illegal, violating well-established legal judgments as to what constituted torture. It is becoming increasingly clear that for many US administrations, signing treaties and publicly subscribing to the ethical treatment of prisoners has often been motivated primarily by a fear that otherwise US soldiers in the hands of the enemy would also be tortured, with consequences that would include the discouraging of military recruitment. In fact, some of those in the US military raised exactly these concerns in their critique of Bush's torture policy.

But the problem lies not merely with such excesses but with the routine activities of this state. It is here that I disagree with the argument of Marvin and Ingle (1999: 199) that all societies are based upon obligatory blood sacrifice, not because they have a rosy-eyed view of the US, but because they overgeneralize from the American experience. Members of many societies try to avoid rivalry and war by trying to nurse their own resources and engage in co-operative relations with other societies. Only some societies are expansionist. The US was born from British colonialism and the rationale for its foreign policy is well captured by the doctrine of Manifest Destiny, notable for its theocratic underpinnings, worship of private property, its preference for an egoistic freedom over collective endeavors, its disdain for substantive equality and its impoverished view of democracy (Pearce 2007).

There is a more critical discourse of sacrifice that links it with justice and injustice. First, the activities of the US have led to the sacrifice of many brave young American men and women who have risked and often sacrificed their lives and health in conflicts in other lands, not, as they have been led to believe, in the pursuit of peace, self-determination, justice and democracy but rather through political strategies oriented to securing US political and economic hegemony. Particular Americans have disproportionately borne the burden of these sacrifices – for example, it was clear during the Vietnam war that while most elite white men kept their sons, including a future vice-president and president, safe in America, many badly schooled sons of poor southern whites and of poor African-Americans were destined for combat in Vietnam and other parts of south-east Asia. But there is an important point to note about this critical discourse of sacrifice. It understands these wartime deaths in a new way, as being a cynical misuse of noble impulse and courageous commitment, a consequence of a system in which state power is at the behest of self-serving limited special interests. This reinterpretation makes possible new ethical judgments and to imagine alternative forms of social arrangements that could produce different outcomes, ones that offer all human beings equal respect and equal protection. In other words, the occurrence of these deaths become what Alain Badiou calls an 'event' (Badiou 2001: 70). Thus, Remembrance Day can be used to argue for new ways of dealing with international and global relations rather than to legitimate new militaristic venture.

In this context, like in the Aztec case, there are readily available statements and documents that can facilitate a shift in perspective on the relation between sacrifice and the US military. A useful starting point is the six articles of the current Code of Conduct for Members of the Armed Forces of the United States.

I
I am an American, fighting in the forces which guard my country and our way of life. I am prepared to give my life in their defense.

II
I will never surrender of my own free will. If in command, I will never surrender the members of my command while they still have the means to resist.

III

If I am captured, I will continue to resist by all means available. I will make every effort to escape and aid others to escape. I will accept neither parole nor special favors from the enemy.

IV

If I become a prisoner of war, I will keep faith with my fellow prisoners. I will give no information nor take part in any action, which might be harmful to my comrades. If I am senior, I will take command. If not, I will obey the lawful orders of those appointed over me and will back them up in every way.

V

When questioned, should I become a prisoner of war, I am required to give name, rank, service number, and date of birth. I will evade answering further questions to the utmost of my ability. I will make no oral or written statements disloyal to my country and its allies or harmful to their cause.

VI

I will never forget that I am an American, fighting for freedom, responsible for my actions, and dedicated to the principles which made my country free. I will trust in my God and in the United States of America. (US Department of Defense, n.d.)

The code assumes monotheism and an unquestioning nationalism. Military personnel must be willing to sacrifice their lives for the defense of their country and to never surrender willingly. The Code of Conduct is seen as a positive mission statement regarding expected behavior in combat or captivity and in a relation of mutual support with the Uniform Code of Military Justice (UCMJ). The UCMJ is a system of punitive laws, a part of which can be used to address serious violations of the Code. Articles 77–134 of this are known as the Punitive Articles. While some of these refer to many of the same offenses to be found in state and federal civilian criminal codes, a large number deal with offenses against military organization and military projects. Desertion, disobedience, mutiny, sedition, rioting and cowardice are all addressed and liable to severe punishment. This means effectively that once personnel are in the military they are obliged to effect their superior's definition of 'defensive action' and how they should conduct themselves. True, there are conditions in which formally they can refuse unlawful orders, but in practical terms authority and discipline generally rule their responses. It indicates how personnel, in effectively surrendering their autonomy, may carry out orders, whatever their content. This has been made all too clear in such incidents as the 'My Lai massacre' and the disgraceful events in Abu Ghraib prison, but it is also just as clear when the military accept such unethical commands as to firebomb cities, drop atomic bombs and invade

---

Sacrifiers: American state functionaries, organized capitalism, ideological apparatuses, gendered and radicalized institutional structure.

Societally superior sacrifier: The corporate capitalist system and its state.

Victims: (a) Military personnel; (b) Working class used up in production processes; (c) Consumers reproducing themselves and some valuing themselves through accumulation of commodities; (d) Those denied an adequate income and meaningful life for selves and children in US and abroad.

Sacrificers: An autocratic military, repressive state apparatus, authoritarian corporations.

Ceremonies: Memorializations of some victims but effacement of others.

Recipient: Global capitalist system articulated and ordered through transnational and national relations.

Cosmic order: Unequal/unjust/class/race/gender systems sustained by unjust wealth distribution, repression and sustained by meritocratic ideology.

Community: Supports 'communities' of the 'respectable', disorders 'communities' of the 'oppressed'.

Social effects: Tensions about middle-class self-identification; class, racial and gender injustices and systemic contradictions and struggles to organize positive change potentially challenge this.

Figure 4.4   US society, sacrifice and repression

other sovereign states because they might constitute a threat. Figure 4.4 offers a radical reinterpretation of sacrifice and the contemporary USA.

Coda

Sacrifice has also been a significant theme in President Barack Obama's communications with Americans. For example, in his Inaugural Address on 20 January 2009 he mentioned the human cost of the American War of Independence, the Civil War, World War Two and the Vietnam War. He refers to the back-breaking contribution of pioneers and immigrants and, unusually, slaves ('the lash') and exploited workers ('sweatshops'), to the development of the United States. In another part of the speech, he called for 'a new era of responsibility – a recognition on the part of every American that we have duties to ourselves, our nation and the world'. These words may seem hackneyed, crying out for the cynical response only too appropriate to similar words from the Presidents Bush. However, they elicited positive responses from many, both because President Obama appears to express genuine concern for the disadvantaged and oppressed, but also because intuitively people realize that no society is possible without sacrifice. And yet, there are serious limitations to Obama's vision: in his acceptance speech at the Democratic Convention in August 2008 he claimed that 'each of us has the freedom to make of our own lives what we will', thus seeming to efface structural advantage and disadvantage; his challenges to corporate capitalism have been weak; his policy in Afghanistan is foolhardy. Nevertheless, there seems little doubt that he is wise, compassionate and courageous, and these qualities may help him move beyond the limits of his current political vision. It is possible that the more he becomes aware that the ruthless egoism he confronts is a natural concomitant of an inherently unjust corporate capitalism, the more he may recognize that a just world requires its demise.

Acknowledgments

This article has been the fruit of many intellectual exchanges over many years. For these discussions and much else I am particularly grateful to Tara Milbrandt, Paul Datta, Tony Woodiwiss and Lorna Weir. I am also grateful to Tony and Lorna Weir for having been able to share with them both the awe-inspiring experience of exploring some of Mexico's ancient pyramids.

Chapter 5

Toward a prospective criminology of state crime

David O. Friedrichs

Preface: from 1908 to 2108

How do we best approach the immense challenges arising out of crimes of states, as criminologists, as scholars and academicians, as citizens, and as human beings? Some historical perspective provides one useful point of departure. This chapter originated in relation to a prepared, opening presentation at the Onati workshop on 'State Crime in the Global Age', in May 2008. For me, at least, that year has significance on a number of different levels. But let me begin with some reflections on 1908, a hundred years earlier. That year, very early in the twentieth century, was a fairly uneventful year in a period of world history preceding cataclysmic events and upheavals. The era between 1908 and 1914 has been characterized as an opulent, unstable age on the brink of disaster, but also a period of dramatic change (Blom 2008). Of course, dates always have an arbitrary dimension to them, and in the interpretation of at least some historians 1908 is better understood as a year near the end of the 'long' century, the nineteenth, rather than the shorter twentieth century, which really begins with World War One and ends with the collapse of the Soviet Union in 1991.

But the world as a whole was pretty much at peace during the year of 1908. State crimes and political crimes certainly occurred – as they have in every year during recorded history – but not in a highly dramatic fashion. Early in the year the United States and Great Britain issued some demands for the end of abuses in the Congo, at that point still the personal fiefdom of King Leopold II of Belgium. This regime has been recognized as guilty of especially monstrous and extreme crimes committed in the name of colonial, imperialist empires (Hochschild 1998). Later that year the Congo was shifted to Belgian government control. During the course of the year Turks revolted against the Ottoman empire, and the people of Crete against the Turkish regime; Austria annexed Bosnia and Herzegovina and Serbia signed an anti-Austrian/Hungarian pact. Almost a century later, both the Congo and the Slavic nations were still implicated in terrible crimes, especially the brutal war crimes in the former country and the 'ethnic cleansing' in the latter area.

Early in 1908 the King of Portugal (and his heir) was assassinated, a failed assassination attempt was made on the Shah in Tehran, and later that year the Sultan of Morocco was deposed. But nothing that year – and nothing associated with the pre-World War One era – provided a clear basis for predicting the monumental state crimes that were to come during the course of the twentieth century. A few years earlier, perhaps, some ominous foreshadowing occurred: the massacre of some 70,000 Herero tribespeople in south-west Africa, for example, by German colonial forces in 1904, and the Bolshevik uprising that was successfully put down in Russia in 1905. In 1908, however, Adolf Hitler was a wholly anonymous young Austrian, trying – unsuccessfully – to gain admission to the Academy of Art in Vienna, and Joseph Stalin was a Bolshevik gangster, captured and imprisoned by the Russian authorities (Kershaw 2000; Montefiore 2007). In that year no one familiar with either of these two individuals could possibly have foreseen that they would become two of the mega criminals of the twentieth century. Automobiles and airplanes were very new technological developments; the first Model T Ford was produced that year, and the first airplane-related death occurred. Important technological breakthroughs that either facilitated certain forms of state crime or elevated exponentially the actual and potential devastation caused by state crime were still in the future.

Altogether, in the twentieth century and the hundred years since 1908, state crimes hardly imaginable at that time have occurred, and continue to occur. Indeed, by some measures state crimes were a more visible element of our global environment in 2008 than they were in 1908. We have an ongoing war in Iraq that arose out of an American invasion five years earlier that is widely viewed as blatant violation of international law, and we have other apparent violations of international law emanating out of the war against international terrorism. We have an ongoing genocide in Darfur, and tragically in many other post-colonial African countries all manner of state crimes are being committed (Mullins and Rothe 2008). We have the President of Iran, a country in the process of developing a nuclear weapon capability, declaring that the state of Israel should not exist. And – in the context of an exceedingly limited and selective review – we have many other state crimes being perpetrated around the world, often (but not exclusively) by non-democratic, repressive and profoundly corrupt regimes.

The preceding is intended to provide a very broad framework for considering the optimal character of the work of criminological students of crimes of states, going forward. What will a retrospective assessment of the twenty-first century – undertaken in 2108 – look like? Obviously we cannot know, and there are many different hypothetical scenarios. But my view here is that it would be difficult to overstate what is at stake in the endeavor of envisioning the worst possible scenarios for state crimes during the course of the twenty-first century, with criminologists playing a role in what should be a broad, multi-disciplinary enterprise. Is it really hyperbole to suggest that the prospects for human beings (our descendants, among others) living in a sustainable world in 2108, and in the extreme case the very survival of humanity, depends in fundamental ways on whether a collective endeavor that anticipates and contributes to the prevention or deflecting of the worst state crimes is successful?

The purpose of the present chapter, then, is to contribute to the development of a provisional framework within which criminologists can hope to address issues of monumental importance.

Reflexive statement

If there were such a word – and there isn't – I suppose I would characterize myself as a 'perspectivist'. In this chapter I propose to offer not a theoretical approach to crimes of states, not empirical data on such crimes, nor new policy proposals to respond to such crimes. What I propose to offer is a perspective on addressing crimes of states that I hope will be useful in some way to students of such crimes.

In the context of the Onati 2008 workshop, the twentieth anniversary of Bill Chambliss' presidential address, 'State-Organized Crime', was surely the most significant anniversary we were commemorating. I will return to this anniversary and its importance in relation to the criminological study of state crime shortly. But for me it also happens that this year was the hundredth anniversary of my mother's birth, in 1908. My own interest in crimes of states is surely driven at least in part by the fact that my mother and father were refugees, in the later 1930s, from a criminal state, Nazi Germany. As it happens, on 3 September 2008, an academic symposium ('Judisches Leben und Akademisches Milieu in Braunschweig') was held in Braunschweig, Germany, where my mother lived between 1912 and 1937, that commemorated the hundredth anniversary of her birth and focused upon her and important people in her life (including my father, a mathematician). It is surely highly unusual that such a symposium would be devoted to a woman who spent most of her adult life as a homemaker in Westchester, New York. But in the 1970s a memoir she originally wrote for her family was published by the Braunschweig archive, and became something of a bestseller there, which led to her being honored with the keys to the city (Friedrichs 1980). When she died in 1994 a substantial obituary was published in the Braunschweig newspaper, and a few years later a street with some 65 homes was named for her. Guidebooks to the city include identification of landmarks associated with my mother.

The city of Braunschweig was something of a Nazi stronghold during the Nazi years, and in fact it was this city that provided Hitler with his German citizenship. Accordingly, people in Braunschweig were grateful that a woman who had come of age as a Jew in their city could – without diminishing the horrors of the Nazi regime – remember many good experiences and fine people, and was agreeable to reaching out to the community of her childhood city in a spirit of reconciliation. A younger brother of mine – a professor of history at the University of British Columbia – gave the keynote address at this symposium. Had I addressed the symposium, I believe my theme would have been the centrality of a cosmopolitan ethic in my mother's whole outlook, one which I myself believe is ultimately necessary for responding most constructively to state crimes of the past, and for attempting to prevent them in the future. Arguably the single greatest challenge going forward in the twenty-first century is the wider embracing of a cosmopolitan ethic, if human beings around the globe are to live in a sustainable environment and in the extreme case if humanity is to survive into the next century. Of course, on some level such a project can be regarded as impossibly utopian, as indeed it is. But if the premise stated here is accepted as valid, then at least every initiative in this direction, if even very partially successful, should be constructive.

Criminological students of crimes of states: pathways to this interest

Why do criminologists – myself and Bill Chambliss included – become interested in crimes of states, as opposed to the more conventional concerns of criminologists? In my own case, as indicated earlier, family history played some role. In addition, I was potently influenced by the political (much more than the cultural) developments of 'the Sixties', with the emphasis on crimes of the powerful, not the powerless. This led to developing a course (and ultimately a text) on white collar crime, with the interest in crimes of states in part emanating out of this. In the case of Bill Chambliss, his early fieldwork in Seattle led to an interest in political corruption, which seems to have been one source for his later interest in state crime (Chambliss 1988b). Stanley Cohen grew up in apartheid South Africa, and was also clearly influenced by his experiences in Israel and growing concern over Israeli policies toward Palestinians, leading to his focus upon human rights violations (Cohen 2001; Downes *et al.* 2007). In the case of John Hagan (2001), it seems likely that his experiences as a war resister during the Vietnam era – addressed in his book *Northern Passage:*

American Vietnam War Resisters in Canada – would have been at least one source of his eventual attention to international tribunals, war crimes and genocide (e.g. Hagan *et al.* 2005). Jeffrey Ian Ross (2006) early in his career studied political violence with Ted Robert Gurr, and moved to crimes of states from an interest in political terrorism. Of course there are many other prominent students of crimes of states, each coming to it from some particular personal and professional background. A number of women – including Penny Green, Martha Huggins, Alette Smeulers, Catrien Bijlefeld, Elizabeth Stanley and Dawn Rothe – have made noteworthy contributions to the literature on the criminology of crimes of states, and have their own accounts on how they got there.

It may be that some readers view this type of reflexive exercise as self-indulgent and irrelevant. But if criminological students of crimes of states have the aspiration to persuade more criminologists to adopt an interest in crimes of states it seems not unhelpful to understand what brought them to this interest themselves.

Criminology and the study of crimes of states

The study of state crime has been addressed in different ways. Altogether we can say that multi-disciplinary, trans-disciplinary, interdisciplinary and purely disciplinary approaches have been applied to this challenging topic. A criminological approach to the study of state crime inevitably has an interdisciplinary dimension, but it seems to me that among criminologists who attend to crimes of states there is a certain tension between those who consciously attempt to maintain a criminological identity, and those who are quite indifferent to such commitments. Surely many criminologists have reservations about addressing crimes of states as a criminological phenomenon, but I will not here address any such reservations. A growing number of criminologists have adopted the view that criminological attention to crimes of states is indeed imperative in these times. The question raised here, one that seems to me is often glossed over in the criminological literature on state crime, is: are there uniquely criminological sources of knowledge that can be brought to bear on state crime and its control?

The conceptual issues in this whole realm have always been quite formidable. In 1967, when Marshall Clinard and Richard Quinney first published their *Criminal Behavior Systems: A Typology*, they included as one type 'political crime'. But this category encompassed both those acting on behalf of the state – for example, in oppressive campaigns against political dissidents – and those acting from outside, against the state – for example, traitors and conscientious objectors. It has longed seemed to me, that it is important to differentiate in this realm between those who are acting from within the state – as state officials in some sense – and those who are acting from outside the state – members of a revolutionary group, for example. My own solution to this problem was to put forth the notion of 'governmental crime' – crime committed by those from within the government – and then to break that down into state crime – crime committed on behalf of the state – and political white collar crime – crime committed for the advantage of political office-holders (Friedrichs 2010).

Another fundamental issue in all of this is the complicated role of law in relation to state crime. Since the state plays a central role in the production and implementation of law, it is obviously problematic to define state crime exclusively in relation to violations of state law. Accordingly, alternative approaches have been put forth, with international law, or a humanistic or moralistic conception of law, as foundations for defining state crime. Some British criminologists, in particular, have argued in favor of adopting a 'social harm' approach in place of a core focus on the concept of crime (Hillyard *et al.* 2004). There are both benefits and drawbacks to adopting such an approach (Friedrichs and Schwartz 2007). But this is one of the intellectual dialogues with which students of state crimes must engage.

If a criminology of crimes of the state is inevitably interdisciplinary, I believe it is most likely to have a measurable impact to the extent that a conspicuously criminological framework is applied. My concern is that when criminologists address state crime issues in 'purely' interdisciplinary terms – that is, with no specific invocation of a criminological framework, criminological terminology and criminological knowledge – this work has little chance of attracting attention either from scholars who address state crime issues from some other discipline (such as international law, international politics or psychology) as well as from criminologists with more conventional concerns. If this work is framed in specifically criminological terms it seems to me that it has a better chance of being viewed as work that can on the one hand offer unique insights to scholars in other disciplines or fields who address state crime issues, and on the other hand be seen as useful in some way for comparative purposes by criminologists focused upon more conventional forms of crime.

William J. Chambliss' 'State-Organized Crime' address – and its legacy

The Onati conference in 2008 allowed us to commemorate some earlier years. For present purposes the most significant anniversary was that it was twenty years since William J. Chambliss' 1988 landmark American Society of Criminology presidential address on 'State-Organized Crime' (as well as the publication of his innovative textbook, *Exploring Criminology*). Chambliss' presidential address was made almost a half-century after another landmark presidential address (in this case to the American Sociological Society, as it was then known), namely Edwin H. Sutherland's (1940) address on 'White Collar Crime' in 1939. Needless to say, Sutherland's address is widely recognized as having initiated white collar crime as a scholarly endeavor within the field of criminology, and I believe that Chambliss' address is recognized as having given fundamental impetus to the study of state crime as a legitimate area of criminological inquiry. This is not to say, of course, that one cannot find some earlier forms of attention to such crime, but the significance of both Sutherland and Chambliss promoting white collar and state-organized crime from the high-profile venue of presidential addresses can hardly be overstated. In his discussion of 'state-organized' crime in *Exploring Criminology* (although not in the presidential address), Chambliss specifically acknowledges Sutherland's 'ground-breaking' work on white collar crime, and argues that state-organized crime is even less well explained by conventional theories of criminal behavior than is the case with white collar crime (Chambliss 1988a). The identification and application of appropriate theoretical frameworks remains one of the ongoing challenges for students of crimes of states.

It is rather striking to note that although Sutherland fully recognized the significance of traditional criminological neglect of the crimes of one important segment of 'the powerful' in society – corporations – to the best of my knowledge he never in any way noted or addressed traditional criminological neglect of another segment of the powerful: state actors, on behalf of the state. He spent a good portion of the 1940s working on his pioneering study of crimes of corporations, published at the end of that decade as *White Collar Crime* (1949). Of course, it was during that same decade that arguably the highest profile of all historical crimes of states – the Holocaust – occurred, as did the landmark, historically unprecedented Nuremberg trials that held the surviving Nazi leadership (and principal operatives) accountable for their crimes. But Sutherland does not allude to this state crime or the trials in this book or in any of his other published writing, to the best of my knowledge. He does compare the propaganda of the utility corporations to that of the Nazis, and did signify that he believed some of the actions of American corporations were helpful to the Nazi cause (Galliher and Guess 2008; Sutherland 1949: 210). In 1943 he published a book chapter on 'War and Crime', but this addressed the impact of war on conventional crime. The book *White Collar Crime* includes a chapter on 'War Crimes', but this addressed violations of wartime regulations by American businesses in the interest of enhancing profits. Sutherland nowhere addresses directly the crimes of state, within or outside the context of war.

It should be noted, however, that crimes of war were not entirely neglected by Sutherland's criminological contemporaries. John Hagan and Scott Greer (2002) have discussed Sheldon Glueck's not widely known work on war criminals and involvement with the Nuremberg trials in the 1940s (it may be worth noting that Sutherland's (1951) last known paper, presented a month before his death in October 1950, was a critique of Sheldon's *Varieties of Delinquent Youth*). I believe it is also little known – and I stumbled on this accidentally myself – that criminologist Donald R. Taft of the University of Illinois addressed the 'Punishment of War Criminals' in a 1946 article in the *American Sociological Review*. In this article Taft, writing in the wake of the atomic bombs dropped on Hiroshima and Nagasaki, expressed concern that the next world war would be fought with such bombs or weapons – legal or illegal – of even greater destructive power. He addressed some contrasts between war crimes and domestic (i.e. conventional) crimes. He goes on to apply what has been learned about the punishment of conventional offenders to the punishment of war criminals, and the potential of such punishment to contribute to the prevention of future war crimes. Altogether, he concludes that the prevention of future aggressive wars and atrocities depends more upon transformation of the world system, and cannot be achieved by punishing war criminals; indeed, he expresses the view that such punishment may facilitate rather than prevent a World War Three. Whether or not one agrees with Taft's conclusions, his article is a notable – if rare – attempt by a criminologist from an earlier era to address crimes of states, and to draw upon criminological knowledge in relation to how the likelihood of future state crimes can be reduced.

For at least 30 years following Sutherland's address only a handful of criminologists addressed white collar crime – aside from Sutherland's own landmark book ten years after the address. In the 1950s only a small number of criminologists (or sociologists) published anything of significance relating to white collar crime, including Marshall Clinard, Donald Cressey, Frank Hartung, Robert Caldwell, Donald J. Newman and Vilhelm Aubert. Not much was added to the criminological literature on this topic during the 1960s either. As it happens, 2008 was also the fortieth anniversary of the publication of *White-Collar Criminal* (1968), edited by Gilbert Geis. This volume was, to the best of my knowledge, the first collection of readings on white collar crime. Due to the relatively thin criminological literature on the topic at this time, Geis included many selections produced by scholars from outside the field of criminology, as well as journalists. Richard Quinney's 1962 dissertation on occupational crime among pharmacists – completed under the supervision of Marshall Clinard – was a rare case of a doctoral student in criminology addressing a form of white collar crime. Indeed, Gil Geis' own paper, 'The Heavy Electrical Antitrust Case of 1961' – first published in 1967 – was arguably the most influential contribution to the white collar crime literature during the 1960s. It is really only during the 1970s – perhaps in some good measure in response to a range of political and cultural developments of that era – that white collar crime begins to be more fully addressed by criminologists. During the decades that followed, a formidable literature on white collar crime has developed, a significant number of criminologists either specialize in white collar crime or address it as part of their work, and a number of white collar crime textbooks have been published. The White Collar Crime Research Consortium has well over a hundred members. Nevertheless, many criminologists who specialize on white collar crime continue to regard it as somewhat marginalized within the field of criminology itself, with less grant support and other broad forms of endorsement. Courses on white collar crime are not a staple of the criminology or criminal justice curriculum, as is the case with, for example, courses on juvenile delinquency. And the influence of white collar crime scholarship in the larger world remains quite modest at best. By some measures, there has actually been a relative decline of criminological investigation of corporate crime over the past 25 years or so.

The pace of criminological attention to crimes of states, in the wake of Chambliss' landmark address, has been relatively greater, by some measures, than the pace of criminological attention to white collar crime following Sutherland's address. In the 20 years since the Chambliss presidential address there has been a significant production of state crime research by criminologists, especially over the past ten years, although of course it also remains quite marginal within the discipline.

But going forward – over the next 50 years or so – can we anticipate an exponential growth of criminological work on state crime? Will the increase of criminological attention to state crime outpace such attention to white collar crime, within the respective historical frameworks? Will those of us who have been addressing crimes of states for some time now be seen by some future generation of critical criminologists as blind to other important manifestations of crime? Some proponents of the 'social harm' perspective – mentioned earlier – have been advancing the claim that poverty and starvation in the world should be viewed as macro-level forms of crime, although these conditions have certainly not been addressed as such by most criminologists, including students of crimes of states.

In 'State-Organized Crime' Chambliss defined such crime as 'acts defined by law as criminal and committed by state officials in the pursuit of their job as representatives of the state' (1989: 300). He specifically excluded from consideration 'criminal acts that benefit only individual officeholders' (such as accepting bribes) as well as such actions as the excessive use of violence by the police in urban ghettoes because this type of activity is not sanctioned by the state. Chambliss chose to address the following specific forms of state-organized crime: piracy, smuggling (of narcotics and arms), assassinations and murder (for example by CIA operatives against foreign heads of state), and violations of civil rights. These are all significant forms of state-organized crimes with, in many cases, some dimension of co-perative activity with non-state actors. But since Chambliss' 1988 address the concerns of criminological students of crimes of states have expanded to include – among other phenomena – genocide, crimes of war, state-corporate crime, the victimology of state crime, and the role of international tribunals.

The year 2008 marked for me, at least, the tenth anniversary of the publication of *State Crime*, Volumes I and II. I was approached about editing such a work by David Nelken, a co-editor of the Ashgate International Library of Criminology, Criminal Justice and Penology, in the fall of 1996, shortly after the first edition of my *Trusted Criminals: White Collar Crime in Contemporary Society* (1996) had been published. (Since Nelken himself had already edited the *White Collar Crime* volume (1994) for this series, that project was no longer available.) I was pleased to accept this invitation because it seemed to me to provide an opportunity to contribute towards the legitimation of 'state crime' as a distinctly criminological topic. At that time the International Library included volumes on many topics that would be obvious candidates for any such series, including street crime, serial murder, sex crimes, organized crime, professional criminals, policing, the sentencing process, and offender rehabilitation. But perhaps in some respects parallel to the situation Gil Geis found himself in with his 1968 work on the white collar criminal, most of the articles reprinted here – although by my criteria relevant to a criminological understanding of state crime and its control – were not produced by criminologists. But at least some of the contributions were from criminologists. The volume included not only Chambliss' presidential address but work by Stanley Cohen, Gregg Barak, Ron Kramer and Dave Kauzlarich; however, most of the work was by scholars who would not be identified as criminologists, but who included law professors, historians, political scientists, economists and sociologists. One criterion for inclusion was that, at least in my judgment, the articles had special relevance for advancing a criminological understanding of crimes of the state. Perhaps as a function of my affinity for commemorative dates, I chose for the first selection in Volume I of this project a chapter of a book published (in English) 100 years earlier, in 1898, by a French judge, Louis Proall, entitled *Political Crime*. Just as students recognize earlier foreshadowing of Sutherland's pioneering initiatives on white collar crime in the work of Marx and Engels in the nineteenth century, and E. H. Ross early in the twentieth century, students of state crime can acknowledge that earlier writers such as Proall laid a foundation for the recognition of certain activities of states as a form of crime.

If I were editing the *State Crime* volumes today, as opposed to more than ten years ago, it seems to me that there would now be a good chance that one could include articles almost wholly produced by self-identified criminologists. Ultimately, there were enough articles to go with two volumes, the first on 'Defining, Delineating, and Explaining State Crime' and the other on 'Exposing, Sanctioning and Preventing State Crime'. One of my aspirations for these volumes has been that they would encourage graduate students in criminology, and younger scholars, who had come to realize that their own interests lay elsewhere than in the study of conventional dimensions of crime and the criminal justice system, that the pursuit of topics pertaining to state crime and their control was a legitimate pursuit. It has been gratifying to me that there are indications that this aspiration was realized, at least in some cases.

And if 2008 was the tenth anniversary of the publication of my *State Crime* volumes, it was also the tenth anniversary of the publication of David Kauzlarich and Ronald Kramer's *Crimes of the American Nuclear State* (1998). To a degree that is quite remarkable, nuclear issues have been almost wholly neglected by criminologists. For me, Richard Harding's 1982 presidential address to the criminology section of the Australian and New Zealand AAS first called attention to this neglect. In light of the fact that the nuclear threat going forward in the twenty-first century is quite certain to be a monumentally important issue, it seems that the Kauzlarich and Kramer book will be recognized, in time, as a seminal contribution to a criminology of nuclear-related crimes. To date, there has been relatively little criminological follow-up on Kauzlarich and Kramer's initiative (but see Kramer's Chapter 8 in this volume and Kramer and Kauzlarich 2010). Rob White's (2008) analysis of the nuclear depletion issue as a form of state crime is one recent exception to this proposition, but much remains to be done.

Altogether, the crimes of states have been recognized as a legitimate area of criminological inquiry in recent years. The publication of Penny Green and Tony Ward's *State Crime* (2004), that provides a critical survey of this terrain of inquiry, strikes me as one important signifier of this status, as is the publication of Alette Smeulers and Roelof Haveman's *Supranational Criminology: Towards a Criminology of International Crimes* (2008). With Dawn Rothe, I have reviewed the evolution of a criminology of crimes of states elsewhere (Rothe and Friedrichs 2006). And Dawn Rothe (2009) has now produced another seminal survey of crimes of the state, *State Criminality*. It is clear now that Chambliss' 'State-Organized Crime' address contributed in a fundamental way to setting into motion this body of scholarship.

Reservations about a retrospective criminology of crimes of the state: and the case of the Holocaust

The criminology of state crime has been essentially – and perhaps inevitably – a retrospective criminology. By this I mean it has focused, for the most part, on state crimes of the past, and the responses to them. Arguably no state crime in the twentieth century – and by certain criteria in all of history – has generated as large a literature as the Holocaust. I have periodically immersed myself in some of this literature over a period of many decades, in part in relation to family history, and also in relation to having co-taught a course on the Holocaust for more than ten years. Indeed, I have made a modest contribution to the immense literature on the topic with my article 'The Crime of the Century? The Case for the Holocaust' (2000). It seems unlikely that I would be teaching about and writing about the Holocaust if I were not myself persuaded of the immense importance of trying to understand it as fully as possible, in all of its multi-faceted dimensions. But it is also the case that I have been struck, and on some level troubled, by the immense scope of the retrospective analysis of (and commemoration of) the Holocaust – especially since the 1960s – an enterprise that has been pejoratively referred to as 'the Holocaust industry', and the relative paucity of analysis and attention both before and during the Holocaust. As one small piece of this, I became intrigued at some point by the question of what German criminologists were writing about during the lead-up to the Holocaust, in the 1930s. The answer, of course, is that – for various reasons – they were focused almost exclusively on conventional crimes, with one conspicuous faction of them applying neo-Lombrosian interpretations to the under-standing of criminality that nicely agreed with the Nazi's conception of inherently criminal people (i.e. Jews) (Wetzell 2000). They certainly were not evaluating the criminality of the Nazi state, and the forces leading toward state criminality on a mass scale.

In addition to the Holocaust, we have in varying degrees some significant retrospective attention to other historical genocides, including the more recent cases of Bosnia and Rwanda, although rather little of this attention has come from criminologists. The ongoing genocide in Darfur, to the best of my knowledge, has attracted very little attention from criminologists, with the work of Mullins and Rothe (2008) and Hagan *et al.* (2005) as rare exceptions to this. But what about future possible genocides? Conceding that analysis of past genocides provides a basic foundation for identifying conditions that could give rise to future genocides, is this a pronounced dimension of literature on genocides?

Towards a prospective criminology of crimes of the state

Where, then, does a criminology of state crime go? More importantly, what is the future of state crime itself? In an apocalyptic vision, state crime on a monumental scale – inevitably involving nuclear weapons – will destroy human existence, and may lead – as Jonathan Schell (1982) suggested in *The Fate of the Earth* – to the 'death of death'. In a utopian vision, enlightened world leaders will do away with all the truly consequential forms of state crime. A realist vision, it seems to me, recognizes the very real and dramatic threats of state crimes in the future, but also the hypothetical possibility of containing or deflecting the worst of such crimes, and toward achieving more effective controls over state crime more generally. A basic question arises, then: can criminological students of state crime identify the most constructive approaches to minimizing the chances of an apocalyptic future?

Accordingly, I here call for a *prospective* criminology of state crimes. Such a criminology would have as its primary focus the identification of potential sites of prospective crimes of states, and the analysis of the most feasible strategies for preventing, subverting or containing future crimes of states. A prospective criminology of state crime not only has to be rooted in a retrospective criminology of state crime, but also must adopt a coherent framework of a rapidly evolving world, including the present character of globalization and post-modernity in the world, and the significance of a post-9/11 world. Is the notion of an 'American empire' (or American hegemony) also a key part of this evolving world, as Peter Iadicola asks in Chapter 3? If we are to adopt a basic framework for characterizing the world in its present and evolving state, it seems to me that Richard A. Falk's (2004b) *The Declining World Order: America's Imperial Geopolitics* is especially persuasive. First, Falk usefully differentiates between several different forms of globalization: corporate, civic, imperial, apocalyptic and regional. He then identifies the most salient 'post-Westphalian' developments: the rise and fall of Euro-centrism; colonialism and decolonialism; the advent of weapons of mass destruction; the establishment of international institutions; the rise of global market forces; the emergence of global civil society; and revolutionary new technologies. Some of the most significant new global trends are identified as well: the resurgence of global religion; the emergence of transnational social forces; the rise of transnational crime; the expansion of legal and illegal migration; globally integrated television; and the militarization of the planet. Here we have, then, a fundamental starting point for identifying the complex confluence of forces most likely to give rise to crimes of states, as well as the most promising potential dimensions that could contain the outbreak of such crime.

A prospective criminology of state crime must also attend to some of the key concepts relevant to addressing the challenges of such crimes going forward: human rights – and the contested character of such rights, and how they are conceptualized; nationalism – an enduring, and some would say pathological, force; sovereignty – increasingly complex in a 'borderless' world; and legitimacy – especially problematic in a multi-faceted, evolving global environment. These are certainly among the core concepts for a prospective criminology of crimes of the state, although there are, of course, other important concepts as well.

With regard to state crime and its control, a prospective criminology of crimes of states must especially contend with the following: the whole matter of 'pre-emption' and the complicated moral conundrums involved with humanitarian intervention; the potential and limitations of an expanding international law; the potential and limitations of international tribunals, and especially the newly created International Criminal Court; the forms of transitional justice (see Elizabeth Stanley's analysis in Chapter 14 of this volume) that most effectively diminish the probability of new outbreaks of state crime; and specifically, the role of truth and reconciliation commissions in this context.

In addition, a prospective criminology of state crime must contend with the ongoing and now expanding dialogue on global governance. Historically, global governance has been an enormously problematic notion. The United Nations is typically recognized as the largest-scale global governance endeavor to date, and the record of the United Nations in relation to preventing or responding effectively to state crime has been one of many failures and much disappointment, although perhaps not a uniformly negative record. Some commentators suggest that global governance is already here, in networks of high-level government officials and diplomats working co-operatively to implement international agreements and policies. But for a prospective criminology of state crime the potential of evolving forms of global governance to both contain and amplify forms of state crimes has to be a primary consideration.

With regard to a prospective criminology of state crime, a fundamental conundrum must be acknowledged. Any endeavors by criminologists to identify sources of potential state crimes have the potential to be co-opted by state entities for their own purposes, and in the worst case scenarios to facilitate the commission of state crimes. One must always be mindful of 'Project Camelot' types of precedents. A prospective criminology of state crime has the potential to become part of an administrative criminology of state crime ('empire's criminology', in Peter Iadicola's term from Chapter 3). However, some counter-strategies in relation to such concerns are possible. Critical reflexivity always has to be maintained in relation to a prospective criminology of state crime. A pragmatic 'cost–benefit' analysis of engagement with state entities takes into account both the risks and the rewards of engagement with state entities. Alternatively, those undertaking a prospective criminology of state crime focus their efforts on engagement with civil society entities. A 'public criminology' is certainly part of all this (see the concluding chapter in this volume).

In conclusion, a prospective criminology of state crime ideally draws upon criminological knowledge to contribute uniquely and significantly to the understanding of crimes of states. Criminological knowledge can contribute measurably to the prevention or effective response to such crimes and the grave harms they pose.

Part Two
The Brutal Realities of State Crime

Chapter 6

Modern institutionalized torture as state-organized crime

Martha K. Huggins

Seeking an explanation for torture

This chapter argues that torture that is nurtured, supported and justified by a political state, whether authoritarian or formally democratic, and by such states' private sector counterparts, is best explained through a systemic model of state torture. Based on prior research (Huggins *et al.* 2002) into torture in Brazil, I concluded that: (a) state torture is not a function of 'deviant' psychology; (b) it is not the product of one particular presidential administration or form of government; (c) changes in government administration will not eliminate state torture; (d) state torture is a product of the 'normal' and rational political organization of states; and (e) formally democratic states can have torture systems. With these premises in hand, by late 2004 – particularly after the Abu Ghraib *60 Minutes II* exposé, the publication of the Taguba (2004) and Fay (2004) reports, and the investigative reporting of Hirsch (2004b) and Brody (2004 and 2005) – it became possible to use the practices at Guantánamo and Abu Ghraib to widen the predictive powers of the 'torture essentials' model I was beginning to develop (Huggins 2002).

'Torture essentials': the model

The ten elements of the 'torture essentials' model provide a synthesized prototype for studying torture by different kinds of political states – from totalitarian, to military authoritarian, to formally democratic, or to state welfare and socialist. The ten conditions associated with state torture are hypothesized to operate in all such political states, although the weight of each factor and how it operates may change with regime types. The 'essentials of torture' are as follows:

1. **Ideology:** Advancing, employing and exploiting ideologies that support and justify torture by the state.

2. **Mislabeling:** Calling torture something other than what it is, which makes less problematic its use by state agents.

3. *Ad hoc* **legalism:** Explaining and justifying state torture, often defining it through executive decree as something other than it is in legislation and judicial decisions.

4. **Bureaucracy:** State torture systems are embedded within *normal* bureaucratic organizations that are formally characterized by rationality, reason in their operation, universal application of rules and regulations, and a formal division of labor, with positions ranked according to differing degrees of social status, power and rewards.

5. **Multiple actors:** Responsibility for torture is diffused across multiple categories and status levels of actors including: (a) *direct perpetrators* of torture, usually a numerical minority, usually with lower systemic power within a state torture system; (b) *facilitators*, a numerical majority characterized by greater systemic status and power; (c) *bystanders*, who are usually structurally outside the torture system, yet nevertheless are 'insiders' insofar as they are witnesses to atrocity and (d) organizational/technical systems for enabling and carrying out torture.

   Torture perpetrators come and go, as do heads of government in formally democratic states. However, as long as facilitators and the organizational arrangements exist for nurturing, justifying and/or hiding torture, new torture perpetrators will replace old ones, accompanied by new or modified enabling ideologies and the *ad hoc* legal arguments for legitimizing torture.

6. **Competition:** Bureaucratic actors and their various sub-organizations compete for social, career and organizational rewards, increasing the probability of state use of torture to secure 'the best' information and/or the 'most important' terrorists in the shortest time; this encourages escalating the amount and degree of violence during interrogations.

7. **Routinization:** Persistence in carrying out an objective encourages its continuation: practice may not make 'perfect' but it facilitates continuation. Bureaucracies are by nature conservative toward change, a feature that encourages routinization. As long as a system of routinized torture continues, impunity for facilitators and perpetrators will further routinize the state torture system. Ignoring state torture

grants implicit and explicit acceptance of perpetrators and facilitators, helping to strengthen the systemic and ongoing nature of torture – its routinization.

8. **Insularity and secrecy:** Isolating and hiding a state torture system provides protection from outside scrutiny, greatly facilitated in the US 'war on terror' by executive branch consolidation of power, often justified by cultivating a culture of fear and associated ideologies about 'national security from terror'.

9. **Censorship and denial:** Deliberately failing or conspiring to allow exposure of facilitators and perpetrators, and/or creating the organizations and technologies for doing so, provide a fertile climate for torture.

10. **Differential impunity:** Impunity, in general, contributes to the longevity of a state torture system; differential impunity, in particular, nurtures the system's invisibility and permanence. In some instances low-level perpetrators and facilitators of state torture may even be punished for involvement in torture, serving as sacrificial and exculpatory 'bad apples' within an allegedly otherwise 'healthy' system (*Mother Jones* 2008a). The higher the status of facilitators, the less likely they are to be denounced or prosecuted.

The 'torture essentials' model does not directly address why people torture (a micro social-psychological question). Rather, as a general model, it is focused on factors that explain the longevity of torture systems. These include the roles of ideology and law in enabling and justifying state torture, and the various types of actors within a state torture system – perpetrators, facilitators and bystanders – and the normal bureaucratic arrangements that facilitate, encourage, routinize, hide and excuse torture.

Illustrating the torture essentials model

I Ideology

Over the years, the United States has fostered and promoted a plethora of 'national security' ideologies (Huggins 1998) – some have become hegemonic, some have not. During the Cold War, regimes and movements were labeled Communist, 'leftist', 'neutralist', or 'fellow-traveling' to justify military intervention against, or support for, oppressive military governments. State abuse of power, including torture, has been nurtured and justified by flexible ideologies that create ever-expanding categories of 'enemy others' (see Moore 2001): when 'good' nations are supposedly threatened by 'evil-doers' anyone might be an 'enemy'. This leads easily to the conclusion that there should be no restrictions on a state's efforts to defend itself, including buying votes, subversive infiltration, military incursions and violent interrogations. Fear, whether or not deliberately instilled – as with fictions about 'weapons of mass destruction' used to justify the US invasion of Iraq – legitimizes interrogatory torture. It is also common for states to argue that when the presumed threat operates outside the law of nations the state's response can also legitimately act outside law, an argument used by the Brazilian military during the 1964–85 period of authoritarian rule, the Argentine generals during the 1976–83 Dirty War, and by the recent Bush administration's war against so-called 'Islamofascism' and other forms of 'terrorism'.

2 Mislabeling

The word 'torture' has been mislabeled or avoided altogether by perpetrators and responsible officials alike, although those with more power have had greater capacity to have their euphemistic definitions of torture legitimated and accepted. For example, the Brazilian police torturers I interviewed in 1993 seldom used the word 'torture', referring instead to it as 'that type of conduct', 'a conversation with our prisoners', or 'conducting research ... and looking for data'. They would admit to having carried out such 'lesser excesses' as 'slapping ... and punching [a prisoner] around a little' or 'hanging [a prisoner] up there', a reference to placing a victim on the notorious 'parrot's perch'.[1] When torture had gone 'too far', the torturer pointed to his having 'commit[ed] a mistake' or 'engaged in "unnecessary" excesses' (Huggins et al. 2002).[2]

In the case of higher officials within a torture system, investigations of US abuse of alleged terrorists also demonstrates a reluctance by United States officials to use the 'T' word, describing such violence as 'degradation', 'staging', 'tough interrogation', 'enhanced interrogations', 'controlled acute episodes', or by designating sets of actions used in interrogation – 'the hard takedown', 'water dousing', 'pressure point technique'. Presumably, all such forms of violence – setting aside the claim that they fall short of torture – are each neatly frozen in time and separate from one another, such that one form of violence does not evolve into another one. The latter might create something that might be defined as torture.

In fact, however, inside a prison and its interrogation chambers, especially during preliminary 'softening up' sessions – where at Abu Ghraib physical or psychological mistreatment was part of the interrogation process – the 'lesser' forms of violence quickly turned into more serious forms, including physically and emotionally disabling torture and even murder (CBS 2004; Hirsch 2004b; see also Browning 1992; Haney and Zimbardo 1977). Violent interactions, however defined and defended, are not static; violence produces more, and usually more serious, forms of violence (see Toch 1996; Warden 1996).[3]

3 Ad hoc *legalism*

A torture-enabling culture is fostered and excused by official rulings and other official decisions, especially at the executive level, which make state torture seem legitimate. In 2002 the Bush administration simply decided that 'terrorist' detainees were not covered by the US Constitution or international law. Under pressure from the State Department, this ruling was revised to apply only to Guantánamo's 'illegal combatants', a status that Bush administration officials assigned to each 'eligible' detainee rather than having it done by military tribunals, as is required by the US-signed Geneva Convention. Attempting in the spring of 2004 to clarify the Bush administration's position on Iraqi prisoners, Secretary of Defense Donald Rumsfeld explained before the Senate Armed Services Committee that at the Abu Ghraib prison the Geneva Convention only vaguely applied to the incarcerated 'in one way or another'. Going on, Rumsfeld argued that the Geneva Convention applies directly to 'the Prisoners of War, [but] the criminals . . . are handled under a different provision of the Geneva Convention' (*New York Times* 2004b), failing to identify the unspecified legal status of 'battlefield detainees'; perhaps these were the 'criminals' to whom the Defense Secretary referred. The Bush administration claimed to accept the Geneva Accords and the UN Convention Against Torture – except when it did not – an illustration of what some legal scholars call 'international law *à la carte*', a version of the White Queen's legal decisions in *Alice in Wonderland*. Such a flexible legal standard makes prisoners vulnerable to state torture, especially when the definition of torture itself shifts conveniently under international, national and local political pressures.[4]

In fact, the UN Convention Against Torture, signed by the United States in 1994, defines torture as 'any act that creates severe pain and suffering, whether physical or mental, intentionally inflicted to obtain information or a confession, or to punish'. According to this standard one could conclude that prisoners in Iraq were subjected to cruel and unusual treatment and torture since they were:

- held for prolonged periods without formal charges;

- held in solitary confinement for sustained periods;

- subjected to psychological terror;

- kept without food and water;

- stripped naked and placed in dark cells;

- attacked by dogs;

- burned;

- prodded with electric poles;
- forced to simulate or perform sex acts;
- subjected to repeated rectal examinations;
- sodomized with light bulbs;
- raped;
- choked until they collapsed;
- beaten, sometimes to death (see *New York Times* 2004a).

A torture-enabling culture is created and legitimized when executive-level lawyers, in collaboration with minister-level executive branch appointees, indicate how to skirt international and national laws against torture.[5] But to claim that Abu Ghraib prisoners were *not* tortured would certainly raise the question as to why the US State Department and CIA lawyers attempted to identify interrogation techniques that would avoid prosecution for carrying out 'rough interrogations'. According to Bush administration lawyers' *ad hoc* legal reasoning, since Guantánamo's 'unlawful combatants' had no status in US Constitutional or international law they had no protection against torture. However, just in case, the lawyers assured the Bush administration that:

- Torture by foreign governments, that is, torture 'by proxy', would not implicate the US, even if information obtained through torture was passed on to US officials (see Jamieson and McEvoy 2005).

- The federal torture statute will not be violated as long as any of the proposed strategies were not specifically intended to cause severe physical or prolonged mental harm.

- An interrogator is guilty of torture 'only if he acts with the express purpose of inflicting severe pain or suffering on a person within his control'.

- Interrogation that 'simulates torture' may be used as long as such acts stop 'short of serious injury' (see *Washington Post* 2004).

Furthermore, a façade of legitimacy was provided by Secretary of Defense Rumsfeld, who was designated to sign his explicit approval for certain forms of prisoner interrogation – presumably in Iraq and Afghanistan, and at Guantánamo – that were otherwise considered 'overly stressful'. Like Humpty Dumpty in Lewis Carroll's *Through the Looking Glass*, when the Secretary of Defense certified that torture was not torture, he made the word 'torture' into what he chose 'it to mean – neither more nor less'.

4 Bureaucratic organization

State torture occurs within normal bureaucratic organizations character-ized by their members' use of reason and rationality in the application of rules, regulations and directives (Weber 1958). Within bureaucratic organizational hierarchy equivalent sets of ranked positions have differing levels of power and authority to make and execute organizational direct-ives. This 'chain of command' is characterized as relying on written rules and regulations, although this may not always be the case in actual practice.

There is no longer much argument that torture took place within multiple, formally constituted, bureaucratic organizations charged with pursuing the administration's 'war on terror'. This torture was neither the work of a few 'bad apples' nor indicative of failures in a 'chain of command'. It was a common practice within the bureaucratic organization of the US national security apparatus, as the revelations of torture by 'waterboarding' revealed. The institutions of modern state systems, presumably governed by reason and universally applied rules, would seem the last place for systemic torture to emerge and thrive. Yet, we find that during the Bush administration's 'war against terror' the practice of 'waterboarding' – strapping a detainee to an inclined bench and covering his nose and mouth with a cloth that is repeatedly saturated with water to simulate drowning – was not only common practice, it was governed by highly bureaucratized 'legal' rules developed and approved at high levels of US government. For instance, no session of simulated drowning 'was to exceed forty seconds'; there 'could only be two sessions [daily]' in which a detainee was waterboarded; 'in each [such] session there could be no more than six applications of water to the cloth [that] last[ed] ten seconds or longer' (Scherer and Ghosh 2009); 'the detainee [had to be] placed on a towel or sheet . . . not placed naked on the bare cement floor, and the air temperature . . . [was to] exceed 65 degrees if the detainee will not be dried immediately' (Shayne and Mazzetti 2009). Despite its brutality, the administration was able to claim that waterboarding was not torture because a state agency – the CIA – had developed guidelines for its use and the state security bureaucracy, using its legal-rational systems of rule-making and dissemination, distributed these through its authoriz-ed chains of command. An additional layer of bureaucratic legitimacy was achieved by mislabeling, that is, by using the term waterboarding, a word that evokes sport surfing more than simulated drowning, rather than calling it by its name in international law – torture. But according to the detailed arguments in US Justice Department 'Torture Memoranda', such interrogatory 'techniques' as waterboarding are strategies of 'extraordi-nary rendition' necessary for securing information from 'high-profile terrorists'.

By making rules for brutalizing prisoners, governments and their corporate associates give torture the appearance of being law-based, controlled, goal-oriented; an instrumental practice that bears no relationship to the common image of the sadistic lone-wolf torturer. This façade of official legitimacy filters down to those conducting interrogations, giving them license to torture, albeit under some other name.

Hierarchy

Torture-permissive guidelines issued at the highest levels of the US government were disseminated to interrogators in Afghanistan, Iraq and Guantánamo. US Justice Department lawyers assured President Bush that as Commander-in-Chief he had the (desired) authority to ignore national and international laws forbidding torture. Donald Rumsfeld approved specific forms of prisoner (mis)treatment. In a 'Gitmoization' of Iraqi prisons, Rumsfeld's top civilian intelligence official, Undersecretary of Defense Stephen Cambone, sent General Geoffrey Miller, then head of Guantánamo's prison complex where torture had become routine, to 'assess' conditions in Iraq. General Miller recommended that prison guards at Guantánamo should 'set conditions for the successful interrogation' of prisoners in Iraq by army and civilian contract intelligence officers. As a result of this assessment, General Miller was placed in charge of Abu Ghraib prison, which became infamous for pictures and prisoner testimonies about torture.

In accordance with the Bush administration's *ad hoc* legality, the torturers, both guards and interrogators, functioned under an explicit chain of command designed to ensure that the people who could be relied upon to render opinions legalizing torture would be in a position to do so. A report by five inspectors general disclosed that Vice President Dick Cheney and David Addington (Cheney's Chief of Staff) selected John Yoo to write a legal assessment of Bush administration interrogation tactics (one of the 'torture memos') because Cheney and Addington 'knew in advance that [Yoo would] approve of whatever they wanted to do ...' (Greenwald 2009a). There is little difference between this and the Brazilian experience where facilitators and torturers were carefully selected by their superiors for their professional aptitude and attitudes toward torture, knowing that selected torture perpetrators would be predictable as long as their violence was regularized by an administrator.

The actions of torturers and guard facilitators at Abu Ghraib were encouraged by rewards and punishments, a typical bureaucratic strategy. The formal and informal normative systems at Abu Ghraib rewarded those who met the goals of obtaining 'information' and punished those who did not. This created a culture in which explicit orders to torture were not needed (see Haney and Zimbardo 1977; Huggins *et al.* 2002, Ch. 10; Zimbardo 1970, 2007; Zimbardo *et al.* 1973, 2000). Any soldier who questioned a chain of command order to 'soften up' prisoners faced the possibility of punishment for insubordination. In essence, Abu Ghraib became an organizational culture wherein potential torturers and torture facilitators had to choose between being rewarded for legalized brutality or facing career and social costs for defying explicit, but more often implicit, mandates to torture (see Johnson 1997; Henry 2004).

This system of rewarding torture is not limited to battlefield prisons. There is a high likelihood that the career aspirations of such political appointees as John Yoo shaped their willingness to authorize torture. Individuals at the lowest levels of a torture system may be even more likely to comply with officials' and organizational mandates because they know that they enjoy relative impunity for the consequences of their actions.

Division and specialization of labor

Our research on Brazilian torturers (Huggins et al. 2002) demonstrated that an important difference between the police who became torturers and those who did not was membership in an elite and/or physically separate (and thus insular) police operation or intelligence unit. Indeed, a person's work or task assignment within a police or military hierarchy was the most important predictor of an actor's perpetrating torture. Quite simply, a person could not torture routinely unless associated with an intelligence or interrogation squad or assigned to some kind of detention facility. In addressing how such specialized violence organizations might shape human conduct, Robert J. Lifton (1986: 425) argues that such organizations are 'so structured . . . institutionally that the average person entering . . . will commit or become associated with atrocities' (see also Huggins et al. 2002, Chs 9 and 10; Jenkins 2000; Morales 1999; Skolnick 1966; Skolnick and Fyfe 1993). This suggests that some responsibility for state torture rests with those who determine the structure and functioning of special-ized units and their technologies, by knowingly creating them and placing, training and overseeing the people who work in them.

A division of labor in which some people directly torture and others facilitate it helps those not directly involved with torture to define themselves as non-torturers. For example, we found among the Brazilian police who interfaced with torture teams a tendency to distance them-selves physically and organizationally from those whom they themselves labeled torturers: as one Brazilian policeman asserted, his team would simply arrest suspects and leave them 'to be "officialized" . . . [my squad] just gave interrogators the material to work on' (Huggins et al. 2002).

5 Multiple actors

Torture typically occurs within large bureaucratic systems that include not only lower- and middle-level direct perpetrators, but also higher-, middle- and lower-level facilitators, all operating within a bureaucratic organiz-ation's formal division of labor (see Mother Jones 2008a). This includes various levels of superiors who knowingly (or even unknowingly) establish and promote torture-facilitating ideologies, structures and environments. Overall, the process protects more powerful facilitators from exposure or blame. For instance, those who facilitated torture at Abu Ghraib have suffered no real blame or censure for their complicity (Earthtimes.org 2005, 2007; Hirsch 2007; Sevastopulo 2005).

The assembly-line (highly segmented, task-differentiated) structure of state torture systems enables those who commit or facilitate torture to avoid facing the real meaning and consequences of their violence. As one Brazilian torture perpetrator told me: 'I never tortured anyone; I just delivered people to the interrogators; I don't know what happened to them after that' (Huggins *et al.* 2002).

The direct *perpetrators* of Abu Ghraib torture – some police and military and some CIA and contract interrogators – could not have tortured regularly without a range of *facilitators* who provided organizational (construction of the 'cold-hot' holding facilities), technical (medical doctors who advised about torture;[6] linguistic (translators), flight (Jeppeson Corporation rendition flights), legal (Justice Department 'torture memos'), financial (US Congressional funding for the 'war on terror'), and moral support (constructed ideologies creating a 'culture of fear'). In the immediate torture environment, facilitators included translators and physicians (see Bloche and Marks 2005; Kater 1989; Miles 2004; Stover and Nightingale 1985; Thieren 2007), psychologists (Concerned Psychologists 2006; Goodman 2008), nurses and medics, guards and dog handlers, among many others (ICRC 2007). The American Red Cross discovered that CIA doctors, nurses and/or paramedics monitored prisoners undergoing waterboarding; medical workers were present when guards confined prisoners in small boxes, shackled their arms to the ceiling, kept them in frigid cells, and slammed them repeatedly into walls (the 'hard takedown'). These Abu Ghraib medical personnel even 'condoned and participated in ill treatment . . . [giving] instructions to interrogators to continue, to adjust, or to stop particular methods' (Rall 2009; see also Taguba 2004; ICRC 2007).

The US torture system's higher-up facilitators included US President George W. Bush and Vice President Dick Cheney, a number of foreign heads of state, high-level US government administrators and assistants, ambassadors, lawyers, chiefs of departments (Horton 2008; Taguba 2004), to name a few. Non-interfering bystanders included in-the-know US military units, members of the media, other governments' agents – including those granting permission for, and those working in, holding facilities for terrorists 'redacted' by the CIA to secret prisons in their countries (ABC News 8 June 2007; Bergen 2008; Global Security 2006). Amnesty International (2006a), Americas Watch (2005) and American Civil Liberties Union (2005) have prepared briefs identifying some powerful US government torture facilitators.

According to the 'Essentials of Torture' model, facilitators such as those described above are indispensible to the long-term stability and protection of a torture system. Just as state torture during Brazil's military-authoritarian period could not have persisted for over 20 years without the active complicity of high-level facilitators, state torture by the post-9/11 US security apparatus depended on compliant participants at all levels of government.

6 Competition

As we found in Brazil, the use and cruelty of torture is nurtured by competition between government agencies and their agents. Within a Taylorized social control system where procedures are not only routinized but also elaborated into jurisdictional subdivision of tasks, competition and operational illegalities become normal. When intra-organizational rivalry takes place as part of a war against state 'enemies', as was the case in Brazil and during the Bush 'war against terror', the ramifications are often violent and lethal.

In Brazil's assembly line of repression, where each separate social control organization, team or squad was competing for rewards for capturing the greatest number or the most high-profile subversives, competition frequently spilled over into violence among the various groups as well as against the captives brought in for interrogation. Intelligence-system 'speed-up', nurtured by a broadly defined 'preventive war' against an expanding category of enemy 'others', encourages competition among state agencies and between them and contractors for intelligence, which creates a hospitable climate for torture. As military and civilian intelligence agencies and their agents vie for the 'most' and the 'best' information from and about 'terrorists' – with each of these categories ('most', 'best' and 'terrorist'), ill-defined and subject to change – 'normal' physical coercion and psychological pressure often devolve into outright physical torture.

In Iraq and Afghanistan today competition between and within US intelligence organizations is exacerbated by conflating interrogation and guard work and by outsourcing much of this labor to private corporations. To label the military contract corporations and their employees 'private' disguises their heavy reliance on Pentagon and CIA funding for their existence. Most military contractors serving in Iraq and Afghanistan receive up to 95 per cent of their funding from the US Department of Defense (*Business Week* 2002). Because they are not fully private, despite being mislabeled as such, employees are easily transformed into torture proxies by the same organizational pressures that affect those in uniform. Of equal importance, these contractees can perpetrate or facilitate torture without immediately implicating the US government, providing a degree of 'plausible deniability' for government actors.[7]

Torture by civilian contract employees at Abu Ghraib was documented in the US army's reports by Fay (2004) and Taguba (2004) which implicated two companies, CACI International (based in Arlington, VA) and Titan Corp (based in San Diego and recently acquired by L3 Communications) for their participation in torture. Steve Stefanowicz of CACI reportedly directed the use of threatening dogs at Abu Ghraib, ordered that a prisoner not receive his prescription painkillers, made a male prisoner wear women's underwear, failed to report abuse, and then lied to investigators about the abuse under his direction. Daniel Johnson, also employed by CACI, is alleged to have directed and participated in prisoner abuse, interrogating a prisoner in an 'unauthorized stress position', according to the Fay Report. Johnson directed Sgts Ivan Frederick and Charles Graner to torture a detainee during an interrogation. Three Titan employees were accused of raping a male juvenile detainee, making false statements about interrogations and failing to report detainee abuses.

Such abuse is not rooted in the irrational intentions and proclivities of those carrying it out. In the case of private military contractors, for example, 'success' is bankable: if interrogation produces abundant information, whether accurate or not, another lucrative government contract is likely to follow. Operating within a brief time-frame for a contractually defined activity, contract employees – unregulated by the Uniform Code of Military Justice – have wide latitude in pursuing contract goals. Corporations providing intelligence (IT) technologies to the Pentagon and CIA have a particular need for a constant and abundant flow of intelligence information. Whether or not such information is correct can be relatively less important than its abundance. Where humans and their information are grist for IT technology operations and development, torture becomes a research and development tool for product development and testing, and thus for securing more military contracts.[8]

7 Routinization

The longer an organizational structure persists in carrying out a particular activity, the greater the probability that such an activity and the organizational arrangements that enable it will become normal. Practice may not make perfect, but it does encourage longevity, particularly when linked to legitimate bureaucratic organizational entities such as government and corporate business. A particularly powerful factor in the routinization of torture is the practice of hiding, ignoring, or failing to effectively punish its various facilitators and perpetrators, thus making it part of ordinary practice.

8 Insularity and secrecy

Torture facilitators and perpetrators are enabled and protected by insularity, secrecy and lies (see *Mother Jones* 2008b). Isolation of torture practices from the rest of society can be promoted at the social organizational level through such tactics as victim kidnapping (CIA 'rendition') and secret holding facilities (CIA 'black sites'), as well as through an organizational division of labor that hides perpetrators and facilitators from outsiders, from each other, and even from their own awareness (see items 4, 5 and 6 above). Justifying ideologies that make state violence appear 'necessary', through the use of mislabeling language and *ad hoc* legalism, make what goes on within a state torture system manageable by insiders and exclusionist of outsiders (see items 1, 2 and 3). Even routinization (item 7), while habituating participants and others to torture, renders it less visible to them. By depicting and dealing with torture as something other than what it is, insularity and secrecy further enable torture systems to strengthen and grow.

Yet if torture systems need secrecy for growth and longevity, why did some Abu Ghraib perpetrators and facilitators take pictures of people being brutalized? This could expose the torture system (as it did for Abu Ghraib). But one Brazilian torturer I interviewed explained that he had taken a photograph of a man being tortured on the infamous 'parrot's perch', because 'police never talk' – a statement much more about the narrow 'culture of police brotherhood' among those in a Brazilian torture room than about the danger of exposure. Since this policeman's situation includes the systemic components of his torture room, where actors are answerable only to each other and to their immediate superiors who directly and indirectly permit torture, snapping pictures is very low risk.

But if this is so, why do torture perpetrators often carry out their violence at night, wear hoods, and place these on their victims? The social psychological answer (Huggins *et al.* 2002, Conclusion) addresses some mechanisms that enable torturers to carry out violence in the first place: as *serial* torturers, darkness, masks and hoods dehumanize their victims and provide a shared 'work persona' for torturers. People without eyes and facial expressions can be more easily abused (see Watson 1973; Zimbardo 1970; Zimbardo *et al.* 1973, 2000); human invisibility goes a long way toward transforming victims into non-human 'material', just as pre-World War Two Japanese medical experimentation teams did when they called their human guinea pigs 'stumps of wood' (Gold 1996; see also Kater 1989). A successful serial torturer must not see his torture victims as human beings nor himself as brutalizing them; of course, this also applies to facilitators.

At the systemic level, detainees' vulnerability to torture is compounded when they are held in secret locations, authorized for Iraq by torture facilitator Rumsfeld at the request of another powerful facilitator, CIA

95

Director George Tenent. In one case, apparently to assist US military officials in Iraq in hiding seventeen 'high-level' prisoners from International Red Cross inspectors, these detainees were subjected to 'extraordinary rendition' (see ACLU 2007; ICRC 2007) – the US government practice of sending terrorists as 'ghost detainees' to another country for imprisonment and interrogation (ABC News 8 June 2007; Bergen 2008; European Parliament 2007).

This practice grew out of the wide-reaching authority assumed by the Bush administration in the 'war against terrorism' after the September 2001 attacks, giving the CIA 'the unusually expansive authority' (*New York Times* 2005) to act without even obtaining case-by-case approval from the White House or the State and Justice Departments for transferring suspects to another country to be interrogated (see ABC News 8 June 2007; Serrano 2005). Since 11 September 2001, through its program of 'extraordinary rendition', up to 80,000 alleged terrorists have been 'through the system' of rendition to off-shore secret prisons (Campbell and Norton-Taylor 2008). A Council of Europe investigator reported in 2006 that 'more than twenty countries, mostly in Europe, had colluded in a "global spider's web" of secret U.S. CIA prisons and prisoner transfers' (Iran Daily 2006; see also Human Rights Watch 2007; ABC News 8 June 2007). Estimates vary as to the number of 'ghost detainees' transferred to such CIA 'black sites', but according to Campbell and Norton-Taylor (2008), 'by its own admission, the US government is currently detaining at least twenty-six thousand people without trial in secret prisons', which include, besides the land-based sites abroad, at least seventeen US ships specifically designated for holding and interrogating high-level detainees.

The complete invisibility of 'ghost prisoners' to outsiders and the lack of any accountability for their treatment needless to say increase these detainees' vulnerability to the kinds of 'overly stressful' interrogation that Rumsfeld was supposed to authorize case by case. However, apparently the CIA itself made the 'call' about the severity of interrogations, at least in the case of some terrorist suspects subjected to 'extraordinary rendition'.

9 Censorship and denial

Evidence of state torture is usually ignored, hidden, denied and lied about and monitoring practices are sidestepped. Many torture regimes use press censorship and even eliminate legislative and other controls, and even elections, and may shut down the judiciary too, in order to avoid public knowledge of government-sponsored torture. This was certainly the case during Brazil's military period. However, in the United States, although formally a democracy, powerful actors can also dismiss, hide, or if necessary lie about interrogators' 'excesses'. For example, when the International Red Cross, Amnesty International and other human rights groups, the family of one American Abu Ghraib guard, and numerous US service personnel reported prisoner abuse in Iraq and Afghanistan, their charges were ignored, dismissed, downplayed, or hidden by US officials.

It took public photographic evidence of Abu Ghraib prisoner mistreatment to force serious general consideration of US treatment of prisoners in Iraq. In the case of those housed at Guantánamo Bay, prisoners and observers continually reported abuses there, most of it denied by the Bush administration. Human Rights Watch has recorded prisoner abuse in Afghanistan, where John Walker Lindh, the 'American Taliban', was tortured in 2001, initially by Afghan allies of the United States but then by US agents themselves. They put Lindh, wounded and stretcher-bound, for several days into a windowless, suffocating, casket-like metal container with little food or medical attention. Lindh, a Taliban fighter, could be so treated because as such he was adjudged at the time to be an 'enemy combatant', outside US constitutional and international law protections.

10 Differential impunity

Impunity, in general, contributes to the longevity of a state torture system; differential impunity, in particular, nurtures the system's invisibility and permanence within government. If facilitators and perpetrators of state torture continually get away with their violence, the message is that there is very little personal, organizational or state threats against continuing it. At the very least, some lower-level torture perpetrators may eventually get negative public and legal attention for their violence, but torture facilitators, especially those at the highest levels of a state torture system, are generally exempted from paying the price for their role as enabler facilitators.[9] As Greenwald (2009a) explains:

> Washington mentality when it comes to lawbreaking [is that] when political crimes become so blatant and extreme that they can no longer be safely excused (Watergate, Iran-contra, Abu Ghraib), then it's necessary to sacrifice some underlings who carried out the crimes by prosecuting them, but – no matter what else happens – the high-level political officials responsible for the crimes must be shielded from all accountability. In ordinary criminal justice, what typically guides prosecutions is the opposite mindset: namely, a willingness to immunize low-level soldiers in order to ensure that the higher-level criminals suffer the consequences of their crimes. But when it comes to crimes committed by political officials in America's Versailles culture, only the pawns are subjected to the rule of law while the monarchs and their highest royal court aides are immunized.

Higher-ups who are (infrequently) alleged responsible for torture under their command are protected by claims of 'chain of command failures', as occurred with Abu Ghraib[10] prisoner mistreatment. Yet the full evidence about the Abu Ghraib prison demonstrates that, rather than torture being caused by a chain-of-command *failure*, the prison's torture system was a *successful* product of organizational interaction and legitimacy, emanating normatively from the highest levels of US government through the military and intelligence systems' chains of command down to those who were told that they could legitimately perpetrate torture or even ordered to do so. Torture perpetrators did not have to 'follow orders' in most cases because their violence had been rendered a necessary and 'legitimate' mechanism for protecting the US against terrorist attacks.

Modern torture as organized crime[11]

Maltz (1995: 19) defines 'organized crime' as violations of law committed by two or more actors who are, or intend to remain, associated for the purpose of committing crimes. He further notes that organized crime 'is the product of a self-perpetuating criminal conspiracy [that] by one means or another obtains a high degree of immunity from the law'. In Maltz's words, the 'objective of most organized crime is power, either political or economic or both'. Based on this definition, it is arguable that torture by the US security apparatus as part of the 'war on terrorism' was, in fact, organized crime.

First, US state torture was criminal. Torture at Guantánamo and Abu Ghraib, despite Bush administration claims to the contrary, is widely recognized by legal scholars as violating international treaties, including the Geneva Accords, that are ratified US law.

Second, war against terror torture involved a conspiracy to consciously manipulate secrecy, through appeals to 'extraordinary executive authority' during a clear and present threat to 'national security'. This conspiracy, orchestrated at the highest levels of the US government, hid torture at Guantánamo, Abu Ghraib and 'black prisons' in participating foreign country locations. When torture was discovered, US government executives and their appointees knowingly mislabeled, redefined and legally manipulated information about the nature and extent of the violence against prisoners in Afghanistan, Abu Ghraib and Guantánamo. By encapsulating torture within an ideology of 'government protection', 'citizen safety' and a 'religious crusade' against 'evil', the United States government sought to transform violations of international law into necessary means to a righteous end.

Third, torture at Guantánamo and Abu Ghraib became organizationally self-perpetuating through the normal operation of government, not due to the uniquely deviant aspects of organizations or their atypical 'rogue' actors or due to a failure in a chain of command. On the one hand, those at the top of government gave formal approval to acts ratified by the

United States as torture in international law. This contributed to torture becoming self-perpetuating through a chain of command that required, hid and excused it. On the other hand, once torture had been incorporated within the operational hierarchy of US government,[12] the order to facilitate or commit torture did not have to be explicitly given – the organizational structure and its interlocking systems of status and power and rewards and punishments fostered torture.

There is no doubt that torture system actors – some elected officials, others appointed or associated with government through private contract firms – clearly intended to remain associated during the post-9/11 phase of the US war against terror. In the process, the willing torture perpetrators and facilitators were in a position to work toward and benefit from the 'objective of most organized crime ... power, either political or economic or both' (Maltz 1995: 19). Defined as an informal institution with a monopoly over the use of force in a given territory, a national security state can disregard its own laws and those of other nations to protect national and world security. In the process such a state has an alternative to employing brute force to over-reach the boundaries of its nation state. Through politicized claims about threats to national security, the US government could 'legitimately' perpetrate the organized crime of state torture without (until discovered) losing its legitimacy as a law-abiding country.

Conclusion: theory, research and torture

'Torture essentials' examines the role of micro-level, middle-range and macro-level actors within a state-organized torture system. It demonstrates that torture facilitators, who typically comprise a majority of those involved in torture, both numerically and in terms of their power, are central actors at each level of a state torture system. If facilitators are the foundation for a state torture system, torture perpetrators are the structure's replaceable *fascia* – they are negatively visible and easily replaced minority actors with relatively little structural or social power. The infrequent trials and the even more infrequent punishment of torture perpetrators (and some of the lowest-level facilitators) – which is the opposite of organized crime's 'street soldiers' who fill courts, jails and prisons – function in the case of torture perpetrators to shift attention from the powerful torture system facilitators: the state torture system's 'king pins' who remain relatively invisible while they are keeping the state torture system alive.

Exploring state torture through the criminological lens of an organized crime framework can reinforce and expand our understanding of torture by revealing how a criminally culpable national security 'protection racket' assisted powerful torture facilitators in carrying out state violence in the name of 'national security'. In the process war, assassination and torture are presented to the public as necessary for strengthening government (read: executive branch) and state against dangerous outside threats. As just one example, in late 2004 Bush administration officials pressured Homeland Security Chief Thomas Ridge to 'raise the "terror alert" level in order to sway the November 2004 U.S. presidential election' (Kornblut 2009; Knox 2009). Bush and Cheney's objective of strengthening executive branch power was facilitated by presidential executive decrees, exaggerating homeland security threats, overriding US Congress, and other forms of *ad hoc* legality, all embraced within a 'protection racket' promising US national and world security.

Afterword

Can legislative drafters and law-makers use legislation to dismantle a state torture system and its 'protection racket'? How can human rights activists and their non-governmental organizations weaken a state torture system? Can other civil society groups play a role in destabilizing state torture systems? Is it even possible to fully dismantle a recidivist torture state? The first three questions give hope; the last, despair. Clearly, any lasting solution to state torture requires government and civil society collaboration: preventive and punitive legislation by government, along with government accountability monitored by independent civil society groups not indebted to the state. An example of the latter, Brazil's Tortura Nunca Mais (TNM) and Argentina's 'Mothers of the Plaza de Mayo' have kept the atrocities of their countries' military governments alive through ongoing investigations into former atrocity facilitators and perpetrators, by demanding and getting trials, and punishment, and by simultaneously pressuring professional associations to censure those who have facilitated or engaged in torture.[13] In Brazil the professional associations of medical doctors, psychiatrists and psychologists, and of lawyers have stripped licenses from their members who facilitated or perpetrated torture during Brazil's military period. Nevertheless, torture continues in Brazil (UN 2001), albeit now used against common criminals. Torture systems are flexible: they can expand and contract as definitions of 'the enemy' change.

The failure to eliminate widespread torture in Brazil raises discouraging questions relevant to recent US experience with torture. Is it realistic to expect the actors and organizations that have directly and indirectly reaped the rewards of a torture state to co-operate in dismantling it? How far can or will a new, more enlightened, government go to weaken a national security state's 'protection racket'? Would the elected and appointed representatives of a government whose chambers and offices have earlier overridden acts of US Congress or bypassed Congress altogether be genuinely willing to work with a new president to weaken and eliminate the torture-related ideological and organizational entities and practices that they had once supported? Without doubt, the greatest challenge for those seeking to dismantle US state torture is to discover the legislation, regulations, past legal cases and other deterrents that could assist in preventing and punishing those who foster, enable, justify and hide torture.

In a step toward eliminating torture against 'high-profile' terrorists, the Obama administration is creating a High-Value Detainee Interrogation Group (HIG) where National Security Council (NSC) and Federal Bureau of Investigation (FBI) interrogators will be 'closely monitored' by the executive branch and operate through the 'strict guidelines' of the US Army Field Manual – earlier US army and CIA interrogation manuals were implicated in torture (NSA online, n.d.). To ensure that torture does not occur at the HIG, an Obama-appointed task force will consult scientific research to 'determine a set of ''best practices'' for interrogation' (Kornblut 2009). At the same time, HIG interrogators will not be legally bound to inform detainees of their rights against self-incrimination – whether or not a detainee is 'Marandized' will be 'decided on a case-by-case basis' (Kornblut 2009).

It is not at all clear that Obama's HIG will be able to prevent the torture of 'high-value' terrorists, given the HIG plan's use of mislabeling, secrecy and *ad hoc* legality, and that the organizations involved have been implicated in the past in enabling (NSC) or practicing (FBI) torture (see Huggins 1998). Moreover, the HIG plan cannot protect 'low-value' detainees against torture. Indeed, being of 'low value' to a state torture system itself renders such detainees vulnerable to mistreatment. In the end, Americans may only discover after many secret interrogations of 'high' and 'low' value terrorists whether an enlightened president who vowed to eliminate torture (presumably only in the US war on terror?) and to hold HIG interrogators to 'professionalism' and 'science', had fulfilled his promises. The president who fails to do so, and who promised careful executive branch oversight of interrogations, will stand exposed and without even 'plausible deniability' to protect him from prosecution as a 'high-profile' torture facilitator.

Notes

1 Parrot's perch torture involves stringing up a person on a rod with hands and feet tied to the rod. The person is beaten, and water is forced into the anus and mouth.
2 Other scholars have demonstrated that those who carry out violence use euphemisms (see, for example, Chandler 1997; Crelinsten and Schmidt 1995; Huggins 2003; Payne 2003; Presser 2008; Scully and Marolla 1985).
3 See also research on college and university 'hazing'. Hazing is defined as 'an abusive, often humiliating form of initiation into or affiliation with a group' http://definitions.uslegal.com/h/hazing/.

4   For a discussion of how such ideologies are instilled and maintained at the small group social psychological level, see Kelman and Hamilton (1989) on authorization, dehumanization and routinization.

5   See Greenwald's (2008) assessment of White House Counsel John Yoo's complicity in torture.

6   Rall reports (2009) that the International Red Cross found that CIA doctors, nurses and/or paramedics monitored prisoners undergoing waterboarding, apparently to make sure they did not drown. Medical workers were also present when guards confined prisoners in small boxes, shackled their arms to the ceiling, kept them in frigid cells and slammed them repeatedly into walls. See also part 3 of ICRC (2007).

7   CACI and Titan, two corporations whose contractees were implicated in Abu Ghraib torture, are ranked 15th and 19th respectively among the 20 corporations that together receive half of all Pentagon information technology contracts (WT 2004). For a discussion of US private military contractors at Abu Ghraib, see Appendix A (www.basicint.org/pubs/Research/2004PMCapp3.pdf).

8   See Isenberg 2004. For a discussion of US private military contractors at Abu Ghraib, see Appendix A of that same report (www.basicint.org/pubs/Research/2004PMCapp3.pdf). See also Amnesty International (2006a).

9   Charles Graner 'got the highest Abu Ghraib sentence – 10 years in prison. No generals or top officials were charged with a crime. However, Brigadier General Janis Karpinski, whose unit was in charge of the prison facility, was demoted' (Earthtimes.org 2007).

10 An alternative to this is Hirsch's *Chain of Command* (2004a).

11 My model for how to do this comes from William Chambliss' study *On the Take* (1988b) and from Kitty Calavita *et al. Big Money Crime* (1997). Both of these research projects connected 'outsider' (i.e. socially disadvantaged and usually criminally defined) actors at the bottom of a vast and far-reaching organized criminal hierarchy to a group of socially and politically prominent actors at the apex of American society and government and to the normal operations of corporate and government bureaucracies.

12 Not new with the war against terror, however, once practiced torture is relatively easy to continue, albeit even under changed organizational arrangements.

13 According to Rall (2009), 'Since 1945, at least 70 doctors around the world have been prosecuted for participating in torture.'

Chapter 7

War as corporate crime

Vincenzo Ruggiero

With recent developments in international affairs, war is increasingly becoming a form of state and corporate criminality, therefore requiring criminological analytical efforts. This chapter analyzes 'war as crime', focusing on the illegality perpetrated by invading states and the criminality of the private enterprises these states involve in their military ventures. After an introductory discussion of corporate crime, some empirical material is provided regarding the direct involvement of private companies in wars: in the form of private 'security' services, armies, and in the hazy area of 'conflict consultancy'. The traits that war and corporate crime possess in common are highlighted, while the definition of 'war as corporate crime' presented in the final discussion is situated within the analytical framework of the study, more generally, of the crimes of the powerful.

Harm and benefit

Since Edwin Sutherland's (1983) original formulation, the concepts of white collar and corporate crime have been the subjects of debate focusing on a number of controversial crucial aspects. Why did Sutherland include under the rubric of white collar crime conducts that are not intentional violations of the criminal law? Why did he lay such emphasis on the social status and respectability of offenders? Why did he not consider that not only are there crimes committed *by* corporations, but also crimes committed *against* them? Responses to the first question highlight that, though often dealt with within the administrative and civil adjudication sphere, the harm produced by white collar and corporate crime could well find its natural treatment within the criminal justice system. These responses allude to labelling processes and imply that criminologists should face this type of crime irrespective of its official definition as crime. In answering the second question, students would stress that the crucial task of Sutherland was to suggest that crime is not the preserve of marginalized individuals or disadvantaged groups, but can also result from learning processes occurring between individuals and within groups who enjoy privileged access to resources and power. As for considering crimes against corporations along with crimes in favour of them, some scholars would claim that the choice to focus on the former or the latter is the result of political sensitivity. Is it so criminologically relevant if employees, say, steal pens and letterhead from the corporation employing them, when that very corporation causes horrendous damage to people and the environment?

It is not the task of this chapter to rehearse such debates, which are well recorded in a wealth of widely known publications (Croall 1992; Nelken 1994; Punch 1996; Ruggiero 1996; Slapper and Tombs 1999). The focus of the following pages is, rather, a related issue whose discussion appears to be far from exhausted. This is the divergence between social, political and legal definitions of white collar and corporate crime. Such divergence brings back, though from a different angle, the questions posed above, suggesting that perceptions of crime as harmful behavior are inspired by the position one occupies in the social system as well as in the political spectrum. That is, the alleged difference between definitions of white collar crime are formulated within distinct social contexts. More precisely, differing social definitions of white collar and corporate crime are the products of collective sensitivity on the part of groups who benefit from that crime and those who are victimized by it. Political definitions, in turn, may be the outcome of contested formulations and appreciations of 'harm' among, respectively, beneficiaries and victims. Finally, legal definitions may be regarded as the jurisprudential seal laid upon the formulations which manage to be victorious in such definitional contest.

It is worth analyzing how the social, political and legal spheres display increasing interconnections at the current moment.

If we consider the social sphere as a public space in which meaning is constituted and contested, we identify an arena where discussion is conducted outside the official hubs and networks of power. In other words, we may regard the social sphere (often termed 'civil society') as an extra-political space exercising control and supervision over groups wielding power and their institutional representatives. The notion implied here is one of supervision from below. It is from below, one assumes, that the identification of corporate conduct as criminal is likely to take shape. Therefore, when scholars posit the existence of a social as opposed to political and legal definitions of corporate crime they also imply that the respective definitions are inherently antagonistic. However, both power-less and powerful actors operate in the public sphere, and at times a symbolic civil war is fought between them in pursuit of consensus, a war utilizing a combination of coercive and dialectical means. The struggle for consensus has 'potentially divisive and destructive consequences', because it takes place outside the legislation and aims to forge a prevailing, unassailable definition of the common good (Taylor 2004: 91). Those who will manage to prove, or persuade others, that their good is also the common good will transcend the social sphere, permeate other spheres and bring with them the new perceptions and definitions they have produced.

Powerful groups manage to 'de-territorialize' their social existence because they take advantage, to put it in the terms coined by Deleuze (2005), of the vectors allowing them to exit their own social territory. In this sense, corporate actors are constantly lying in ambush, experimenting and innovating; their existence is never tranquil, keen as they are to transfer the definitions they forge time after time of their conduct into the legal and political spheres. I will return to this point in the final section of this chapter.

My argument is that the distinctions between social, political and legal definitions of corporate crime are becoming more blurred than we are prepared to accept. Let us see this process in more detail.

In the analysis of Taylor (2004), there are two vital extra-political, secular spaces that have played a crucial role in the development of society in the modern West: first, the space of market economy, and second, the public sphere. The latter, however, brings together groups of people who have already carved out a private space for themselves as economic agents. The market economy comes to constitute a sphere in which people are interconnected not only objectively but also in their mutual understanding. In this sphere, entrepreneurs are seen as benefactors, and narratives about them, 'their rise from rags to riches', are 'recounted again and again, offering example and inspiration' (Taylor 2004: 151). They gain respect and admiration because, presumably, they create wealth and contribute to the public well-being. Contrary to Taylor's opinion that such an economic sphere retains its independence from the public one, the two spheres tend in reality to overlap as entrepreneurs strive to prove that their activity, their freedom and their individualism possess an inherent capacity to benefit the collectivity and contribute to the freedom of all.

Economic activity is constituted by a succession of breakthroughs which, initially condemned, and after generating resistance and repression, may slowly gain acceptance within the prevailing sensibility. It seems that entrepreneurs bear an original sin which, according to the specific devices offered by different contexts, is either 'purged', removed or displaced. The history of the enterprise itself coincides with the history of this removal or displacement. The risks and uncertainty connoting economic activity put entrepreneurs in a moral limbo: there can be no judgment in relation to the ethical values expressed by enterprise, because risk and uncertainty in themselves suffice in allowing the ethical stretching of values.

In a different perspective, the criterion 'who benefits?' offers another possibility to entrepreneurs to stretch values and make their conduct acceptable. Using this criterion, four types of enterprise can be distinguished according to the prime beneficiaries of their conduct, respectively: its workers, its owners, its clients and the public at large (Blau and Scott 1963). In deviant entrepreneurial behavior an attempt is constantly made to confound the identification of 'who benefits'. The act of deviating may be justified when it appears to benefit less the perpetrators than the clients or the public at large.

I believe we can now identify some common traits shared by corporate crime and contemporary war. Corporate criminals mobilize the variable risk when justifying their violations: the risk of losing their investments, that of succumbing to competitors, and even the risk of breaching regulations which are too complex or whose existence they just ignore. Risk, in brief, puts values and violations in a different ethical framework. The variable 'who benefits', in its turn, can provide rationalizations to entrepreneurial crime: illegally generated profits will be invested and eventually create new jobs. War, similarly, supposedly staves off the risk of being victimized by rogue states and groups, while the benefits of invading an inimical country will be shared by entrepreneurs, who will consequently access new markets, while labour, thanks to the trickle-down principle, will enjoy part of the wealth thus generated.

The crimes of the powerful are said to occur in contexts in which the growth of corporate actors causes a structural change in society whereby 'natural persons' play an increasingly insignificant role. In such contexts interactions become largely asymmetric, in that corporate actors are in the position to control the conditions in which their relationships with natural actors take place. The former hold more information regarding the nature of their relationship and the way in which this can be altered (Coleman 1982). War can be equated to state and corporate crime for the similar asymmetric position that decision-making groups occupy *vis-à-vis* natural persons, who become victims even when they are unaware of having been victimized, and even when victimization is disguised under heroism and patriotism.

It is time to link the two hypotheses I have formulated so far. First, I have argued that neat distinctions between social and political definitions of corporate crime are becoming increasingly difficult to identify. Powerful actors, in other words, are able to impose their own definitions within the social sphere, and while making them widely acceptable are then capable of translating them into political concepts and sensibilities. In this way, conduct that might be regarded as criminal may slowly find acceptance within social and political spheres where the criminal characteristics may no longer be perceived. Second, I have suggested that contemporary wars share a number of traits with corporate crime, although such traits tend to fade away from the collective perception. When the need and the benefits of waging war are objectified, the capacity to inflict pain upon 'the other' increases, and such pain vanishes from the public sensitivity: it becomes inadmissible to political discourse (Feldman 1994). International conflicts, moreover, become more and more asymmetric in nature, and as corporate criminals resort to an ideological use of variables such as risk and benefit to pursue legitimation for their conduct, so do advocates of war to try and legitimate theirs. A provisional conclusion could be that corporate crime, wars, and in general the crimes of the powerful share one crucial common denominator: the power to make their criminal nature not definable as such.

I have mentioned that corporations keep experimenting with new economic conducts and striving for their collective acceptance. Processes of privatization encourage such experiments, whereby corporations indeed 'lie in ambush': forcing ethical limits, seizing novel opportunities, and constructing a rationale according to which any given good or item, including collective well-being, can be subjected to negotiation, acquisition or predation. Contemporary wars are at the same time the result and the leading promoters of these processes; they become private affairs which turn even institutional violence, once the domain of state monopolies, into a good, a commodity among others. As we shall see below, wars are triggered by, and at the same time generate, predation. In the past markets have always attempted to hide their violence, whereas now they seem to have stopped doing so, as violence and material interest coincide and form one single commodity. Let us see some examples.

The bellicose corporation

Business and violence are linked in numerous fashions. International development agencies and world financial organizations are the vehicles that allow these links to be formed. In the autobiography of an 'economic hit man' (Perkins 2004: ix) the mechanism is described whereby money is funnelled from the World Bank, the US Agency for International Development (USAID) and other aid organizations into the coffers of large corporations and 'the pockets of a few wealthy families who control the planet's natural resources'. This takes the form of loans to build infrastructure (electric generating plants, highways, ports, airports or industrial parks) in developing countries. It is the task of advanced countries to demonstrate that such economic operations will result in growth for their developing counterparts, thus justifying the loans. Prediction studies, in this respect, are paramount, with gross national product being a critical factor. Measurements of 'growth', however, say little about wealth distribution and collective well-being, as profits of economic activity may be concentrated in small enclaves and mainly appropriated by influential families. Among the conditions of international loans is that structural and infrastructural work is carried out by companies operating in advanced countries, so that the finances, in fact, never leave such countries. 'Most of the money never leaves the US; it is simply transferred from banking offices in Washington to engineering offices in New York, Houston or San Francisco.' Although immediately transferred to corporations, the money is turned into debt for the 'aided' country. When completely successful, such operations create payment defaulters who can compensate creditors with permission 'to install military bases, or access to precious resources such as oil'.

> My job was to encourage world leaders to become part of a vast network that promotes US commercial interests. In the end, those leaders become ensnared in a web of debt that ensures their loyalty. We can draw on them whenever we desire – to satisfy our political, economic, or military needs. In turn, they bolster their political positions by bringing industrial parks, power plants, and airports to their people. The owners of US engineering/construction companies become fabulously wealthy. (Perkins 2004: xi)

Debts can also be paid through the sale of forests or other resources, as in the case of Ecuador, which can only honor its foreign obligations by selling its rainforests to oil companies, or the case of countries in the Amazon region, beneath which 'there is a sea of oil'.

> Thus, out of every $100 worth of oil torn from the Amazon, less than $3 goes to the people who need the money most, those whose lives have been so adversely impacted by the dams, the drilling, and the pipelines, and who are dying from lack of edible food or potable water. (Perkins 2004: xx)

Failure to bow to the exploitation of resources may result in heads of states being overthrown, or in open aggression, which not only grants access to resources, but brings along a plethora of related business and predatory opportunities. This process has been depicted as military neo-liberalism (Retort 2005). Iraq is a case in point, showing how the barriers insulating military strategies from high-risk financial strategies are increasingly eroded (Balakrishnan 2005).

The invasion of Iraq has been likened to a form of neo-liberal shock treatment, whereby from the very beginning war presided over a transition from a centrally planned economy to a market economy. Market forces had to be introduced in key areas of the economy, while all restrictions addressed to foreign corporations had to be abolished. 'Economic opening to multinational competition bankrupted a substantial proportion of Iraqi-owned local enterprises' (Schwartz 2007: 27). Coercive economic 'development', however, incorporated illicit elements. Let us examine some detail.

In late April 2004 it was revealed that less than 5 per cent of the $18.4 billion earmarked for the reconstruction of Iraq had actually been spent. Occupation officials reassigned $184 million appropriated for drinking water projects to fund the operations of the new US embassy, while $29 million was moved from projects such as 'democracy building' to pay for administrative expenses. 'Of the $279 million earmarked for irrigation projects none had been spent, nor had the $152 million allocated for dam repair and construction ... the same for road and bridge construction' (Chatterjee 2004: 11). Less than 1 per cent of the Iraqi labour force had been employed in reconstruction projects, and no trace was found of the money that was not spent. Immediately after the invasion of Iraq, numerous contractors associated with multinational corporations took a leading role in 'reconstructing' the country and 'installing democracy': payments for their work, it was assumed, would derive from the country's oil reserves.

> In the oil wells, employees were Indian and Pakistani working for the Al Kharafi Company, a Kuwaiti subcontractor working for Kellogg Brown and Root (KBR), a subsidiary of Halliburton. In 2003, Halliburton won contracts that range from cooking meals, delivering mail, and building bases, to repairing Iraq's oil industry. That year these contracts totalled more than $8 billion. (Chatterjee 2004: 16)

Paul Bremer, the American proconsul in Baghdad until June 2004, arrived in Iraq immediately after the official end of hostilities. He controlled a budget of $6 billion remaining from the UN Oil for Food program, sequestered and frozen assets, and at least $10 billion from resumed Iraqi oil exports. These funds were transferred into a new account held at the Federal Reserve Bank in New York, called the Development Fund for Iraq (DFI), and was intended to be spent by the Coalition Provisional Authority (CPA) in a transparent manner for the benefit of the Iraqi people.

The US Congress also voted to spend an additional $18 billion of US taxpayers' money on the redevelopment of Iraq. By June 2004 the CPA had spent about $20 billion of Iraqi money, compared with $300 million US.

The reconstruction of Iraq, the largest American-led occupation program since the Marshall Plan, was largely 'paid by the Iraqis themselves' (Harriman 2005: 2). Many financial irregularities were described in reports written by auditors, who referred more than a hundred contracts, involving billions of dollars paid to American personnel and corporations, for investigation and possible criminal prosecution. CPA was accused of not keeping accounts and awarding contracts without tender: pilfering was said to be rife.

The mandate of CPA was to relaunch the Iraqi economy by engaging foreign companies as the key players in the reconstruction of the country. A number of legal orders were issued that permitted foreign ownership of state-controlled Iraqi assets. The electricity, telecommunications and pharmaceuticals industries were sold off, along with banks, mines and factories, and the new foreign owners were allowed to take their profits out of the country. This economic 'restructuring' occurred amid large-scale malpractice and corruption.

The development model being promoted in Iraq is based on contracts known as production sharing agreements (PSAs), which have existed in the oil industry since the late 1960s. Oil experts agree that their purpose is largely political: technically, they keep legal ownership of oil reserves in state hands, while practically delivering oil companies the same results as the concession agreements they replace. PSAs are effectively immune from public scrutiny and lock governments into economic terms that cannot be altered for decades. In Iraq's case, these contracts could be signed while the government was weak, the security situation dire, and the country still under military occupation. As such the terms are likely to be highly unfavorable, but could persist for up to 40 years. Production sharing agreements have been heavily promoted by oil companies and by the US administration. Their use in Iraq was proposed by the Future of Iraq project, the US State Department's planning agency, prior to the 2003 invasion, and their implementation represents a radical redesign of Iraq's oil industry, transferring it from public into private hands (Platform 2005).

An auditing board sponsored by the UN recommended that the United States repay as much as $208 million to the Iraqi government for contracting work in 2003 and 2004 assigned to Kellogg, Brown and Root, a Halliburton subsidiary. The work was paid for with Iraqi oil proceeds, but the board said it was either carried out at inflated prices or done poorly (Iraq Occupation Focus 2005).

Meanwhile, the auditors' investigations into financial abuse under Bremer's CPA in Iraq's South-Central region found hard evidence of mendacity and theft. Two men were arrested in the US: Philip Bloom was charged with conspiracy, fraud, money-laundering and other offences. He was accused of having rigged bids and bribed CPA officials who awarded his companies contracts worth $3.5 million.

If Bloom was described as a small-time wheeler-dealer, Robert Stein, his alleged co-conspirator, was more powerful, being the CPA's Comptroller and Funding Officer for the South-Central region. Stein was convicted of fraud and sued for embezzlement in previous business dealings with the US military. Being a private contractor, not a federal employee, it was odd that he was entrusted with the $82 million reconstruction budget. Stein kept the value of the contracts he awarded and the payments he authorized just below the threshold above which senior approval was required. Because he was spending Iraqi money, he was not subject to the tight standards that would have applied had he been spending American taxpayers' dollars. 'In return for allegedly granting Bloom's companies contracts, including to build a police academy at Babylon and to rehabilitate the Karbala library, Stein and his wife are accused of receiving $683,285 from Bloom.' Some $267,000 was transferred into their personal bank accounts. 'Other payments went directly to creditors in Stein's hometown in North Carolina': some to jewellers, some to a local estate firm, some to local car dealerships (Harriman 2006b: 14).

It is unlikely that the full extent of corruption under the CPA will ever be known, because the former CPA did not maintain complete accounting records in respect of contractual commitments. As Harriman (2006b: 14–15) notes, 'Across Iraq, much of what hasn't been stolen has been skimped on. Schools, clinics, sewage projects, all described as completed by the US embassy, will soon need major repairs as well as regular maintenance work carried out by trained staff.'

Foreign interests were and are not confined to the larger sectors of economic activity. In the ancillary economy foreign labour was hired, providing basic services to the military and large businesses. Such labour enjoyed no union protection or representation, as unions were banned because they were deemed vehicles of civil disorder.

Contractors and subcontractors are part of a specialized network that offers services and goods in war situations. They move from conflict to conflict, 'setting up chow halls from an empty field to a thousand army camps in a matter of days' (Chatterjee 2004: 45). In 2006 it was revealed that 100,000 individuals working for government contractors were operating in Iraq (not counting subcontractors), a figure approaching that of the US military force there (Merle 2006). These companies were hired by large corporations such as Halliburton (once led by US Vice-President Dick Cheney), which has contractors in Saudi Arabia and Kuwait, which in turn have subcontractors in India (Brody 2006). Overcharging is routine, with large companies winning contracts from governments who are unwilling or unable to assess the costs of the war efforts for taxpayers. In some cases, ancillary services are intimately linked with warfare operations, as exemplified by a subsidiary of Halliburton winning a $30 million contract to help build a new permanent prison for terror suspects at Guantánamo Bay (Cornwell 2005). In other cases, contractor services possess an explicit military nature, such as contracts are required to protect key civilian 'principals', or train civilians in conflict zones to provide support for the occupation forces. A good example of this is a consultancy firm Creative Associates International, a Washington-based company operating in Iraq, that had previously been hired to provide military training to the Contra's anti-Sandinista guerrillas in Nicaragua.

In Iraq, however, the inability to properly restore the oil industry compounded the chaotic situation, adding social and political unrest to widespread feelings of national humiliation. 'Reconstructing' the country, therefore, slowly became synonymous with making it 'safer', and private security companies responded to the growing demand on the part of the occupying forces and the businesses these generated. Let us see some examples.

The industry of death

The cost of 'rebuilding' Iraq increased constantly due to the continuing war situation. The US embassy, for example, cut its budget for reconstructing the water and sanitation system by more than $2 billion, largely to pay for security and to repair what the insurgents and US marines destroyed. Security costs can add 25 per cent to budgets. At one point there were twice as many private mercenaries as British troops in Iraq. To pay them, development projects across Iraq were scrapped and scaled back (Harriman 2006a, 2006b).

British companies have been among the most successful security contractors. The services offered by London-based Janusian Security Risk Management include armed guards and armored vehicles, and its structure mimics that of the military, with employees being ranked according to experience and training. The company owns military equipment such as Kiowa helicopters and trains pilots to fly them in Iraq. Another British firm, Rubicon International, hires former members of special forces such as the SAS, who are regarded as extremely well trained, low profile and effective: 'la crème de la crème' (Chatterjee 2004: 108).

The service officially provided by private military contractors ranges from advice, training of local forces, armed site security, cash transport, intelligence services, workplace and building security, war zone security, weapons procurement, vetting, armed support, air support, logistical support, maritime security, cyber security, weapons destruction, prison supervision, surveillance, psychological warfare, propaganda tactics and covert operations. Mercenaries do not operate under military jurisdiction, and are largely exempted from prosecution when they commit crimes against civilians of the occupied nation.

In 2005 British private military company Aegis Defence Services announced profits of £62 million. The firm has seen turnover rise more than a hundred-fold in the past three years, thanks largely to contracts for the US Pentagon in Iraq. Aegis Defence Services is run by Lt Col Tim Spicer, the former Scots Guards officer at the center of an arms-running scandal implicating the British government in a military coup in Sierra Leone that brought the pro-British regime of Ahmed Kabbah to power in 1998. According to Spicer, three-quarters of the company's record profits

came from contracted work in Iraq. Officially, Aegis co-ordinates communications between US-led coalition forces in Iraq, civilian contractors
and their private security guards. Among the functions of the company is
to pass on information about the activity of insurgents, providing a daily
intelligence service to contractors, as well as tracking the position of their
vehicles. Estimates for the value of Aegis's contract range up to £230
million. In 2004 the firm, which employs 900 staff in Iraq, was awarded a
deal with the UN to provide security for the constitutional referendum
and elections. Spicer said he is now looking for new contracts in other
countries, including Russia and China, adding, 'Wherever people operate
– in extractive industries, shipping, aviation – anywhere where there is a
threat, there has to be an interface between the forces of law and order
and commercial operations. That is something that we have developed'
(Thompson 2006: 11).

According to estimates, as of 2009 there were between 25,000 and 35,000
private military personnel in Iraq. The US army, which is by far the largest
force in the country, employs one private military worker for every ten
soldiers.

Dyncorp, a high-profile US security contractor, provides not only police
trainers – individuals with appropriate experience to re-establish a police
force in occupied Iraq – but also experts in 'justice and prison functions'.
The company employs recently retired police officers, prison guards and
'experienced judicial experts'. Previously working in Bosnia, Dyncorp
troops are active in Afghanistan and have also been involved in
defoliation missions over coca crops in Colombia as well as in border
control between the US and Mexico. 'Dyncorp attracted a mixture of
ordinary policemen from the US who jumped at the opportunity to double
their salaries, as well as a few Soldiers of Fortune magazine readers –
macho, swaggering types who walked around Iraq wearing Oakley
sunglasses, Kevlar helmets, and flak jackets, thinking that they owned the
place' (Chatterjee 2004: 112).

In 2007, Dyncorp was hired by the US State Department to help equip
and provide logistical support to international peacekeepers in Somalia,
giving the US a significant role in the mission without assigning combat
forces, and thus avoiding the political scrutiny associated with sending
uniformed soldiers into harm's way (Tomlinson 2007).

Companies operating in war zones can play a variety of roles due to the
grey areas war itself generates. The boundaries between providing a
security service and actively participating in military operations are
vague. Employees of such companies share not only a physical space but
also a national and political culture with the members of official armies.
Employees often include fighters hired from developing countries for
security functions, for intelligence work and for tasks such as interrogation of prisoners. For example, new job opportunities were generated with
the opening of American-run prisons holding Al-Qaida suspects in

Afghanistan and at Guantánamo Bay. 'Easily the most known of these contracts were carried out in the now infamous torture chambers of Abu Ghraib' (Tomlinson 2007: 139).

Private security companies, whose duties in Iraq increasingly mirrored those of the military, in some instances claimed the right to arm themselves with heavy military-style weapons. Charged with the front-line responsibility of defending infrastructure projects, homes, personnel and even US military convoys, the companies' operatives became prime targets of insurgents' attacks (Behn 2005).

The private security and military industry is composed of a maze of companies whose operations are difficult to control due to the international scope of their interests. Tony Blair was accused of trying to privatize the war in Iraq because his government actively encouraged security firms to go to Iraq by giving them multi-million-pound contracts. Private companies were expected to take over duties that could have been performed by British forces (Sengupta 2006). Such companies are often registered as businesses in developing countries and work mainly on a subcontracting basis, which renders accountability and the monitoring of responsibilities impossible. As a result, numerous incidents were reported of contractors firing against civilian vehicles they believed were a threat as potential suicide bombers. According to other reports contractors, who frequently travel in unmarked vehicles and do not have reliable communications with military units, were fired on by US counter-insurgent forces in apparent cases of mistaken identity (Miller 2005).

A final area in which military services are contracted to private companies is the area of translations and interrogations. Among the beneficiaries of such contracts is CACI International from Arlington, Virginia.

> With the new contracts, CACI immediately started soliciting on its web site for interrogators to be dispatched to Afghanistan, Iraq and Kosovo. Would-be interrogators were told that they would have to be comfortable working under 'moderate supervision', providing intelligence support for interviewing local nationals, and determining their threat to coalition forces . . . Candidates must have at least two years' experience as a military policeman or similar type of law enforcement/intelligence agency experience, whereby the individual utilized interviewing techniques. (Chatterjee 2004: 139–40)

Discussion

In terms of sheer scale, the financial scandal detected in Iraq ranks as one of the greatest in history. The money that was placed in the trusteeship of the US-led coalition by the UN, and was to be used in a 'transparent manner' benefiting the people of Iraq, was instead appropriated by private foreign companies, or just disappeared (Macrae and Fadhil 2006). In this respect an initial reflection can be made.

Some traditional criminological analysis has given attention to the relationship between war and common crime. Bonger (1936), for example, argues that war increases all the factors that may lead to crime: family life is ripped apart, children are neglected, destitution spreads, while scarcity of goods generates theft and begets illicit markets. Crime is also caused by the general demoralization, and violent behavior increases as a mimetic outcome of the spectacle of 'killing, maiming and terrible destruction' (Bonger 1936: 105). Crime statistics swell despite the fact that a large part of the male population in the age range of the most represented offenders' group is sometimes in military service, and thereby outside the jurisdiction of the ordinary courts. The dark figure of crime in its turn is assumed to go up, due to the weakening of institutional agencies such as the police and the judiciary.

War is, therefore, criminogenic for those who do not fight, but as Bonger (1936: 105) suggests it also pushes the very individuals who fight to commit a variety of offences, though 'the figures of the crimes committed in the field will probably never be published'. This perspective overturns functionalist analysis: war is described less as an event encouraging supreme integration and solidarity than as a normless condition conducive to egoism and to the dangerous weakening of social bonds.

Bonger's analysis, however, focuses on how war is conducive to conventional criminal activity. More recently, calls for students of crime to be attentive to the conditions shaping the relationship between war and crime are prompted by the 'incidence and ferocity of wars and ethnic conflicts which show no sign of abating' (Jamieson 1998: 480). A criminology of war, therefore, will focus on mass, devastating victimization, violations of human rights, and other forms of state crime; moreover 'states of emergency usher in massive increases in social regulation, punishment and ideological control, new techniques of surveillance and, with that, a corresponding derogation of civil rights' (1998: 480).

'Crimes in war' and 'war crimes' are central areas of investigation. The former are exemplified by conventional predatory offences, interpersonal violence and illicit market operations, while the latter tend to be included under the rubric of state crime (Hagan 2003; Ruggiero 2006). In the cases examined above, however, war also seems to provide an ideal environment for corporate crime to prosper. As a provisional conclusion, therefore, we can state that war is criminogenic not only for powerless individuals but also for powerful actors: what remains to be highlighted is that extending our logical argument, war is also a form of corporate crime.

We have seen how states, by involving business operators, have played a crucial role in the development of mercenary companies and private armies, thus expanding their violent capacities. 'Western states are facilitating new modes of delivering terror and violence that are also likely to increase, rather than reduce, the incidence of state-corporate crime' (Whyte 2003: 575). The concept of state-corporate crime (Michalowski and Kramer 2006) may be appropriate to describe offences that are the product of complex relations between states and corporations. This concept, however, should be coupled with some insight into the way in which war can simply and straightforwardly be conceptualized as corporate crime. In this respect, it may be useful to return to the dynamics sketched above, namely the relationships between the social, political and legal spheres and their respective definitions of what corporate crime is and what it is not.

I have already argued that powerful actors may be able to shape definitions favorable to their conduct within the social sphere and transfer them into the political sphere. Their criminality, in this way, may no longer be perceived as such, nor will it be contested in the political arena. In respect to war, we encounter examples of how this 'transferral' of definitions and sensibilities takes place when we analyze the function of general purpose technologies, whose development would have occurred more slowly, or not at all, in the absence of military and defence-related procurement (Ruttan 2005). The mixture of technology development and death makes the criminality inherent in war disappear, as war comes to be accepted as a natural component of progress and as such rationalized. There are, finally, other crimes inherent in contemporary wars that require yet further mechanisms of rationalization. I am referring, first, to the fact that contemporary wars are forms of unauthorized violence, as they are not legitimized by international organizations. When they are, international organizations themselves are often the spokespersons of the powerful nations in favour of war and aggression. Second, the means utilized are themselves illegal, for example the use of translators-interrogators-torturers, of phosphorous bombs against civilians, and the handling of prisoners through extraordinary rendition. Rationalizations for such conducts, which violate international agreements and conventions, are achieved when new legal definitions are formulated.

New practices forge new understandings and rationales for action, in the sense that improvisation and experimentation modify the way in which practices are perceived and defined. Once adopted, certain conducts seek to find hospitality in a modified collective imaginary. By imaginary we may mean the way in which people understand their existence, relate to others, and develop their expectations: how they imagine their social surroundings and how they deal with it. We may also refer to the social imaginary as 'that common understanding that makes possible common practices and a widely shared sense of legitimacy' (Taylor 2004: 23). Illegal practices pursue similar legitimacy, and once their perception has been modified within the social and the political spheres, it is jurisprudence that, in providing its final seal, turns them into future potential routine. Above I have hinted at the possibility for corporate actors to utilize the vectors available to them to exit their social sphere, namely to innovate and avoid repetitive conducts and routines. These vectors can be described as 'escape lines' (Deleuze 2005) as they show the routes to new conducts whose outcome may be unknown and will only become clear after repeated experimentation.

War and corporate crime seem to be inspired by a similar 'experimental' logic, according to which some illicit practices are adopted with the awareness that they are indeed illicit, but with an eye to the social and institutional reactions that might ensue. It is the intensity of such responses that will determine whether violations are to become part of a 'viable' routine or are to be carefully avoided. Some violations possess a 'founding force'; namely, they are capable of transforming the previous jurisprudence and establishing new laws and new types of legitimacy (Derrida 2003).

War and the crimes of the powerful restructure the legal and the political spheres. The law chases the economy, and in the face of continuous violations by the latter, new founding laws are permanently required (Rossi 2006). Examples of this 'founding force' are far from being confined to economic activity. Recent episodes, already mentioned, of torture, military invasion, secret flights, kidnappings by secret services and the use of prohibited weapons appear to confirm that the crimes committed by powerful actors rewrite the international law and refound the principles of justice. This is perhaps the logic of contemporary powerful states, exemplified by the administration of George W. Bush in the following manner: solutions do not emerge from a judicious study of discernible reality. 'When we act, we create our own reality ... we are history's actors and you, all of you, will be left to study what we do' (Jenkins 2006: 11).

In sum, then, war and the crimes of the powerful encapsulate a normative element, and while challenging legality they may end up establishing new norms and legislations. Only the future will tell whether this dynamic can be challenged, so that alternative normative elements are identified capable of establishing norms and legislations genuinely favorable to the common good.

Chapter 8

From Guernica to Hiroshima to Baghdad: the normalization of the terror bombing of civilians

Ronald C. Kramer

Monday, 26 April 1937 was a beautiful, clear day in the ancient Basque (Euskadi) town of Guernica (Gernika). It was a market day and the town was filled with people from around the area. But at this time the Basque campaign of the Spanish Civil War was raging and the rebel forces of General Francisco Franco, along with their fascist German and Italian allies, were engaged in a 'new kind of warfare, a war waged against civilians' (Kurlansky 1999: 197). At 4.40 p.m., when the center of Guernica was most crowded, a deadly air display began when new modern attack aircraft from the German Condor Legion and the Italian Aviazione Legionaria bombed and strafed the town. Up to a thousand people were killed in the vicious attack, and much of Guernica, the symbolic capital of the Basques, was destroyed by the 'thermite rain' of the incendiary devices dropped by Nazi bombers (Patterson 2007). Guernica was not the first time that civilians had been bombed from the air, but as Patterson notes: 'It was the first time that a completely unmilitarised, undefended, ordinary civilian town in Europe had been subjected to this sort of devastating attack from the air' (2007: 17). The purpose of the bombing was to break the will of the Basque people and eliminate their 'appetite for resistance' to Franco's Nationalist insurgents (Graham 2005: 71).

The terror bombing of a civilian population is a moral and a legal *state crime* because it violates the 'long-standing and widespread' moral principle and international legal norm of 'noncombatant immunity' (Conway-Lanz 2006: 2). This principle is found in both just war theory and the legal rules of international humanitarian law (the laws of war). The bombing of civilians has also been defined as *state terrorism*: systematic state violence against civilians in violation of international laws (Selden and So 2004: 6). And Markusen and Kopf (1995) have even classified the Allied terror bombing campaigns against Germany and Japan during World War Two as *genocidal*.

What also makes the terror bombing of Guernica sociologically relevant, however, is that it was labeled as 'deviant' by a wide variety of social audiences worldwide at the time. As Englehardt (2008a: 2) points out: 'The self-evident barbarism of the event – the first massively publicized bombing of a civilian population – caused international horror. It was news across the planet.' Patterson (2007: 38) has observed: 'Many attacks since then, including the ones we have grown used to seeing in Iraq and the Middle East in recent years, have been on such a scale that Guernica's fate seems almost insignificant by comparison. But it's almost impossible to overestimate the outrage it caused in 1937.' The global outcry stemmed as much from what the attack presaged, as from the actual damage inflicted. As Kurlansky (1999: 200) notes: 'The world was horrified – outraged at the ruthless massacre of unarmed civilians but also terrified at its first glimpse of the warfare of the future.' From the bombing of Guernica came perhaps the most famous painting of the twentieth century, Picasso's *Guernica*. First installed in the Spanish pavilion at the Paris World's Fair in June of 1937, the massive panel both expressed the horror of the world at the bombing as well as its definition of the act as 'criminal'. According to Patterson, 'Picasso's painting . . . made Guernica the most famous image of total war, and articulated the terror of it so potently that the picture has become almost synonymous with a sense of outrage and condemnation' (2007: 2). Quickly the little town of Guernica became a cultural symbol and the very word itself 'carried an accumulation of horror at everything connected with the bombing of undefended civilian towns and homes' (2007: 34).

Within a decade, however, in the context of the massive violence of the global human catastrophe that was World War Two, the terror bombing of civilian populations, often referred to as 'area bombing', became both commonplace and morally acceptable to many of the same political leaders and publics that had condemned the horror of Guernica. The wartime erosion of social and moral restraints on the state crime of bombing civilians was evidenced on all sides by the tragedies of the air attacks on the coastal cities of China, the Blitz of London, the bombing of Rotterdam, the firestorms of Hamburg, Dresden and Tokyo, and finally to 'the most extreme and permanently traumatizing instance of state terrorism', the atomic bombings of Hiroshima and Nagasaki (Falk 2004a: 45).

The area bombing of civilians in Germany and Japan by the Allied nations during World War Two in particular wrought 'a revolution in the morality of warfare' (Schaffer 1985: 3). While the German and Italian attack on Guernica and the Japanese bombardment of civilians in China in 1937 brought forth a 'chorus of outraged condemnation' from around the world that 'reached unprecedentedly high levels' (Bess 2006: 90), the Allied terror bombing attacks on Germany and Japan became normal and acceptable to many people by 1945. This appears to be a prime example of what Vaughan (1996, 2007) calls 'the normalization of deviance'. According to Vaughan, the normalization of deviance occurs when actors in an organizational setting, such as a corporation or a government agency, come to define their deviant acts as normal and acceptable because they fit with and conform to the cultural norms of the organiz-ation within which they work. Even though their actions may violate some outside legal or social standard and be labeled as criminal or deviant by people outside the organization, organizational offenders, such as state officials, do not see these actions as wrong because they are conforming to the cultural mandates that exist within the workgroup culture and environment where they carry out their occupational roles.

During the course of World War Two social definitions and cultural mandates concerning the terror bombing of cities began to change and the moral constraints on this practice almost completely collapsed in just a few short years of what came to be called 'total war' (Conway-Lanz 2006; Markusen and Kopf 1995; Patterson 2007). Once 'normalized' – that is, culturally approved – this form of state terrorism, the 'most barbaric style of warfare imaginable' (Englehardt 2008b: 161), would continue to characterize American war fighting right up to the present. As Selden (2009: 93) observes: 'The strategy of killing noncombatants through airpower runs like a red line from the bombings of 1944–45 through the Korean and Indochinese wars to the Gulf, Afghanistan and Iraq wars.'

This chapter provides a theoretical account of how, after the outrage over Guernica, the terror bombing of civilians developed during World War Two and became normalized – culturally accepted and approved by many political and military leaders and the American people. The account draws on an integrated model for the analysis of organizational deviance developed by Kramer and Michalowski (1990, 2006) and refined by Kauzlarich and Kramer (1998). This theoretical schema, an effort at theory elaboration (Vaughan 2007), links three levels of analysis – macro, meso and micro – with three catalysts for action: motivation (goals), opportunity (means), and formal social control (sanctions). The objective is to inventory and highlight the key factors that contribute to or restrain organizational deviance at each intersection of a catalyst for action and a level of analysis. This model views the organization as the key unit of analysis, nested within an institutional and cultural environment, and engaged in social action through the decisions of individual actors who occupied key positions within the structure of the organization. According to this schema, organizational deviance is most likely to occur when pressures for organizational goal attainment intersect with attractive and available illegitimate organizational means in the absence or neutraliz-ation of effective formal social controls.

Drawing on this approach, this chapter demonstrates that over the course of World War Two, the socially constructed morality of nationalistic and imperialistic war goals, the 'technological fanaticism' of the bureaucracies charged with military planning, the legitimation of state violence through the failures of international law, and a variety of social, psychological and emotional factors all contributed to the overall erosion of social and moral constraints on the state crime of terror bombing. The social and cultural forces that developed during the war resulted in a 'normalization of deviance' that continues to provide normative support and institutional benefits for the illegal military targeting of civilians from the air within various state organizational structures and the general culture down to the present.

The social construction of the morality of war goals

The primary goal of the United States and its allies during World War Two, of course, was to win the war. The 'precision bombing' of military and war-related industrial targets, with its attendant collateral damage, and then the 'area or strategic bombing' of enemy civilian populations to destroy their morale, were two of the means to that ultimate end. But by 1944 military victory was all but assured in both the European and the Pacific theatres. At this point secondary war goals emerged to the forefront: ending the war as quickly and decisively as possible, and by accomplishing those objectives saving the lives of Allied military personnel. Gradually, the majority of American political and military leaders came to believe that the accomplishment of these national goals necessitated a change in the use of air power from a sole reliance on precision bombing to an increasing use of terror bombing of enemy civilian populations, including the utilization of newly developed atomic weapons (Biddle 2002; Schaffer 1985; Walker 2004). As Walker points out: 'The primary objective of the United States had always been to win the war decisively at the lowest cost in American casualties, and the [atomic] bomb was the best means to accomplish those goals' (2004: 92).

Some historians argue that the area bombing campaigns and the use of atomic weapons did help to shorten the war somewhat and thus they did save some American lives (Bess 2006; Walker 2004). After the atomic attacks on Japan, and in the early post-war period, however, President Truman, Secretary of War Henry Stimson and others who had participated in the decision to drop the atomic bombs, created an elaborate narrative that the bombings of Hiroshima and Nagasaki had been the *only way* to end the war short of a costly invasion of Japan, and that the lives of up to a million soldiers had been saved by shortening the war and avoiding the invasion. While some historians also support these assertions (Frank 1999; Newman 1995), others have challenged them (see Kort 2007 for an overview of the controversy). Walker (2004: 109), for example, argues that the bomb 'was not necessary to prevent an invasion of Japan' and that it 'saved the lives of a relatively small but far from inconsequential number of Americans'. And in his massive study of air power and military coercion in war, which includes both the conventional and atomic bombing raids of World War Two, Pape (1996: 314) flatly asserts that the evidence shows that 'strategic bombing does not work'. Despite the debate among historians about the truth of the claims that the bombings 'worked' by ending the war and saving lives, it is important to point out that according to the principle of noncombatant immunity found in both the just war moral tradition and the international laws of war, it is never permissible to target innocent civilians or noncombatants to accomplish war aims or save the lives of military combatants.

In the latter stages of World War Two and in the post-war Truman-Stimson narrative, the goals of shortening the war and saving the lives of American boys were presented as self-evidently 'good' and 'just'. The entire conflict, of course, in a nationalistic fervor, was defined as the 'Good War' (Terkel 1984; Wood 2006). Defeating what was to most the obvious 'evil' of Hitler and the Fascists, whose own state crimes during the war were massive, exacting 'just retribution' for the 'sneak' attack on Pearl Harbor and other Japanese atrocities during the war, and defending freedom and democracy at home against the criminal aggression of the Axis powers were such clear moral goals that any means necessary to accomplish them came to be viewed as acceptable and legitimate to most American leaders and the public. In their comparative analysis of the Holocaust and Allied strategic bombing practices, Markusen and Kopf (1995: 195) refer to this as the 'healing-killing paradox', the concept that 'an evil means is justified in the service of a valued, noble cause'. They note: 'Moral qualms that might be aroused by the evil nature of the means are assuaged or neutralized by a preoccupation with the worthiness of the goal to be attained by use of such means' (1995: 195). In his study of the strategic bombing campaigns of World War Two, Schaffer (1985: 176) makes much the same observation:

> The concept of just retribution, the notion that the military and political objectives of the air war justified the means employed, the view that it was proper to exchange the lives of civilians connected with the Japanese war effort for the lives of American servicemen, and the hope that destroying cities with nuclear bombs might convince nations to abolish the institution of warfare all supported what was done. Along with technical and political considerations and the belief that American public opinion favored harsh treatment of Japanese civilians, these moral attitudes outweighed, in the minds of the men who made key decisions, the moral objections that a few people raised.

Thus, the social construction of the goodness and morality of the war in general, and the specific objectives of shortening the bloody conflict and saving the lives of 'our boys in uniform', overwhelmed and short-circuited any attempt to critically evaluate the morality and legality of the terror bombing of the civilian populations of the 'evil' enemy as a means to those legitimate ends. The interpretive claims made by Stimson and Truman can be viewed as the linchpin of what Cohen (2001) calls a 'culture of denial', a culture in this case that served to neutralize blame for the atrocity of Hiroshima and Nagasaki and legitimate the atomic attacks, and by extension all forms of terror bombing during the war, in the eyes of the American people and the world. Lifton and Mitchell (1995) have cogently analyzed this unfolding process of denial related to Hiroshima. And as Cohen (2001: 101) points out: 'Cultures of denial encourage turning a collective blind eye, leaving horrors unexamined or normalized . . .'.

In addition to this 'interpretive denial' (Cohen 2001), a number of historians have documented that the United States also shared with its adversaries certain other nationalistic and expansionist motives. The war 'propelled the U.S. to a hegemonic position' that provided a unique opportunity for American leaders to pursue these 'imperial' designs (Selden 2009: 91). Enhancing the economic power and geopolitical position of the American empire also became central goals of US wartime policies, including the policy of terror bombing (Gerson 2007; Zinn 1980).

The United States has been an imperial project from its earliest years (Anderson and Cayton 2005; Ferguson 2004; Nugent 2008; Wright 2008). Throughout the nineteenth century, American growth relied on expansion through force, including enslavement of Africans, expropriation of Native lands in the name of 'manifest destiny', claiming North and South America as an exclusive American sphere of influence (the Monroe Doctrine), expansionist war with Mexico, and using American warships to ensure Asian trading partners (Beard and Beard 1930; Kolko 1984; Sewall 1905/1995; Williams 1959/1988, 1969). As the nineteenth century drew to a close, structural contradictions in American capitalism provoked an intensification of America's imperial reach through formal colonization in Cuba, Puerto Rico and the Philippines. The United States would soon abandon its brief experiment with formal colonization as too economically and politically costly. The United States became an 'informal' empire as opposed to a formal or colonial empire. As Selden (2009: 91) points out: 'In contrast to earlier territorial empires, this took the form of new regional and global structures facilitating the exercise of American power'.

World War Two provided a unique opportunity for the US to greatly expand this informal empire by confronting and defeating rival imperial powers and by creating some of these new regional and global structures. A clash of imperial ambitions precipitated the 'Day of Infamy' at Pearl

Harbor. This clash of imperial ambitions necessitated the decisive defeat of Japan and the complete destruction of Japanese militarism and imperialism. The firebombing of Japanese cities and the use of the atomic bombs were viewed as important means to accomplish these goals, in addition to exacting just retribution for wartime atrocities (Gerson 2007; Zinn 1980).

As the war progressed and it became clear that the United States would be able to exercise hegemonic power in the post-war era, American leaders began to plan for the construction of new global institutions that would greatly advance their imperial designs. As Zinn (1980: 414) notes: 'Before the war was over, the administration was planning the outlines of the new international economic order, based on partnership between government and business.' This new international economic order would enhance and expand the informal, Open Door imperialism the United States had been practicing since the early years of the twentieth century (Williams 1959/1988).

Even as World War Two was putting the United States into a position from which it could dominate the world, American political and military leaders recognized that the Soviet Union, their wartime ally, would be their chief rival in the post-war period. The contest for power and domination between the Soviet Union and the United States that would later be dubbed 'The Cold War' was already under way before the 'hot' war against fascism was over. American officials increasingly came to view Stalin and the Soviets as a threat to their post-war imperial designs in both Europe and East Asia. And the perception of this threat would be an important factor in the most momentous decision of World War Two: the decision to drop the atomic bomb.

A number of historians have argued that the decision to use the atomic bomb was motivated more by political factors related to the perceived Soviet threat than by purely military factors. Alperovitz (1965, 1995) presents persuasive evidence that American leaders dropped atomic weapons on Hiroshima and Nagasaki in an effort to impress Stalin with the power of the bomb and to intimidate the Soviet Union in the coming post-war contest for domination. He argues that Japan was on the verge of surrender in the summer of 1945 and that Truman and his advisors were well aware that alternatives to using the bomb existed. Nevertheless, Alperovitz contends, for diplomatic considerations US leaders decided to use this powerful new weapon on Japan. To gain political leverage over the Soviets in the post-war period, the United States carried out the terror bombing of two cities using atomic weapons.

Another political factor that is alleged to have played a role in the decision to drop the atomic bomb was the threat of Soviet expansionism in the Far East. Once the war in Europe was over, Stalin had pledged to enter the Pacific war by attacking Manchuria, eventually driving the Japanese out of China and perhaps becoming involved in a prospective invasion of the Japanese homelands. As Hasegawa (2005) points out, alarmed by the prospect of Soviet territorial gains in East Asia and a shared occupation of Japan, American leaders hoped to use the atomic bomb to end the war quickly before the Soviet Union could enter the fight and become a major player in the endgame in the Pacific. Again, imperial rivalry rather than military necessity appears to have driven the decision to bomb civilian populations with a new weapon of mass destruction.

While some scholars have concluded that the use of atomic weapons against Japan was both a moral and a legal crime (Boyle 2002; Falk 2004a; Gerson 2007; Grayling 2006; Lifton and Mitchell 1995; Zinn 1980), the majority of Americans did not see it that way at the time, and still do not draw that conclusion today. Considerations of the morality and legality of the decision to use the atomic bomb, or of area bombing during World War Two in general, were overwhelmed by the social construction of the morality of the 'good' war. To most political and military leaders, and to the majority of the American people, the goals of winning the war as quickly as possible, saving the lives of American boys in uniform, and exacting a just retribution on the evil German and Japanese empires, were paramount and justified the use of any means, including the terror bombing of enemy civilians. A culture of denial developed in which other nationalistic and imperialistic goals were either not recognized or interpreted within the mythic idealism that has, since the earliest days of white colonial settlement in North America, imagined every act of expansion as part of a noble 'civilizing mission'.

The mythic ideals of political leaders in the United States are usually drawn from a broad historical, cultural narrative often referred to as American exceptionalism (Fiala 2008; Hodgson 2009). American exceptionalism generally portrays the US as a nation of exceptional virtue, a moral leader in the world with a unique historical mission to spread 'universal' values such as freedom, democracy, equality, popular sovereignty, and increasingly global capitalism. This mythic cultural conception of exceptionalism 'thoroughly informs US constructs of its identity' (Ryan 2007: 119). According to Hodgson (2009: 159), the 'myth of American exceptionalism' often takes a 'missionary' form shaped by a 'God-given destiny' to 'spread the benefits of its democratic system and of its specific version of capitalism to as many other countries as possible'. Americans have always viewed their country as a 'city set upon a hill' with a special duty and destiny to spread their values and wisdom, their freedom and democracy, to the rest of the world. This myth of American exceptionalism has often shielded the American people from a critical examination of their history and the imperial motives that so often drive US foreign policy.

World War Two, the 'Good War', only reinforced the mythic idealism at the heart of American exceptionalism. In *Worshipping the Myths of World War II*, Edward W. Wood Jr (2006: 143) points out that one of the myths of that war is the idea that 'When evil lies in others, war is the means to justice.' In the end, the healing–killing paradox prevailed. Americans had come to believe more strongly than ever that the fight against evil and the advancement of America's exceptional ideals justified any of the means, including violent means, we select to accomplish our national goals. In the wartime environment, conformity to these cultural mandates helped to make the bombing of civilians, even with the most horribly destructive weapon that humans had ever devised, a normal and acceptable act.

Weapons technology, military planning and technological fanaticism

A second factor in this normalization of terror bombing was the way in which the destructive technology of air power came to be applied to wartime aims within US political and military institutions and organizations such as the White House, the War Department, the Joint Chiefs, the Army Air Force, the Manhattan Project and the Interim Committee. As Selden (2009: 87) notes, in all of these social settings, 'Technology was harnessed to the driving force of American nationalism.'

Throughout the war, an instrumental rationality that fixates on the most effective and efficient means to accomplish pre-given and unquestioned ends developed within the institutions and organizations associated with military planning that led inexorably to the terror bombing of civilian populations. Organizational and bureaucratic imperatives concerning the development of technologies of mass destruction increasingly came to drive the war planning process and moral and legal concerns about these technologies were pushed aside. As Jackall (1980: 355) points out, 'The rational/technical ethos of bureaucracy transforms even those issues with grave moral import into practical concerns.' Thus, the instrumental rationality of the organizational form itself appears to be partially responsible for the state terrorism of bombing civilians. Again, Jackall observes: 'The very rationality which makes bureaucratic structures effective administrative tools seems to erode moral consciousness' (1980: 356).

Sherry (1987, 1995, 2009) has developed a compelling analysis of this rational bureaucratic process in its association with the development of American air power. He terms it 'technological fanaticism' and argues, that 'among policymakers, if not in the public at large, a technological fanaticism often governed actions, an approach to making war in which satisfaction of organizational and professional drives loomed larger than the overt passions of war' (Sherry 1987: xi).

The very concept of 'precision bombing', which American political and military leaders clung to for much of the war, implies a faith that advances in technology allowed attacks to be carried out on military and war-related industrial targets with only minimal and unintentional 'collateral damage' to civilians and noncombatants. As Conway-Lanz (2006: 19) points out, both during and after World War Two, 'many Americans tenaciously clung to the optimistic assumption that violence in war could still be used in a discriminating manner despite the increased destructiveness of weapons'. Buttressing this assumption was the fact that the advancing technology of air power provided both a physical and a psychic distance from the people being harmed for scientists and military personnel (Markusen and Kopf 1995; Sherry 1995). As Sherry (1995: 81) observes:

> By virtue of their economic and technological superiority, Americans could act out war's destructive impulses while seeing themselves as different from their enemies. Rarely witnessing the human costs to the enemy, scientists could press new technologies on the armed forces, air force crews could incinerate enemy cities, and battleships could pummel Japanese-held islands from miles offshore. The intricate technology of war provided physical and psychic distance from the enemy.

Within the organizational settings in which World War Two military planning took place, then, an instrumental rationality concerning the application of the new technological means of mass destruction through the use of air power to the unquestionable moral goals of the war took hold. As Selden (2009: 87) points out, 'What was new was both the scale of killing made possible by the new technologies and the routinization of mass killing or state terrorism.' This technological fanaticism aided the developing culture of denial and served to override and displace moral and legal concerns over the use of terror bombing within the various political and military bureaucracies charged with wartime decision-making. It also provided the optimistic assumption that air attacks could be carried out in a discriminating way, as well as physical and psychological distancing from the actual consequences of bombing civilian populations. Technological fanaticism, therefore, was one more factor in the dynamic social process that spawned terror bombing during the war and allowed it to become normal and acceptable.

Laws of war: the absence of enforcement and the legitimation of violence

Despite the long-standing principle of noncombatant immunity, or any of the formal legal standards found in the laws of war as they existed at the time, the terror bombing of civilian populations became widespread during World War Two, including the atomic bombings of Japan. The

127

final factor that influenced the normalization of these bombing attacks on civilians was the weakness of international law itself. The primary weakness of international law in general is the lack of any effective enforcement mechanism. While a plethora of laws and legal standards have been promulgated over the years (particularly with regard to conduct during war), states have been unwilling to give up enough sovereignty to allow for any formal controls or coercive enforcement tools to be created that may be able to effectively punish or deter violations of these standards. Absent of any effective formal legal controls, the compelling drive to achieve nationalistic and imperialistic goals during the course of the war through the effective and available means of terror bombing was not deterred by the mere existence of the legal principle of noncombatant immunity.

While no effective coercive enforcement mechanisms existed under international law at the time of actual hostilities, following the war there was an important effort to hold states and political and military leaders to account for their actions during the conflict that constituted 'war crimes' broadly conceived. The international military tribunals at Nuremberg and Tokyo prosecuted, convicted and then sanctioned a number of German and Japanese government officials for 'illegal' acts they had allegedly engaged in during the war. Space does not permit an extended discussion of these international tribunals but it is important to note that the aerial bombardment of civilian populations, whether to destroy their morale or for any other purpose, was not one of the crimes that was prosecuted. As Jochnick and Normand (1994: 89) point out: 'In order to avoid condemning Allied as well as Axis conduct, the war crimes tribunal left the most devastating forms of warfare unpunished.' They go on to argue that the decision not to include terror bombing among the war crimes to be prosecuted at Nuremberg or Tokyo helped to legitimate this behavior: 'By leaving morale bombing and other attacks on civilians unchallenged, the Tribunal conferred legal legitimacy on such practices' (1994: 91). So even the most significant effort in history to actually enforce the laws of war, along with its undeniably important humanitarian accomplishments in advancing the legal categories of 'crimes against peace' and 'crimes against humanity', failed to even define the bombing of civilians as a crime let alone punish the behavior or attempt to deter it in the future with formal sanctions. Thus, the legal legitimacy conferred upon terror bombing by the international military tribunals helped to normalize the practice and ensure that it would continue to be an acceptable practice in the future.

But alongside the failure to control terror bombing due to a lack of formal enforcement mechanisms, there is an even more fundamental way in which international law legitimizes state violence and contributes to its normalization. As Jochnick and Normand (1994: 56) have convincingly argued, the laws of war provide 'unwarranted legitimacy' and 'humanitarian cover' for violence during wartime due to the way in which states have created and codified an elastic definition of 'military necessity' within the codes and conventions that constitute this body of law. Through overly broad and unchallenged conceptions of military necessity and military objectives, international law has legitimized and facilitated state practices during war such as terror bombing. During World War Two the Allies did not openly violate the laws of war as much as simply interpret them in such a way as to justify and 'legalize' their resort to the aerial bombardment of civilian populations in Germany and Japan. Jochnick and Normand (1994: 89) conclude:

> In both World Wars the laws of war played analogous roles. In each conflict the law served as a powerful rhetorical device to reassure anxious publics that the conflict would be confined within just limitations. The First and Second World Wars both saw the law subverted to the dictates of battle, reduced to a propaganda battle-field where belligerents traded attacks and counterattacks. And in the end, the law ultimately failed to protect civilians from horrifying new weapons and tactics. The scope of permissible violence expanded under a flexible definition of military objective and military necessity that eventually, and predictably, justified relentless terror bombing campaigns.

In several ways, then, international law played a significant role in the development and normalization of terror bombing. By the failure to create effective mechanisms to enforce the legal standards that purport to provide immunity for noncombatants, and by the refusal of the Allies to include area bombing as a war crime to be prosecuted by the military tribunals formed after World War Two, the international legal community helped to institutionally facilitate and culturally legitimate the targeting of civilians by air during wartime. Furthermore, the elastic definition of military necessity that was deliberately written into the laws of war over the years has allowed states to interpret their bombing behavior as 'legal' and provided them with a rhetorical device to assure their publics that the deaths of innocent civilians in such attacks are regrettable but necessary to accomplish military aims. Thus, terror bombing becomes normalized and culturally approved.

The erosion of constraints: social psychological and emotional factors

After the horror and international outrage generated by the air attack on Guernica, and despite the plea of President Roosevelt on the eve of the war for all of the belligerents to refrain from the 'bombardment from the air of civilian populations or unfortified cities' (Grayling 2006: 24), the terror bombing of noncombatants became commonplace during World War Two. The social and moral constraints on the bombing of civilians that seemed to be in place prior to the war eroded quickly during the course of that conflict. Selden (2009: 87) notes: 'The most important way in which World War II shaped the moral and technological tenor of mass destruction was the erosion in the course of war of the stigma associated with the systematic slaughter of civilians from the air, and elimination of the constraints that for some years had restrained certain air powers from area bombing.' General Curtis LeMay himself, who was in charge of the latter stages of the air war in the Pacific, later reflected on 'how moral compunctions against city bombing had disintegrated in World War II as retaliation and re-retaliation led the Allies to all-out strategic air warfare whose ultimate expression was the raids on Hamburg and Tokyo and the atomic bomb attacks' (quoted in Schaffer 1985: 217).

A large part of the erosion of the stigma associated with, and the elimination of the constraints on, area bombing during the war can be attributed to the factors discussed above. Despite these cultural, organizational and institutional factors, some American political and military leaders still had moral qualms about the practice of targeting civilian populations during the latter stages of the war. Schaffer (1985: xi) found evidence that during the war 'the moral issue' was raised by some officers within the US Army Air Force and that some 'American generals based military decisions at least partly on moral concerns'. In the earlier years of the war, the concept of precision bombing, with its stricter definition of military targets and its comforting notion that civilian deaths were unintentional, had provided some protection to these individuals. With the adoption of area bombing in 1944–45, however, the moral concerns were raised anew. A number of additional social psychological and emotional factors help to explain the further erosion of these social and moral constraints. As Schaffer (1985: 189) points out:

> . . . it is clear that several elements interacted to produce the result. Pressures of time and the availability of information, the presence of key individuals and of persons sharing their points of view, the need to appear tough, and other group psychological phenomena combined with rational appraisals of military and political circumstances to produce a wide range of reactions, including no reaction at all, to the moral issues that arose from American bombing.

In addition to the factors that Schaffer documents, racism, ideological dehumanization, and a variety of strong emotions also appear to have played important roles in overriding social and moral constraints on the targeting of innocent civilians (Bess 2006; Markusen and Kopf 1995). Bess has argued that it is particularly important to understand the human and emotional context in which the 'choices under fire' of political and military leaders during World War Two were made:

> If we put ourselves in the place of the Allied leaders in 1945, we have to make the leap into a very different mental world from that of today. We have already seen ... how the Allies gradually came to adopt the Orwellian logic of strategic incendiary bombing, in which the killing of masses of noncombatants could be rationalized as morally acceptable and even as 'merciful', since it hastened the war's end and the earliest possible cessation of the carnage. The wartime context, moreover, was unequivocally one of brutalization, dehumanization of the enemy, racism, and hatred on all sides. To lose sight of this fact is to miss one of the key realities of the Second World War: though most of the war's major decisions were certainly built on logical analysis, no judgment was made in a detached rational vacuum. On all sides, the wartime leaders could not help but make their decisions as human beings, subject to such emotions as outrage, fear, bitterness, and the desire for revenge. This is not to suggest that most of what they did was primarily motivated by such emotions: it was not. But it does call attention to the broader human context within which all wartime policies were unavoidably being shaped. This was a time of hard, cold, often grimly brutal resolutions, in which the deaths of large numbers of human beings had become commonplace, and in which the more humane considerations that normally characterize peacetime decision-making necessarily took a back seat (Bess 2006: 202).

To fully understand the erosion of the social and moral constraints against attacking civilians through the air during World War Two, then, these additional social psychological and emotional factors must be taken into account. When they are added to the broader cultural and structural factors already discussed, a clearer understanding of the development and normalization of terror bombing emerges.

Conclusion: the normalization of state terrorism

This chapter has argued that the aerial bombardment of civilian populations that took place during World War Two was a form of state crime. It was state crime because it violated the moral and legal principle of noncombatant immunity and other standards of international law in existence at that time. The state officials who ordered these terror attacks on innocent civilians could have, and should have, known that the practices that they were engaged in were immoral under just war theory and illegal under the laws of war. Such attacks had generated international outrage as late as the 1937 bombing of Guernica; and the bombing campaigns of World War Two were controversial even at the time they took place and the decision-makers were fully, and perhaps criminally, aware of the moral and legal objections that were being raised about them.

From a sociological perspective, however, it is important to point out that the political and military officials who approved and carried out these terror bombings did not see themselves as criminal, nor did the vast majority of the publics they served. Those who thought otherwise, such as Vera Brittain (1944), were a small minority. The state officials who engaged in these criminal acts did not make a calculated decision to violate any laws. Instead they were enmeshed in a culture of denial. They were conforming to cultural mandates concerning ending the war, saving American lives, and advancing national interests that were derived from the mythic idealism of American exceptionalism. They utilized the technological means at their disposal within bureaucratic settings that were dominated by a form of instrumental rationality that erodes moral consciousness. They interpreted international law through the lens of an elastic concept of military necessity and were never forced to contemplate the threat of formal legal sanctions. In a few short years during the war, bombing civilians, even with a new weapon of mass destruction, had become normalized.

Both the leaders and the majority of citizens in the Allied nations during the course of World War Two had come to view the illegal aerial bombardment of the civilian populations of Germany and Japan as necessary, acceptable and even normal. And since then terror bombing, what Englehardt (2008b: 160) describes as the 'religion of air power', has become an important part of the American way of war to the present. As Vaughan (2007: 11) points out, some organizational offenders may come to define their deviance as 'normal and acceptable: it is not a calculated decision where the costs and benefits of doing wrong are weighed because the definitions of what is deviant and what is normative have been redefined within that setting'.

Winning World War Two, the 'Good War' against evil, and purportedly winning it generally through the use of air power and specifically through the use of the atomic bomb, helped to cement the normalization of the state crime of bombing civilians. As Falk (2008: 228) observes: 'The winners in a war such as World War II, which was, in the deepest sense, widely regarded a just war, exerted a strong influence in determining which practices in war are to be tolerated.' The bombing of civilians and the use of atomic weapons would now be tolerated. They had become normal and acceptable. The concept of the healing–killing paradox had been validated (Markusen and Kopf 1995). In the immediate post-war period, the Truman-Stimson narrative concerning the necessity of the use of the atomic bomb to end the war without an invasion, thus saving over a million American lives, would further cement the normalization of the use and threat to use nuclear weapons.

The normalization of terror bombing that emerged during World War Two has continued to exert an enormous influence on the conduct of US foreign policy ever since. In the early 1950s, three years of bombing and shelling reduced Korea, North and South, to a 'shambles' (Zinn 1980: 481). The total tonnage of all airborne ordnance during the Korean War was 698,000 with a death toll of between 2 to 3 million (Young 2009: 157). In Vietnam, from Lyndon Johnson's Operation Rolling Thunder in 1965 to Richard Nixon's Christmas bombing of North Vietnam in 1972, described by Carroll (2004: 150) as 'terror bombing pure and simple', the use of air power was incredible. Some 8 million tons of bombs were dropped on Indochina during the Vietnam War (compared to 2 million tons in all of World War Two), and the death toll was between 2 and 4 million (Young 2009: 157). The 'shock and awe' bombing of Baghdad in March 2003 and the increasing use of air strikes to battle insurgents and suspected terrorists in Iraq, Afghanistan, and other parts of the Middle East, South Asia and Africa are only the most recent examples of how normal and acceptable this way of war, this religion of air power, has become for both American political and military leaders and the US public.

Thus, the bombing of civilians has become a normal and acceptable way of warfare for the United States since World War Two. Those who are concerned to reduce or prevent this form of state crime, such as peace movement organizations and leaders of the international political community, must understand that that effort will not succeed merely by changing elected or appointed government officials. After six decades, the bombing of civilians is deeply rooted. As Englehardt (2008b) observes, it has indeed become a 'religion' and will continue as long as the cultural, organizational, institutional and social psychological factors analyzed above remain in place. Changing those factors will be difficult. But only by challenging the 'myth of morality' attached to US imperial goals (Lens 1971/2003), dismantling the culture of denial, eradicating technological fanaticism within the military-industrial complex, eliminating the elastic definition of military necessity in the laws of war and in the culture more generally, rejecting the euphemism of 'collateral damage', strengthening the ability of the United Nations to enforce the standards of international law against nation-states, and rebuilding the social and moral constraints on air warfare at the cultural, organizational and personal levels, can a broad-based international peace movement have a chance to put an end to the slaughter of innocent civilians by the state terrorism of aerial bombardment.

Chapter 9

The neo-liberal state of exception in occupied Iraq[1]

David Whyte

[T]he state of exception has today reached its maximum worldwide deployment. The normative aspect of law [is] obliterated and contradicted with impunity by a government violence that – while ignoring international law externally and producing a permanent state of exception internally – nevertheless still claims to be applying the law.

Georgio Agamben[2]

Hey, we won the war!

John Shaw, senior official at the US Department of Defense,
responding to accusations that he rigged a bid for the Iraqi
telecommunication network on behalf of a
consortium of his business associates[3]

In two earlier writings I have argued that the routine lawbreaking and corruption that dominated the Iraqi reconstruction can only be understood as a technique of domination (Whyte 2007a, 2007b). Systematic fraud and bribery served a useful purpose for the Anglo-American occupation as part of a broader economic strategy designed to provide structural advantages to western firms entering the Iraqi economy. Routine corporate criminality, facilitated by the government of occupation, was an important means of producing and reproducing (neo)colonial power relations. This systematic corruption of the reconstruction economy unfolded in a liminal space opened up by the suspension of Iraqi sovereign law and the establishment of impunity for all US nationals (and some categories of the nationals of all Coalition states). The legacy left by this corrupt 'reconstruction' is a major and ongoing humanitarian crisis that has created human suffering on a staggering scale. According to UN Under-Secretary-General for Humanitarian Affairs, John Holmes, 'At least four million people do not have enough food while around 40 per cent of the 27.5 million population do not have access to clean drinking water, and 30 per cent do not have access to reasonable health services.'[4] The cumulative effect of the economic restructuring and the concomitant weakening of public services has been a decimation of health, education, electricity distribution and food and water supplies.

This chapter explores the extent to which the criminal transformation of the Iraqi economy depended upon a 'state of exception', a specific moment of state/law/power in which the state suspends the rule of law under emergency conditions. This approach opens up a new way of thinking about the structure of the *legal* power and the structure of state violence. Insofar as it reveals how sovereign authority is constantly negotiating and reconstructing the boundaries of the law – sovereign authority always exists in an indeterminate space that does not correspond clearly to fixed legal boundaries. But this structure only becomes apparent to us at particular moments. The invasion and occupation of Iraq was one of those moments.

A state of exception?

In *State of Exception*, Georgio Agamben (2005b) argues that the tendency of governments to resort to non-lawful means under the pretext of a 'war on terror' is nothing new. In a historical analysis that includes Napoleon's state of siege in 1811, Lincoln's suspension of *habeus corpus* in 1861, the Italian states of siege in Palermo, Naples and Milan in the latter half of the nineteenth century, Roosevelt's assumption of extraordinary powers in 1933 and the Third Reich's suspension of the Weimar Constitution, Agamben maps out the resort to 'state of exception' as a regular feature of modern states.

Insofar as the state of exception depends upon the suspension of law to impose a new force of law, its relationship to the rule of law cannot be defined easily; it exists neither as a lawful state nor as a state of complete lawlessness. Rather a state of exception is a state of limbo that exists in an indeterminate space somewhere between law (insofar as a sovereign authority issues a decree or order that, by virtue of the fact it has been made by the sovereign, claims a legal source) and non-law (insofar as the normal rule of law or the normal rules of legal procedure have been suspended or erased).

For Agamben, the state of exception represents something fundamental to state power. It is not merely a result of bad government, or a pathological condition, but is (following Schmitt's famous statement (1950/2003) that the sovereign is 'he who decides on the state of exception') the very foundation of state sovereignty. Starting from this point Agamben shows how the state of exception has become an almost permanent condition in the most powerful and advanced states. His argument is that the US detention centres of Abu Ghraib and Guantánamo represent the highest stage of development of the state of exception, and rather than being understood as aberrations or the extremes at the margins of state power, they represent the latest manifestations of an ever-present core of state/law/power. The state of exception that is so clearly discernible at Abu Ghraib and Guantánamo should therefore be interpreted in terms of what it tells us about the structure of state power, rather than what it tells us about a specific situation.

A key aspect of Agamben's analysis of sovereign power is the relation between the sovereign and its ability to reproduce the space between law and non-law in which a 'secret solidarity between law and anomie' is revealed. There are similarities here with Klein's (2007) analysis in the sense that the deliberate creation of chaos is intended to shock a subjugated population into compliance with extreme economic measures. Power is thus extended through the deliberate creation of an anomic state.

The state of exception normally occurs under conditions of national emergency involving a security crisis or challenge to state sovereignty (whether real or imagined), when the state invokes the right to suspend the normal rule of law as a matter of *necessity*. Agamben argues that the concept of necessity derived directly from Carl Schmitt is the figure that enables the state of exception to appear 'as an "illegal" but perfectly "juridical and constitutional" measure that is realised in the production of new norms (or of a new juridical order)' (Agamben 2005b: 28). As Hannah Arendt noted in the context of the Third Reich, suspension of the law is generally justified using a principle of *raison d'état* (literally, 'reason of state', which is normally equated to the 'national interest') – an overriding concern that requires the state to use extreme means to defend its integrity (Arendt 1965/1977). So, in the case of the 2003 invasion and occupation of Iraq, Saddam's fictitious weapons of mass destruction acted as the *raison d'état*; and self-defence against 'terrorism' – sometimes refined as a 'ticking bomb' scenario – acts as the *raison d'état* for the extension of police counter-terrorism powers, the suspension of *habeus corpus* and the legitimization of torture. It is not difficult to deconstruct those narratives of necessity and see how they are almost entirely fictional, but this is not the point. The point is that the state always needs to locate its resort to exception – which is, by definition, a resort to extreme measures – in the context of a legitimating narrative.

The state of exception, as Aradau (2007) has noted, represents a fundamental shift in the political structure: namely, the collapse of law into *nomos* (the concrete requirements of the space in which legal decisions are taken). Thus, the legal authority to take decisions is transferred from political fora to administrative or bureaucratic officials. For example, in Guantánamo the law functions through the bureaucracy and administrative practices of the prison itself. Key decisions about prisoners and how they are to be processed do not result from statute or constitutional decision. That is, such decisions are no longer made in political fora but occur 'at a distance' from the heart of government. This is a form of law that is technically oriented and that seeks to control a particular space according to the requirements of the specific situation, rather than according to any political rationale or government policy. The implications of this transformation of this process is that law imposed by the state of exception is highly bureaucratic on the one hand and on the other is deformalized and subject to the requirements of specific spaces and situations (Aradau 2007: 496–7).

All of this raises fundamental questions for understanding state crime. For how can we define the state as criminal if the very foundation of state sovereignty is the ability to suspend the law so that power is enacted in liminal, anomic spaces? If the core of state power is its ability to suspend the rule of law, how could we apply the rule of law to states? Moreover, if we conceptualize state crime as 'deviance' from a particular set of norms, what does this mean when the exception has become the norm? Those are questions that this chapter returns to in the conclusion. In the meantime, this chapter begins to explore those questions through a discussion of the rule of law in post-invasion Iraq.

Suspending the normal rule of law

The power vested in the Coalition Provisional Authority (CPA) following the 2003 invasion of Iraq, and the strategy it subsequently employed, provides us with a formidable example of a state of exception in action. Paul Bremer's position as the bureaucratic head of the CPA carried with it the authority to both make and administer the law, to set the budget for reconstruction and to spend revenue, to allocate funds to government ministries, to write the new constitution and to design the new political system. Of course, each of those roles was comported in close consultation with the White House, the State Department and the Pentagon (who did not necessarily agree on key questions), but the autonomy and concentrated power that was vested in Bremer is astounding. In the bureaucratic structure of the CPA we find the collapse of political and legal authority into the figure of the bureaucratic official; in other words, the negation of the separation of powers that is supposed to characterize modern liberal democracies.

The legally binding administrative orders issued by the CPA created a trade regime that eradicated 'protections' for local industry and opened the way for product dumping on Iraq, permitted privatization and full foreign ownership of a wide range of state-owned Iraqi assets, industries and banks and generally created a WTO-compliant regime that protected foreign capital at the expense of local business. Neo-liberal reforms imposed by the CPA radically transformed industrial policy, import and export rules and the structure of taxation. Together those reforms represented a formidable crowbar that had the single purpose of prising open the Iraq economy for global (but mainly US) capital. *The Economist* described the CPA's policies as a 'wish-list of foreign investors'.[5] The final order made by Bremer was the decree that those reforms would have a lasting and binding authority on future Iraqi governments.

In March 2003, anticipating the Anglo-American occupation of Iraq, the British Attorney General Lord Goldsmith had issued a legal opinion on the economic governance of Iraq that was unequivocal about the occupiers' obligations under international law. Goldsmith reminded the UK government that 'Article 43 of the Hague Regulations imposes an obligation to respect the laws in force in the occupied territory "unless absolutely prevented"', and issued a clear warning that 'the imposition of major structural economic reforms would not be authorised by international law'.[6] The occupiers, then, were well aware of their legal obligations under international law. They chose not to observe them (see also Kramer and Michalowski 2005).

The Iraqi constitution at the time of the occupation enshrined the principles of central planning by national authorities and asserted that private enterprise must be compatible with those principles. Thus, the transformation of the Iraqi economy should not merely be regarded as a matter of policy but should be considered a constitutional matter, which effectively destroyed Iraq's distinctive political and social identity and obliterated the existing (constitutional) legal order. It is this feature of the occupation that made many of the policies and actions of the CPA unambiguously illegal under international law (although this argument is yet to be developed in any international legal forum). Moreover, given the amount of work that went on in the CPA debating and writing a new constitution for Iraq, there can be little doubt that key CPA personnel were well aware that they were involved in a process that breached the Geneva and Hague rules.

If CPA officials were wilfully ignoring their obligations under international law, as seems most likely, they did so in the knowledge that their government was fully committed to ensuring the legal impunity of its officials. At the beginning of the occupation, the United States government made a remarkable decision to ensure that actions taken by its own personnel in Iraq would remain outside the reach of normal legal procedures. On the same day that the CPA was created by United Nations Security Council Resolution 1483, George W. Bush signed and issued Executive Order 13303. The order, which passed almost entirely without comment in the US media, never mind in public debate, declared a state of emergency under which all personal legal liabilities of the occupiers would be suspended. The text of the order read as follows:

I, GEORGE W. BUSH, President of the United States of America, find that the threat of attachment or other judicial process against the Development Fund for Iraq, Iraqi petroleum and petroleum products, and interests therein, and proceeds, obligations, or any financial instruments of any nature whatsoever arising from or related to the sale or marketing thereof, and interests therein, obstructs the orderly reconstruction of Iraq, the restoration and maintenance of peace and security in the country, and the development of political, administrative, and economic institutions in Iraq. This situation constitutes an unusual and extraordinary threat to the national security and foreign policy of the United States and I hereby declare a national emergency to deal with that threat.

As a result of this 'unusual and extraordinary threat' (although it is hardly clear from the text of the order whether the threat is from the risk of judicial process or the business of occupation itself), US citizens were exempted from any 'attachment, judgement, decree, lien, execution, garnishment, or other judicial process' with respect to the proceeds from the sale of petroleum, or any interests in Iraqi petroleum held by the United States government or any national of the United States.[7] The order quite clearly sought to exempt US citizens from judicial process in the US and in Iraq.

From the text it is clear that the order also intended exemption from international law. In what looks like a nod to Article 64 of the 1949 Geneva Convention, Executive Order 13303 notes that judicial interference or financial instruments are likely to obstruct 'the orderly reconstruction of Iraq'. Article 64 had broadened the remit of the 'public order and safety' clause in the Hague rules to permit occupiers to maintain 'the orderly government of the territory'. Bush's order, then, rather clumsily attempts to connect the immunity of US personnel to orderly reconstruction. But this cannot be considered consistent with either the spirit or the letter of Geneva or Hague. The legality of Executive Order 13303 has subsequently been challenged by academic lawyers (see for example Kelly 2004), but this challenge has failed to provoke public debate.[8]

The terms of the exemption provide immunity first, from prosecution for the theft or embezzlement of oil revenue, and second, from any charges of safety, human rights or environmental violation. In effect, Executive Order 13303 ensured that any offence that might be committed in the course of producing Iraqi oil would be shielded from prosecution. Now to all but the closest observer of the CPA in its early period, the significance of providing immunity from the first category – the theft or embezzlement of oil revenue – might not be immediately obvious. But its significance, particularly in the first 14 months or so of the occupation, is that it placed the management of upwards of 30 billion dollars worth of Iraqi oil revenue held in the Development Fund for Iraq (DFI) and spent by the CPA beyond any legal scrutiny.

Executive Order 13303 deliberately provided a cover of immunity for the use and abuse of DFI funds made available to the CPA by United Nations Security Council Resolution 1483. This is significant, since it was those funds that were used to finance the entry of western corporations into the reconstruction economy.

Any doubts as to the application of Bush's order in Iraqi law were eradicated on 23 June 2003 by Paul Bremer. CPA Order 17 declared that all CPA personnel, and personnel who were members of Coalition forces along with their property, funds and assets, 'shall be immune from Iraqi Legal Process'. The order also declared that 'all Coalition contractors and their sub-contractors as well as their employees not normally resident in Iraq, shall not be subject to Iraqi laws or regulations in matters relating to the terms and conditions of their contracts in relation to the Coalition Forces or the CPA'. Once again, there is a nod to the provisions of the Hague and Geneva rules. Thus, the order notes that states are contributing personnel, equipment and other resources to the Coalition in order to contribute to 'the *security and stability* that will enable the relief, recovery and development of Iraq'.[9]

Order 17 was extended again in June 2004 as one of the final acts of the CPA. Taken together, Executive Order 13303 and CPA Order 17 provided a *carte blanche* provision of immunity from prosecution for white collar and corporate crimes in Iraq. Executive Order 13303/CPA Order 17 represent very simply and clearly an act of suspension of the law. The effect was a state of limbo between law and lawlessness that produced fertile conditions for US capital to exploit newly opened markets in 'reconstruction', security and the production and sale of Iraqi oil: a liminal space in which a particular form of a 'state of exception' provides those companies and their employees with legal immunity.

Those specific provisions of immunity, granted by government order, were supported during the CPA's term of office between 2003 and 2004 through the deliberate circumnavigation and obstruction of external auditing procedures. The establishment of the International Advisory and Monitoring Board (IAMB), the body required under the terms of United Nations Security Council Resolution 1483, was deliberately delayed by the US authorities and prevented from receiving its mandate until a full five months into the CPA's term of office (Iraq Revenue Watch 2003). In addition, investigative and enforcement powers were denied IAMB after successful lobbying by US government representatives (Lawson and Halford 2004: 7). Subsequently, the CPA took eleven months to appoint its internal auditor, the Special Inspector General for Iraq Reconstruction (SIGIR) (Iraq Revenue Watch 2003). Those delays were crucial in hindering the ongoing audit of CPA activities. The CPA and the US government continued to block audits and investigations throughout the Authority's term of office.[10]

In another explicit breach of UNSCR 1483, the CPA failed to meter oil production and export and did not keep an adequate record of oil export income. In addition, the CPA kept no list of companies it issued contracts to. One report by IAMB (2005a) found evidence of incomplete DFI accounting records; untimely recording, reporting, reconciliation and follow-up of spending by Iraqi ministries; incomplete records maintained by US agencies, including disbursements that were not recorded in the Iraqi budget.

The systematic obstruction of auditing procedures preserved the zone of liminality in which few records were kept and few mechanisms of accountability existed. This disruption to the operation of audit procedures constituted clear breaches of both the specific requirements of UNSCR 1483 and the norms of international accounting. It was estimated that in the first year of occupation, between \$8.8 billion and \$12 billion of DFI revenue remained unaccounted for.[11]

Law-making violence

In many ways, the transformation of the Iraqi economy can be understood as a *prima facie* example of a 'state of exception'. But what has been described here is more complex and nuanced than Agamben's account of the structure of state/law/power.

In the state of exception imposed on Iraq, we find an entirely different structure from that of Guantánamo or Belmarsh – or indeed, more generally in anti-terror legislation that introduces special powers or suspends *habeas corpus*. In those cases the state imposes a state of exception to enable the diminution of the legal status of the individual. The individual is captured in a legal limbo, with no political or legal rights; a state of 'bare life'. Where the status of an entire territory or nation-state is the target of the state of exception, then a very different set of dynamics comes into play.[12] In occupied Iraq the general aim was socio-economic reordering. In Guantánamo and Belmarsh, where the focus is on the recategorization and absolute control over particular individuals, this is not so immediately clear; although, of course, we cannot imagine the existence of such places were Britain and the US not involved in a global struggle for socio-economic dominance. This is a state of exception that seeks the control of a territory and its socio-economic structure as opposed to the eradication of individually created rights or the arbitrary condemnation of individuals to the status of *homo sacer* (although the latter clearly may facilitate the former and *vice versa*).

One consequence of this tendency to focus on the individual object of power is that state power is conceptualized in negative or controlling terms. This is a feature of the concept of state of exception that Lemke (2005: 9) has drawn our attention to: 'Agamben pursues a concept of power that is grounded in the categories of repression, reproduction and reduction, without taking into account the relational, decentralised and productive aspects of power.' In reflecting upon this point, it is significant that the suspension of law in occupied Iraq was imposed using both positive and negative functions of law. That is to say, it sought to create a very particular social order, at the same time as it imposed coercive or controlling measures. In this sense, the state of exception that we find in the transformation of the Iraqi economy cannot simply be understood in terms of the 'state as policeman' (Coleman *et al.* 2010) or embodied in the 'figure of the police' (Agamben 2000).

Of course, the imposition of a new legal order in occupied Iraq was partly based upon a 'negative' dynamic of law. Indeed, it might be said that the overbearing dynamic in the context of the transformation of the Iraqi economy was not a formal (or even informal) suspension of law, but obliteration of the law. And this might be described in entirely negative terms. But it is crucial to recognize that the (negative) obliteration of the law was coupled to a creative or positive reconstruction of the legal basis for economic activity. On the face of things, the law created new possibilities for economic activity – especially for economic activity by foreign multinationals. Now those positive or creative capacities created by CPA law fatally weakened indigenous industry and indigenous capital. Enforced debt dependency shackled the Iraqi economy to the economic prescriptions of international donors and lenders and ensured that the occupiers' neo-liberal reforms would remain institutionalized under future Iraqi governments (Herring and Ragwala 2006: 252–7). This dynamic, best described as the creative destruction of the Iraqi economy, is a contradictory one, and one that cannot be simply understood in the negative terms invoked by categories of 'suspension' or 'eradication' of law.

In this sense, the year zero approach to the Iraqi economy, which swept aside international and national law in order to establish the foundations of a neo-liberal economic infrastructure, cannot simply be understood as part of the continuum of historical cases that Agamben draws our attention to, but more closely approximates to what Benjamin (1978) called 'law-making violence', whereby the previous rule of law is obliterated and a new law created as a result of the ability of a social group to violently enforce its will. Revolutionary transformation – the disposal of particular sets of social relations and their replacement with new sets of social relations – is, for Benjamin, always premised upon law-making violence. Thus, the disposal of political and military elites, their replacement with new elites and the social and economic transformation that followed can be understood as a supreme act of law-making violence.

Moreover, this obliteration of law was given legitimacy by a particular form of humanitarian discourse that does not fit closely to Agamben's typical necessity justifications. While the framing of Executive Order 13303 draws upon a *raison d'état* of protecting US national interests, more general claims as to the necessity of reconstructing the economy are based upon the premise of promoting economic success and survival for the

Iraqis, as opposed to some kind of defense against an external or internal threat. Discourses of economic liberation were important in both Coalition and Iraqi government sources supporting reform. Here, the basic claim was that the reforms would free the Iraqi people from the 'tyranny of the planned economy'. Saddam's economic policies were in such discourses represented as key mechanisms of political and social repression (Whyte 2007b). The Coalition, then, invoked an economic as well as a political humanitarianism. In this context, the concept of 'necessity' is framed rather differently, whereby the rationale used to support economic transformation is made with reference to economic necessity. The reasoning behind the suspension of law, then, is rather more circumspect and connected more closely to what we might call a 'civilizing mission'.

Civilizing the brutes

For Santiago (2006) the legitimate authority for the expansion of the US empire in its earliest moments was provided by the demarcation of a notional line between the inside/civilized notion of self and the outside/savage notion of self. As long as the Native American was on the other side of the divide, theft of land, brutalization and genocide would remain legitimate. Boiled down to its most simple logic, otherness or being outside of civilization justified – in law and in practice – the most extreme measures of violence and expropriation.

The notion of civilization has, certainly since the colonization of the Americas, always projected a 'civilized' social order based upon a very specific set of economic relationships. As Ellen Meiksins-Wood shows in *Empires of Capital* (2003), early ideological justifications for the colonization of the Americas rested on the idea that land and property could be legitimately taken by colonizers if it was not 'productive'. This justification for the violent expropriation of Native American populations was later transformed by English liberal philosopher John Locke into the efficient production of value, whereby land could be seized if it did not produce value (or, more accurately, the type of value that counted in the European money system: Meiksins-Wood 2003). The Marshall trilogy, the colonial doctrine that legitimized the military conquest of the North American frontiers, developed the lasting jurisprudential justifications for the colonization of territories that the Native American inhabited. The Marshall trilogy promoted dispossession of the Native Americans, since their lack of civilization 'would leave the country a wilderness', or in Lockean terms would not produce the right type of value.[13]

As Laura Nader (2005: 200–1) argues, commenting upon the relationship between colonization and a legal civilizing mission, legal imperialism often exhibits an internal cultural logic that views all other legal cultures as basically empty. Legal systems that do not conform to our standard of civilization can therefore be treated as blank canvases that lack law and lack the means to develop. The Anglo-American strategy in Iraq did precisely this and mobilized a civilizing mission that provided the rationale to treat the country's economic and legal system as a blank canvas. Just as the US Patriot Acts and the cages of Guantánamo, not to mention the UK Anti-Terrorism Acts and the cells of Belmarsh, have effectively erased any legal status of the individual, so the Anglo-American invasion and occupation of Iraq instantly erased the nation's legal status and replaced it with a new system of law in the name of civilization and progress.

To be useful in such contexts, then, the concept of the state of exception must incorporate a broader understanding of necessity than that captured by *raison d'état*. On one hand, this is the notion of a lack or a deficit in the ability of the indigenous US peoples to fully exploit their environment (Nader 2005). In the context of the contemporary global economy, they cannot afford to hold themselves back. The civilizing mission – always one dripping with rhetorical benevolence – is now drowning in a very different rhetoric of economic survival: it is only by full incorporation into the global economy that survival can be made possible.

On the other hand, law is becoming more responsive to the infrastructural needs of global economic restructuring. This point is developed later in this chapter. For the time being it is enough to note that we can see, most strikingly in the US, the intensification of 'market patriotism' (Whyte 2007c) whereby the national interest is explicitly aligned with a universalizing, civilizing rationale that subjugates us all, to paraphrase Thomas Frank (2000), to 'one market under God'. And 'one market under God' could well have been the motto of the CPA, for it describes precisely the occupation's enterprise. The first priority for the government of occupation in its first year was not the protection of public assets or the protection of the rights or living conditions of the Iraqi people, but the imposition of a neo-liberal economy on Iraq.

Lex mercatoria as an alternative set of norms

Audi (2004–05) has argued that the rationale for the overnight transformation of the Iraqi economy can be found in a new 'standard of civilization'. Insofar as this standard of civilization seeks universal adoption of the neo-liberal terms and condition of entry into the global economy, it boils down to little more than the Washington Consensus. Thus, 'the implementation of liberal, market oriented reforms becomes the prerequisite for a country's integration into international society' (2004–05: 338).

If there is a general principle of international law that has always existed, it is one that is based upon the promotion of values of 'civilization'. If we can put aside the oxymoronic qualities and hypocrisies of the western concept of civilization for a moment, it is important to recognize the enduring centrality of an idea of a universal 'civilization' in international law. Thus, Article 38 of the International Court of Justice statute asserts a jurisprudential benchmark of 'general principles of law recognized by civilized nations'. Now, of course, there is some controversy about what 'civilized' constitutes here, but if there is one common theme that runs through bodies of rules and norms that have been described as a 'standard of civilization', they are rules for the functioning of a global economic system (Panezi 2007). The standard of civilization is most clearly expressed in the mysterious, imprecise, legal concept of *lex mercatoria*, which supports liberalized markets and 'free' trade, and in contractual, trade and property relationships that have their origins in the eleventh-century legal system used by European merchants. Infrastructurally, the rules and norms described as *lex mercatoria* have expanded rapidly as international transactions have intensified (de Sousa Santos 1995). The neo-liberal institutions, the World Bank and the IMF, have been key sites of the new *lex mercatoria*, as have the institutional structures of trading blocs such as the European Union and NAFTA. To this we can add the predominance of US-initiated and organized fora for dispute resolution at an international level that are established and guided by the norms of American informal law (among them, for example, the International Chamber of Commerce: Heydebrand 2001).

In articulating a position that reeks of the end of history thesis, David Fidler (2001: 147) argues that the new 'standard of civilization' is given force by a 'liberal victory' that is clearly discernible in international law and international relations: 'In international law, liberal dominance appears in the prominence given to free trade, democratic governance, human rights, the rule of law, and good governance.' According to Fidler, international lawyers must get over their embarrassment with eighteenth and nineteenth-century colonialist association with the term 'standard of civilization', since the world is now moving gradually, but assuredly, towards a new 'civilizational pluralism' (2001: 154). In this account, the progress towards this neo-liberal standard of civilization appears as consensual, guaranteed by the evolution of mutually agreed-upon processes and procedures. Now Fidler wrote this piece a matter of months before the September 2001 attacks on the World Trade Center and the Pentagon. And perhaps, without those events, his analysis might have had more persuasive power as a portent of a smoothly running legal order, organized around a relatively consensual agenda. But, given the long history of how the US has dealt with those who stand outside the standard of civilization, it is the long march of US imperialism rather than the sudden events of September 2001 that reveals the naivety of Fidler's analysis. After all, Iraq was hardly the first time a military invasion or coup, initiated or backed by the US, produced a wholesale transformation of an economy resistant to US capital into an economy open for business.

The shock therapy experiments of Chile and Indonesia stand as key examples. But to those we might add the low-level military operations in the 1980s in Nicaragua and Guatemala, the war to defeat the Left as part of Plan Colombia, the invasions of Panama, Grenada and Haiti and the ongoing military blockade of Cuba. All of those military operations aim to consolidate a US political and economic and legal hegemony, and specifically establish US-friendly economic policies as a standard of civilization.

If Fidler and his colleagues'[14] narrative about a steady, consensual, transition to a universal law of the market tells us something important, it is about how US legal scholarship provides intellectual support for US global hegemony. Just as academics such as Alan Dershowitz, Harvard's own professor of torture, obediently concocted a new line in novel, if entirely spurious, legal justifications for torture and for the existence of Guantánamo Bay,[15] so a handful of US lawyers emerged to justify the illegal economic transformation of Iraq. The new *lex mercatorialists* find in the complex of common practice norms, rules and transnational institutions a normative structure that is apparently strong enough to brush aside the Hague and Geneva agreements and the terms of the US Security Council agreement that presumably applies to the occupying forces.

Challenging *lex mercatoria*

There is, however, good reason to doubt the legal status or even the existence of *lex mercatoria*. Without devaluing the hegemonic significance of this legal architecture, what we are describing here is by no means a linear or logically integrated process of law-making. Those norms have developed over at least five centuries and in its contemporary context *lex mercatoria* can be said to have multiple sources of varying political and juridical status. These include international treaties, established custom in TNCs and other transnational organizations, the decisions of international courts, the United Nations and its various subcommittees and affiliated organizations, NGOs and so on. Moreover, each of those sources incorporates its own conflicts, debates and unresolved battles whose protagonists may or may not have popular support and may indeed be challenged by counter-hegemonic groups. It is therefore important to understand this standard of civilization not as a closely coupled system that has developed smoothly or rationally, but as contested terrain involving hegemonic struggles in an unfathomable range of sites, with outcomes that invariably contradict and conflict with other outcomes. In this sense, *lex mercatoria* cannot seriously be considered consensual. Neither does *lex mercatoria* have a hierarchy of rule or decision-making processes that can be located in time or space. It emanates from customary sources of law, but this point itself raises questions about the relationship between custom, norm and law, particularly if those customs have been arbitrarily imposed 'from above'.

Boaventura de Sousa Santos (1995: 290–4) argues that we can challenge *lex mercatoria* on two main grounds. First, its validity has been the subject of some debate between civil law scholars and common law scholars, the latter disputing its legal status, largely because a major source of *lex mercatoria* has not been the courts or law-making authorities, but private bodies such as corporate in-house lawyers and American corporate law firms. Second, in the absence of a developed institutional architecture capable of guaranteeing, at a global level, the regulation and reproduction of a new global regime of (capitalist) accumulation, the American law firm has played a central role in the production of a set of commercial and trade rules commonly known as *lex mercatoria* (see also Gessner 1998). This indicates that *lex mercatoria*, rather than being based on a universal set of norms, is emerging as a highly parochial US-centric normative structure.

It is therefore not credible to claim that *lex mercatoria* constitutes a truly global legal normative framework. The growing significance of the Chinese economy on the world stage provides evidence of an entirely separate set of normative standards and values, exemplified by the *guanxi* system of exchange. Moreover the current US-led assault upon Hawali and Hundi systems of exchange provide evidence of the ongoing struggles between competing norms. *Lex mercatoria* might be better described as part of a set of 'faked rules and institutions' that aim to extend the structural power of capital by relinquishing the law's role in constraining market actors. Those faked rules and institutions are, in turn, based upon a fake legal consensus (Mattei 2003: 4).

Yet the lack of a convincing claim to embody a standard of international law has not prevented the new *lex mercatorialists* proclaiming *lex mercatoria*'s integrity as a legal standard. For Audi (2004–05), Iraq remains a lawless space until it complies with the new standard of civilization. For as long as it exists on the wrong side of the boundary between civilized and uncivilized economy, it cannot claim the protection of international law more generally. This is a circular argument that Kafka would have been proud of: Iraq can be subject to a suspension of law and forced to swallow the prescriptions of the neo-liberal order, precisely because it remains outside the protection of international law. And it remains outside the protection of international law because it has not become fully integrated into the neo-liberal order. Just as the inmates of Guantánamo find themselves in legal limbo, in a state of 'bare life', under the command of a law that eradicates their legal status and yet at the same time determines precisely their conditions of existence, so it goes for the Iraqi nation state.

In the case explored earlier, we find a set of legitimating narratives that are too complex to be described as *raison d'état*, for they are based upon the premise of a civilizing mission as well as upon the granting of political freedoms, and they are openly connected to the creative destruction and reconstruction of an economic and political system, rather than simply being based upon the survival or integrity of the sovereign. But *lex mercatoria* is a law that is not really law, for it is an ephemeral, arbitrary and highly contentious body of rules that can make no credible claim to universal application. It is a fake law. Yet it is this law, the arbitrary law of the occupier, that sweeps aside the international laws of war, and the sovereign law of the Iraqi constitution. Those laws, which once appeared as concrete law, are turned instantly to dust by an act of military force. And this is how, in Iraq, a fake law came to be imposed by a fake legal authority.

Conclusion

This chapter has argued that Agamben's formulation of the state of exception does not fully describe the structure of state/law/power in the case of occupied Iraq. Insofar as Agamben limits himself to understanding the consequences of the relationship between sovereign power and anomie for the individual, it does not contemplate the connection of law – and indeed the liminal spaces created in the state of exception – to the deeper structures of social inequality that the law supports in capitalist social orders. As Santiago (2006: 21) has noted, 'Agamben's argument privileges a liberal interpretation of the law that situates the emergence of the state of exception in the relationship between the state and the individual.' But states of exception are always connected to a project of power that constitutes (unequal) social relations in general terms as well as constituting legal relations between the individual and the state.

Lex mercatoria – to the extent that it can be said to exist in the practices and norms of international business – raises further problems for the adequacy of Agamben's formulation. The state of exception addresses what might clearly be described as doctrinal law. It describes the suspension of statutory or common law that has a concrete and clearly definable status in the process of juridical decision-making. But, as we have seen, *lex mercatoria* cannot be described in this way. For even if we accept that it is indeed a body of (fake) law, it remains largely based upon normative standards of practice; it cannot yet be considered international/ universal law. What happened to the Iraqi economy in the immediate aftermath of the invasion was an attempt to establish a new set of commercial practices that would effectively eradicate local control over the economy, decimate Iraqi industry and precipitate a humanitarian crisis that is ongoing in Iraq. Insofar as frequent reference was made to the reforms as part of an effort to bring Iraq closer to the conditions required for membership of the WTO, those practices were introduced with reference to international institutions and the normative standards that they promulgate, but not with reference to international law.

Because of its narrow focus on legally (and illegally) constituted power, the state of exception begins to lose meaning when it is applied to structures that are not clearly definable in legal terms. This is precisely the problem that has plagued scholars of 'crimes of the powerful' for at least six decades, and it is a problem that shapes Green and Ward's (2004) definition of state crime, which overtly links a concept of state deviance to a concept of international norms, rather than law. The problem we always confront when thinking about 'state crime', then, is the relationship between the norm and the state. But what might a failure to comply with the normative standards of the fake law of *lex mercatoria* – if it were linked to human rights standards – mean in Green and Ward's terms? Would this constitute state deviance?

To return to the key issue at stake here, the transformation of the Iraqi economy was not merely the result of a formal suspension of law (although suspension of the legal responsibilities of coalition personnel was part of the strategy), but resulted from a combination of obliterating law (or at least the occupiers' obligations under international law), and what might be called the 'higher loyalty' of coalition officials to the norms of the neo-liberal market. In the conceptual universe occupied by the US governing elite, it was Saddam's planned economy that constituted the exception: an economically uncivilized and barren space that had hitherto stood outside and in opposition to neo-liberalism. The aim of the occupation was not merely to impose a law of exception, but to establish a global norm – the new *lex mercatoria*.

The conclusion to Colin Dayan's (2007) study of the role of the Eighth Amendment of the US constitution in legalized brutalization of slaves, and subsequently prison populations, argues that rather than imposing an exception, it is more useful to understand how exceptional measures exist as the norm:

[I]t might seem at first that the rules for the treatment of Iraqi prisoners were founded on standards suited to war or emergencies, based on what the political theorist Carl Schmidt called the urgency of the 'exception'. They were meant to remain secret and to be exempt from traditional legal ideals and the courts associated with them, but the ominous discretionary powers used to justify this conduct are not exceptional; they are routine and entirely familiar to those who follow the everyday treatment of prisoners in the United States – in prison and in court. (Dayan 2007: 4–5)

This uncovers a different way of conceptualizing the relationship between the norm and the exception; rather than being ontologically separate, they exist as points on the same continuum of power. There is resonance here with an enduring characteristic of the state that has been brought to light by some key British criminology texts. In the classic

Policing the Crisis (Hall *et al.* 1978), the authors document a shift towards the exceptional state in late 1970s Britain and Northern Ireland that culminated in the routine resort by the police to 'informal' (illegal) strategies of quasi-judicial swoops on suspects, detention and torture (1978: 288). And a decade and a half later, Paddy Hillyard's (1993) *Suspect Community* documented how the 'exceptional powers' invoked by the British state to fight terrorism were gradually normalized by practice and legislation.

We should not lose sight of the truism that Anglo-American ruling elites are less interested in imposing a state of exception in Iraq than they are in maintaining and where possible extending their ability to rule. A state of exception is ultimately not a project of legal power, but a project of power. In some situations it corresponds to a means of defending, and finding new ways of consolidating, the social order. In other situations, as in the case of the Iraqi economy, it assists the wholesale destruction of the social order and its replacement with something else.

Insofar as it is able to reveal the core of a brutal relationship between the state and the law, the concept of the state of exception provides a useful way into interpreting the hidden structure of state power. However the state of exception is not the end of power, but a means to achieve a particular end. In advanced capitalist states, the state of exception has a range of simultaneous functions: as ideological or propaganda supports, as a means of expanding or enhancing state security apparatuses, legitimizing colonial reach externally, and so on. But all of those functions are connected to the preservation or deepening of a social order that continually seeks to expand its capacities for capital accumulation.

Notes

1   I would like to thank participants in seminars at the Universities of Lincoln and Keele where this argument was first presented, and to Jose Atiles-Osoria and Ray Michalowski for their useful comments on drafts of this chapter. All errors and matters of interpretation are mine alone.
2   Agamben 2005b: 87.
3   *Los Angeles Times*, 29 April 2004.
4   *Irin News*, 4 April 2008.
5   *The Economist*, 27 September 2003.
6   Memorandum from Lord Goldsmith, Attorney General to the Prime Minister, 26 March 2003, reproduced in Kampfner (2003).
7   The full text of this Executive Order 13303 can be found in Office of the Press Secretary, White House Press Release, 22 May 2003, published online at: www.whitehouse.gov/news/releases/2003/05/20030522-15.html
8   This raises a key question about the status of international law: if this was so flagrantly illegal under international law, why have the institutions of international law been non-responsive? We might say precisely the same thing

about the military invasion of Iraq, which was quite ambiguously a crime of aggression, the 'supreme crime' as defined in Nuremberg. Zolo's (2006) response to such questions is convincing. He argues that history shows that international law has always been imposed selectively and arbitrarily by those who hold the power to impose law. From Nuremberg to Baghdad, international law 'produces an asymmetrical and retributive form of justice from which consideration of the winners' crimes is systematically excluded' (Toscano 2008: 129–30). In fact, international law has provided a means of extending the power and influence of the most powerful states. Toscano argues that selective criminalization of war legitimates the low intensity conflict and humanitarian wars of the victors, and that if there is a principle at the core of international law, it is the 'normalization of the great-power aggression' (2008: 133).

9 My emphasis; see note 6 for source of text.
10 *Washington Post*, 16 July 2004; *Financial Times*, 22 June 2004; KPMG Bahrain (2004; IAMB (2005b).
11 The lower and upper limits of those figures are derived from SIGIR audit analyses by investigative journalists. See Reuter's report, 'Audit Shows $8.8 billion in Iraqi funds missing', 19 August 2004, available at: www.msnbc. msn.com/id/5763483/print/1/displaymode/1098; also Harriman (2006a).
12 I am very grateful to Jose Atiles for pointing this out to me in conversation.
13 This argument and direct quotes can be found in Johnson v. M'Intosh, 21 US 543, 590 (1823).
14 For the classic statement of the new *lex mercatoria*, see Mustill (1988); for a complex sociological legitimization of *lex mercatoria*, see Teubner (2002).
15 In an infamous article in the *San Francisco Chronicle*, Dershowitz followed in the footsteps of his intellectual forebear Carl Schmitt by proclaiming his own support for a state of exception. In an article supporting judicial torture warrants (Dershowitz 2002: A-19) he observed, 'Every democracy, including our own, has employed torture outside of the law.'

Chapter 10

China's aid policy toward economically weakened states: a case of state criminality?

Dawn L. Rothe

Over the past decade, a growing body of literature on state crime has focused on the descriptive and etiological factors of the worst atrocities that have resulted from government policies and actions: crimes against humanity (e.g. enslavement, forced disappearances), genocide (e.g. intent to destroy in whole or in part an ethnic population), human rights violations (e.g. obstruction of humanitarian food aid), and war crimes (e.g. targeting civilian populations). A key concern for analysts of state crime is the presence or absence of potential control mechanisms that can act as barriers to state criminality and/or as after-the-fact mechanisms of accountability. For example, post-controls such as international military tribunals, *ad hoc* international criminal tribunals, and the International Criminal Court have been used to hold a select few high-ranking government officials accountable for their crimes. Other international institutions such as the United Nations have used sanctions as an attempt to control ongoing wrongful state behavior. Likewise, others have identified international financial institutions (IFI) such as the International Monetary Fund (IMF) and the World Bank Group (WB) as potential mechanisms to control and/or constrain state criminality through the withholding of loans (Ross 1995, 2000; Rothe and Mullins 2006).

Even though over the last twenty years researchers of globalization have linked IFI policies to the production of grave human rights violations, criminologists who study state crime have given this topic little attention until 2002 when Friedrichs and Friedrichs suggested that harms caused by the policies and practices of IFIs could be operationalized as crimes of globalization.

Informed by Falk's (1993) observation that globalization is driven by the interests of capital over people, 'crimes of globalization' refer to mass social harms – especially within developing countries – that occur as latent consequences of the development and expansion of global capital. Friedrichs and Friedrichs (2002) highlight the role of international financial institutions, transnational corporations and states in the context of crimogenic tendencies within globalization. The privileging of transnational corporate interests and the interests of powerful states, coupled with the arrogance with which these institutions implement a 'top-down' form of globalization, results in immensely harmful consequences that conflict with the ideology and promotion of human rights. Examples of these harms include the implicit role of the IMF and WB policies in a WB-financed dam in Thailand (Friedrichs and Friedrichs 2002); the Rwandan genocide (Rothe *et al.* 2009); the Senegalese *Le Joola* sinking (Rothe *et al.* 2006); the Ugandan illegal expropriation of the Democratic Republic of Congo gold (Mullins and Rothe 2008); and how IFI policies contribute to the exposure of women to risky lifestyle choices that often increase their vulnerability to HIV infection (Ezeonu and Koku 2008). Moreover, since international financial institutions work closely and co-operatively with high-level government officials in both developed and developing countries, the crimes of globalization they facilitate are inevitably intertwined with crimes of the state (Rothe and Friedrichs 2006).

While some scholars have noted the potential of IFIs to act as a control over state criminality through their ability to withhold loans as well as through anti-corruption campaigns, others, such as Freidrichs and Freidrichs (2002) have noted that they are also problematic and criminal through their policies and practices that have created criminogenic conditions that have facilitated state crime and/or caused social harms. Perhaps the most problematic aspect of viewing these IFIs as controls over state crime is the criminogenic conditions they themselves often create and/or enable. This is not to say that the state itself is not criminally liable for subsequent crimes committed, merely that one cannot ignore the complicit and/or implicit role that other agencies play in the criminal act(s). Subsequently, the states that commit atrocities are committing state crime and IFIs, because they impose policies that cause harm directly and/or create conditions for state governments to commit crimes, can be considered as criminal (i.e. crimes of globalization).

Furthermore, within the research on the interrelationship among globalization, IFIs and crimes of globalization, there is some recognition that these financial institutions operate within an environment that lacks control or constraint mechanisms against their actions or policies (Bracking 2009; Ezeonu and Koku 2008; Friedrichs and Friedrichs 2002; Friedrichs 2007; Rothe *et al.* 2006; Rothe *et al.* 2009). Nonetheless, this body of work has failed to examine the growing role of China's 'independent foreign policy' and its potential to be a viable alternative for these economic and/or politically weakened states, potentially reducing or constraining the negative consequences of IFI policies: thus, acting as a constraint to IFI policies and practices, relating to both crimes of globalization and international controls for states and organizations.

I aim to fill this gap by analyzing China's growing role within Africa as it relates to China's economic involvement along with the practices of IFIs within this same region. I begin with a review of literature concerning international institutions and crimes of globalization where IFIs were active agents in crimes against humanity, genocide and/or avoidable atrocities. A brief discussion of the WB and IMF is then followed by a detailed discussion of the emerging role of China in these and other African states to identify policies that contrast with those of the IFIs. In closing, I explore the potential of China as a control mechanism over the actions of IFIs.

Controls, international finance institutions and crimes of globalization

Controls

The issue of controls of state agencies has generated a small yet noteworthy amount of literature within the state crime literature. This has included the conceptualization of external and internal controls. For example, Ross (1995, 2000) suggested that external controls are those that lie outside of the state apparatus and are imposed on the state itself, and internal controls are those that arise within the state and are directed against itself (e.g. domestic laws and self-regulation). External controls provide powers of review or sanction by organizations both domestic (e.g. external review boards, extra-agency competition, public opinion, media) and/or international (e.g. media, the World Court of Justice, the United Nations). Controls at the international level can occur by means of economic or political sanctions or threat of military actions. It has been suggested that economic organizations such as the World Bank (WB), the International Monetary Fund (IMF) and the World Trade Organization (WTO) represent potential controls on criminal states through the manipulation of financial assets, trade agreements and trade sanctions. In the case of international financial organizations, for example, Ross has suggested that the ability to operate as a control of state crime lies within their capability to grant or withhold needed economic capital. Yet not all commentators concur. Barak (2000: viii) suggests that these controls are problematic as they are subject to 'burnout, especially since the benefits of regulating these kinds of crimes seem to be dwarfed by the costs' of control. Moreover, the willingness of these economic institutions to act as a control when not in their self-interests has been brought into question

(Bracking 2009). As previously noted, the most problematic aspect of viewing these IFIs as controls of state crime is the criminogenic conditions they themselves often create and/or enable.

International finance institutions

The World Bank

The World Bank is not a 'bank' in the commonly used sense of the term. Rather, it is a specialized financial agency, composed of 184 member countries. The World Bank, conceived during World War Two, initially helped rebuild Europe after the war. Its first loan of $250 million was to France in 1947 for post-war reconstruction. It once had a homogeneous staff of engineers and financial analysts, based solely in Washington, DC. More recently, the Bank became a Group, encompassing five closely associated development institutions: the International Bank for Reconstruction and Development (IBRD), the International Development Association (IDA), the International Finance Corporation (IFC), the Multilateral Investment Guarantee Agency (MIGA), and the International Centre for Settlement of Investment Disputes (ICSID) (Rothe *et al.* 2009).

The World Bank is a closed system based upon investment. Votes allocated to member countries regarding specific programs are linked to the size of their shareholdings. Initial membership in the Bank gives equal voting rights but there are also additional votes. These depend on financial contributions to the organization by member states, implying undemocratic decision-making. For example, the US holds 16.4 per cent of total votes, Japan 7.9 per cent, Germany 4.5 per cent, and the UK and France both hold 4.3 per cent. Rwanda holds .08 per cent of total votes. Within the Multilateral Investment Guarantee Agency the US has 15 per cent of total votes, Germany has 4.2 per cent of the total votes, and France and the UK both hold 4 per cent of total votes. By contrast, Rwanda has 398 votes, which constitutes 0.18 per cent of total votes and Senegal has 525, only 0.25 per cent of total votes (World Bank 2004).

Once its original mission of post-war European reconstruction was completed, the WB turned its lending practices to development issues. While its rhetoric was often focused on human rights, human dignity and infrastructure development, its operational concerns strongly focused on producing returns for investors. Through the 1970s and 1980s, debtor countries were frequently unable to meet repayment demands. Therefore, during the 1980s the Bank went through an extensive period focused on macro-economic and debt rescheduling issues. During the latter part of the 1980s, social and environmental issues assumed center stage and an increasingly vocal and active civil society in Europe and the Americas accused the Bank of not observing its own policies in some high-profile projects. While the WB often did not respond directly to the critiques and more human rights-focused concerns of these populations, it did begin considering the need for debt restructuring. Yet, as with other actions, the WB did not simply accede to the vocal minorities demanding global policy changes. In return for debt reallocation or admission into forgiveness programs, it demanded that macro-structural political and economic changes occur within the debtor states. In many cases the Bank also required recipient countries to adopt certain political measures, such as policies that would foster 'democracy', by which they meant opening state holdings to private ownership.

In addition to providing financing, the World Bank Group offers advice and assistance to developing countries on almost every aspect of economic development. Since the mid to late 1990s, the Bank Group utilizes private sector development (PSD) as its strategy to promote privatization in developing countries. Thus, all other strategies must be co-ordinated with the push towards privatization. Although impoverished governments around the world rely on the World Bank as a contributor of development finance, it is often criticized by NGOs for undermining the national and economic sovereignty of recipient countries through its pursuit of economic liberalization. The Bank also operates under the marked political influence of certain countries, notably the United States, whose corporations profit from advancing their access to additional markets as well as specific resources available in less economically, politically and militarily empowered states, such as cheap labor, gold and diamond mining, peanuts, and electric industries. Moreover, having a notable political influence on the World Bank's policies of restructuring, the G8 states' priorities are directed toward private ownership policies. Consequentially, economic enterprises funded by the World Bank are often detrimental to the people they are allegedly designed to help, as was the case with the dam in Thailand.

The International Monetary Fund

The International Monetary Fund (IMF) is also composed of 184 member countries and is headquartered in Washington, DC. The IMF was established in 1945 to promote international monetary co-operation, ensure good governance, foster economic growth and provide temporary financial assistance to needy countries. It 'is the central institution of the international monetary system – the system of international payments and exchange rates among national currencies' (IMF 2006: 1). Additionally, since the IMF was established, its above-stated purposes have remained unchanged, but its operations such as surveillance (a dialogue among its members on the national and international consequences of their economic and financial policies), financial assistance (loans), and technical assistance (structural adjustment policies) have changed during its history. The IMF is the international system that encourages countries to adopt what it believes to be 'sound economic policies', or what most commentators refer to as neo-liberal economics. While it may appear that the IMF and WB are similar in their functions, they nevertheless differ: the WB is a reconstruction and development institution and the IMF maintains a system of payments and receipts between countries to reduce the potential of unpredictable variations in the exchange values of state currencies – closer to a bank in the common usage. Additionally, while both promote similar policies of neo-liberalism, they typically assist different members and have different goals.

Although the IMF is an international organization, its members do not have equal voting power. During the Bretton Woods Conference in 1944, which established the institution, a compromise was adopted between two approaches to determine voting power of states: (1) based on members' contribution and (2) based on the legal principle of equality. The result was a system where each member country would get one vote for every $100,000 of quotas, plus 250 basic votes. To date, the number of basic votes has not been changed, while there have been successive quota increases. Consequently, the ratio of basic votes to total votes declined from 11 per cent in 1945 to 2 per cent, despite a fourfold growth in membership. The quotas are important because they determine decision-making power and who has access to financing. Thus, the small quotas of developing countries mean a limited share of voting power and access to IMF resources.

The approval or voices that are represented in these 'sound policies' are not equally distributed. For example, the US has 371,743 total votes comprising 16.83 per cent of all votes, Japan has 133,378 votes or 6 per cent of the total, Germany has 130,332 or 5.9 per cent of the total votes, followed by France and the UK, both with 107,635 or 4.87 per cent of the total votes. Rwanda holds 1,051 total votes and Senegal holds 1,868, which make up only 0.09 per cent of the total institutional votes. The pattern holds true for other African countries as well (see Table 10.1).

Crimes of globalization

The concept of crimes of globalization was first introduced by Friedrichs and Friedrichs (2002). Crimes of globalization have characteristics of 'state crime, political crime, white-collar crime, state-corporate crime, and finance crime', but do not fit neatly into any of these categories (2002: 18). Specifically, these crimes 'involve cooperative endeavors between international financial institutions, transnational corporations, and state or political entities that engage in demonstrably harmful activities in violation of international law or international human rights conventions'.[1] As later noted by Rothe and Friedrichs (2006), the policies and practices of IFIs can have deleterious effects, specifically structural adjustment

Table 10.1 Quotas and voting power of selected industrial countries in 2000

	GNI (PPP)	GNI (billion $) at market exchange rates	IMF quotas (million SDRs)	Votes
Austria	214	204.5	1,872.3	18,973
Belgium	282	251.6	4,605.2	46,302
Denmark	145	172.2	1,642.8	16,678
Finland	127	130.1	1,263.8	12,888
France	1,438	1,438.3	10,738.5	107,635
Germany	2,047	2,063.7	13,008.2	130,332
Greece	178	126.3	823.0	8,480
Ireland	97	86.0	838.4	8,634
Italy	1,354	1,163.2	7,055.5	70,805
Luxembourg	20	19.2	279.1	3,041
Netherlands	412	397.5	5,162.4	51,874
Portugal	170	111.3	867.4	8,924
Spain	760	595.3	3,048.9	30,739
Sweden	213	240.7	2,395.5	24,205
United Kingdom	1,407	1,459.5	10,738.5	107,635
European Union	8,864	8,459.4	64,339.5	647,145
United States	9,601	9,601.5	37,149.3	371,743
Memorandum items				
World	44,459	31,315	212,666	2,172,350
All industrial countries	24,793	24,994	130,567	1,347,885
Developing countries and transition economies	19,666	6,321	82,099	824,465

policies (SAP) imposed on countries such as Argentina, Senegal and Rwanda that destroyed the way of life of large numbers of indigenous peoples or the knowing acceptance of Rwanda and Uganda's illegal exporting of resources. SAPs are imposed on borrowing states supposedly to create socio-economic conditions more conducive to economic health and growth. These can include, but are not limited to, opening government-owned industries to privatization, acceptance of currency re-evaluations and reductions in social or other governmental spending programs in ways determined by the lenders. Indeed, SAPs are driven by neo-liberal economic principles emphasizing free markets and private capital.

Nonetheless, as noted by Rothe and Friedrichs (2006), IFIs may not intend to do harm. After all, they claim that their central mission is to alleviate economic and other forms of suffering. However, the privileging of transnational corporate interests and the interests of powerful states, coupled with the arrogance with which these institutions implement a 'top-down' form of globalization, results in immensely harmful consequences. While these institutions claim to promote 'structural adjustments' that will ease the social problems associated with harsh impoverishment, these policies often destabilize the economic structures of targeted economies (Friedrichs and Friedrichs 2002; Rothe et al. 2006, 2009). As stated by Kwamena Bartels (2001: 1), Ghana's minister for works and housing, in May 2001:

> After 20 years of implementing structural adjustment programmes, our economy has remained weak and vulnerable and not sufficiently transformed to sustain accelerated growth and development. Poverty has become widespread, unemployment very high, manufacturing and agriculture in decline and our external and domestic debts much too heavy a burden to bear.

The political economy of development and IFIs 'builds a process in which poverty is, in a counterintuitive sense, not reduced but embedded and reproduced' (Bracking 2009: xiii). Moreover, since IFIs work closely and co-operatively with high-level government officials in both developed and developing countries, the crimes of globalization they facilitate are inevitably intertwined with crimes of the state (Rothe and Friedrichs 2006). Simply, the driving ideologies and policies of these organizations may act as catalyst for state criminality.

Criminologists face the challenge of examining and explaining how these different cognate forms of crime interact and have reciprocal influences. Following Friedrichs' (2004) call to criminologists to engage with the literature of globalization, Rothe, Muzzatti and Mullins (2006) conducted research that explored the interrelations between international institutions such as the IMF and WB, legacies of colonialism, and foreign policies that set the stage for atrocities, state victimization and state crime.

Exploring the circumstances leading to the sinking of the ferry Le Joola, the authors show that in the wake of the sinking, it became clear that the state of Senegal itself held liability for the ferry's failure; the government readily admitted its errors and several ministers either stepped down or were removed from their positions. However, despite unequivocal governmental responsibility, Rothe et al. suggest that this was not simply a case of state crime. Rather, a thorough investigation and analysis of the reasons and forces behind the Le Joola sinking suggested that international institutions bore culpability for the disaster. In response to imposed SAPs, the Senegalese government was forced to cut spending in many areas, including its ferry programs, which were central to transportation in the country, especially in light of the geographic location, governmental cuts mandated by the IFIs, and lack of alternative travel. This had a direct impact on the upkeep of the Le Joola and its return to open waters with only one of the two functioning engines when it capsized, resulting in 1,863 passenger deaths – one of the worst maritime disasters in history. Based on this analysis, Rothe et al. argue that scholars need to examine how western capitalism and international finance lenders and institutions dominate the choices available to governments of developing states, and the criminogenic conditions to which IFI policies contribute. They suggest that focusing attention on the economic contexts generated by the pro-capital, non-human emphasis of the IMF and World Bank are essential to understanding such crimes.

A similar analysis by Rothe, Mullins and Sandstrom (2009) explored the role of IFI policies in the conditions leading to the Rwandan genocide. While the IMF and WB did not seek to instigate economic collapse through the forced currency devaluation or the changes in the coffee market, or to catalyze genocide in Rwanda, their systematic inattention to the deteriorating economic conditions and growing insecurities caused by their IFI policies, and the increased use of IFI funds to purchase unprecedented weaponry, along with their acceptance of sub-standard invoicing, set the stage for political, social and economic disaster. The authors suggest that not only did the IMF and WB knowingly violate their own standards, as well as international human rights principles, by imposing rigid conditions tied to aid packages, they served to facilitate rather than constrain criminal activities.

During the build-up to the genocide (the early 1990s), monies from IFIs earmarked for commodity imports were diverted by the government toward the acquisition of military hardware. After October 1990 the Rwandan armed forces expanded from 5,000 to 40,000 men, requiring a sizeable influx of outside money to pay the new recruits and to provide weaponry. International financial institutions became wary of such large military expenditures and demanded that the regime decrease military spending. At the same time, however, they allowed the government to account for the sums loaned by the WB and the IMF by presenting old invoices based on a flawed accounting system for all imported goods (Toussaint 1999). By using invoices rather than receipt-based accounting, which is the standard for IFI accountability, for imported goods, the dates and amounts were easily altered. This strategy allowed the regime to finance massive arms purchases that would later be used in the 1994 genocide. For example, trucks imported for the army were put on the Transport Ministry's account and fuel used for militia and army vehicles was recorded on the Health Ministry's account (Toussaint 2004). When the IMF and WB suspended lending at the beginning of 1993, they failed to freeze the large sums of money held in accounts in foreign banks, which the Habyarimana regime used to buy more arms. The arms purchases enabled the armed forces to organize and equip the militiamen in preparation of the upcoming genocide. Rothe *et al.* (2009) suggest that in the analysis of the Rwandan genocide, the policies and practices of external controlling bodies, especially the IMF and WB, served to facilitate rather than constrain criminal activities.

The interconnectedness of crimes (including crimes against humanity committed by states and paramilitaries/militias) and policies of the IFIs have also been illustrated in the cases of Uganda and the Democratic Republic of Congo (Mullins and Rothe 2008). One of the widespread criminal actions within the DRC has been the wholesale looting of the country's rich mineral resources (large deposits of diamonds, copper, gold, zinc, and silver, among others) by foreign powers and regional ethnic militias. The IMF and WB have indirectly facilitated the criminogenic practices of illegal exporting through confiscation, extraction, forced monopoly, price-fixing, and the removal of resources from a sovereign territory without the consent of the government. Consider that in 1995, 3.09 tons of gold were exported from Uganda totaling 23 million US dollars, while only 0.0015 tons were produced within the legal borders of the state. In 1996 exports increased to $60 million, valued at $105 million in 1997. Ugandan gold production peaked at 0.0092 tons in 1998 and its export of gold peaked in 1999 at 11.45 tons. Similar gaps between production and export were also noted in diamonds. Uganda has no indigenous diamond production. According to the Diamond High Council in 1997 Uganda exported US$120,000 in diamonds, $1,440,000 in 1998, $1,810,000 1999 and $1,260,000 in 2000.

With the discrepancies of Ugandan exports and their native production and/or actual resources, Mullins and Rothe (2008) state that the government of Uganda acknowledged to the IMF that the volume of gold exports 'does not mirror production levels and may indicate some exports are "leaking over the borders" from the DRC'. Yet the IMF proclaimed the increase in exports as a strengthening of the Ugandan economy, increasing its assessment grade for balance of payments status. Due to these revenues, the World Bank lauded Uganda as a success story for what its structural adjustment programs could accomplish. The paradox is that the SAPs did nothing to increase Ugandan economic health and can be seen as providing motivation for the government's corruption and engagement in illegal mineral expropriation. Thus, not only did Ugandan leadership profit from their organized criminal activity, they were rewarded by the IFIs for doing so.

Additionally, structural adjustment reforms have coincided with a sharp slowdown in states' economic growth and have led to a reduction in the progress on major social indicators (life expectancy, infant and child mortality) in the vast majority of countries that have turned to them for aid since 1980 (Weisbrot 2007). Moreover, for almost twenty years economically weak countries have had little choice but to seek out aid and development finance from IFIs. In particular, since the 1980s African states have had to rely heavily on IFIs, making IFIs the purveyors of advice for development as well as the authors of conditions for aid receipt: free markets, privatization of industries, currency devaluations, removal of tariffs, deregulation, good governance, anti-corruption initiatives, and cuts in governmental spending. Contrary to the dominant model, economically weakened states have succeeded more often where the IMF and World Bank have had the least influence on local economic policy.

China's growing role in African economic structures

Prior to the 1980s China's economic and political influence in Africa was minimal. However, since the 1990s, it has become the major provider of economic aid to a significant number of states within Africa. A major difference between China's economic aid and debt forgiveness and that of the IFIs is that China maintains a policy of not interfering in sovereign affairs. Indeed, this policy has garnered significant concern by western governments, claiming that China's lack of strings for the economic aid fosters non-democratic regimes and human rights abuses. Nonetheless, for the first time in nearly two decades economically impoverished countries in Africa are now getting a choice: between finance from IFIs that has multiple conditions, strings and mandated adjustment policies, and from China that comes with no broader economic or social policy strings – a soft policy approach.

Currently China is providing economic aid, directly or through debt forgiveness, to over 40 African states, including, but not limited to, Angola, Chad, Democratic Republic of Congo, Ethiopia, Gabon, Gambia, Ivory Coast, Kenya, Mozambique, Nigeria, Rwanda, Senegal, Sierra Leone, South Africa, Sudan, Uganda and Zambia. Debt forgiveness, not considered to be aid by the Chinese regime, has been increasing as well. For example, since 2000 China has canceled the debt of 31 African states: in 2000, US$1.2 billion in African debt was canceled and in 2003 an additional $750 million was forgiven (Eisenman and Kurlantzick 2006). In 2002 China gave $1.8 billion for development aid to its African allies.[2] Furthermore, according to the Beijing Summit of the Forum on China–Africa Co-operation Report (2006b), by 2009 China had committed to doubling the amount of its assistance to Africa and canceling government interest-free loans that have fallen due in 2005 with its African allies.

The amount of aid China has committed and continues to commit to Africa far outweighs that of IFIs. For example, according to World Bank figures, in 2006 the WB provided US$2.3 billion to sub-Saharan Africa, yet China committed approximately $8.1 billion that same year just to Nigeria, Angola and Mozambique. The International Rivers Network noted in 2007 that China Exim, the official export credit agency of China, loaned at least $6.5 billion to African governments, primarily for infrastructure projects (Bank Information Center 2007: 1).

According to French (2006), China has approximately 900 investment projects on the African continent overall, which include a new rail network in Angola, Great Nile Petroleum, coal-fired thermal power stations in Zimbabwe, Nigeria and Sudan, and a communication satellite for Nigerian telecommunications and internet service. Chinese banks have also aided Zimbabwe's small and medium enterprises (SME) where the Ministry of SME Zimbabwe has now set aside $12 billion to be disbursed to encourage industries such as textiles, soap, tile and fiberglass. The Zimbabwe Iron and Steel Company is also being refurbished with China's financial assistance (Eisenman 2005). Most recently, in February 2007 Chinese President Hu Jintao announced that the Chinese government would write off a substantial amount of Sudanese debt and provide an interest-free loan of $13 million for infrastructure projects, while simultaneously announcing a new pledge of $5.2 million in humanitarian assistance for Darfur.

China's growing international presence and involvement in Africa has expanded well beyond economic aid. It has established the China–Africa Business Council, under the auspices of the United Nations, to boost trade and development in Africa and has contributed to international construction projects in Ethiopia, Tanzania and Zambia.

China has also increased the number of export goods that are eligible for zero tariffs from African states from 190 to 440 (Beijing Summit 2006a, 2006b). China committed US$3 billion in preferential loans and $2 billion preferential exports buyer's credit to African countries. From these and the projected credits, the amount of trade has grown significantly (see Figure 10.1). Additionally, China signed trade agreements with ten African states, and according to Premier Wen Jiabao Chinese mutual trade

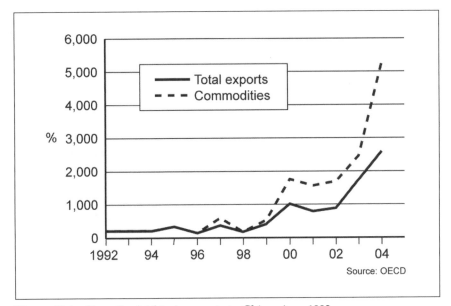

Figure 10.1 Growth of Africa's exports to China since 1992
Source: World Bank, NBS Staff Estimates, 2007

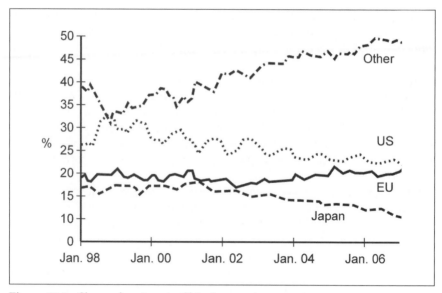

Figure 10.2 Share of regions in China's export, per cent
Source: World Bank, NBS Staff Estimates, 2007

with Africa will double to $133 billion by 2010 (Center for International Finance and Development 2006: 3). Since 2000, China has formally recorded a fivefold increase in trade with Africa, which was up from US$1.06 billion to $40 billion in 2005 and $55 billion in 2006 (McLeary 2007). (See Figure 10.2.)

A key issue here, and significant difference between China's aid and that of IFIs, is the independent domestic and foreign policy recognition.

Discussion of IFIs' and China's roles

While it may well not be the intention of IFIs, the lack of recognition of sovereignty and the push for a westernized model of market economy and privatization produces conditions that render these nations worse off than before they sought the assistance of IFIs. Furthermore, the conditions of international aid receipt have become one set of many threats to the sovereignty of post-colonial states. An-Na'im remarks that 'sovereignty and stability of African states are constantly contested . . . by the forces of diminished sovereignty over vital national economic and social policy under current structural adjustment policies and unfavorable global trade relations' (2003: 13). Such continual dependency and subjugation is highly problematic as post-colonial states attempt to more fully integrate themselves into the international political community and global markets.

Many international observers have questioned the effectiveness of the remedies embodied in IMF-supported adjustment programs – especially those backed by the enhanced structural adjustment facility (ESAF), established in 1987, through which the IMF provides low-interest loans to poor countries with specific demands that must be followed. As noted by the IMF (1999: 1), 'some even described these remedies as part of the problem rather than the solution'.

A key issue here, and a significant difference between China's aid and that of IFIs, is the independent domestic and foreign policy recognition; at this point China seems willing to honor states' sovereignty without making external demands on governments and domestic decision-making processes. For example, the Ghanaian parliament passed a budget in 2003 that included a provision to increase the import duty on poultry products to protect its domestic farmers that were being priced out of the Ghanaian market because of subsidized European poultry. Upon receiving news of the legislation, the IMF 'reminded' the Ghanaian government of the limitations placed on restrictions for trade. The legislated increase was removed two weeks later (Thomson 2007: 4). Ghana had pointed out its intention to review the trade liberalization policies in its Poverty Reduction Strategy Paper[3] (PRSP), and implemented an alternative policy, yet 'was pressured by the IMF to revert back to trade liberalization' (Thomson 2007: 5). However, when the aid is provided by China, countries are able to introduce import quotas as a way to protect domestic production without restrictions being mandated by the Chinese government. For example, in 2006 the government of South Africa introduced import quotas for 31 categories of Chinese textiles until 2008. Under IMF guidelines, such restrictions on imports are not tolerated (French 2006).

User fees for health and education have also been required as conditions for WB program eligibility. Specifically, in 1998 the Operations Evaluation Department noted in an internal review of the Bank's health, nutrition and population lending that 75 per cent of the projects in sub-Saharan Africa included the mandated use of or expansion of user fees. In the case of Ghana, the implementation of fees for health services resulted in charges where a visit to a specialist cost the individuals ten times the average daily wage (Thomson 2007: 3). As a result there were substantial declines in the population's use of healthcare services, leading to additional humanitarian issues. The WB has noted the problem of their own policies, dating back to a 1994 report that stated that with the introduction of user fees in Zambia, 'vulnerable groups seem to have been denied access to health services' (in Thomson 2007: 3). Nonetheless, the report and recognition was followed by a new health project initiative to increase the implementation of user fees.

On the other hand, China has been economically supporting the advancement of education and health in African states. In the 2006 *Declaration of the Beijing Summit of the Forum on China–Africa Co-operation (FOCAC)* (Beijing Summit 2006b) China pledged to further support

Africa's education and health structures. This included building 30 hospitals in Africa and providing US$300 million in grant monies to provide artemisinin (an anti-malaria drug), along with building malaria prevention and treatment centers and an additional 100 rural schools in Africa. China also stated that it would continue to help African countries establish quarantine and public health emergency response mechanisms and send medical teams to address current health crises (e.g. malaria and AIDS) (Beijing Summit 2006b: SUNS #6135). Unlike IFIs' mandated user fees, the grants and aid provided by China came with no state requirements mandating fees for its citizenry or other forms of economic or political restructuring. Nor does China demand changes in states' governmental structures.

Summary

In the final analysis, the stated requirements of so-called good governance and democratization of IFIs has had negative effects (see Friedrichs and Friedrichs 2002; Rothe *et al.* 2006, 2009). Nonetheless, in cases of atrocities that have been linked to policies of IFIs (e.g. Senegal, Rwanda, and the WB-financed dam in Thailand), there has been no oversight or agency of control to respond to these remedies that can become part of the criminogenic conditions, much less scrutinize the actions of these institutions, save for the work of some NGOs with little to no political leverage to actually impact on IFI policies.

Unlike most organizations, where there are checks and balances or a populace to which they answer, IFIs have no formal external monitoring system. While states are bound by international laws and treaties, IFIs are currently not included as actors that fall under the jurisdiction of these laws or any controlling agency. Yet there are documents that prohibit the direct manipulation of a state's economic processes and ownership structures that violate core human rights standards: the 1974 Declaration on the Establishment of a New International Economic Order (UNGA 3201/s-vii); the Convention on Economic, Social and Cultural Human Rights (2003); the Maastricht Guidelines (1997); and the Norms on the Responsibilities of Transnational Corporations and Other Business Enterprises with regard to Human Rights Agreement (2003). For example, the United Nations International Covenant on Economic, Social, and Cultural Rights (1966) holds that 'all people have the right to self-determination . . . and freely pursue their economic, social, and cultural development . . . In no case may they be deprived of its own means of subsistence.' However, IFIs, though often violating these basic principles, are not held accountable by any external body or extant international institution of control.

I suggest that China's ideology of an independent foreign policy, or soft diplomacy, may do more than empower these post-colonial and economically weakened states. China may also fill an important niche within the international economic sector. I view China's growing role in Africa as an example of its power to be a potential offset, or constraint, against the mandated policies of IFIs. While there may indeed be latent consequences of China's involvement in Africa (e.g. supporting regimes that are committing atrocities, as in the case of Sudan and Zimbabwe), I see this as no different from other countries supporting totalitarian and/or harsh regimes. The difference here lies in China's willingness to provide aid and/or loans without the strings and SAPs that have had additional negative consequences beyond that of a particular state's actions or crimes. In other words, China's loans, debt forgiveness and aid have not come with demands for restructuring economic systems, privatization, or other mandated adjustments to a sovereign state system.

The ability of China to act as an option for post-colonial and economically weakened states is indeed real. As noted by the Beijing Declaration, 'China will overtake the World Bank as the continent's main financial provider' (Beijing Summit 2006b). Consequentially, the potential for China to act as or be perceived as a constraint against some of the harmful and interventionist policies of IFIs is a growing reality. Simply, China may act as a control for IFI policies, providing a much-needed balance to the dominant policy of development, restructuring and neo-liberalism to date. In part, I base this on the WB and the Export-Import Bank of China (China Exim) agreement of understanding to collaborate on projects in Africa (Wroughton 2007: 1). The news release announcing this partnership suggests that the Bank's decision to team up with China Exim is part of its growing concern and strategy to avoid competition with its rapidly growing Chinese counterpart.

Additionally, after some twenty years, since the late 1980s, of making 'bail-out' and 'structural adjustment' loans to indebted and impoverished countries, the IMF has been confronting a crisis of confidence and legitimacy for the past two years. Demand for its services has been shrinking and in early December 2007 the IMF announced major lay-offs to counter its growing losses. Indeed, in 2007 the institution posted its first loss in decades – about $100 million. In part, this is a result of three or four of the IMF's biggest customers pulling out.

In 2005 Argentina withdrew from the IMF program and paid back its loan. This decision post-dates (11/2004) China's announcement and subsequent investment of nearly $20 billion (£11 billion) in Argentina over the next ten years, with $100 billion planned investment in Latin America over the next decade. Serbia withdrew in 2007 having unexpectedly paid back the IMF in 2006. Again there is a correlation with Serbia's relationship with China, where trade between the two countries was worth more than $788 million in 2007, according to figures of the Serbian embassy in China. Indonesia also paid back IMF loans; as with the other countries, in 2004 the trade value with China stood at $13 billion, up 31 per cent from 2003's $10.2 billion, and almost matching Indonesia's $13.5 billion export–import flow with the United States. All of this comes at the same time that development bankers have recently been suggesting that:

[S]ome of the conditions that are attached to lending to developing countries may have to be diluted in order not to be replaced as the lender of choice by creditors such as China. After all, good or bad, China's assistance does not come with restrictions for good governance, economic reform, or interference in sovereign political affairs. (IMF 2006)

Conclusion

Defenders of the WB and IMF might suggest that developing countries voluntarily enter into agreements with these institutions and can choose whether to accept their policy recommendations and how to implement them. However, their compliance with the demands of IFIs is not purely or genuinely 'voluntary', particularly given the nature of the contemporary global economy. While indigent states previously had few options for development aid and other forms of humanitarian assistance, the emergent role of China is an alternative to the policies of IFIs.

I am not implying that there will be no negative consequences to China's increasing role and presence in these countries. I am not arguing that China is or even has the potential to be the best global citizen. In fact, the Chinese record on human rights is troubling and I do not necessarily believe that China will insist upon high standards in this realm on behalf of the countries it aids. China's increasing penetration of African economies presents a multitude of issues for global politics and international relations. Nonetheless, it appears that the growing competition has indeed acted as a constraint mechanism where IFIs are reconsidering their policy-mandated aid conditions. Under these circumstances, China's practices and involvement in post-colonial or economically vulnerable states make it a more than viable option for countries to avoid what often become criminogenic loan conditions. It is becoming a source of pressure that may compel IFIs to adjust the demands and contingencies they place on loans, thus reducing or constraining the negative consequences of IFI policies.

Simply, China's growing role in Africa and the international political scene may provide a much-needed catalyst of competition for IFIs, inadvertently then acting as a constraining mechanism. Perhaps this will be the result of a larger constraint mechanism – fear of China's competition in relation to the impact on the dollar as the currency of the world (Campbell 2008). At this time, however, more scenarios will have to play out before we will fully realize the impact of China's aid on these weakened states, as well as on IFIs.

Nonetheless, it may well be that the future will see a shift in the mandated *laissez-faire* policies of IFIs to one based on universalism, self-determination and the rights of countries to run their own economic affairs, thus offering policies more aligned with the sovereign states' needs as against the drive for more global capital. In return, we may see countries coming back to the IFIs for assistance, rebalancing any negative consequences of China's non-interventionist policies where issues of human rights may continue to surface.

If China is successful in acting as a constraint against IFI policies, and these institutions readjust their neo-liberal economic policies, then IFIs may be able to act as a counterforce against any negative consequences of China's aid. The subsequent realization by IFIs of previous unsuccessful ideologies that have long dominated their practice of lending might bring about a balance between the two, where sovereign needs and human rights take center stage in policy formations and loan receipt, thus reducing the criminogenic environment and conditions. If successful as a constraint mechanism *vis-à-vis* a rival force, China's current role could, as a latent consequence, add further legitimacy to the idea that human rights should be justiciable conditions. I agree with An-Na'im's assertion that 'there was a time when civil and political rights too were nonjusticiable and nondeterminant, but they were made justiciable and sufficiently determinant through imaginative development of judicial mechanisms and remedies. The same can happen to economic, social and cultural rights' (2003: 106).

Notes

1   For a more complete discussion of the typology see Friedrichs 2004.
2   Since 2003, Beijing has stopped officially reporting its aid and debt forgiveness, making a complete and accurate tally impossible.
3   The PRSP is an economic plan formulated by receiving countries, although heavily influenced and monitored, which is used as a means for defining WB and fund policy conditionality.

Chapter 11

Framing innocents: the wrongly convicted as victims of state harm*

Saundra D. Westervelt and Kimberly J. Cook

In 2003, we began interviewing death row exonerees about their post-exoneration lives. Our inquiry was prompted by the substantive growth in academic attention to cases and causes of wrongful convictions of the innocent since the publication of Radelet, Bedau and Putnam's *In Spite of Innocence* (1992) ten years earlier, and a substantive dearth of attention to the lives and experiences of exonerees after their release from prison. Our examination began with one primary question: what is the impact of a wrongful capital conviction and incarceration on those individuals who have been exonerated and released? Several sub-questions followed: what are the primary issues and obstacles they confront upon release? How do they cope with these issues? How do they rebuild their lives? What factors affect their abilities to cope and rebuild effectively?

We drew our initial guiding theoretical frameworks in this investigation from the social psychological literature on trauma management and recovery. We did not overtly set out to contribute to the state crime literature. But, because our approach has been inductive, rather than deductive (Westervelt and Cook 2007, 2008), we have continually re-mained open to the emergence of new ways of understanding and framing what our participants tell us about their lives. As coding of our 18 interviews with death row exonerees progressed, one story that emerged speaks to the state crime literature, and most particularly to the discussion of the victimology of state crime as forwarded by Kauzlarich,

* Modified from Westervelt, S. D. and Cook, K. J., 'Framing innocents: the wrongly convicted as victims of state harm', *Crime, Law and Social Change*, Volume 53–54, DOI: 10.1007/s10611-009-9231-z, Springer, 2010. With kind permission from Springer Science and Business Media.

Matthews and Miller in their 2001 article 'Toward a Victimology of State Crime'.

Much has been written on the nuances of defining state crime (see Michalowski, Chapter 2 in this volume), with most definitions falling within two broad categories: legalistic definitions that encompass acts defined as criminal by the state and 'social harms' definitions that include, more broadly, socially injurious acts committed by the state that cause harm or violate human rights (whether legally defined as 'crime' or not) (Kauzlarich *et al.* 2003; Matthews and Kauzlarich 2007; Michalowski 1985; Rothe and Friedrichs 2006). Kauzlarich *et al.* (2001) argue, however, that such debates over conceptual categories and definition can easily lose focus of the very real victims of state crimes and the very real harms they suffer.

Kauzlarich *et al.* (2001: 175, 190) argue that regardless of whether state crimes are defined as 'illegal, socially injurious, or unjust acts', they cause harm and produce victims. Taking a victimology of state crime perspective shifts the discussion away from more confining debates over what constitutes state crime and encourages examination of the actual harms experienced by victims. Thus, they and others argue for the importance of a sociology of 'state harms' rather than 'state crimes' (Matthews and Kauzlarich 2007). Our revelations as to the array of injuries and injustices confronted by exonerees post-release speak directly to this victimology perspective. Whether the result of wilful, malicious, illegal conduct by state officials, public pressure on and tunnel vision by police, an imbalance of resources in favor of the state, or sheer carelessness by investigating and prosecuting parties, wrongful convictions cause harm and produce victims.

Framing exonerees as victims of state harms

Kauzlarich *et al.* (2001: 176) define state crime victims as: 'individuals or groups of individuals who have experienced economic, cultural, or physical harm, pain, exclusion, or exploitation because of tacit or explicit state actions or policies which violate the law or generally defined human rights'.

This definition certainly applies to innocents convicted of crimes they did not commit. In an attempt to lay groundwork for research into the victimology of state crime, Kauzlarich *et al.* (2001: 183–9) also offer six propositions that characterize state crime victims and the harms they suffer. We use these propositions to examine exonerees as victims of state harms and to bring focus to the role the state plays in constructing the harms with which they struggle. They are as follows.

1 Victims of state crime tend to be among the least socially powerful actors.

'Even a cursory examination of state crime reveals large power differentials between the victim and victimizer' (Kauzlarich *et al.* 2001: 183). State harms typically are inflicted by state officials who exercise power to inflict harm on vulnerable people who have little recourse to defend themselves or resist the harm being inflicted on them (Matthews and Kauzlarich 2007; Michalowski 1985). This is certainly the case with regard to those wrongly convicted, in particular of capital offenses. In the process by which individuals are selected for the application of lethal force by the state, the 'victims' (exonerees) and 'perpetrators' (state agents) are not equally matched. Prosecutors are relatively well-funded and have broad discretionary powers to bring charges against defendants without worrying too much about access to the material resources needed to pursue cases. The average defendant in a capital case is poor and relies on an underfunded attorney, often court-appointed, with a heavy caseload and limited time, resources and knowledge to adequately represent his/her client. This is certainly the situation in the majority of exonerees in our study. It is not a level playing field where both prosecutors and defendants have equitable resources to collect the evidence, challenge the evidence, and present the evidence in search of 'truth' (Givelber 2002).

The state also maintains control over representations of the crime and defendant to the public via its relationship with the media. Media outlets rely heavily on police and prosecutors' offices for information about crime and defendants (Fishman 1978). Not surprisingly, then, media accounts of criminal investigations are often laden with official constructions of what happened, what evidence is available, and what type of person the suspect is. Such constructions legitimate activities of state agents involved in the investigation and prosecution while relying on stereotype, innuendo and fear to create biased images of marginalized, uncooperative or 'typical' suspects (Martin 2002). Defendants lack the ability to combat such constructions in the media, which then follow them into the courtroom when they face the jury.

2 Victimizers generally fail to recognize and understand the nature, extent and harmfulness of institutional policies. If suffering and harm are acknowledged, they are often neutralized within the context of a sense of 'entitlement'.

State officials responsible for the illegal and/or unethical acts that result in wrongful convictions are rarely held accountable (Scheck *et al.* 2000; Weinberg *et al.* 2006). Police are protected by an internal culture that discourages whistle-blowing and an external culture that views criminal activity through a police-friendly lens (Surette 1992; Walker 1999; Westley 1970). Criminal justice officials operate mostly with a presumption of guilt, a presumption shared by the general public who believes that the police only arrest guilty people (Fisher 1993; Givelber 2002). If a police officer's testimony conflicts with a suspect's, such as about whether the suspect was physically abused during an interrogation, those within and outside the system are predisposed to believe the officer. Thus, police are insulated from inspection and accusation.

Prosecutors also rarely face punishment for legal violations and/or unethical activities in the pursuit of a prosecution; more often they are rewarded for high conviction rates and their dogged pursuit of 'justice' (Gershman 1986; Rosen 1987; Weinberg *et al.* 2006). Prosecutors are immune from civil liability unless they can be shown to have pursued an innocent person with wilful and malicious intent, a high standard indeed (Gershman 1986). The judiciary partially shields prosecutors from punishment through use of the harmless error doctrine that allows the judiciary to admonish prosecutors for overstepping bounds while maintaining that their behavior did not significantly impact the outcome of the case: in essence, turning a blind eye to misbehavior (Gershman 1986; Weinberg *et al.* 2006).

A second method by which state agents deny and neutralize the harmfulness of their policies and actions is by continuing to deny the actual innocence of individuals, even upon their exoneration and release from prison. In numerous cases in our sample, prosecutors in particular continued to insist on the guilt of exonerees in public statements immediately on the heels of an exoneration or release. This holds true even in cases in which the exoneration and release were based on DNA evidence. Exonerees consistently note the unwillingness of state officials to recognize or apologize for their failures. These denials of the actual innocence of exonerees reveal a refusal by state officials to recognize that they have committed harmful errors, and a reluctance to examine their policies and practices. This only further victimizes the exoneree struggling to reintegrate into a community influenced by continued insistence by state officials that they are criminals, despite their exoneration.

3 Victims of state crime are often blamed for their suffering.

'Victim blaming is unfortunately a common reaction to those most wounded by state crime' (Kauzlarich *et al.* 2001: 186). This is quite common among victims of wrongful convictions. Exonerees often hear from family, friends, community members and state officials that they are responsible for their own plight: that if they did not do what they were convicted of, they most certainly had done something along the way to deserve such a punishment, or they are responsible for their convictions because they did not mount an aggressive defense. This latter argument, of course, wholly overlooks the significance of proposition (1): that victims of state harm tend to be among the least socially powerful actors.

4 Victims of state crime must generally rely on the victimizer, an associated institution, or civil social movements for redress.

Exonerees often must depend on the very police, prosecutors and judges whose misconduct, carelessness or oversight led to their wrongful convictions to re-examine the investigatory process, retest the evidence, and retry the case to secure an exoneration. An exoneration requires that the state reassess its earlier behavior, one reason why the average time between a conviction and exoneration is from seven to nine years. Following an exoneration, exonerees must go back to the state again to request expungement of their records or compensation for their wrongful convictions (if available in their state), processes that are costly, time-consuming and fraught with obstacles. The sheer irony of forcing exonerees to ask those who wrongly convicted them to uncover and repair their mistakes and provide them with redress via an expungement or compensation is not lost on several of the exonerees in our study. For example, Alan Gell notes:

> You got to hire a lawyer to do an expungement. And you know, again I'd like to have it done. But the truth of the matter is, is if I had fifty million dollars I wouldn't pay a damn lawyer a penny to do it. I think the governor should expunge it on his own. It shouldn't cost me to expunge, to expunge what should've never been there . . . You know I didn't ask to be arrested . . . I didn't ask to be snatched up . . . You know, that was a mistake made by them. To learn that you later have to, you know, ask the Governor to forgive you or ask the Governor to pardon you, it just, I think they've got that whole process backwards. It's not supposed to be me go to him and say, umm, 'will you please pardon me for not doin' what y'all said I did'.

Exonerees receive little help from the state. A few receive some help from non-profit organizations focused on their needs, but most are aided mainly by family members, friends and attorneys. Or for some, their needs go unmet.

5 Victims of state crime are easy targets for repeated victimization.

'The harm incurred by most victims of state crime does not decrease [over time] rather it merely takes another form' (Kauzlarich *et al.* 2001: 187). Once the actual wrongful conviction is identified, the ripple effects of that conviction and incarceration can be felt far into the future and take many forms. In some instances, the revictimization of exonerees comes directly at the hands of state officials. Several exonerees in our study have noted being subject to police surveillance after their release, and they fear attempts by officials to bait them into activities that could land them back in prison.

State officials also directly influence the revictimization of exonerees when they fail to publicly acknowledge actual innocence, fail to take responsibility for their own misconduct and abuses, fail to provide an apology, and fail to provide meaningful assistance towards establishing new lives for those they have harmed. Revictimization also includes poor health, lack of access to health care, stifled family relationships, inability to have children, feelings of bitterness and anger, drug and alcohol addiction, poor job skills, unstable employment, lost time in building financial security through home-ownership and retirement funds, and no immediate savings to secure a degree of comfort in the future. Many exonerees live a life of uncertainty marred by continual reminders of how the painful past continues to impact their future.

6 Illegal state policies and practices, while committed by individuals and groups of individuals, are manifestations of the attempt to achieve organizational, bureaucratic or institutional goals.

It is important to conceptualize wrongful convictions as 'the product of organizational pressures to achieve organizational goals ... [and to consider how] the organizational climate itself fosters, facilitates, or encourages such behavior' (Kauzlarich *et al*. 2001: 188), rather than the consequences of a few 'bad apples' in the justice sytem.

Within the organizational context of policing, investigations are typically premised on the belief that police are building a case against a guilty person. This 'confirmatory bias' creates a tunnel vision resulting in the selection of evidence that supports the guilt of the suspect, minimizing evidence that might be exculpatory, and molding a crime narrative to fit a theory developed very early about what 'really happened' in a case (Fisher 1993; Givelber 2002; Lofquist 2002; Martin 2002).

Prosecutors also work within an organizational context characterized by a presumption of guilt, tunnel vision and public pressure. Additionally, prosecutors are elected officials judged by conviction rates who are often inadequately challenged by underfunded or underprepared defense counsel. The outcome is an organizational context conducive to wrongful convictions. In some jurisdictions, the pursuit of convictions becomes the primary objective to the point that an 'ends justifies the means' mentality sets in (Martin 2002; Weinberg *et al*. 2006).

Finally, the incarceration and execution of the condemned are presented as meeting the presumed institutional goals of retribution and incapacitation (Paternoster *et al*. 2008). Executions are publicly announced and celebrated as the ultimate power of the state to exact 'justice' (Garland 1990). Politicians and public opinion makers claim that executions achieve the explicit goal of deterrence (Paternoster *et al*. 2008), and guards and prison officials who carry out executions believe that they are simply fulfilling the will of the people (Johnson 1998). Thus, victims of wrongful convictions in capital cases are as much victims of these entrenched institutional cultures as anything else.

A catalogue of harms: struggling with exoneration

The state's role in producing the trauma felt by exonerees is obfuscated by criminal justice officials who publicly deny responsibility and media outlets that broadcast images of tearful, joyous exonerees embraced by grateful and loving friends and family on their day of release. Little attention is given to the challenging journey that awaits them or the state's role in it.

Since 2003, we have completed 18 life-story interviews with death row exonerees, 17 men and one woman, chosen from a list of death row exonerees maintained by the Death Penalty Information Center (Westervelt and Cook 2007, 2008). Participants spent an average of 9.9 years in prison, ranging from 2 years to 26 years, and an average of 5.2 years actually on death row, with a range of 1 to 18 years.[1]

Confronting the possibility of death by court order

Exonerees often discuss the fear, anger, loneliness and feelings of inhumanity that come with facing execution for crimes they did not commit. Juan Melendez, for example, spent more than 17 years on death row in Florida. He notes:

> That was one of the hardest parts of being there was when they kill somebody. You got to recognize this, you livin' in a cell. You got a man next door to you for nine years ... ten years. You become attached without even knowing it. And now they come, they snatch him, they kill him. Then you think, 'I'll probably be next'. So that was the part that I say was the hardest part for me in there, when they kill people.

Walter MacMillian was held on death row while *awaiting* trial in Alabama. He believes the state held him in prison, rather than the customary county jail lock-up, in order to intimidate him into confessing. His cell was diagonally across from the execution chamber, and a prisoner was killed only a few days after he initially arrived to 'the row'. He said:

> Boy, they executed a lot of guys while I was down there. They executed one guy about four days after they got to keep me down there. That's why they done that, I think, to try to scare me, you know. They put me up high, upstairs, so I could look right over there ... look right at the building with the chair in it, you know, what they

execute in ... And I just reckon they just done that to try to irritate me ... make me, you know ... try to make me give up, I reckon.

Shabaka Brown came closest to death than any of the exonerees we interviewed, coming within fifteen hours of his own electrocution in Florida. When he realized the prison guards were measuring him for his burial suit, he lashed out, assaulted the officer, and lost some of his teeth in the brawl. He said:

The most telling thing during that time was when they took me out of that cell. And they had a civilian with them, with the Lieutenant. And the civilian had a tape measurer in his hand. And they took the handcuffs off me, and asked me to raise my hands, like that. And the tape measure went around my chest, and around my waist, and the inseams of my leg. And then it struck me. Son of a bitch's measuring me for a burial suit, you know. And I struck out. I mean, 'cause I was standin' there, and they was doing this so mechanically. I mean, it was almost like ... arghhh [bangs on table] ... I was an inanimate object. And for some reason, something just ... [shouts out in frustration]. And I was determined right then and there that if they were going to kill me, they were going to do it with some damn dignity.

Finally is the experience of Sabrina Butler, the only female exonerated from death row in the US. Butler was sentenced to death in Mississippi; at the sentencing hearing, the judge announced her execution date would be 2 July 1990. That hearing was seared into her consciousness as a traumatic life experience like none other. She did not understand or absorb the rest of the proceedings that day. She was not informed, in a way that she could grasp, that the execution date would be stayed pending appeals in the State Supreme Court. As the day approached, she became increasingly anxious and agitated. She heard from no one. She worried about what was likely to happen. She told us:

July the 2nd of 1990 was my death date. And when that day came ... I was the scaredest person in the world. That is a feelin' that I wouldn't wish on my worst enemy. I stood there at the little old door ... one slot had glass in it. And you just stand there and look. And I thought, by me watchin' TV, and stuff, that they was gonna come and get you, and you was gonna have this ball and chain on. And these people gonna be walkin' beside you. You goin' down this long hall, you know what I'm sayin.' ... And I was scared to death, and the girl [in the cell next to her] kept tellin' me, 'Sabrina, they're not gonna do nothing' ... 'You know, I was standin' there cryin'.' I kept telling her, 'Yeah, they gonna kill me. They gonna kill me. Somebody call my mama, or somethin' and tell 'em that,' you know, 'I love 'em.' You know, I was just sayin' everything 'cause I was scared [emotional]. And she kept tellin' me, 'Don't cry. Don't cry. Don't cry. It's gonna be alright. It's gonna be alright.' That whole day, I just sat in my room. I couldn't sleep. I couldn't eat [crying]. That is the most humiliating, scary thing that any person could ever go through. I was scared to death because I thought that they was gonna kill me for somethin' that I didn't do. And I couldn't tell nobody to help me. Wasn't nobody there, you know, on that day. I don't never wanna go through that no more. I don't care what. I don't never wanna go through that anymore.

Problems of everyday living

The problem that looms most immediately upon release is housing. With only an hour or a day's notice of impending release, exonerees have little time to plan for life after prison. Relying on their defense networks or family members for immediate housing is typical. Shabaka Brown lived with his post-conviction defense attorney for six months. Sabrina Butler was essentially 'kicked to the curb' – no phone call, no transportation, and no one to pick her up: 'They didn't give me jack! They just took the handcuffs off me and sent me out the door ... Didn't get nothin' but "goodbye, we'll holler at ya".'

The most frequently mentioned problem facing exonerees is finding employment. While some manage to keep themselves gainfully employed most prefer occupations with relative isolation from the public. Exonerees are stymied in searching for meaningful employment by required criminal background checks, despite their exonerations. To have civil rights restored upon exoneration and the wrongful conviction expunged, exonerees must hire an attorney, which they cannot afford. To skirt the requirement of reporting their felony convictions on job applications, some enclose their exoneration paperwork or write 'Not Applicable' on the forms. Such strategies have proven futile. For exonerees living in small communities, stigma can impede their employability. Kirk Bloodsworth and Sabrina Butler faced employment problems because they were such recognizable figures. Butler had been offered a job at a local grocery chain and was filling out the employment paperwork when an assistant manager recognized her and terminated her immediately.

Upon release, most exonerees have serious health problems (such as malnutrition, arthritis, asthma, muscular atrophy, digestive disorders, skin rashes, diabetes, hepatitis). Rebuilding their health is difficult because access to healthcare is largely determined by employment. The self-employed exonerees struggle to pay insurance premiums and may have pre-existing conditions that put premiums out of range. They seek help from Social Security or disability coverage and often are denied. As Alan Gell explains:

I went to the Department of Social Services, and I was like, you know, I hadn't got no money. I hadn't got no job. I was just let out of, you know, out of prison, off of death row. There's not healthcare for me whatsoever and I got these health problems. I got mental problems. I got some, you know, physical problems as far as like, uh, my foot being broken and never set. Is there any way I can get any help from you? And they refused. I mean, they told me that, you know, the only way I could do it is if like I was a senior citizen or, umm, if I was pregnant.

Furthermore, the basics of everyday living confound exonerees. They must relearn how to eat with utensils, how to grocery shop, how to sleep (especially with a significant other). Juan Melendez reports problems finding his way around buildings and frequently getting lost; that after nearly 18 years confined to a 5 ft by 7 ft cell, his sense of direction has suffered. In the first weeks after his release, Alan Gell reports having problems sleeping in the dark, because it is never truly dark in prison. Depending upon the length of incarceration, they may return to a world dramatically different from the one they left. Using modern technology may be difficult. Several exonerees had never seen a cell phone, CD player, DVD, computer, self-serve gas pump, or ATM machine, except on TV.

These practical problems become obstacles to social reintegration which ripple throughout their lifetimes: no home equity, no retirement funds, no prescription coverage, ruptured family relationships, and in some cases reincarceration or early death. They are problems they face alone and without assistance from social service agencies, relying solely on the aid of family, friends, advocates and attorneys willing to provide legal services, often for free. The state offers no post-exoneration aid to negotiate these difficulties, and in some ways only throws up additional obstacles upon release by requiring exonerees to secure their own legal services to have records expunged, civil rights restored and rights to compensation pursued. In many cases, they do not know when (or if) they will be released and thus are not able to make even the most basic plan as to how to manage these practical issues when they get out.

Feelings of grief and loss

Exonerees report spending a significant period of time after prison grieving over losses they incurred during or due to their wrongful incarcerations: the loss of time, loss of feelings of security, loss of loved ones, and loss of self.

Juan Melendez said that after spending '17 years, 8 months, and 1 day' on death row for a crime he did not commit, 'I became an old man in there'. Melendez, Delbert Tibbs, Gary Gauger, Greg Wilhoit and several others lament their loss of time with loved ones, especially children. Several exonerees went into prison leaving small children behind, and returned to grown children and even grandchildren they hardly knew. Some re-establish familial relationships after release, though others interact with their children infrequently and see their relationships as irreparable. Others, like Gary James, imprisoned for 26 years, spent the better part of their childbearing years behind bars and lament the lost opportunity to have children: 'I would like a family, but it's kind of, like, unrealistic, you know. I don't have no kids ... I don't think I'm gonna have none. You know, at this point ... that's the only thing that I want. I would like to have at least one.'

Several exonerees describe a lost sense of security, especially when in public places. They have been under surveillance after release and are vulnerable to police who resent their exonerations. The general public may see this as paranoia, yet to exonerees this is a legitimate fear in the wake of their wrongful capital convictions. For example, returning to Arizona where his wrongful conviction took place, Ray Krone describes taking the following precautions:

> So I have been back to Arizona. I traveled in groups. I didn't drive in a car or get by myself anywhere. I was actually in a bar one night havin' some drinks and some trouble started. And I got the hell out of there quick! ... I was very careful where I went. I took one of those little microphones ... a little recorder along with me in my pocket, just in case I ever did get stopped I was gonna have that thing runnin', but nothin' happened.

The most profound grief is revealed by exonerees who still mourn lost loved ones. Four of our participants were accused of killing family members. They suffered the loss of their family members at the same time they were being tried, convicted and sentenced to death for those murders. Sabrina Butler recounts her confusion and feelings of helplessness while being interrogated by police at the hospital on the night her son died: 'I'm sittin' here holding [her deceased baby]. And everybody's askin' me [what happened]. I could have said I was a elephant! I don't know what I said ... Everybody was askin' me, "What happened?! Who did this?!" ... I don't know what I said, what I didn't say ... And nobody would help me. *Nobody*.' She still visits his grave every year on his birthday with a candle and a toy. Scott Taylor was convicted of killing his wife and toddler and five others in a fire and describes, with tears in his eyes, how he was unable to mourn their deaths until he saw their gravesite for the first time on his ride home from prison the day of his release. Gary Gauger's pain was the most palpable as he describes managing the grief over the loss of his parents, whom he was convicted of killing:

The only way I could say I maybe had grieved a little bit was about a month and a half, two months after my arrest, I had a dream. And I was speaking with my mother. And then I realized, I said, 'Oh, wait a minute, but you were killed.' And then she faded away. I asked for a hug [Gary begins to cry – whispering] Man, I didn't want to do this [deep breath and silence] . . . um, I asked for a hug and then she faded away, and I started crying. And I woke up crying, and I . . . that, I suppose would have been the . . . [speech slurs, crying] . . . Oh man, oh man. I don't even wanna come close to that. Um . . . that was as close as I had come to mourning their murders, their deaths. I would call that . . . I probably had four or five emotional episodes since then. This is pretty close to one right now. I feel like I'm a plastic barrier holding back the ocean. You know, not much substance and a lot of weight.

Debilitating grief and anger haunt other exonerees whose loved ones died while they were incarcerated. Kirk Bloodsworth lost his mother, his primary supporter, merely five months before his exoneration and release. Fifteen years later, he still cannot discuss her death without crying: 'Five months, that's all it was, five months, and she was gone. I had to view her body in handcuffs, shackles and leg chains for five minutes before her funeral. It had literally killed her, this mess.'

Finally, exonerees report a feeling of loss of self and identity upon release. Their socially constructed self-concept was based on their family relationships, employment, friendships, most of which have evaporated or disintegrated. They struggle to carve out new identities through new relationships, new jobs, new spirituality, and even through the 'exoneree' identity itself. Gary Gauger articulates how profound this is: 'My life is no longer my own. I really feel sometimes, I was actually murdered the same day my parents were, and this is like an alternate life I'm living. 'Cause the difference is just so abrupt and different.'

Again, exonerees are given no resources with which to manage these losses post-release. They are not provided with access to counseling services or even names of individuals willing to aid them. They receive no decompression time in a halfway house after release, a resource made available to parolees in some states – no time to adjust to life as an 'exoneree' and to seek assistance for the practical problems of life awaiting them. Instead, they are thrust into their new lives, often in full view of searing media and public scrutiny and often with little to no time to prepare.

Negotiation of stigma and reintegration

Most exonerees experience painful stigma after release. Several were fortunate to return to communities that readily accepted them. However, in spite of actual innocence, many exonerees return to communities that are extremely hostile. A few, like Perry Cobb, move away from where they were tried, hoping that anonymity will insulate them from stigma. But with limited resources and families rooted in particular places, some exonerees return to neighborhoods and towns that know them well. Kirk Bloodsworth was greeted with fear from his neighbors, suspicion from people he had known since childhood, and messages of hate written in the dirt on his truck – 'child killer'. Sabrina Butler cannot find employment in her small town of Columbus, Mississippi where her name is well known. She was rejected by her church when she tried to seek sanctuary there. She feels the searing glare of hatred from community members while grocery shopping or about town, so she rarely goes out: 'I'm this person . . . this heinous murderer that stomped my baby . . . they have just destroyed my life! And I'm angry. I am very angry because I can't get back what they took from me!'

Managing this social rejection can lead exonerees to retreat and isolate themselves. Some retreat into substance abuse, while others rarely leave their homes. Gary Gauger describes his tendency to choose isolation: 'I hate to even have the phone ring. I don't like to talk to people on the phone. So, what's the point? I can't write letters. I can't talk on the phone. I don't like to visit. I don't like to go anywhere. I don't like to leave the house.' Aside from an apology from state officials, acceptance is what exonerees want most. Kirk Bloodsworth explains what exonerees need most upon release: 'A hug. He needs to be loved . . . That was what I wanted more than anything. I wanted to be loved again. I wanted people to respect me. And I didn't want people to think I was a child killer anymore. Out of everything, you know, that was the biggest thing . . . I wanted love and acceptance.'

In many cases, the stigma and social rejection exonerees face is stirred by vocal police and prosecutors who insist on the guilt of exonerees at the very moment they are being released based on evidence of innocence. Such public pronouncements fuel suspicions and fears in the communities to which exonerees return and seal their fates as subjects of harsh social judgment.

This is a relatively short reporting of the harms suffered by these victims at the hands of the state, but the account does provide insight into the variety and depth of the injuries with which they struggle as well as the degree to which the state not only creates these harms but aggravates them after exonerees are released.

Discussion

Using Kauzlarich et al.'s (2001) victimology framework to examine the experiences of death row exonerees brings focus to the role the state plays in producing and in some instances exacerbating the harms exonerees face. These are not harms of their own making. State agents actively seek to evade responsibility for these harms, while engaging in activities that maintain and enhance the very harms they have created.

Our hope is that framing innocents in this way will draw attention to the very real damage suffered by those wrongly convicted of crimes they did not commit and the role the state plays in creating and maintaining their struggles. We believe exonerees benefit from promoting an understanding of their experiences as state victimization. This is not a problem that 'has no name', rather it is a problem that can no longer remain subterranean. Exonerees benefit when society acknowledges, understands and embraces them as human beings. Wrongly convicted individuals benefit when their stories are compiled, preserved, analyzed and disseminated as part of larger public debates about state policies and the impact of deadly practices. It is possible that by documenting and recognizing their struggles, the state might alter its practices and pass laws that guarantee automatic expungements and compensation, healthcare, educational opportunities, and post-trauma therapeutic assistance. It is possible, though less likely, that public officials will be held accountable for their actions and the harms their actions have generated when the stories of these wrongly convicted are known more widely.

For scholars, analyzing these experiences is one avenue to examine the direct role that state officials play in generating harm, and how that harm is manifest for victims. Expansive research into the array of criminal activities and human rights violations perpetrated by states reveals the incomprehensible amounts of harm generated to large numbers of people around the world (Green 2005; Green and Ward 2000; Kauzlarich et al. 2003; Kramer and Michalowski 2005; Lenning 2007; Matthews and Kauzlarich 2007; Rothe and Friedrichs 2006; Ward 2005). Revealing that to public gaze prefaces any discussion of what can then be done about it. For scholars, activists and public officials, recognition that wrongful convictions are harms often generated by state agents and institutional contexts creates an opportunity for change.

The similarities between the harms outlined by Kauzlarich et al. (2001) and those suffered by exonerees lend credence to the need to extend the state crime literature to include the wrongly convicted. Wrongful convictions have yet to be theorized as a form of state crime. The time has come. We offer here a place to begin in thinking about wrongful convictions as state crime.

Framing wrongful convictions as state crime is partially dependent upon the definition of 'state crime' with which one begins. Chambliss' (1989: 184) original definition is indicative of those offered from the legalistic perspective: 'acts defined by law as criminal and committed by state officials in the pursuit of their jobs as representatives of the state'. Such a definition restricts the discussion to outright illegal activities committed by state officials, primarily police and prosecutors, in the pursuit of prosecutions that result in the wrongful conviction of the innocent. Though limiting, such criminality has, nonetheless, been documented in wrongful conviction cases. Police have been found to beat false confessions out of suspects, threaten suspects with execution if they did not confess or provide information, and fail to give exculpatory evidence over to prosecutors, as required by law (Fisher 1993; Leo 2008; Protess and Warden 1998; Radelet *et al.* 1992; Zimmerman 2002). Scientists working in police labs have been known to falsify, fabricate and destroy evidence (Castelle 1999; Luscombe 2001). Prosecutors, too, have fabricated and falsified evidence and withheld exculpatory evidence from the defense (Radelet *et al.* 1992; Scheck *et al.* 2000; Weinberg *et al.* 2006).

These illegal activities, however, represent only one extreme of a broad continuum of behaviors engaged in by state agents that can result in a wrongful conviction. Thus, thinking about wrongful convictions as state crime solely from within this rather narrow legalistic discussion is limiting. Legalistic definitions leave out an array of human rights violations and 'socially injurious acts' committed by state agents that result in 'socially analogous harm' (Michalowski 1985; Rothe and Friedrichs 2006). The social harms approach recognizes that nothing is inherently criminal and that a legally bound definition of state crime is a state-constructed label, requiring state officials to criminalize the activities of other state officials (Matthews and Kauzlarich 2007; Rothe and Friedrichs 2006). Use of the social harms perspective frees researchers to consider analogous types of behavior, though short of illegal, that cause equally serious forms of harm. Kauzlarich *et al.* (2001: 175) offer one possible definition of state crime from within this more inclusive social harms approach: 'illegal, socially injurious, or unjust acts which are committed for the benefit of a state or its agencies, and not for the personal gain of some individual agent of the state'.

In the case of wrongful convictions, police and prosecutors (and judges on occasion) have been found to engage in a wealth of activities that fall short of criminal behavior but nonetheless have resulted in the convictions of innocent people. These include practices that result from carelessness, sloppiness, short-cutting, cynicism, routine processing, stereotyping, tunnel vision, and/or the presumption of guilt. For example, police provide inducements to falsely confess, feed information to witnesses, conduct misleading line-ups and photo arrays, lose and contaminate evidence, ignore conflicting evidence or alternative leads due to tunnel vision, and mishandle informants (Radelet *et al.* 1992; Scheck *et al.* 2000; Westervelt and Humphrey 2002), to name a few. Prosecutors fail to provide complete files to the defense, lose evidence, mishandle witnesses, use inflammatory and misleading evidence at trial, intentionally exempt people of color from juries, mischaracterize evidence in court, and provide inappropriate information to the media (Weinberg *et al.* 2006; Westervelt and Humphrey 2002). And, of course, these most likely occur within a context marked by an unequal distribution of resources between the defendant and his/her defense counsel and the prosecution (Givelber 2002).

This is a brief look at how wrongful convictions could be examined as yet another form of state crime. We encourage further consideration along these lines. We advocate for an examination of wrongful convictions as state crime that takes into account the full picture of how wrongful convictions are produced, including the individual, organizational, contextual and societal factors that produce these harmful outcomes.

Conclusion

Rather than recognizing the role that state agents and organizational contexts play in the production and perpetuation of wrongful convictions, state officials (with some notable exceptions) more often deny responsibility and even claim that exonerations are evidence of how well the system works. Ray Krone discusses what he sees as this failure of accountability:

> I think that is [lack of accountability] actually truly the root cause because that's what allowed [the prosecution] to keep thinking, 'I can get away with this.' And others see, 'Well, we can get away with this.' All to get a conviction . . . It ain't about, 'I'm saving society because I got this murderer off the streets here.' It's about getting a conviction. And I know somewhere, in all these cases you've reviewed, I know somewhere along the line, a police officer, prosecutor, somebody in them offices had to look and say, 'Wow, I wonder why this shit don't add up right? Ah . . . who cares.' . . . And they're dangerous. They talk about taking dangerous people off the streets. They tell the jury to send this dangerous person . . . take 'em out of society. I tell you, prosecutors like that are dangerous. Police officers like that are dangerous.

When asked to comment on the claim that his exoneration demonstrates that the 'system works', Kirk Bloodsworth adamantly responds:

> No sir! No ma'am! No way! No how! The system didn't work. *I* worked. I got *myself* out. . . . I had a smart attorney who believed me. But, even he, he did what I told him to do. He said, 'You're either crazy or you're innocent.' And I said, 'Well, I'm both. Go do it.' I took three blood tests and the rest is history . . . So, but the prosecutor, the day I got out, this is what she says, 'Although we're releasing Mr Bloodsworth, we're not prepared to say he's innocent. However if we had had this evidence in 1984, we wouldn't have prosecuted him.' So what does that mean? You know what I mean?! [angrily] They won't even own up to their stuff! And this is the . . . the . . . the, I call it

ostrich-and-the-sand-thing, where they hide their head . . . stuck their head in a hole and tried to hide from the world, and they're the one's that's doin' the most damage to a lot of 'em because it's all about . . . their arrogance.

So, for exonerees who have been through the experience of a wrongful capital conviction and death sentence, the system is broken. It is not a matter of the 'rotten apple' or specific individuals who have fallen short of their ethical obligations. Rather their cases point to the 'contaminated orchard' where the entire system – from arrest to prosecution to incarceration and ultimately to post-exoneration – inflicts injury, trauma and irreversible damage to them, where the final insult is an inability by anyone to 'own' the state's role in the tragedy. Thus, framing innocents as victims of state harm puts a very real face on the need for changes in state acknowledgment and policy to more effectively address the needs and challenges faced by innocents when they finally are released.

Note

1   Interviews with exonerees were conducted in person (except one completed by correspondence) and lasted between two and five hours each. Interviews focused primarily on life once they left prison. All participants were compensated for their interviews.

Acknowledgments

Funding for this research has been provided by: The External Proposal Development Incentive Program, Office of the Associate Provost of Research, The University of North Carolina at Greensboro, and the American Sociological Association's Fund for the Advancement of the Discipline Award supported by the American Sociological Association and the National Science Foundation.

Chapter 12

Prosecutorial overcharging as state crime?

Lauren N. Lang

In the early morning hours of 14 March 2006 a woman reported that she had been raped by three men during a party in Durham, North Carolina. This all too frequent crime report quickly mushroomed into the media circus that became known as the Duke Lacrosse Rape Case. The subsequent prosecution ultimately culminated in the dismissal of all charges against members of the Duke University Lacrosse Team and the disbarment of Michael Nifong, the District Attorney of Durham County, North Carolina for prosecutorial misconduct.

Specifically, District Attorney Nifong was charged by the North Carolina Bar Association with making statements to the media that he 'knew or reasonably should have known ... had a substantial likelihood of prejudicing the criminal adjudicative proceeding'.[1] The charges also allege that Nifong and Dr Brian Meehan, the president and director of a DNA analysis company, discussed and 'agreed that the final [DNA analysis] report would not include all of the results of the tests and examinations performed by [the DNA lab] but would be limited only to the "positive" results', meaning that 'potentially exculpatory DNA evidence and test results ... would not be provided to the Duke defendants', their lawyers, and other player suspects. According to the North Carolina Bar, this resulted in Nifong failing to comply with mandated discovery requirements, and him making 'misrepresentations and false statements of material fact to the court'.

The disbarment of the District Attorney for violating the very laws he was sworn to prosecute is an anomaly. In fact, the Center for Public Integrity, an investigative journalism group, found 2,012 cases since 1970 in which appellate courts dismissed or overturned trial court rulings or verdicts due to prosecutorial misconduct. Yet, according to the Center, in that same time-frame only 44 prosecutors appeared before a state bar to answer allegations of prosecutorial misconduct. Likewise, an investigation by the *Chicago Tribune* found that between 1963 and 1999, 381 state murder defendants received new trials due to prosecutorial misconduct but no prosecutor was disbarred or publicly sanctioned.

The Duke Lacrosse Rape Case and the findings of the *Chicago Tribune* and Center for Public Integrity pose an interesting question for the study of state organized crime: does prosecutorial misconduct constitute an ongoing practice of law violation by agents of the state?

This chapter seeks to answer that question by examining one specific function of a prosecutor: filing charges. Specifically, it demonstrates that we can identify a pattern of 'overcharging', defined as 'the practice of pleading unnecessary counts or overloading the charging documents to induce a guilty plea to lesser charges before trial' (Schons *et al.* 2001: 19).

Prosecutors, unlike other attorneys, have unique ethical duties that require them 'not [to seek to] win a case, but that justice shall be done'[2] (Berger v. United States, 1935: 295 U.S. 78, 88). One of the most important functions of prosecutors, and the source of incredible power over individuals, is the decision of whom to charge with what crime(s). At least initially, prosecutors have virtually unfettered charging discretion[3] but 'prosecutors must not misuse the charge selection process by "overcharging"' (Bordenkircher v. Hayes, 1978: 434 U.S. 357, 364). A prosecutor pleading unnecessary counts or overloading the charging documents to induce a guilty plea to lesser charges before trial is abusing the process' (Coleman *et al.* 2001 quoted in Schons *et al.* 2001: 19).

Methodology

To conduct a preliminary study of 'overcharging', 200 cases were drawn at random from the 995 felony cases opened by the Santa Barbara County Public Defender (hereafter, Public Defender) in 2005 in Santa Barbara, California. At least initially, the Public Defender was appointed to represent the defendant charged with a felony crime in a Complaint.[4] The charges contained in either the Complaint or Information were compared to the ultimate outcome of the case to see if there was a pattern to the charges dismissed.[5] Additionally, in an effort to explore any discrepancy between the charges filed and what the defendants were arrested for by the police, in 20 per cent, or 40, of the 200 cases a search was done for the booking sheet.[6] Sixteen booking sheets were found and arguably in five of the cases more serious charges were filed than those the defendants were booked into jail for, but in three of the cases less serious charges were filed.

Data

In some of the 200 cases multiple defendants were charged so that the total number of persons/defendants in the study was 233. At the time of disposition, the Public Defender represented 169 or 72.53 per cent of the 233 defendants. Private counsel, either hired or appointed due to a public defender conflict, represented 64 or 27.47 per cent of the defendants. Ninety-nine or 42.5 per cent of the cases had at least one charge of violating drug laws.

Seventeen, or 7.3 per cent of the defendants had their cases dismissed in total by the District Attorney, while another 61 (26.18 per cent) had their cases reduced to a misdemeanor or infraction. A shockingly low number of defendants (four or 1.72 per cent) were tried by a jury. All four were convicted and received prison terms. Eight defendants had strikes alleged under California's 'three strikes and you're out' law.[7] The strikes were dismissed against four of the defendants (50 per cent) and in the other four either found true by a judge or jury or admitted.

In addition to prior strike convictions, under California law sentences can be enhanced for felons previously sentenced to prison who face a new felony charge. Punishment for the new felony charge can be increased by one year for each prior prison term served (California Penal Code Section 667.5(b)). Fifty-nine of the one-year prison priors were alleged, some defendants had several alleged, and 45 or 76.27 per cent were dismissed.

Duties of prosecutors

In general, '. . . it is the duty of the prosecutor to do justice, not merely to "win" convictions' (American Bar Association 1993: 61). Further, although the 'line separating overcharging from the sound exercise of prosecutorial discretion is necessarily a subjective one . . . the key consideration is the prosecutor's commitment to the interests of justice, fairly bringing those charges he or she believes are supported by the facts without "piling on" charges in order to unduly leverage an accused to forgo his or her right to trial' (American Bar Association 1993: 77).[8]

Despite the above language in the ABA guidelines, the United States Supreme Court has not been receptive to arguments that 'overcharging' violates a defendant's right to 'due process' under the 14th Amendment to the United States Constitution, as demonstrated by Bordenkircher v. Hayes (1978, 434 US 357). In that case, the Kentucky prosecutor, on the record, threatened to file amended charges subjecting Mr Hayes to life in prison as a habitual offender if Mr Hayes did not plead to lesser felony charges and accept a sentence of five years in prison (Bordenkircher v. Hayes, 1978: 434 US 359).[9] Mr Hayes, whose non-violent crime consisted of passing a forged check in the amount of $88.30, refused the prosecutor's harsh pre-trial offer and was convicted at trial and sentenced to life under Kentucky's version of 'three strikes and you're out'.[10]

On appeal, the Sixth Circuit Court of Appeals held that the prosecutor's actions violated due process for the prosecutor to 'threaten a defendant with the consequence that more severe charges may be brought if he insists on going to trial' (Hayes v. Cowan, 1976: 47 F.2d 42, 44). The United States Supreme Court, however, was not impressed with the argument that the prosecutor's admitted vindictive motive in filing the additional charges violated due process and reversed the Sixth Circuit decisions, ruling 'that the course of conduct engaged in by the prosecutor in this case, which no more than openly presented the defendant with the unpleasant alternatives of forgoing trial or facing charges on which he was plainly subject to prosecution, did not violate the Due Process Clause of the Fourteenth Amendment' (Bordenkircher v. Hayes, 1978: 434 U.S. 361–2).[11]

Conclusion

What then do we make of this seeming conflict between the ethical guidelines suggesting that prosecutors should not overcharge and the United States Supreme Court ruling that would seem to suggest that anything goes in the rough-and-tumble world of plea bargaining? Is it possible that the ABA and California District Attorney Association are more ethical than the United States Supreme Court? And what implications does this have for the study of state organized crime? Indeed, given the Bordenkircher decision, does overcharging even fit into a definition of state organized crime? After all, the highest law of the land has ruled that, for all intents, there is no such thing as 'overcharging'. Given this, how can we even consider overcharging under the rubric of state crime?

The answer to the question whether overcharging qualifies as state organized crime depends on the definition of state organized crime. If state organized crime is defined as activity by government agents in violation of the laws of its sovereign, then overcharging, given the Bordenkircher decision, would not qualify as state organized crime. However, if state organized crime is defined as a pattern by government actors in violation of their ethical duties, then given the CDAA and ABA guidelines overcharging may very well qualify as state organized crime. Specifically, since these organizations set forth the standards of normative behavior for prosecutors, it is legitimate to consider violation of these standards as deviant acts, whether or not they arise to the status of criminal acts. Criminology has a long tradition of examining deviant acts that were accepted as legal, even if distasteful, by law (Green and Ward 2004). Given this, prosecutorial overcharging is certainly as legitimate a topic for criminological inquiry as any other form of deviance.

A more compelling question is, how does prosecutorial overcharging fit into the social harm model?[12] Though overcharging may not be a 'crime' *per se* – a violation of the laws of the sovereign – inducing defendants to forgo jury trials and to plead to greater sentences by overcharging undoubtedly causes untold 'harm' on the defendants and their families. Indeed, if the social harm model can be applied on a micro scale to overcharging and 'harm' is defined as unfilled human needs, then surely overcharging is such a harm. Arguably, there is a universal human need to be free, particularly free from repressive state actions. Insofar as overcharging results in defendants agreeing to longer periods of incarceration than their crimes warrant in order to avoid even longer prison terms, prosecutorial overcharging would seem to clearly fit the definition of repressive state action.

But does the data show a pattern of overcharging? We believe that it does. While it is hard to generalize about just eight cases in a study of 233, the fact that half of the strikes alleged under the three strikes law were dismissed calls for a study of 'strike' cases, to examine whether there is a pattern of alleging strikes to compel plea bargains to lesser charges and thereby deprive defendants of their constitutional right to a trial. The 50 per cent dismissal rate in this study could well indicate that the draconian punishments of the three strikes law offer prosecutors an opportunity to use the law as a bludgeon to compel defendants to settle rather than face 25 years to life in prison.

Perhaps the clearest pattern of overcharging can be seen in the over 75 per cent dismissal rate of the one-year prison priors. There is clearly a pattern of allegation in the Complaint or Information and then dismissal as part of plea bargaining. Such a pattern of overcharging – overloading the charging documents to induce a guilty plea before trial – is in violation of the prosecutor's ethical and statutory duties and should be considered a form of state organized crime.[13]

In view of the Supreme Court's ruling that overcharging is an acceptable legal practice, are there any strategies to confront and reduce the commission of this state crime? Unfortunately, the obvious strategy to combat overcharging is through legislative changes to abusive sentencing schemes (such as three strikes) that distort the criminal justice system by subjecting individuals to life sentences for petty crimes. Given the fear of legislators of appearing 'soft on crime' the prospects of such action seem dim. Indeed, as we write California is in the worst depression since the 1930s and yet despite that and a Federal Court Order to release up to 40,000 of the 170,000 prisoners held by the California Department of Corrections, legislation is stalled in the California State Assembly. If the current budget crisis is not sufficient impetus for the California State Legislature to release non-violent offenders, then prospects are indeed very bad for any change to California's Penal Code that would curb prosecutorial overcharging.

Notes

1 North Carolina State Bar v. Michael B. Nifong, Amended Complaint filed January 2007 by the North Carolina State before the Disciplinary Hearing Commission of North Carolina. Reported in http://news.findlaw.com/nytimes/docs/duke/ncbnifong12407cmp.html

2 The prosecutor is 'the representative not of an ordinary party to a controversy, but of a sovereignty whose obligation to govern impartially is as compelling as its obligation to govern at all; and whose interest, therefore, in a criminal prosecution is not that it shall win a case, but that justice shall be done. As such, he [or she] is in a peculiar and very definite sense the servant of the law, the twofold aim of which is that guilty shall not escape or innocence suffer.'

3 'In our system, so long as the prosecutor has probable cause to believe that the accused committed an offense defined by statute, the decision whether or not to prosecute, and what charge to file or bring before a grand jury, generally rests entirely in his discretion.'

4 In California, criminal cases are initiated by the District Attorney filing a formal charging document called a Complaint. Complaints typically contain notice to the defendant of the date, jurisdiction and type of crime, i.e. which law they are charged with violating.

5 After the preliminary or probable cause hearing, Information is filed that supersedes the Complaint. Most of the cases in the study settled prior to the preliminary hearing.

6 When a defendant is booked into the County Jail, law enforcement files with the jail a 'sheet' listing the arrest charges.

7 In 1994 California passed what is probably the most draconian of repeat offender sentencing schemes in the United States. The 'three strikes and you're out' sentencing scheme provides that upon conviction for any felony, if the defendant has twice been previously convicted of a 'serious' or 'violent' felony they can be sentenced to 25 years to life in prison. Additionally, punishments are doubled for any felony committed after conviction of one strike. According to the California Department of Corrections and Rehabilitation website, as of 31 December 2007 there were 41,748 people in California prisons pursuant to the three strikes law.

8 See also at page 76: 'Although there are many different conceptions of what "overcharging" actually is, the heart of the criticism is the belief that prosecutors have brought charges, not in the good faith belief that they fairly reflect the gravity of the offense, but rather as a harassing and coercive device in the expectation that they will induce the defendant to plead guilty.'

9 While cross-examining Hayes during the subsequent trial proceedings the prosecutor described the plea offer in the following language: 'Isn't it a fact that I told you at that time [the initial bargaining session] if you did not intend to plead guilty to five years for this charge and ... save the court the inconvenience and necessity of a trial and taking up this time that I intended to return to the grand jury and ask them to indict you based upon these prior felony convictions?'

10 Interestingly, after Mr Hayes' conviction, Kentucky repealed its habitual offender law replacing it with a 'persistent felony offender sentencing' scheme,

under which Mr Hayes would not have been subjected to enhanced sentencing. At the time of Hayes' trial the statute provided that '[a]ny person convicted a ... third time of felony ... shall be confined in the penitentiary during his life' (Ky. Rev. Stat § 431.190 (1973) (repealed 1975)). That statute has been replaced by Ky. Rev. Stat § 532.080 (supp. 1977) under which Hayes would have been sentenced to, at most, an indeterminate term of 10 to 20 years (§ 080 (6) (b)). In addition, under the new statute a previous conviction is a basis for enhanced sentencing only if a prison term of one year or more was imposed, the sentence or probation was completed within five years of the present offense, and the offender was over the age of 18 when the offense was committed. At least one of Hayes' prior convictions did not meet these conditions. According to his own testimony, Hayes had pleaded guilty in 1961, when he was 17 years old, to a charge of detaining a female, a lesser included offense of rape, and as a result had served five years in the state reformatory. In 1970 he had been convicted of robbery and sentenced to five years' imprisonment, but had been released on probation immediately.

11 Although Bordenkircher seemingly involved the opposite of 'overcharging' – i.e. the Kentucky prosecutor undercharged initially and tried to use the threat of greater charges to compel a guilty plea – analytically the United States Supreme Court treated the situation the same as if the prosecutor overcharged: 'As a practical matter, in short, this case would be no different if the grand jury had indicted Hayes as a recidivist from the outset, and the prosecutor had offered to drop that charge as part of the plea bargain.'

12 The authors are not criminologists and as such do not pretend to fully comprehend the academic concept of social harm but rather introduce the analysis here so that more serious scholars might expand upon or criticize their work.

13 At the presentation of this paper at the workshop on 'State-Organized Crime' (29–30 May 2008 at the International Institute for the Sociology of Law in Onati, Spain), it was astutely suggested by one of the participants (whose son is a prosecutor), that all the data showed is the benevolence of prosecutors in plea bargaining: prosecutors simply file charges as allowed or dictated by the legislature and then in the exercise of their 'discretion' dismiss enhancements or charges to reflect the true gravity of the defendant's conduct. While such an argument may have merit, in a social harm model it simply shifts the focus from the actions of the executive (prosecutors) to the actions of the legislature in passing draconian sentencing laws as advocated by the prosecutors. The bottom line is that the harm suffered by defendants and their families is due either to 'overcharging' by prosecutors or to the legislature passing unreasonable sentencing laws. The harm is real nonetheless!

Appendix A

1. Total number of defendants: 233[1]

---

[1] There were 238 total defendants in the sample population (200 cases). However, cases for five of those defendants were transferred to other counties.

    a. OPD cases: 169 (72.53%)
    b. CDA cases: 45 (19.31%)
    c. Private attorney cases: 19 (8.15%)
       i. Total number of CDA and private attorney cases: 64 (27.47%)
2. Total number of cases dismissed or reduced to misdemeanor or infraction: 61 (26.18%)
3. Total number of cases dismissed: 17 (7.3%)
    a. OPD: 11 (64.71)
    b. CDA: 4 (23.53%)
    c. Private attorney: 2 (11.76%)
       i. Total number of CDA and private attorney cases dismissed: 6 (35.29%)
4. Total number of felony cases reduced to misdemeanor or infraction: 44 (18.88%)
    a. OPD: 29 (65.90%)
    b. CDA: 10 (22.73%)
    c. Private attorney: 5 (11.36%)
       i. Total number of CDA/private attorney cases reduced: 15 (34.09%)
5. Total number of jury trials: 4 (1.72%)
    a. 100% of cases
6. Total number of strikes alleged: 8
    a. Total number of strikes dismissed: 4 (50%)
    b. Total number of strikes found true: 4 (50%)
7. Total number of prison priors alleged: 59
    a. Total number of prison priors unpunished/dismissed: 45 (76.27%)
    b. Total number of prison priors punished: 14 (23.73%)

Appendix B

Note: These statistics have been computed independent of the larger sample study. The below computations are a separate independent analysis.

1. Total number of public defender cases: 169[2]
    a. Total number of OPD cases reduced or dismissed: 40 (23.67%)
       i. Total number of cases reduced to misdemeanor or infraction: 29 (17.16%)
       ii. Total number of cases dismissed: 11 (6.51%)
2. Total number of CDA and private attorney cases: 64[3]
    a. Total number of CDA and private attorney cases reduced or dismissed: 21 (32.81%)

---

[2] These statistics are solely based upon the total number of OPD.

[3] These statistics are solely based upon the total number of CDA and private attorney cases.

     i. Total number of cases reduced to misdemeanor or infraction: 15 (23.44%)

     ii. Total number of cases dismissed: 6 (9.38%)

3. Total number of CDA cases: 45[4]
   a. Total number of CDA cases reduced or dismissed: 14 (31.82%)
     i. Total number of cases reduced to misdemeanor or infraction: 10 (22.22%)
     ii. Total number of cases dismissed: 4 (8.89%)
4. Total number of private attorney cases: 19[5]
   a. Total number of private attorney cases reduced or dismissed: 7 (36.84%)
     i. Total number of cases reduced to misdemeanor or infraction: 5 (26.32%)
     ii. Total number of cases dismissed: 2 (10.53%)

---

[4] These statistics are solely based upon the total number of CDA cases.
[5] These statistics are solely based upon the total number of private attorney cases.

Part Three
Responding to State Crime

Chapter 13

The politics of harm reduction policies

William J. Chambliss, Jonathan William Anderson and Tanya Whittle

The criminological study of state crime typically focuses on the harmful consequences of state violations of domestic or international laws. Contrary to the view that state crimes are always harmful, however, this chapter suggests that in some cases states may cause less harm by violating international laws than by conforming to them. Specifically, we examine how several European nations, by violating United Nations resolutions governing the sale and use of drugs, have caused less harm than if they had conformed to the prohibitionist and highly punitive model of drug control promoted by UN anti-drug resolutions created in accordance with US interests.

Beginning in the 1960s, the United States pursued an active policy of exporting US drug policies through United Nations conventions. This US policy resulted in four major UN conventions: the Convention on Narcotic Drugs of 1961, the 1971 Convention on Psychotropic Substances, amendments to the 1972 Protocol amending the 1961 Convention, and the United Nations Convention Against Illicit Traffic in Narcotic Drugs and Psychotropic Substances of 1988. The 1988 Convention reiterated the substance of the earlier conventions but added new methods of dealing with illicit international traffic, especially through financial interference (Silvis 1996). Throughout the creation and implementation of these Conventions, the United States used its political muscle to ensure conformity with the US vision that drug problems are crime problems to be addressed by crime control strategies, rather than public health problems to be addressed by policies of harm reduction.

In addition to calling for the conventions, the United States employed a number of other tactics to encourage and at times coerce UN member nations into implementing its 'drug war' policies. Charles Siragusa, a US narcotics agent wrote in his 1966 memoirs: 'Most of the time, though, I found that a casual mention of the possibility of shutting off our foreign aid programs, dropped in the proper quarters, brought grudging permission for our operations almost immediately' (Gardner 2000: 12).

In 1980, the United States suspended most foreign aid to Bolivia when it deemed the Bolivian government unresponsive to American concerns about cocaine. According to the *National Drug Strategy for Prevention of Drug Abuse and Drug Trafficking* (1984: 22 cited in Gardner 2000: 12), 'U.S. decisions on foreign aid and other matters should be tied to the willingness of the recipient country to execute vigorous enforcement programs against narcotic traffickers.' The effect of US pressure to bolster prohibitionist policies has also been felt elsewhere. On 15 March 1995 the World Health Organization (WHO) issued a press release in anticipation of a two-year study of cocaine, which had involved dozens of experts in nineteen countries. WHO noted that it was 'the largest global study on cocaine use ever undertaken' (Gardner 2000: 12). However, a report was never issued. WHO spokesman Gregory Hartl asserted that the report was peer-reviewed for 'two to three years' and determined to be 'technically unsound' (Gardner 2000: 12). Others contend that the unreleased report was critical of current drug policies and asserted that many of the beliefs about the dangerousness and addictiveness of cocaine were unfounded. An anonymous former UN International Drug Control Program official disclosed that the report was not issued because the United States threatened to withdraw funding from the section of WHO responsible for it. WHO records indicate that Neil Boyer, the American representative to the organization, expressed concern that the WHO substance abuse program was 'headed in the wrong direction'. He cited the cocaine study and 'evidence of the WHO's support for harm-reduction programs'. He concluded that 'if WHO activities relating to drugs failed to reinforce proven drug-control approaches, funds for the relevant programs should be curtailed' (Gardner 2000: 12). In keeping with this approach, the International Narcotics Control Board, which was created to develop and implement political and economic pressure strategies designed to compel other nations to abandon harm reduction drug programs, aimed at addressing drug problems through treatment and decriminalization in favor of a US-like 'war' on drugs.

The US government also employs carrots as well as sticks to coerce nations into following their drug policies. For instance, the United States agreed to share the proceeds from confiscated property such as cash, houses, boats and airplanes resulting from US-led drug raids in other countries. Thus, incentives to co-operate with US policies include avoiding the loss of foreign aid and obtaining additional income from confiscation of property for foreign law enforcement agencies. To understand the practical consequences of US strategies we need to consider the types of drug policies the United States has sought to limit.

Safer injection rooms and heroin maintenance

Two related harm reduction programs, designed to reduce health risks to users, have generated the greatest controversy with relation to the international conventions – safer injection rooms and heroin prescription programs.

Safer injection rooms, known also as 'tolerance areas' and 'shooting galleries', are areas where intravenous drug users have access to clean injection equipment, medical attention and counseling (CCSA 1996). Safer injection rooms in three European countries – Germany, Switzerland and the Netherlands – have proven to be successful in reducing the trans-mission of diseases, overdoses and vein damage. In some studies, addicts have reported engaging in unsafe sex less often, presumably as a result of counseling and hygienic services. Where safer injection rooms operate, public drug use has declined and fewer discarded syringes are found in the streets (Killias and Rbasa 1998). In Frankfurt, reductions in property and drug crimes are attributed to the city's overall harm reduction policy, of which safer injection rooms are a part (Lindesmith Center 1999). The success of the programs has led to their implementation by city and national governments in Italy, Spain, Portugal, Luxembourg, Norway, Canada and Australia, and calls for their implementation elsewhere (CCSA 1996).

The success of heroin maintenance programs in Switzerland and the Netherlands has lead to calls for their implementation in Germany, Denmark, Luxembourg, Australia, Canada, the United States, and else-where (Cooper-Mahkorn 1998). The success of heroin maintenance pro-grams in Switzerland has led to studies in the United Kingdom, Germany, Spain and Belgium (FDHA 2008). Additionally, the UK has prescribed heroin to addicts for decades, although it is a practice carried out only by individual doctors.

Despite the success of these programs the United Nations steadfastly follows the US logic of opposing them. The United Nations International Narcotic Control Board's annual report for 1999 states:

> The Board believes that any national, state or local authority that permits the establishment and operation of drug injection rooms or any outlet to facilitate the abuse of drugs (by injection or any other route of administration) also facilitates illicit drug trafficking ... By permitting drug injection rooms, a Government could be considered to be in contravention of the international drug control treaties by facilitating in, aiding and/or abetting the commission of crimes involving illegal drug possession and use, as well as other criminal offenses, including drug trafficking. (INCB 1999: 26)

US response

Both safer injection rooms and heroin prescription programs have earned the criticism and warnings of the International Narcotics Control Board (Mann 1999). Oddly enough, safer injection rooms, which unlike heroin maintenance programs do not supply the drugs, are apparently of greater concern to the Board (Mann 1999). For example:

> The Board expressed concern over Germany's and Luxemburg's injection room programs and compared drug injection rooms to 'shooting galleries' when urging against the Australian program. In the view of the Board, such establishments would provide an outlet for illicit drug abuse and facilitate or encourage illicit drug trafficking (Mann 1999: 1A).

The criticism of the programs by the INCB, as well as the United States Congress, has come despite the success of the programs in improving the health of addicts, reducing crime and saving money (Boller 1998). The INCB's annual report for 1999 states:

> The Board believes that any national, state or local authority that permits the establishment and operation of drug injection rooms or any outlet to facilitate the abuse of drugs (by injection or any other route of administration) also facilitates illicit drug trafficking. (INCB 1999: 26)

The report continues:

> By permitting drug injection rooms, a Government could be considered to be in contravention of the international drug control treaties by facilitating in, aiding and/or abetting the commission of crimes involving illegal drug possession and use, as well as other criminal offenses, including drug trafficking. (INCB 1999: 62)

While safer injection rooms and heroin maintenance have had significant beneficial social results, they are primarily medical programs that have been adopted for health policy reasons. In fact, whether the facilities and their services exist for medical reasons is one key factor in whether or not they violate the UN Conventions.

International response

Among industrialized European countries there is a growing consensus that the criminalization of drug policies fostered by the US through UN treaties and agreements does not work and is counter-productive. Instead of criminalizing drug use, European nations have increasingly adopted 'harm reduction' strategies, which aim at reducing drug-related harm without requiring abstention from drug use (CCSA 1996: 62). The strategies focus on 'reducing the negative consequences of drug use for the individual, community and society while the user continues to use drugs', at least temporarily (CCSA 1996: 9). The primary concern remains the reduction of the 'adverse health, social, and economic consequences of drug use without requiring abstinence' from drugs (CCSA 1996: 9). The health and social well-being of individuals is the primary objective, and harm-reducing services are not denied if individuals are unable or unwilling to change their behavior (Westermeyer 2008: 2).

Preliminary studies have indicated that harm reduction programs are effective not only in reducing the incidence of disease but in some cases also decreasing criminal activity and increasing the social well-being of addicts among other benefits. This, in turn, has encouraged other countries to consider and implement similar programs.

Despite their success and growing popularity, governments choosing to adopt harm reduction programs have encountered a somewhat unexpected obstacle: the United Nations. Harm reduction policies have been challenged by the International Narcotics Control Board of the United Nations, which claims that the programs violate international drug control conventions. On 23 February 2000 the INCB warned that safer injection rooms, like those being implemented in Germany, Switzerland, Luxembourg and Spain, could violate the international drug conventions (Reuters 2000). Nevertheless, on 25 February 2000 Germany, despite the Board's warning, passed a law allowing addicts to inject their own heroin in safer injection rooms where clean swabs and needles are provided, together with counseling for addicts (Reuters 2000).

Rogue states

Switzerland

Like the Netherlands, Switzerland has been a pioneer in experimenting with harm reduction strategies. Some Swiss cities began to experiment with safer injection rooms as early as the 1980s, and in 1986 the first officially supported facility was opened in the city of Bern (Boller 1998). By the 1990s Switzerland had also begun to experiment with the state provision of heroin to confirmed addicts, in settings similar to those of the safer injection rooms. In 1992 official studies of the prescription of heroin began. Both safer injection rooms and heroin prescription in Switzerland were part of a general shift towards a 'health-orientated drug policy' by the Swiss medical association (FMH) which 'emphasized the definition of addiction as a disease' (Lindesmith Center 1999: 6).

Prior to the heroin trials, Switzerland already had 'one of the world's most comprehensive and well-supported array of addiction treatment services' and more than 30 per cent of heroin users in Switzerland were in methadone maintenance programs (Drucker and Vlahov 1999: 46–7). Heroin prescription was developed as a type of 'last resort option' to reach addicts for whom methadone and other types of conventional treatment had failed. Patients were required to be over 18 years old, although most were significantly older. Furthermore, they were required to have been injecting heroin on their own for over two years and have failed at least two prior treatments. Most had been addicted to heroin for over ten years and had numerous treatment failures (MacCoun and Reuter 1999). As Benedikt Fischer, a scientist with the Centre of Addiction and Mental Health, stated, 'The idea is not to replace methadone but to provide an alternative – a last resort option when conventional treatment doesn't work' (Vittala 1999: 9). Precautions were also taken to prevent the diversion of the prescribed heroin to the black market. Injectable heroin had to remain on site, although a limited number of addicts were permitted to bring home a few heroin-laced cigarettes at night.

The results of the heroin trials were overwhelmingly positive. The mortality rate of participants was 1 per cent compared with 8.9 per cent of those out of treatment. Drug-related deaths in Switzerland dropped from 419 in 1992, the first year of the studies, to 159 in 1999 (Boller 1998; Herde 2000). No overdose deaths occurred among program participants who stayed in the program (MacCoun and Reuter 1999).

Heroin prescription also effectively reached addicts who had failed with previous treatments. It is reported: 'More than 70 per cent of all patients enrolled stayed in HAT [heroin-assisted treatment] for a year and nearly 60 per cent for two years or more' (FDHA 2008: 12). This was a high rate relative to those found in methadone programs, especially considering that all the participants had previously failed other treatments. Of those who 'dropped out', about half entered other forms of treatment, including both methadone and abstinence based therapies (FDHA 2008; Drucker and Vlahov 1999).

Studies of the program reported a number of additional benefits: 'After improving their health, participants were able to find work and accommodations; they also were able to reduce their indebtedness' (Boller 1998: 9). Unemployment fell from 44 to 20 per cent (MacCoun and Reuter 1999). Additionally, 'Treating a heroin-dependent in a HAT centre ... saves society 47 francs per day, mainly in the form of costs for criminal proceedings' (FDHA 2008: 3). Information provided by the Swiss Federal Office of Public Health (2007) showed considerable drops in the criminal activity of the program's participants (MacCoun and Reuter 1999; Vittala 1999). The crime rate dropped among all patients over the course of treatment. There was also a sharp drop in the use of non-prescribed heroin (MacCoun and Reuter 1999). The participating addicts were also significantly less likely to be victims of crime (Killias and Rbasa 1998).

The World Health Organization (WHO), taking a somewhat critical stance, argued that the reported benefits may have resulted from the 'intensive medical and psychosocial services' that were provided in addition to the prescribed heroin. Nevertheless, the WHO also recognized 'it is medically feasible to provide an intravenous heroin treatment program under highly controlled conditions where the prescribed drug is injected on site, in a manner that is safe, clinically responsible and acceptable to the community'. The WHO further recognized the improvements in mental health and social functioning and decreases in illegal activity and illicit heroin use noted above (Rusche and Caltrider 1999: 532).

The authorities in Switzerland have concluded from the data that heroin causes very few problems when used in a controlled manner and administered in hygienic conditions (CCSA 1996). In 1997 the Swiss government approved a large-scale expansion of the program that will potentially accommodate 15 per cent of the country's estimated 30,000 addicts (MacCoun and Reuter 1999). The Swiss people also approved by referendum a continuation and expansion of heroin therapy programs (Drucker and Vlahov 1999).

Germany

Germany, like Switzerland, has promoted safer injection rooms. Frankfurt, one of seven German cities that operate safer injection rooms and other low-threshold drug services, has reported a drop in overdose fatalities from 147 in 1991 to 44 in 2007, while they remain steady in the rest of Germany (Welle 2008). The rate of HIV infection among drug users has dropped from 63–65 per cent in 1985 to 12–15 per cent in 1994. Frankfurt also reported a decrease in drug-related criminal activity: 'cases of street robbery declined from 1,761 in 1991 to 1,407 in 1997; cases of car break-ins declined from 28,672 in 1991 to 19,495 in 1997; general heroin offenses declined from 1,109 in 1991 to 631 in 1997; and cases of heroin trafficking declined from 1,211 in 1991 to 220 in 1997' (Lindesmith Center 1999: 27).

A preliminary survey in Frankfurt in 1995 revealed that individuals who injected in public were significantly more likely to derive income from drug dealing and 'various illegal activities' than those who injected in the safer injection rooms. Furthermore, those surveyed at the open drug scenes on average derived a greater portion of their income from illegal activity than those found at the safer injection rooms. This survey also noted that the facilities reduce public annoyance and ensure 'both better hygienic conditions for consumption and immediate help in case of an overdose' (Kemmesies 1999: 53).

Australia

With the success of safer injection rooms, heroin prescription and other harm reduction methods in Europe, the programs have gained support in other countries. Provincial and city governments in Australia have been among the most eager to replicate the positive results of harm reduction. Until recently, Australia has followed more traditional prohibition policies. However, high rates of heroin addiction, HIV and AIDS have fostered increasing support for harm reduction programs (Gardner 2000). Australian harm reduction programs are often referred to as 'harm minimization' programs because they involve supply reduction strategies: they are tough on drugs, not drug addicts (UNODC 2008). The movement has also been fueled by comparisons with the Netherlands, which has for decades embraced much more progressive, harm reduction oriented methods. The Royal Australasian College of Physicians reported that more than 2 per cent of Australians aged 14 and over had used illicit injectable drugs at some point in their lives; the comparable figure for the Dutch population was 0.3 per cent (Gosch and Busch 1999).

In 2001, Sydney established a safer injection room for heroin addicts (UNODC 2008). Programs involving the prescription of heroin are also being initiated in Australia (CCSA 1996). These programs are being implemented along with other drug treatment programs, including a significant expansion of methadone maintenance and safe needle distribution.

The decisions to implement both safer injection rooms and heroin prescription studies were supported by the Australian Medical Association, which issued a statement to that effect in July 2000 (AAP Newsfeed 2000). Kerryn Phelps, the Association's president at the time, stated that 'we feel that the more options that are available to people who have problems of drug addiction, the better' (AAP Newsfeed 2000). She argued that it should be 'easier to get into a rehabilitation program than it is to score on the street' (AAP Newsfeed 2000).

Although they have widespread support and other safer injection rooms were planned in Canberra and Melbourne, the plans for safer injection rooms and heroin prescription trials were opposed by Prime Minister John Howard and the Federal Cabinet on the grounds that the rooms send the wrong message to young people. However, indications are that it was not so much a concern for what message was being sent as a concern over possible international sanctions that guided their opinion. In December 1999 the United Nations' International Narcotics Control Board (INCB) threatened an embargo against Australia's US$160 million poppy trade (which accounts for part of the world's legal supply of medical opiates) if the nation did not prevent state and city governments from proceeding with safer injection room trials.

Despite the warning of the INCB and the United States, and their subsequent failure to gain the approval of the Prime Minister, the cities have moved ahead with their plans for safer injection rooms. Since the establishment of the safer injection room in Sydney, it has been found that there are a number of social benefits. Arrests for heroin and other opiates is down from 11,223 in 1999–2000, before the establishment of the safer injection room, to 3,239 in 2001–2002 (Drug Enforcement Administration 2004). It is believed that since its establishment the safer injection room in Sydney helped prevent 2,000 drug-related deaths (UNODC 2008).

Canada

Similar to their counterparts in Australia, health experts in Canada are also calling for both safer injection rooms and heroin prescription trials (CCSA 1996). Health officials in Vancouver have recognized the need for safer injection rooms. The reasons in Canada are similar to those elsewhere: the failure of other programs. Vancouver is currently faced with the worst hepatitis C epidemic among needle users in the western world and has continually high rates of AIDS infection (Mickleburgh 2000: 17).

The health officer of the province of British Columbia, Dr Perry Kendall, stated: 'We have to stop looking at this as a criminal issue rather than a health issue' (Mickleburgh 2000: 16). Canadian health and drug policy experts pointed to the success Australia has had lowering the rate of hepatitis C infection with their harm reduction strategies (Mickleburgh 2000). It is approximated that there are currently 60,000 to 90,000 opiate addicts in Canada, and the spread of HIV has reached epidemic proportions (NAOMI 2008). It is further estimated that each opiate addict costs the Canadian criminal justice and health systems US$45,000 per year (NAOMI 2008).

The North American Opiate Maintenance Initiative (NAOMI), a group of researchers and clinicians, has implemented a pharmaceutical grade injectable heroin maintenance study in Vancouver and Montreal (Gartry et al. 2009). Data released from the study show that the illicit use of heroin by study participants dropped by approximately 70 per cent. The number of study participants and the time spent by participants in illegal activity also dropped notably. The amount of money spent on drugs decreased by 66 per cent, and the medical status of participants increased by 27 per cent. Furthermore, the heroin assisted treatment had higher retention rates than the methadone maintenance therapy (NAOMI 2008).

England

England, unlike the countries discussed above, made heroin and other drugs available through prescription in the early 1900s. Physicians in the UK, often through drug dependency clinics or community drug teams, prescribe oral methadone, injectable methadone, injectable heroin, am-phetamines, cocaine and other drugs (CCSA 1996; Economist 2000). Smokable drugs may also be prescribed in the Mersey region of England (CCSA 1996). Few British doctors exercise their privilege of prescribing heroin for addict maintenance (MacCoun and Reuter 1997: 23). Contrary to widespread claims, this program was already greatly curtailed before the heroin epidemic of the 1970s (Uchtenhagen *et al.* 1997). However, the practice of prescribing heroin to addicts is reportedly increasing, as a result of the success of heroin prescription elsewhere (Rogers 2000). A study released by the Royal College of Psychiatrists showed a 75 per cent drop in theft among addicts given prescribed heroin (Rogers 2000).

Portugal

In 2001 Portugal decriminalized all drugs including cocaine, heroin and marijuana. In 2007 Glenn Greenwald conducted an extensive research into the social and political consequences of Portugal's decriminalization, and concluded:

> ... decriminalization has had no adverse effect on drug usage rates in Portugal which, in numerous categories, are now among the lowest in the EU, particularly when compared with states with stringent criminalization regimes ... drug related pathologies – such as sexually transmitted diseases and deaths due to drug usage – have decreased dramatically (Greenwald 2009c: 11).

Politically, Greenwald concluded: 'Except for some far-right politicians, very few domestic political factions are agitating for a repeal of the 2001 law ... there is no real debate about whether drugs should once again be decriminalized' (Greenwald 2009c: 27).

Medical marijuana

That marijuana has beneficial medical purposes is no longer in question. The National Academy of Science's Institute of Medicine, a non-profit organization that provides health policy advice under a congressional charter, conducted an eighteen-month review of scientific literature on marijuana and concluded that marijuana can ease pain, nausea and severe weight loss associated with the AIDS virus. The institute also recommended further research into the use of marijuana in treating other ailments. The report noted the dangers of smoking marijuana – including lung damage and low-birth weight babies – and suggested that it should only be used if other therapies fail. However, the report noted that addiction was a relatively minor problem that was likely to affect only a few users (Altman 2000). A committee for the National Institutes of Health concurred with the National Academy of Sciences' conclusion that there is evidence that marijuana can be helpful in treating patients who have not responded well to other therapies (*Medical Industry Today* 2000).

The *New England Journal of Medicine*, the *Lancet*, and *New Scientist* have all noted the strong and persuasive evidence that marijuana works as medicine on a number of illnesses (Altman 2000). In 1997 the *New England*

Journal of Medicine called for an end to the federal ban on medical marijuana calling it 'misguided, heavy-handed and inhumane, based more on reflexive ideology and political correctness than compassion' (McMahon 1999: A1).

In April 2000 the University of Iowa's colleges of nursing and medicine sponsored a two-day conference aimed at aiding healthcare professionals and providers in obtaining and properly using medical marijuana (Altman 2000). The American Medical Association lent its support for the conference by awarding participating doctors with credits toward their continuing education (Altman 2000). In response to changing medical wisdom regarding the benefits of marijuana, a number of nations have experimented with various forms of decriminalization and/or legalization.

Despite the evidence for the effectiveness of medical marijuana, just as it has done with decriminalization, safer injection rooms and heroin prescription, the International Narcotics Control Board has held that permitting medical uses of marijuana sends the wrong message, and is a step down the road towards legalization (INCB 1999). The Board, however, has not yet to threaten sanctions against countries that adopt medical marijuana laws.

England

It has been estimated that in England there are at least 10,000 seriously ill patients illegally using marijuana to relieve their symptoms. GW Pharmaceuticals, which currently operates a legal marijuana farm in the UK, is conducting full-scale clinical trials on patients to have 'cannabis-based' medicine available for oral prescription within three or four years (*Economist* 2000). The GW Pharmaceuticals trials are designed to determine the efficacy of the drug to relieve acute pain and spasticity associated with multiple sclerosis and other neurological disorders without involving inhalation of smoke (*Medical Industry Today* 2000). If these trials receive the Medicines and Healthcare products Regulatory Agency (MHRA) approval, the British government is likely to change laws that currently ban the possession of cannabis-based prescription drugs but will not necessarily affect other marijuana laws (GW Pharmaceuticals 2009).

Even as England is moving towards the possible legalization of medical marijuana, due to the increased potency of skunk available on the street market, cannabis and resin were reclassified in January 2009 from class C drugs to class B drugs (Home Office 2009). Cannabis laws have been hardened even though there has been much support for the decriminalization of marijuana in the UK, and a report by the Police Foundation, a charity for law enforcement officers, stated that prohibition of marijuana 'produces more harm than it prevents' (Reid 2000: A26). Cannabis was reclassified as a class C drug from a class B drug in 2004, which lessened the penalties associated with possession, supplying, dealing, production and trafficking. This reclassification was reversed in January because of the increased potency of skunk available on street markets. The maximum penalty for possession of class B drugs is five years' imprisonment, and fourteen years imprisonment for supplying, dealing, production or trafficking, as compared to the lesser maximum penalty of five years for possession of class C drugs (Home Office 2009).

Canada

The initiative for medical marijuana has come from a different source in Canada, as compared to England and the United States. Jim Wakeford, an AIDS patient in Toronto, won the right to smoke marijuana as treatment from a Canadian court. However, after two of his caregivers were arrested attempting to buy marijuana on his behalf, Mr Wakeford returned to court in January 2000 to ask the federal government to supply him with the drug (Tyler 2000). Wakeford pointed out that marijuana obtained through the black market can carry contaminants that are potentially dangerous for patients with suppressed immune systems (Tyler 2000). On 6 April 2001 Canada's health minister introduced guidelines to make Canada the first country in the world with a government-regulated system for medical marijuana. The initiative came partially as a result of a court order in another case (Lee-Shanok and Gamble 2001). The guidelines increased the amount of marijuana a person can possess and grow for medical purposes, and allowed third parties to grow and supply marijuana to the ill if they pass government inspections (Lee-Shanok and Gamble 2001). Furthermore, in August 2003, following a July court ruling, Canada started distributing medical marijuana to eligible patients. These patients may obtain medical marijuana from Health Canada, grow it themselves, or 'designate someone else to grow it for them' (Health Canada 2009).

Medical marijuana in the United States

In the United States, more and more states have recognized the medical value of marijuana. Thirteen states have laws legalizing marijuana for medicinal purposes. Eight of these states enacted their medical marijuana laws through ballot measures. While the laws explicitly permit patients with specific diseases to smoke marijuana with a doctor's recommendation, the laws do not state how patients may obtain the marijuana, except by growing it themselves. Selling and giving away marijuana remains a federal crime.

In 1992, despite the medical opinions and state-level laws, the Drug Enforcement Administration refused to reclassify marijuana from Schedule I to Schedule II, a category classifying certain drugs as having 'currently accepted medical use in treatment' (*Medical Industry Today* 2000). As a consequence of the DEA's ruling, many doctors in states that permit doctors to recommend medical marijuana remain fearful of doing so (Altman 2000). In several states dispensaries were shut down and their operators arrested by federal authorities. However, a change in US policy towards medical marijuana was signaled in March 2009 when Eric Holder, United States Attorney General, announced that federal raids and prosecutions of medical marijuana distributors will no longer occur unless both state and federal laws are broken (Leinwand 2009).

General harm reduction: the Netherlands example

The Netherlands is arguably the foremost leader in the full adoption of the harm reduction approach into a prohibitionist framework. In 1976 the Netherlands passed the Revised Opium Act. This legislation laid the cornerstone for a shift in Dutch drug policy from prohibition and moral rejection to 'education, prevention, general "youth policy" and measures specifically targeted at drug users, such as social assistance and psycho-medical therapy' (Silvis 1996: 23). The Act, while formally a criminal law bill, was primarily sponsored by the Dutch Minister of Public Health, reflecting the notion in Dutch policy that drugs are a public health and welfare issue, and criminal law 'is of limited and secondary importance' (Silvis 1996: 34).

The Dutch approach followed the recommendations of two committees assigned to study the drug problem. Both the Hulsman Committee and the Baan Committee (formerly titled the Working Group on Narcotic Substances, the official Dutch government committee) were composed of scientists, social scientists, law enforcement officials, representatives of the ministries of justice and public health, and other government officials (Silvis 1996). The reasoning and conclusions of these committees were very similar to official drug policy committees in other countries in the 1960s and 1970s, such as the Advisory Committee on Drug Dependence in the USA (1968), the National Commission on Marihuana and Drug Abuse in Canada (1973), and the UK Commission of Inquiry into the Non-Medical Use of Drugs (1972). However, the Dutch government was unique in following the recommendations of its advisory committees. Both committees specifically rejected the use of law enforcement as the 'main answer' to the problem of illicit drugs. The Baan Committee suggested that penal law should exist in the context of 'general social drug policy' and recognized that certain forms of drug use could be tolerated. The committee further noted that social costs of criminalizing the use and 'other-than-wholesale' trade of marijuana would outweigh any possible benefits.

As MacCoun and Reuter (1997: 48, 51) have noted, the Netherlands policy of 'de jure prohibition and de facto legalization' of marijuana is designed to create a 'systematic application of discretion' aimed at harm reduction. They note that the intended benefits are 'to [avoid] excessive punishment of casual users [and] to [weaken] the linkage between soft- and hard-drug markets' (MacCoun and Reuter 1997: 49). Hence there is a significant difference between the 'law-on-the-books' and the 'law-in-action'. The Dutch Opium Act complies with the criminal nature of the international treaties, yet is primarily health related (Silvis 1996).

The relatively limited enforcement of the criminal drug laws stems from a recognition that heavy enforcement may reduce the visibility of the drug use and drug sales but may increase the harmful effects of the drug problem. As opposed to a 'legality' principle that formally requires the prosecution of any detected crime, the Dutch apply the principle of 'expediency', which allows discretionary powers to the police and prosecution (Silvis 1996).

The discretion of the police and prosecutors is limited, however, by officially published guidelines, produced by the prosecutors of the High Courts. The possession of illegal drugs for personal use, including marijuana, is subject to criminal punishment. However, in practice there is usually no punitive reaction at all. The punishments for trafficking, especially heroin and cocaine, are more severe. And, as the guidelines intend, the laws against trafficking are more uniformly enforced. However, the guidelines create an exception for marijuana, establishing a form of *de facto* decriminalization. The guidelines create an official agreement of 'non-intervention in the retail market of cannabis under certain circumstances' (Silvis 1996: 47). This practice depends upon the agreement of the police, prosecutor and mayor in each town or region.

Most towns have accepted the sale of marijuana in coffee shops, and some Dutch courts acknowledge that cannabis dealers in coffee shops should not be prosecuted provided they act in accordance with certain requirements. These requirements include not selling to minors, not promoting the business by advertisements, not selling large amounts, not selling other illegal drugs, not selling to foreigners, and not causing other public disturbances (Silvis 1996).

The guidelines establish an explicit preference for dealing with personal possession through medical or socio-medical approaches, and are supported by a strong network of drug-related social services. In many ways these services attempt to alleviate the negative effects created by the illegality of use, as opposed to the harmful effects of the drug use itself (Silvis 1996).

In a *Science* magazine article, MacCoun and Reuter (1997) compared numerous studies evaluating the results of Dutch drug policy with that of the United States and other countries with strict prohibitionist policies. They found that in the first seven years after the policy was instituted in 1976, there was little to no effect on usage rates. Usage rates among adolescents in the Netherlands, however, did increase from 1984 to 1996. Meanwhile, in the United States adolescent usage rates increased from

1976 to 1979, and then decreased until 1992, whereupon rates again began to rise steadily. Throughout the first two decades of the Dutch policy, usage rates in the Netherlands have remained at or below those of the United States. The authors note further that depenalization of marijuana in US states in the 1970s, as well as decriminalization of marijuana in Australia, and of all drugs in Spain and Italy, have had a 'similarly modest effect'. They hypothesized that the increase in use that occurred seven years after deregulation was a result of greater commercialization of the cannabis coffee shops, not of deregulation itself. Since 1992, usage rates have risen, but on parallel with the United States and most other wealthy western nations (MacCoun and Reuter 1997).

While the *de facto* decriminalization of marijuana has had no detectable influence on marijuana usage rates, it does appear to have significantly limited the connection between marijuana use and the use of other drugs. In the Netherlands, of those people aged twelve and over who have used marijuana, 22 per cent have also used cocaine. In the United States that figure is 33 per cent. Furthermore, while the Netherlands had an epidemic of heroin use in the early 1970s, there has been almost no recruitment of new heroin users since 1976. This data would suggest that Dutch policy might in fact have reduced the likelihood that marijuana users will try other drugs. Furthermore, there is no evidence to suggest that the Dutch policy has resulted in any increase in property crime or violence (MacCoun and Reuter 1997: 50).

Conclusion

Having surveyed the various 'harm reduction' policies of European nations we are left with two choices. On the one hand, if the creation of harm reduction strategies is in fact a violation of international law as prescribed in UN conventions, treaties and agreements, then we are faced with the apparent absurdity that states can only be 'law abiding' if they choose policies that cause greater rather than lesser harms. On the other hand, if the various harm reduction strategies adopted by 'rogue nations' are preferable to strict compliance with international law, we find ourselves confronting a kind of 'justified lawbreaking', in which our guide becomes not law, but harm. There is a possible third route. If harm reduction programs can be shown to be legally defensible by UN agreements on health and scientific research, then one could argue that the United States is in fact the 'rogue nation' because its policies of criminalizing drug use and trying to force this standpoint on other nations violates the intention of UN resolutions designed to improve the health of human populations. There is substantial evidence from harm reduction programs that suggests that this latter interpretation offers a potential pathway to rethinking policy. This rethinking, however, can only become reality if states, NGOs and state crime analysts, concerned with establishing harm reduction rather than crime control as the guiding beacon for the creation of international drug policy, come together to create a forceful social movement that can counter current laws so heavily weighted toward the US vision of the drug problem as a crime problem. Once this rethinking is accomplished, it will become clear that US policies promoting the criminalization of those who use or are addicted to drugs is the real state crime, not the policies that reduce harm by decriminalizing drugs.

Chapter 14

The globalization of transitional justice

Elizabeth Stanley

The growth of transitional justice has been dramatic. Over the last two decades in particular, there has been an escalation of domestic and international efforts to address past state crimes, conflict and repression, sometimes years after violations have occurred (Teitel 2000). Since the 1970s, practices – including international trials, domestic trials, truth commissions, reparations and lustration schemes (in which perpetrators are excluded from public employment) – have evolved to establish the accountability of individuals for previous harms. This global 'justice cascade' has been such that over the last three decades there have been almost 40 international courts and tribunals and over 35 truth commissions established to deal with the past (Sikkink and Walling 2006). Doing nothing, it seems, is not an option and this upward trajectory of truth and justice measures does not look set to reverse (Sikkink and Walling 2007).

The escalation and international 'success' of these measures is reflected in the way that transitional justice has been widely promoted by influential institutions and politically powerful states. The United Nations (2004) has firmly supported transitional justice measures and has condemned the use of blanket amnesties for perpetrators (Bell *et al.* 2007), and a number of states across North America, Europe and Australasia have begun to claim truth-telling, prosecutions and reconciliation measures as vital ingredients for conflict resolution (Leebaw 2008). There appears to be something of a 'feel-good' factor about transitional justice, and many international actors have wanted to support and be involved with such efforts. External or international funding for transitional justice initiatives has been relatively forthcoming,[1] despite the fact that the outcomes of transitional justice processes (in terms of highlighting truth, building peace, relieving trauma or encouraging reconciliation) are still unknown, assumed or contested. The issue, now, is not whether transitional justice should be done, but how (Nagy 2008).

This chapter assesses the role of internationals,[2] and their related norms and ideals, in the development and implementation of transitional justice mechanisms (specifically truth commissions and court processes) after state crimes. To this end, the chapter explores three points: (i) how knowledge and practice of transitional justice has been increasingly subject to global transfer; (ii) how western norms and values have begun to dominate the transitional justice landscape, and the impact of that domination; and (iii) how transitional justice mechanisms have been employed in ways that have secured the dominant position of powerful external states and their values.

In making these points, this chapter does not seek to minimize the role of local people, social conditions or structures in the development and practice of transitional justice. Domestic actors are centrally placed to develop, maintain or subvert transitional justice. However, internationals have increasingly taken a dominant role within institutions of truth and justice. Thus, it is this international participation that this chapter seeks to examine.

From the outset, it is also worth noting that internationals can work in inspiring, collaborative and inclusionary ways. They may provide vital independent assistance to troubled transitional states. Further, international norms and laws can be developed to recognize and benefit often overlooked victims of state crimes. For example, it seems likely that the recognition of rape as a crime against humanity would not have gained traction in most states around the world; the 'top-down' consolidation of relevant laws was vital to challenge discrimination and provide redress for victims of these violations. It is acknowledged, then, that some international actions can be valuable and supportive, and that local populations can also operate in discriminatory, disempowering or harmful ways. Notwithstanding these contradictions, this chapter exposes some real concerns about the general nature of international involvement in transitional states.

The global transfer of transitional justice knowledge and practice

The international support for transitional justice is reflected and consolidated through the development of a growing academic, policy and practitioner literature. Over the last decade, transitional justice has become a key focus for specialist research organizations and training courses. Perhaps the best known of the latter is the International Center for Transitional Justice's (ICTJ) 'essentials course'. Run within luxurious New York and Parisian surroundings, this course aims 'to equip busy professionals with the basic knowledge required to conceive and implement transitional justice policies and programs that are in line with international best practices'.[3] Similar toolkit provisions have also been developed by the United Nations. The *Rule of Law Tools for Post-Conflict States* have, since 2006, covered the topics of hybrid courts, reparations, prosecutions, truth commissions, legal systems and the justice sector. These tools, distributed across UN stations, 'can stand on [their] own' but they are also produced to fit 'into a coherent operational perspective' (UNHCR 2008: 5).

The global transfer of transitional justice knowledge and 'best practice' has therefore become increasingly common (Hayner 2001), so much so that 'transitional justice goals and methods' have become standardized (Lutz 2006: 333), 'institutionalized and mainstreamed' (McEvoy 2008: 16). Further, those who propel theories, debates and provisions often tend to be western scholars and practitioners (like this author), who temporarily engage with countries, rather than those who have grown up, lived and worked in 'resource-poor and war-torn societies' (Lundy and McGovern 2008: 275).

In some instances, this global transfer of knowledge and resources has brought significant benefits for local organizations working to deal with the past. International funding, for example, can enable local transitional justice workers to have some element of independence from government workers or powerful pressure groups (Cassel 1995). Moreover, coalition support can ensure that local workers are exposed to the accumulated international knowledge on transitional justice – those who have engaged in comparative problems elsewhere are able to exchange their ideas and enthusiasm with those tasked with the issues of dealing with previous violence (Hayner 2001).

However, the consolidation of institutionalized norms has also resulted in an increasingly formalized approach to transitional justice. Rather than reflecting the diversity of conflict resolution practices worldwide, transitional justice has come to represent a small, albeit growing, franchise of the criminal justice enterprise: a rolling out of official, centralized systems of control and conflict resolution. Under this framework, service positions to establish and run transitional justice initiatives – including police investigators, forensic investigators, prosecuting staff, defenders, judges, researchers, court administrators, translators and transcribers, truth commissioners, victim support personnel, security guards or prison guards[4] – have become increasingly common.

While transitional justice has brought a range of potential employment opportunities for internationals and local people alike, the formalization of transitional justice has enhanced the dominant involvement of internationals.[5] For example, many countries emerging from conflict may not have the legal capacity (in terms of personnel or legal knowledge) to undertake international law trials. Taking a prosecutions route, therefore, often ensures the requirement of international judges, lawyers, support staff, and so on. Similarly, the demands for truth commissions to get the numbers 'right' about the extent of violations, as discussed below, can also present a need to engage international analysts and IT professionals. In these circumstances, the involvement of external 'experts' becomes justified; indeed, it becomes a perceived necessity if transitional justice programs are to be undertaken 'correctly'. However, this formalization of transitional justice often means that local workers can be displaced and become dependent on internationals to take action.

Of course, there are plenty of international policy-makers and practitioners who are keen to offer their advice, knowledge and resources – across multiple states – and who enjoy substantial rewards for doing so, in terms of building their own social, cultural and economic capital.[6] The repercussions of this international involvement, in terms of how past state crimes are responded to and how transitional justice practices might entrench global power inequalities, form the focus for the rest of this chapter.

The dominance and consolidation of western norms

Internationals, particularly from North America and Europe, dominate the discourse of transitional justice. Offering advice on 'what works', they increasingly set the boundaries of discussion or the frames of reference about transitional justice. This dominance, and its impact, is discussed here with reference to two issues: first, the normalization of international legal norms, and second, the ascendancy of measuring and classificatory methods to deal with trauma and suffering.

Normalizing international legal norms

As highlighted previously, the set of transitional justice tools on offer has quickly become 'normalized' (Bell *et al.* 2007) and 'imposed' to provide pre-set western-acceptable standards of resolving 'conflict in a particular way' (Cunneen 2008: 295). One significant element of this standardization has been that transitional justice norms continually emphasize compliance with international legal norms (Nagy 2008). The privileging of legal knowledge, standards and practitioners makes sense: after all, law represents order, respectability and a sense of civility; as a means to deal with confusing, multi-layered conflicts, it is enticing (McEvoy 2008). During transitions from mass violence and unrest, ideas of 'objectivity, certainty, uniformity, universality, rationality', among others, are 'particularly prized' (McEvoy 2008: 20). Further, the use of law invokes the development of state institutions of policing, courts and prisons that are knowable and comfortable to internationals.

On closer inspection, however, the 'prize' of law is somewhat tarnished. One reason for this is that the law may not hold much legitimacy within populations that have previously suffered as a consequence of the decisions and practices of legal practitioners. In Timor-Leste, for example, law had been used over decades by the Indonesian regime to bolster their authority, quash opposition and violate rights. Timorese populations were afforded no protection from the law. Consequently, some local people have not viewed the law as the most plausible tool to deal with past state criminality (Stanley 2009a).[7] Similarly, others have not been enamoured with the idea that the law could provide accountability for previous state crime while police personnel continue to engage in human rights violations.

In such circumstances, the law may appear as an imposition to some local populations. This issue is intensified when internationally led legal practices take attention away from traditional, local customs and laws to deal with conflict. A number of authors (Cunneen 2008; Drumbl 2007; McEvoy 2008) have identified how the westernizing force of law has meant that other options – the 'bottom-up' initiatives – are quickly obscured, changed or de-legitimized.

Even local ventures can be undermined by international legal norms. For instance, the Rwandan genocide trials, operational over the last decade, have faced local challenge because they have given dominance to 'a Western legal system inherited from Rwanda's Belgian colonizers' (Longman 2006: 209). For many Rwandans, these processes – like the International Criminal Tribunal for Rwanda – have been out of reach, 'alienating' and unconnected to local reconciliatory endeavors (Longman 2006: 209). Similar critiques have even been directed to the use of *gacaca*, the traditional method of dispute resolution for minor crimes in Rwanda, to deal with previous crimes. As Waldorf (2006: 425) notes, this grassroots approach was subverted into a 'formal institution, intimately linked to the state apparatus of prosecutions and incarceration, and applying codified, rather than customary, law'. Hence, it was transformed from a local practice that dealt with issues of responsibility and restoration to a standardized institution that focused on guilt and retribution (Drumbl 2007). This transformation occurred for two main reasons: first, the Rwandan government wished to centralize transitional justice initiatives, as a means to build their own control at a local level, and second, *gacaca* did not correspond to donors' 'expectations of what justice normatively should be' (Drumbl 2007: 95) – in particular, *gacaca* could not tick the box of due process for international funders. Consequently, despite many international and local actors operating with the best of intentions, dominant western notions of justice continually undermined local feelings of ownership of, or inclusion in, these transitional mechanisms. In doing so, these initiatives lost the opportunity to promote true reconciliation between victims and perpetrators who continue to live alongside each other (Drumbl 2007).

Alongside the concerns of local participation and ownership, the centrality of international legal norms to transitional justice bodies has also led to other opportunities being lost. For instance, western legal norms – that focus on individual accountability, individual forms of suffering, as well as civil and political violations – have been critiqued on the basis that they do not offer opportunities to understand or challenge the social, institutional or structural bases of violations (Stanley 2009a). While an individualizing approach can be useful, in that it highlights which particular people were directly responsible for violations or which people were victimized, it can also be problematic or unhelpful.

Individualism feeds into the myth that the voices of individuals, through storytelling or court testimonies, will somehow be able to solve economic, social and political problems (Hamber 2006). It hides the structures of power in which state crimes take place and the causes of violations are regarded as exceptional deviations from 'normal' state/institutional behavior or from 'normal' international relations (Orford 2006). Thus, individualism tends to disregard economic, social or cultural violations that pervade lives across 'post-conflict' societies and shifts attention away from the international networks of power that nurture inequalities and state crimes. In addition, the focus on civil and political violations will invariably ignore other, frequently private, forms of violence (such as sexual violence or 'domestic' violence) that can increase in the move to more democratic situations (Nagy 2008).

A growing aspect of transitional justice, therefore, is how it takes attention away from other opportunities to understand, and deal with, violence and trauma. Local, potentially more suitable, actions to respond to harms are invariably overlooked while the dominance of international legal norms – that individualize complex social problems – also has the impact of relieving the beneficiaries of such systems from taking any corrective action. As Evans (1998: 16–17) details, these practices are 'convenient for those who most benefit' from existing structures; they undermine the opportunity to learn lessons about international levels of complicity in violations and can mean that the underlying causes of violations go unaddressed (Orford 2006).

In summary, modern legal practices are manipulated to fit diverse conditions, sometimes with 'ambivalent consequences' (Bell *et al.* 2007: 151). Moreover, the legal process impacts on how we talk about, or even envision, transitional justice. Dealing with the technicalities of complex legal arguments narrows the boundaries of what we see as 'transitional justice' (McEvoy 2008). Meanwhile, a host of ongoing issues – from how state crimes are structurally or institutionally propelled and sustained to what victims require in the wake of their violation – go unaddressed.

Classifying trauma and suffering

A further aspect of transitional justice measures that has become particularly entrenched is that of the measurement and classification of human rights violations. Transitional justice is increasingly positivistic and technological in its focus – the issue of how many people were killed, or injured, during conflict has become a central part of official programs. Offering clear, irrefutable facts on how many people have been directly affected can certainly expose the truth and challenge the denials of a previous regime, and subsequently many transitional justice mechanisms increasingly spend significant amounts of money and time trying to get the classifications, measurements and numbers right. These efforts, reflecting 'modern' approaches to understanding social issues, are often supported and enhanced by international donors and workers.

Indeed, a small international industry offering IT systems, data gatherers and analysts has emerged to support and undertake this work. For example, the non-profit Human Rights Data Analysis Group (HRDAG, operating under the Benetech company) has developed software, collection strategies and statistical techniques to measure atrocities and to map mortality figures. Working for truth commissions (including those in Ghana, Guatemala, Haiti, Sierra Leone, South Africa and Timor-Leste), the International Criminal Tribunal for the former Yugoslavia as well as non-governmental organizations, HRDAG has engaged in a range of services for transitional justice bodies including designing methodologies, building database systems, training data inputters, analysing statistics and providing on-site consultants. They offer 'complete technical solutions' to the issue of transitional justice data analysis.[8]

While highlighting the extent of suffering and trauma is an important aspect of much transitional justice work, the reliance on classifications and figures can be sanitizing, distracting and sometimes harmful. The issue of who is classified, and how – and who decides which kinds of harms are noted while others are omitted – can be particularly contentious. After all, the ability to classify, and to make decisions on how categories are formed, is a significant indicator of power (Cohen 1985). The capacity to place individuals into particular categories of experience can provide relief for victims but it can also silence them or force them into remedial action to gain some recognition.[9] The focused classification, for instance, on particular kinds of violations, which involve pre-defined acts, can mean that some victims are omitted from the count completely while others have to make their stories fit to ensure that they will be defined as a victim (Stanley 2001). It can also lead to situations in which victims sense that they are in a hierarchy of suffering, and have to compete against each other for recognition.

In addition, from an onlooker perspective, the focus on numbers, rather than the experience of violation, can sanitize suffering and cut out complex or difficult-to-hear experiences. As Taussig (2003: 88) highlights, 'numbers numb', they 'drain the meaning out of the stuff being numbered' and they 'flatten our understanding of the social world and the imagination that sustains it'. Violence is constructed as a medical, scientific or technological problem rather than a political, social or cultural problem (Taussig 2003).

The sustained approach to get the 'numbers right' may operate, therefore, to create artificial understandings about the nature of violence and suffering (Hamber 2006). Focused on mapping the extent of certain forms of violence during a particular period in history, transitional justice measures can fail to understand the continuation of conflict and harm in the present day. For instance, the South African Truth and Reconciliation Commission made a distinction between political and criminal violence, and mapped the extent of the former over 34 years (from 1960 to 1994). As Hamber (2006: 219) states, this created an 'artificial break'; the public focused on 'the *difference* between past and present violence . . . rather than the *continuities* and structural underpinnings of the cause of both "types" of violence'. The outcome was that South African institutions and groups became less likely to develop complex or dynamic ways of thinking about, and preventing, ongoing forms of violence (Hamber 2006). Thus, the institutional need to categorize violations meant that the nuances of criminal behavior and experience were missed.

The pragmatic solution of acknowledging the scale or extent of violence through the collation and analysis of hard data also presumes a certain, linear outcome – that providing irrefutable data *will* provoke change. Yet, the underpinnings of violence are frequently historical, social and political, and the collation of individual experience does not address those things (Hamber 2006). So, while the exposure of violation statistics may represent an 'end product' for transitional justice, and can signify a job 'well done', it will not necessarily lead to reconciliation, peace or even truth (Nagy 2008).

The technological problems faced by those mapping violations can also begin to dominate; professionals are so busy with getting the numbers right that they lose 'sight of what [or who] the measurements were for' (Taussig 2003: 86). At the same time, the costs and resources spent getting the figures right are not necessarily appreciated by victims of violations. In Timor-Leste, for example, many victims viewed violation statistics as a sideline to other effective transitional justice institutions, or to social and political change (Stanley 2009a). Besides, many Timorese victims have still not seen or heard about the CAVR[10] report despite its publication on the internet in 2005. While internationals can dwell on CAVR findings and the massive scale of loss in Timor-Leste, victims do not enjoy the same access to their nation's truths. In such circumstances, transitional justice is *'externalized'* as it ultimately resonates more with international audiences than local victims-survivors of state crime (Drumbl 2007: 128).

Transitional justice as a route to dominance

It seems that the ways in which transitional justice is done do not always reflect the interests of those who have been subject to human rights violations. Established boundaries, on how violations will be discussed or exposed, or how information is collated and processed, can regularly undermine attempts to understand the nature of complex forms of violence. These ideas are taken further in this section, which assesses how transitional justice mechanisms have been employed in ways that have secured the dominant position of powerful external states and their values. In particular, this section addresses three main concerns: first, the way in which internationals can appropriate transitional justice bodies for their own ends; second, how transitional justice bodies fail to address the role of powerful states and corporations in violations; and third, how the discourse and practice of transitional justice can be applied by international actors as a legitimizing cover for other harmful acts or omissions.

The appropriation of transitional justice

This chapter has already shown that internationals have taken an increasingly dominant role in transitional justice. This in itself does not have to be a 'bad' thing – some internationals can be vital additions to programs that deal with the past. However, it is all too evident that the dominance of internationals and the way in which they approach their work can undermine, exclude and harm local groups.

Certainly, internationals can work as if they are 'the experts' in the field while locals are reduced to being mere observers (Patrick 2001). This has been particularly apparent in Iraq. Here, local populations were excluded from transitional justice measures by the decision of the US-led Coalition Provisional Authority (CPA) to 'go it alone' (Stover *et al.* 2006). The resulting programs that included the removal of former Ba'ath members from authority positions (what was termed de-Ba'athification) were unsound from the outset. As Stover *et al.* (2006: 249) argue, 'The CPA never understood – or even listened to – the people it was seeking to help.' Ultimately, the 'expert' decisions of the CPA created new tensions and increased hostilities towards the regime; it further destabilized Iraq.

Even those transitional justice bodies that are created to increase local ownership can be affected by international dominance. In Timor-Leste, for example, the United Nations created a 'hybrid court' (the Special Panels for Serious Crimes) to bring serious human rights violators to account. On paper, the court offered significant opportunities to include local populations in transitional justice decision-making and practices. However, ultimately, it was operationalized to facilitate the exclusion of locals. For example, local populations were not consulted about the court's development, very few Timorese were employed by the court and, as a

223

consequence of poor communication strategies,[11] most Timorese did not know that the courts even existed (Stanley 2009a). Such modes of working, reflecting short-term administrative priorities – 'justified in the name of efficiency, professional expertise or simply "getting the job done"' (McEvoy 2008: 28) – underpinned local claims that internationals were more concerned with selling an image to the outside world, and facilitating their own professional and political ambitions, rather than with addressing local needs (Pouligny 2006). Without true local participation,[12] the legitimacy of these institutions is certainly brought into question (Stover *et al.* 2006).

Constructing political myths about conflict and violence

The exclusion of local populations from the establishment and practice of transitional justice measures will invariably mean that approaches to truth and justice hold less resonance for those they are meant to serve. However, this issue is also linked to how truths about the past are collated and represented. For example, most transitional justice bodies have failed to expose the transnational nature of human rights violations, and how external states are often directly involved in, or supportive of, violations. Truth commissions and trials tend to focus on human rights abuses as an internal, localized problem, such that 'the international community is absent from the scene of violence and suffering until it intervenes as a heroic savior' (Orford 2006: 862). In doing so, these mechanisms sideline the issue of how internationals create the conditions that lead to violence, conflict and unrest. In these situations, transitional justice is defined and managed by powerful states, and other powerful actors, for their own ends – to legitimize their own ideals, institutions or regimes (Leebaw 2008).

In this context, contemporary transitional justice programs embody new forms of victor's justice: highlighting the attempts of those who wield most power to sustain discourses about their own innocence, and conversely, to manage discourses about those who are cast as 'the perpetrators'. For instance, the ICTY refused to consider NATO violations during the bombing of Kosovo; the ICTR has been charged with covering up war crimes undertaken by the Rwandan Patriotic Front; and the jurisdiction of the ICC has been subverted by the 'opting out' of dominant states, including the US, Russia and China (Boraine 2006; Drumbl 2007; Nagy 2008). In short, transitional justice mechanisms tend to criminalize those state crimes that have occurred in, or involved, less powerful states. Through such circumnavigations, the role of powerful actors (or those whom they support) in violations is downplayed. Inevitably, for many onlookers, an idea is propelled that violence emerges in or by states that are 'troublesome', powerless and usually elsewhere.

This issue has been clearly illustrated in the recent establishment of the Iraqi Special Tribunal by the US administration. This tribunal held no jurisdiction to consider crimes committed by the US and their allies since the invasion (Bell *et al.* 2007). Consequently, there has been no 'justice' for the violations emanating from US-led actions in Iraq, from the illegality of the intervention itself to killings, torture, disappearances, the corruption of the 'oil for food' program or other violations (Boraine 2006; Nagy 2008). Moreover, transitional problems are cast as being Iraqi problems rather than the issues of 'occupation, insurgency, and the war on terror' (Nagy 2008: 280).

This concern of who is excluded from, and who is included in, investigations of violations, has also emerged within the work of truth commissions. Despite their opportunities to provide more complex, detailed truths about how violations emerged and were sustained, commissions have rarely questioned the role of outsiders in human rights violations. For example, commissions have failed to provide significant detail on the role of the US in Central and Latin America, or the other global political and economic networks that have underpinned violence elsewhere (Stanley 2009a).

Transitional justice institutions can, therefore, 'function to construct political myths, whether deliberately or inadvertently' (Leebaw 2008: 111). This is clearly an issue that powerful states are able to manipulate; however, it is also an aspect that provides space for other actors (such as businesses) to facilitate their own positive identities. Transitional justice mechanisms have similarly failed to consider how violations are often propped up by corporate actions. Thus, the Nuremberg trials did not examine the corporations who produced Zyklon B; the serious crimes process in Timor-Leste did not attend to the role of British Aerospace, or other companies, in providing military equipment and arms for Indonesian officials; the South African Truth and Reconciliation Commission glossed over the direct involvement of companies like Anglo-American Corporation (which is majority-owned by UK institutions) in repressive policies, particularly through their dismal health and safety protections and the suppression of trade unions; and the jurisdiction of the International Criminal Court will not apply to non-state parties, unless cases are referred to prosecutors by the Security Council.

The position of transitional justice bodies, in setting the boundaries on who is officially made responsible for violations, frequently allows external powerful players to disengage from testimonies of violations, and to distance themselves from the causes of violence. In this respect, transitional justice mechanisms are fit for global industry. Promoting truths within limits, they raise no challenge to the companies (and global, economic conditions and norms) that sustain forms of harm and violence for economic or political gain.

Transitional justice presents, therefore, an 'orthodox' response that keeps 'inside the circle of officially accepted and acceptable' responses to violations (Mathiesen 2004: 104). In this implementation of transitional justice bodies, there is just an *impression* that violations have been countered. While making no challenge to the structures of dominance and inequality in which state crimes flourish, the performance of transitional justice creates an appearance of the rule of law, justice and human rights. In doing so, transitional justice is not involved in 'problem solving . . . but people solving' as it focuses on addressing social consensus rather than social problems (Mackenzie and Green 2008: 151).

Transitional justice as a legitimizing discourse

The third point in this section relates to how the discourse and practice of transitional justice can be applied by internationals as a legitimizing cover for their other harmful acts and omissions. This can be clearly identified when we consider when transitional justice options are considered and supported. Transitional justice bodies have regularly been used as *'ex post facto* face-savers for the international community' in situations when the 'international community' has not offered any previous protection for civilians (Bell *et al.* 2007: 156). The failures of international actors to act decisively in situations of mass killings or genocide (from Cambodia to Rwanda to Timor-Leste) are retrospectively compensated through their support of trials or commissions. Thus, the discourse and practice of transitional justice can be a short cut for international actors to sustain a human rights dialogue without addressing the concerns of human rights support or protection.

Transitional justice presents, then, an opportunity for certain actors to co-opt, incorporate or pursue progressive values. The global language of transitional justice – that emphasizes human rights, accountability, reconciliation, individual healing, among other values – provides a degree of legitimacy for those who propose relevant bodies. The appropriation of the language of transitional justice is useful for states that want to market themselves in positive ways or wish to provide a 'cover' for other violating activities (Stanley 2008). In the case of Iraq, for example, Bell *et al.* (2007) contend that the US administration employed a transitional justice discourse to legitimize their broader, violating actions under a rubric of building peace and democratic values. The discourse of transitional justice – shaped by western values on transition, democratization and the rule of law – was useful to build the US identity as a progressive force, rather than an occupier. It operated to build the US's hegemonic status (Bell *et al.* 2007).

It appears that the discourse of transitional justice also performs as a significant ideological tool, to bolster legitimacy for interventions or harmful conduct. Related to this, it is perhaps of no surprise to see that transitional justice is now often employed as part of a longer 'checklist' of international interventions to attain peace, order, 'good governance' or security in 'troublesome' states. International interventions, to deal with 'failed states' or 'weak states' or states that are 'terrorist breeding grounds', have been dovetailed with transitional justice practices.[13] In this context, internationals may provoke justice but they may also 'be more willing to make compromises about justice' (Sriram 2004: 24) to fulfil other economic, strategic or political motives of state-building or social transformation. In other words, the discourse of transitional justice – like the 'totalising discourse' of human rights (Rajagopal 2008: 66) – can be employed as a 'way in' for internationals to pursue their other interests. Transitional justice is not politically neutral.

Of course, the issue of how internationals pursue wider programs of change also has repercussions for the success, or otherwise, of transitional justice bodies. In particular, how internationals participate in broader programs of reconstruction, or construction, of state institutions can have a major impact on the local population's sense of well-being and justice. If state-building measures are such that local people endure increasing violence, insecurity or poverty, then their perceptions of transitional justice will be downgraded (Stanley 2009a). This places a burden on those involved in transitional justice to question how their efforts actually impact on victims' lives, and how their work is connected to broader aspects of institutional[14] or redistributive change (Stanley 2009a).

In terms of these latter issues, internationals have considerable influence, not only in providing aid or development opportunities but also by structuring wider economic opportunities through reconstruction or state-building practices. Yet, international decision-making in terms of the economy has not always resulted in equitable or fair consequences for most of the world's population (Mackenzie 2006; Pogge 2002; Woods 2000). For example, the continued emphasis by international financial institutions on strategies of privatization, foreign investment and export production, has undermined rather than enhanced local capacities for sustainable development (Mani 2002). These global bodies can work in ways that embed economic frameworks that deepen structural inequalities further (see Whyte 2007a).

In such circumstances, when the discourse of transitional justice is articulated to provide a cover for further violence or inequalities, the whole value of democratization, the rule of law or other western norms is called into question. If transitional justice bodies are devalued (if there is a dissonance between the rhetoric and practice of rights and justice), then there may well be cynicism about the supposed benefits of transitional justice altogether (Bell *et al.* 2007; Boraine 2006). When transitional justice bodies fail, for example, to bring violators to account, local populations will undoubtedly critique the nature of the rule of law (Sikkink and Walling 2007). Similarly, when victims continue to struggle to acquire food, clean water or safe housing, they may well downgrade the value of official acknowledgements of previous suffering.

Conclusion

This chapter has highlighted some of the repercussions of a formalized transitional justice 'system' which has reflected and developed the norms and values of powerful states and mainstream international institutions. All too often, as detailed above, transitional justice has been applied in ways that hold little value for those they are meant to serve – they can be harmful, limiting, exclusionary and colonizing experiences. While giving the performance of justice, they can be operationalized to build further injustice.

International transitional justice workers can face multiple charges, such as:

- They have facilitated the expansion of the control and punishment industry.

- They have consolidated a professionalized, formalized, western legal approach to transitional justice that has paralysed 'ground-up' forms of dealing with violence or conflict, narrowed the 'truths' about violations, and created a dependency on internationals.

- They have ignored, excluded or silenced those populations they are meant to serve, thereby undermining the support for transitional justice among local populations.

- They have co-opted the discourse and practice of transitional justice for their own ends, such that transitional justice is established as a cover for wider strategies of dominance or power.

- They have focused on transitional justice to the exclusion of other preventative actions for human rights violations or other actions of social justice, development, aid or trade.

Clearly, many of these charges may well reflect the unanticipated consequences of international involvement. Yet these outcomes can mean that the whole idea of transitional justice – which does have the potential to be progressive and useful – is devalued.

To reiterate, this chapter does not argue that internationals should withdraw from transitional justice. Local populations regularly request external assistance to pursue truth and justice and this should not be dismissed. Nor does this chapter propose that local endeavors of transitional justice are always good or useful. In many states, for example, local practitioners of transitional justice will treat certain vulnerable groups – such as women – in problematic ways (for example, by treating female victims as outcasts for speaking publicly about their victimization or by continuing to propound violence against women to maintain order)

(Bell and O'Rourke 2007; Franke 2006). Local cultures and traditions of dealing with conflict are not necessarily wholesome or perfect. All those engaged in transitional justice need to be much more thoughtful about their own role as well as the nature of programs they pursue (Lutz 2006).

Nonetheless, it seems evident that internationals have to work in more collaborative and inclusionary ways with local populations in transitional states. This is vital if justice processes are to have a chance of relevance or success. The legitimacy of transitional justice bodies is dependent on the inclusion of local populations, and from the discussions above it seems that internationals could do far more to ensure locals may participate in, and have their aspirations and ideas reflected in, relevant initiatives. This may sometimes mean that local models of justice – which include traditional processes of dealing with crime and conflict at community levels – take prominence while western models – such as the use of individualized prosecutions or legal classifications – become less dominant.

When legal processes are pursued, there would also be value in internationals engaging in 'legal humility' (McEvoy 2008): to be clear about the limitations of law and to continually emphasize to local populations that legal processes will invariably be partial and limited in their scope. We know that law does not work well in developed states – consider, for instance, the low levels of prosecutions and convictions for rape in western jurisdictions – thus, the possibilities of law to deal with state crimes and repression must be measured and grounded (McEvoy 2008). Law can only provide one small element of transitional justice. Subsequently, transitional justice bodies cannot be operated in isolation from other initiatives of development, human rights and social justice. The success of transitional justice initiatives is dependent on and contextualized by other institutions, programs and interventions (Orentlicher 2007). Victims require 'multiple', culturally relevant 'pathways to justice' (Roht-Arriaza 2006: 8). This means that many institutions and groups (at grassroots, national and international levels) have to be motivated to build the diverse elements of justice.

Finally, at a time in which internationals continually demand accountability for state crimes and gross human rights violations, they have to be prepared for all of the consequences that this position entails (Cryer 2005a). Many victims in transitional states require assistance to deal with the violence and suffering they have endured, and internationals could do far more to provide resources and support to them. Similarly, if powerful states and mainstream international institutions wish to create a global human rights culture, they cannot continue to renege on the issue of preventing state crimes from occurring in the first instance, and nor should they take transitional justice as an opportunity to embed their own values or to pursue their own 'victories'.

Notes

1 This international funding and support is not always consistent and, despite 'grand statements to the contrary', potential donors can also act with complete 'indifference' towards truth and justice bodies (Schabas 2006: 23), particularly if such initiatives conflict with their strategic, political or economic interests.

2 Unless stated otherwise, 'internationals' refers to those working within the United Nations, international financial institutions or official representatives of external governments. These powerful bodies have 'developed their own internal cultures, discourses, rationalizations, and futures' that mean that workers are likely to perpetuate dominant policies and practices (Mackenzie 2006: 167).

   Still, internationals are capable of diverse action and they can work in contradictory ways – while alleged perpetrators may be pursued for arrest and prosecution by certain UN workers, they may also enjoy support and protection from external governments; similarly, workers within the same institution can work 'against' each other. Further, some internationals, and their traditions, will have more power than others. Western state actors, as well as western notions of justice and accountability, continue to have significant sway on transitional states. Given these dimensions, wherever possible, the chapter will highlight the role of particular actors within specific transitional sites.

3 From the ICTJ website: www.ictj.org/en/workshops/courses/index.html. To clarify, I do not denigrate the intentions, commitment or capabilities of these trainers and workers.

4 Some transitional justice bodies, such as the ICTR, the ICTY and the ICC, have formed their own exclusive detention units for the individuals sentenced under their courts.

5 Donor governments will also regularly bolster their own industries or professionals by supplying their own workers or equipment produced in their own countries (such as office furniture, trucks or IT equipment) – rather than providing 'cash without strings'.

6 In Timor-Leste, for example, dozens of international transitional justice workers enjoyed the opportunity to earn good salaries as well as build their careers through their professional experiences. These individuals often lived quite separate, much wealthier lives from the Timorese they were to serve. This latter idea also emerged during the recent film on the International Criminal Tribunal for the former Yugoslavia, *Carla's List*. In this film, legal prosecutors are shown catching personal jets, with their designer luggage, across Europe – ostensibly to place pressure on non-compliant politicians to release indicted individuals. The apparent decadence of this exercise, cast against the footage of desperate victims and their families, highlighted the chasm of experience and benefit between those who work for many transitional justice measures and those who are their subjects. This issue remains, regardless of the intentions and the commitment of those who intervene.

7 Alternatively, local populations can have high expectations that the law will make amends. As shown in Stanley (2009a), numerous victims of torture held hopes that the law would bring Indonesian perpetrators to account. The

subsequent failure of the courts to do this has increased concerns, among victims, about the motives of internationals who failed to prevent violations during Indonesian occupation and failed to secure accountability.

8 See their website at: www.hrdag.org/.

9 Within victims' attempts to be recognized, some victims will have more capacity (in terms of education, skills, legal knowledge, financial ability or media 'friendliness') than others to represent themselves and to attain acknowledgement or redress for their suffering. Conversely, some perpetrators are also more able to resist recognition or denigration than others. It is evident that those who tend to be prosecuted, placed before truth commissions or subject to lustration are those who have lost their status or those who have to renegotiate a new space for themselves under changed political conditions. For example, during the South African Truth and Reconciliation Commission, the vast majority of those who applied for amnesty were black; white officers did not feel the same need to renegotiate their position or comply with TRC proceedings.

10 The Commission for Reception, Truth and Reconciliation (CAVR is the Portuguese acronym that was commonly used).

11 Communications, including meetings and documentation, were often undertaken in English or were heavy in technical jargon. Such activities excluded local populations who were not fluent English speakers or those with limited education.

12 I say 'true local participation' as it is evident that some forms of local participation can also operate in exclusionary ways. Lundy and McGovern (2008) detail, for instance, that elite NGOs in Bosnia and Sri Lanka have operated to dominate the local landscape of those who claim to speak for victims. This issue can produce a 'fictitious view of local participation' (Lundy and McGovern 2008: 283) as some professionalized workers can take attention, and funding, away from other worthy projects. Local groups are certainly not exempt from marginalizing less powerful actors (such as women or children) from transitional justice.

13 As I have detailed elsewhere (Stanley 2009b), given the conditions in many contemporary transitional states, these issues are not easy. The most recent examples of countries emerging from a violent past – such as Sierra Leone, Cambodia, Timor-Leste, Guatemala, Afghanistan and Iraq – have marked a significant shift from the 'first generation' of transitional states such as Argentina or Chile (Lutz 2006). The latter examples marked transitions from dictatorships to civilian governance in countries with functioning state institutions; the former cases illustrate shifts from widespread, complex conflict to a situation of volatile peace. Further, in more recent cases, transitional justice workers have been faced with destroyed social and institutional infrastructure, and the prospect of dealing with thousands of victims, perpetrators and bystanders (Lutz 2006).

14 Boraine (2006) highlights that the reformation of institutions should be at the top of the 'transitional justice' list. If a transitional state does not make a challenge to the institutions (such as the police or army or legal services) that enabled or undertook violations, then it will be far less likely to move towards peace or conflict resolution, regardless of how successful transitional justice bodies are seen to be.

Chapter 15

The reason of state: theoretical inquiries and consequences for the criminology of state crime

Athanasios Chouliaras

Critical criminology, by adding meso- and macro-level analyses to the traditional micro-focus that has dominated criminological inquiry, brought to the surface new objects of inquiry: the state and its legislative production. The importance of this focus on the state is easily conceived insofar as the state possesses the 'monopoly of legitimized physical coercion' (Weber 2002: 43–4, 1056) or, from a different perspective, 'decides on the exception' (Schmitt 2005: 5). In that sense, the state performs a dual function: as the principal guarantor of human rights, materializing a promise to put an end to private vendetta; and as the most serious menace to human rights, reserving for itself the prerogative to suspend or even violate them. The pivotal role of the state not only in the regulation but also in the generation of crime is corroborated by the growing literature on state crime.

Generally speaking, it is a common belief among scholars that state crime presents two key features: organizational dimension and political nature. Although the former is sufficiently elaborated in the criminological literature, this is not the case with respect to the latter.[1] Nevertheless, I argue that it is the latter characteristic that provides the distinctive element of state crime when contrasted with other forms of organizational crime (for example corporate crime). It is this same aspect that facilitates an analysis of state crime in terms of both extraordinariness and banality. It is exactly the political perspective that lays the groundwork for the conception of state crime as an exception but also a reaffirmation of the rule.

In this context, the resort to political philosophy and especially to the theory of state proves to be indispensable.[2] The doctrine of *raison d'état* epitomizes a long intellectual effort to analyze politically the ambiguous role of state with respect to human rights. Accordingly, after presenting the above-mentioned doctrine as one of the most sophisticated attempts to explain in the higher level of abstraction the conditions under which state crime flourishes (aetiology), we consider its potential utility for the criminology of state crime.

The reason of state as an art of government

The elaboration on the doctrine of the reason of state has traditionally taken place within the field of political philosophy and political theory as they touch on the 'art of government' (Lazzeri and Reynié 1992: 9). Its importance becomes unquestionable for every discipline focusing on state, as it sketches the broader framework within which specific policies are designed, crime policy included.

It is now a widely shared tenet that this doctrine lays on the foundations of the modern state. In his course given at the *Collège de France* under the title *Sécurité, Territoire, Population*, Foucault accomplished one of the most innovative analyses in this perspective (Foucault 2004a). Faithful to his original intention to develop a genealogical analysis of power,[3] advanced as the most adequate method for the critical comprehension of the modern society, he employed the terms 'government' (*gouvernement*) and 'governmentality' (*gouvernementalité*), defined as the most general technology of power, in order to address the problem of state, but without limiting his analysis to the structure and function of the latter.[4] Foucault has repeatedly made clear that the target of his analysis is not institutions, theories or ideology, but practices (Foucault 1991: 75). What is more, the originality of his work consists in the perception of power in relational and not in ontological terms.[5] Consequently, de-institutionalization, de-functionalization and strategic analysis of power relations are the three conditions that ensure the necessary distance from the institution under examination in order to shed light on the technology of power standing behind it and conveyed by it (Séglard 1992: 120–3).

The concept of governmentality expresses three things: (a) a set of institutions, procedures, analyses, thoughts, calculations and tactics enabling the exercise of a particular form of power whose target is the population and whose means is the mechanism of security; (b) a tendency in the West, leading to the predominance of the technology of power called government[6] over earlier control strategies of sovereignty and discipline, which is also accompanied and supported by the development of specific apparatuses and a body of knowledge; (c) a procedure through which the state of justice of the middle ages became the administrative state of the fifteenth and sixteenth centuries (Foucault 2004a: 111–12).

In particular, Foucault describes how at the end of the sixteenth and the beginning of the seventeenth centuries a variety of factors were conducive to the rupture of the traditional – spiritual – way of government ('pastoral model') and led to the search for a new technique of exercising sovereignty ('political model').[7] A hallmark of this evolution was the emergence of a new type of government according to the reason of state. In general terms, this is strictly connected with the innovative idea that the sovereign, as the legitimized holder of power, should employ a technique in the exercise of government that derives from a new reasoning imposed by the state. That is due to the fact that emergent state claims a totally new duty, the performance of which nobody else bears: 'neither God in relation to the nature, nor the soul in relation to the body, nor the pastor or the father of family in relation to his flock or his children' (Foucault 2004a: 242). This new *modus operandi* in the public sphere cannot be constructed by reference to an already existing model, either from the side of God or of nature. The situation demands radical changes, given that a new entity comes into sight: the state, which inaugurates a novel, genuine dyad composed of the state and the population.

Foucault traces the first authentic formulation of the new government in the work of Botero – *Della Ragione di Stato* – who writes: 'the State is a solid domination over people' and the reason of state 'is the knowledge of the appropriate means for the foundation, conservation and expansion of this dominion' (Foucault 2004a: 243). Based on this and other similar definitions given by the theorists of the reason of state of that time (Bacon, Palazzo, Chemnitz), one could deduce its basic elements: (a) the reference is made exclusively to the state and not to the nature or the divine order; (b) it is articulated around the relationship of substance-knowledge – the reason of state is an art that encompasses a practical dimension of action (*modus operandi*) and a cognitive aspect enabling the performance of this action; (c) it has a preservative function, as it facilitates the detection of all the necessary actions and means for the maintenance – or restoration in case of rupture – of its integrity. Even when the enlargement or expansion of the state is mentioned, this should be captured in terms of perfecting the maintenance of the state (Foucault 2004a: 263).

Thus, the purpose of the reason of state is the survival of state *qua* state (Foucault 2004a: 264). There is no other further, ultimate objective that would offer an external criterion for that evaluation of its development. Using the terminology springing from systemic theory, it could be argued that the new theory is constructed as a closed auto-referral system capable of producing all the necessary elements for its maintenance and reproduction (*autopoiesis*) (Luhmann 1998: 54–9). Immediate consequences of this new perception of politics are the following: (a) total absence of the problem of origin, foundation or legitimacy of power; (b) total absence of any problem related to the end of history (Foucault 2004a: 265–6).

So, if the state is the regulatory idea of this ground-breaking governmental rationality, then the question that persists is, what is the state?

According to Foucault, this should be explained in two ways: (a) as a principle of intelligibility of the existing reality; and (b) as a strategic objective. The former means that the state offers the general scheme through which it is now possible for the first time to reflect on public affairs (*res publica*) taking into account the totality of the elements, practices and institutions that compose it (sovereign, territory, law, population, etc.). This is the new milieu of the politics. The second means that the state is the final outcome of this new way of reflection. It can be visualized as the tangible result of this intellectual activity; it is 'the end of the operation of rationalization of the art of government' (Foucault 2004a: 295–6). In other words, the state is the correlation of a specific form of government performed according to the reason of state.

Therefore, the reason of state is the rationalization of a practice that is conducted taking into consideration two factors: the state as it is and the state as it should be. The art of government aims at setting down principles and rules, the application of which would imbue the state as it stands (*sein*) with its ideal conception (*sollen*) (Foucault 2004b: 6). In this context, politics are coined as knowledge ('mathesis'), the rationale form of the art of government (Foucault 2004a: 295). On the other hand, the government according to the reason of state can be defined as a finalist multi-faceted action ensuring that the state will be rendered solid, permanent and, of course, mighty *vis-à-vis* every threat, internal or external (Foucault 2004b: 6).

This new way of reflecting on state, as something autonomous, leads to its conception not only in terms of specificity but also in terms of plurality. Since the state represents an end and a value *per se*, disconnected from any other external objective, there can only be a plurality of states. More particularly, there is a plethora of absolute units without interdependence and subordination that do not come under a wider structure, 'a form of universality', like the one embodied by the church or the Roman empire of the middle ages (Foucault 2004a: 298–300). The government, according to the reason of state, produces teleologically conflicting interests and competition among states in almost all the fields of state activity. As every state aspires to its own maintenance and enlargement, it seeks to dominate in the emerging domains of commerce, monetary circulation, colonial expansion, control of the open sea (as is the case of Spain). Within this framework, the concept of force emerges as the novel element of the political reason. The main objective of politics becomes the calculation and employment of forces, which at the same time introduces a dynamic perspective. The real problem of the new governmental rationality is not the maintenance of the state within a general order, but the reproduction of certain relations of power, namely the development of a 'dynamic of forces' (Foucault 2004a: 302–4). Naturally this bears implications in both the internal and the external performance of the organizational action of state.

Concerning the external manifestation of the state, governance according to the reason of state will lead to the auto-limitation of states. The mutual need to restrict the concurrence among them, within the perspective not only of the prevention of the reduction of their force – that could lead to their disappearance – but also of its enlargement, ultimately generated the structure of Europe. The Treaty of Westphalia (1648) is the legal expression of that necessity, as it codified the concurrence and relations among states. Three instruments were created for the assurance of the balance: war, conducted under the pretext of justice ('just war theory') and defined as 'the continuation of politics by other means' (von Clausewitz 1873), the systematic development of diplomacy through the establishment of permanent diplomatic delegations among states, and the creation of the institution of permanent armies. This politico-military complex, which brings about not only war but peace as well, becomes a central mechanism of security (Foucault 2004a: 304–13).

Internally, governance according to the reason of state finds its ideal mechanism of security in the police. During the seventeenth and eighteenth centuries the term 'police' is applied to express the totality of means through which the augmentation of the force of the state and the maintenance of order are pursued (Foucault 2004a: 320–2). In particular, policing the state focuses primarily on the quantity and activity of people forming the population of a state, their immediate, vital necessities, the issue of public health and the circulation of products and merchandises. Statistics become a basic instrument in this activity as they offer 'knowledge of the State over the State' (Foucault 2004a: 323).[8] In general terms, the main object of interest of the police is society, provided that it has become commonsense that individual activity is the constituent element of the force of state (Foucault 2004a: 330). Thus, the job of the police is the articulation and administration of techniques of power with a view to increasing the state's control over its inhabitants (urban regulation, good function of mercantilist system, effective exercise of the sovereign governmentality). It is important to stress that this policing function does not form part of the judicial power, insofar as these activities are not narrowly prescribed by the law. Instead, policing is better understood as the mechanism through which the sovereign state exercises governmentality. The fundamental role of policing the state within the wider context of concurrence of states in combination with the absence of a limited object for this internal activity offers the breeding ground for the emergence of the police state (Foucault 2004a: 326; 2004b: 8–9). In other words, 'the police is a permanent coup d'État' that follows its own rationality in disregard of any sense of legality (Foucault 2004a: 347).

This is why Foucault approaches the reason of state in terms of the theory of *coup d'état*, developed at the beginning of the seventeenth century. As he explains, the *coup d'état* is not the seizure of the state by a group at the expense of another group that possessed it until that moment; it is the suspension of law and legality. In that sense, the *coup d'état* does not represent a rupture with regard to the government according to the reason of state, but its potential manifestation/form of materialization. The latter is not by definition contrary to the provisions or dictates of the positive, moral, natural or divine law; nevertheless, if necessity indicates so, this may occur. In other words, when the application of law is not beneficial for the state, then the state is not obliged to follow it, in the name of its conservation and reproduction. Hence, the *coup d'état* is dramatic, immediate, without rules and in case of necessity an action of the state for its own sake. 'The coup d'État [should be defined] as the affirmation of the reason of State, as the auto-manifestation of the State' (Foucault 2004a: 267–8). Consequently, two are its constituting elements: necessity and violence (Foucault 2004a: 268–9).

Throughout the sixteenth and seventeenth centuries, alongside the formulation and manifestation of the reason of state as police state, there emerged a counteraction in the form of an incessant effort to limit the state *via* the cultivation and promotion of the 'juridical reason'. The theories of social contract and of natural law and natural rights were developed as a basis for constraining the new governmental rationality. Foucault explains that these theories of law can offer an external limit to the reason of state. This is due to the fact that they vindicate the existence of law – and of basic human rights – whose content is presumably set by nature and therefore can be claimed to have validity everywhere. In theory, whenever the government transgresses this law, the sovereign loses legitimacy and the subject peoples are released from their duty of obedience (Foucault 2004b: 9–12).[9]

The problematic of the reason of state in the political and juridical literature

Although it would be inaccurate to allege that there is only one version of the theory of the reason of state, all versions share some minimum common elements. The presentation of these will help to delineate the reason of state as a dynamic concept, developed and reformulated under different circumstances. At the same time, it will render obvious that the essence of the doctrine remains surprisingly valid in the present state of affairs. There are four basic precepts at the core of the reason of state: (a) the concept of necessity; (b) the predominance and furtherance of the state interest; (c) the potential violation of the moral and legal norms; and (d) the concept of secrets.

The concept of necessity constitutes one of the three key concepts applied by Machiavelli to build his interpretation of politics: '*virtù, fortuna, necessità*' (Friedrich 1957: 20; Meinecke 1983: 39). Of course, this frame is not coined randomly, but is based on a specific anthropological foundation (Lazzeri 1992: 95). It is composed of the ideas of ambition, envy and conflict. Machiavelli proposes a conflictual model of society and politics as causally linked with the inherent qualities of human nature (ambition and envy) (Lazzeri 1992: 97–8). Although such interpretations predate Machiavelli, his originality consists in the way that it is formulated: the conflict is not proposed as an exceptional situation but as a permanent one. Given that conflict is consubstantial to human relations, 'the necessity is everywhere and therefore nowhere in particular' (Lazzeri 1992: 104). In that sense, the concept of the enemy becomes universal (Lazzeri 1992: 105).

The predominance of state interest over every other personal or joint interest, and its furtherance, represent the ultimate objective of the new technique of government according to the reason of state. It is sufficient here to reiterate that the doctrine of the reason of state indicates the organizational requirements that should be met in order to ensure the maintenance and enlargement of the state. It is at this point that the crucial question concerning the compliance of means to be chosen with the dictates of moral and legal norms enters the equation. This issue encapsulates the entire problematic of the theory of reason of state (Lazzeri 1992: 93).

Meinecke, in his pioneering book on the history of the idea of the reason of state, starts with the observation that it constitutes the 'maxim of the political action' and the 'most profound and difficult concept of political necessity' (Meinecke 1983: 3–4). The action under the reason of state introduces a causal and simultaneously teleological connection between an end and a value: the furtherance of the state and national community interest as well as the affirmation and extension of its force. Regarding the means, they can be chosen unconditionally, without taking into account the dictates either of morality or of positive law, which could potentially also threaten the *status quo* (existing relations of power) (Meinecke 1983: 4–5). Meinecke summarized the problematic of the reason of state by using the contradiction between *'kratos'* and *'ethos'*, namely between political action guided by the desire of power and one guided by the imperatives of morality. In that sense, the reason of state is characterized by an enormous ambiguity and a profound rupture, given that one of its aspects appertain to the nature and the other to the spirit. The first aspect corresponds to political necessity and introduces the causal element, whereas the second answers to ethical imperatives and brings in the teleological element (Meinecke 1983: 6–8). Thus, the state interest is not only served when the maintenance and growth of its force is promoted, but even more when that is achieved in a way that satisfies the interests (necessities) of national community also: that is, through the promotion of some moral and legal norms. In the opposite case, there is a strategic contradiction between the means and the end (Meinecke 1983: 11–12). In that context, Meinecke observes that with respect to the end, the reason of state may serve the interests of both the state and national community (i.e. security), but the means used frequently infringe on morality or law (Meinecke 1983: 13).

In the same vein, Foucault observes that the government according to the reason of state is not necessarily violent in its ordinary operations, as it may function within the legal frame and through law. But when necessity demands so, it transforms into *coup d'état*, which is synonymous with violence: 'there is a necessity of the State that is superior to the law'. Politics is not inscribed within legality or a system of norms. Politics, even when it makes use of the legal system, is something that is connected to necessity; and necessity 'renders law mute'. Therefore, 'not government according to legality, but reason of State according to necessity' (Foucault 2004a: 268–9).

Friedrich, in the introductory chapter of his book, underlines that the problem of reason of state should be subsumed into the broader issue of 'politics and morals'. He posits:

> Only when there is a clash between the commands of an individual ethic of high normativity and the needs and requirements of organizations whose security and survival is at stake can the issue of the reason of state become real. For reason of state is nothing but the doctrine that whatever is required to insure the survival of the state must be done by the individuals responsible for it, no matter how repugnant such an act may be to them in their private capacity as decent and moral men. (1957: 4–5)

Adopting a political rather than a moral approach, he examines how the deeper thinkers of constitutionalism addressed the question: 'can you justify the violation of the law, when the survival of the legal order is at stake?' (Friedrich 1957: 14).

As far as the concept of secret is concerned, the literature appears unanimous that it forms part of the core of the reason of state. Bobbio observes that the use of secret constitutes the essence of the art of government (1999a: 352) and Chrétien-Goni that it actually marks its birth (1992: 135). The institution of *arcana imperii* (secrets of power) brings about a profound rupture between the sovereign and his subjects (Chrétien-Goni 1992: 137). It is created by the necessity to obscure 'the illegality of all sovereignty as *monopoly of violence*'. In that sense, the technique of secret and the process of decipherment that by definition accompanies it offer the foundations of political communication (Chrétien-Goni 1992: 142). Bobbio, on the other hand, analyzes the political institution of secret in relation with the authoritarian state and in contradiction to democracy (1999a, 1999b, 1985). The public and transparent exercise of power is one of the basic criteria used to draw the dividing line between the constitutional and the absolutist state (Bobbio 1985: 112). In the latter case the secret is the rule of political action, given that decisions are taken in a small isolated circle, away from the knowledge and control of the public (Bobbio 1985: 120). Contrarily, in the former the secret is the exception and is only justified likewise the exceptional measures in general, that is, for a limited time (Bobbio 1985: 111).[10] This is due to the fact that democracy is also defined as 'the governance of the public power in public' (Bobbio 1985: 108, 1999b: 339ff.). Hence, public in this case is synonymous with manifest, clear, visible, and contradicts with private, obscure, secret, invisible (Bobbio 1985: 108).

It goes without saying that the problematic of the reason of state subsumes to the broader debate on the relation between ethics and politics. What is more, even though political philosophy appears in ancient Greece,[11] this debate actually comes along with the creation of new entities, the territorial states, which, as explained above, constitute a principle of intelligibility of the existing reality and a strategic objective. Thus, the question concerning the due relation between the state, understood as the milieu *par excellence* of the political action, and Christian morality gets radicalized (Bobbio 1999c: 125–6). It is redundant to say that the question of morality (or later legality) of political action appears when the latter seems to contravene the former. It is in that case that they should be justified (Bobbio 1999c: 124). In this framework, one could distinguish generally two positions that correspond to the two main versions of reason of state: rigid and flexible.

According to the first version, which belongs to dualist theories, there are two types of actions: final actions that possess an intrinsic value, and instrumental actions that acquire a value by reference to an end endowed with an intrinsic value. In the first case, the criterion of judgment is internal, whereas in the second it is external, depending on their adequacy to achieve the end. Politics constitute the sphere of instrumental actions, while morality the sphere of final actions. They are two separate and independent spheres: morality is apolitical, politics is amoral. The basic principle of this version is that 'the end justifies the means', which originates from Chapter XVIII of *Prince* of Machiavelli. The ultimate end, of course, is no other than the maintenance of the state (Bobbio 1999c: 136–9).[12]

As far as the second version is concerned, which subscribes to the monist theories and represents a flexible monism, there is only one normative system: morality, which is accessible to human reason by revelation or through the observation of nature. The imperatives of morality are general and therefore not applicable to all cases. That is why every moral norm provides for its exception in concrete cases (for example, the rule 'do not kill' does not apply in the case of legitimate defence). Thus, the violation of the norm is justified by the exceptionality of the situation within which the sovereign has to act. In that case, the justification of the 'immoral' action is detected in the same normative system, which permits the suspension of the rule in exceptional cases. This second version was the privileged field of intellectual production of the theorists of the reason of state, who tried to save the principle of the unique moral code and, at the same time, offer to the sovereign a solid argument for the justification of his actions committed in violation of morality (state of necessity) (Bobbio 1999c: 129–31; Senellart 1992: 15ff.).

It is safe to say that the bulk of the literature on the reason of state was produced as a reaction or critique to the first, Machiavellian reason of state (Foucault 2004a: 250). This second version either contests openly the anthropological foundation of Machiavellian theory[13] or merely endeavors to conciliate politics with ethics.[14] This is not the place to provide a detailed account on that aspect. However, it is of major importance to describe briefly the way in which it was attempted to eliminate the possibilities of the eruption of the first version and to circumscribe the second. This brings us before a lengthy procedure that dates back to the end of the seventeenth century and lasts up to the present day, as it aspires to the limitation of the sovereign through its subjection to the rule of law.

The doctrine of the rule of law

I have already described how the government according to the reason of state during the sixteenth and seventeenth centuries, as it was deprived by a limited object, led to the emergence of the police state. Potentially unlimited in its function, this state could only be effectively confined internally and not externally (juridical reason). This is what started happening from the end of the eighteenth century and continued through the promotion of the thought of economists. As Foucault explains, the police state would be vehemently criticized by the latter in terms of efficiency and not of legitimacy. They would propose a new method of government in accordance with the principles of political economy, capable of ensuring the prosperity of the nation. More particularly, 'political economy' should be understood as a general reflection of the organization, distribution and limitation of public power in the society. Its gradual introduction to the governmental rationality provokes its auto-limitation and finally its transformation. The result of this process is the shift from the art of government according to the reason of state to the modern one inspired by the principles of liberalism (Foucault 2004b: 349ff.).

This internal refinement of the art of government would be guided by the developing economic reason, based on the principle that there is a new kind of naturality ('*naturalité*') immanent to the population and to human relations. The concept of a civil society would be forged in order to express a novel, tangible reality resulting from the human transaction and the creation of different interests within the population. In this context, civil society would be conceived as the necessary correlation of the state.[15] As Foucault eloquently observes, 'it is naturality that will be opposed to the artificiality of politics, of the reason of State, of the police' (Foucault 2004a: 357). This entails a radical change regarding the role of the state, which is now determined by its juxtaposition *vis-à-vis* civil society and not through an auto-referential procedure. From now on the former would be in charge of the management of the latter. This management should respect and guarantee the 'naturality of society', understood as sponta- neous, natural processes from which the latter arose. So, the new rationality of governmentality aims at the security of economic processes. But, at the same time, this state intervention should respect the liberty of individuals (Foucault 2004a: 356–81). In this line, the new imperative is not to govern too much ('*ne pas trop gouverner*') and the ideal form of government is the 'frugal government' (Foucault 2004b: 15).

One of the main issues is to express the limitation of governmental rationality in legal terms. This endeavor can be realized in two ways: axiomatic or revolutionary, and radical. The first, which consists in the development of the basic tenets of the traditional theory of public law, entails the legal definition of all rights considered inherent to the human nature (positivation of natural rights).[16] Departing from the concept of human rights, coined in bills of rights and constitutions, we finally arrive to the limitation of governmentality. The second, which is the innovative aspect of the new art of government, results from the introduction of the principle of utility into governmental action. In this case, the point of departure is the same governmental practice as has been developed historically and traditionally. The consideration of the possibilities and *de facto* limits of the government is a practical way to realize what is contradictory or absurd for a government to do or not to do (Foucault 2004b: 41–2).

These two parallel procedures bring forth two different concepts of law and freedom. In particular, in the revolutionary approach, the law is defined as the solemn expression of the general will. It is the statutory provision and regulation of the part of rights conceded to the power and the part reserved to the individuals. According to the radical approach, the law consolidates the division between a sphere of intervention of public power and a sphere of independence of individuals. Respectively, in the first case, freedom is defined as the exercise of some fundamental rights that cannot be derogated, whereas in the second, freedom is defined as the independence of civilians toward rulers (Foucault 2004b: 43).

Of course, these developments could not leave untouched the purpose of politics. If the predominance and service of state interest is the main characteristic of government according to the reason of state, now governmental rationality should take into consideration a variety of factors: individual and collective interests, social utility and economic profit, good function of the market. Thus, in this new complex environment, the government should aim at the management of different and in many cases conflicting interests. In this sense, the legitimate government should only intervene for the accommodation of all the above-mentioned interests (Foucault 2004b: 46–7).

If freedom is one of the key words of the liberal art of government, then security is another. The exercise of individual freedoms, and the free function of market, can only be legitimate as far as they do not represent a danger for the collective interest. In other words, the problem of security is strictly linked with the determination of the limits beyond which the exercise of individual freedoms can become detrimental for the public good. Therefore, at the very heart of the liberal art of government lies the search for equilibrium between freedom and security (Foucault 2004b: 67).

The reason of state nowadays: from emergency criminal law to a permanent state of exception

Keeping equilibrium between actual freedom and security proved to be a stimulating intellectual exercise; however, it was an unattainable objective in practice. Critical criminology and critical penal theory were always on the alert so as to spot authoritarian deviations on crime policy and to call for the respect of the rule of law or constitutional principles. It is safe to say that the security imperative has for the time being prevailed (Rothe and Muzzatti 2004; Welch 2006). The date 9/11 is a symbolic one, marking a paradigm shift from the democratic constitutional state to a permanent state of exception.

This change did not occur out of the blue. Its roots date back to the decade of the 1970s. Key words in this process are 'emergency or exceptional criminal law' (Ferrajoli 1984, 1995: 807ff.; Moccia 1997), 'authoritarianism' (Scraton 1987), 'new penology' (Feeley and Simon 1992, 1994) and 'criminal law of the foe' (Jakobs 2003; Krasmann 2007; Zaffaroni 2006). Although these concepts were coined in different cultural contexts, they address a common reality: the gradual shift from a crime policy designed to deal with crime as an integral part of everyday life to one developed under exceptional and alarmist conditions, given the alleged existence of a permanent state of necessity (emergency). In other words, we witness a process of normalization of exception, which presents two central aspects: (a) the target group is every time broader: individuals involved in terrorist or organized crime acts, the underclass, and the enemy, respectively; (b) the common denominator of all these penal models is the doctrine of the reason of state that prevails over the juridical model guaranteeing individual rights and civil liberties. Additional consequences of this process are the perversion of basic concepts and principles of criminal law (such as the principle of legality, presumption of innocence, principle of proportionality) and, of course, the curtailment of individual rights.

Agamben carried out the most abstract theoretical conceptualization of the existing state of affairs. Building on the work of Foucault, he focuses his investigation on the intersection between the juridical model and the biopolitical model (Agamben 2005a: 25). The basic investigation hypothesis is that nowadays the exception has become the rule; since it is the state that 'decides on the exception' (Schmitt 2005: 5), a new analysis of its structure is required (Agamben 2005a: 32).

The final outcome of this research is the outline of the reason of state in terms of a state of exception, which tends to appear as the dominant paradigm of government in contemporary politics (Agamben 2005b: 2). The basic characteristic of the latter is its indeterminacy:

> the state of exception is neither external nor internal to the judicial order, and the problem of defining it concerns precisely a threshold or a zone of indifference, where inside and outside do not exclude each other but rather blur with each other. The suspension of the norm does not mean its abolition, and the zone of anomie that it establishes is not (or at least claims not to be) unrelated to the juridical order. (Agamben 2005b: 23)[17]

In this context, the broader allegation that 'the state of exception appears as a threshold of indeterminacy between democracy and absolutism' (Agamben 2005b: 3) is completely understandable and justified.

The practice of extraordinary renditions and unlawful detentions (Amnesty International 2006b, 2006c, 2008; Sadat 2005), 'ghost detainees' and 'disappearances' (Human Rights Watch 2004a), systemic abuse and torture at Bagram Air Force base in Afghanistan (Human Rights Watch 2004b), at Abu Ghraib prison in Iraq (Human Rights Watch 2004c; Smeulers and Van Niekerk 2009) and at Guantánamo Bay in Cuba (Fletcher 2004; Maxwell and Watts 2007), the invasions of Afghanistan (Ferrajoli 2004a) and Iraq (Ferrajoli 2004b; Kramer and Michalowski 2005; Kramer et al. 2005), and so on, are distinguishing examples of this expanding zone of indifference or anomie. They are characteristic instances of suspension or distortion of every norm (national or international) and consequently they represent a clear breach of the judicial model, which nowadays pretends to have universal application. At the same time, it is important to note that the very people who commit these acts repeatedly declare their devotion to the judicial model, and they justify its suspension on the grounds of necessity (emergency). At the end of the day the only thing they achieve is the expansion of the category of the oxymoronic: the protection and expansion of the judicial model, based on the idea of rule of law and liberal democracy, is promoted through practices that in reality render both ideals moribund. Excessive use of force, lack of transparency, exceptionalism and actuarialism are the predominant traits of public action. The modern belligerent policies are presented as legal although they are materialized through the use of illegal means. The noble desire to deliver justice is monotonically reiterated, but stripped of any sense of fairness. Unfortunately, but logically, these are impossible equations. The protection of a narrowly defined state interest (national security) is the end that justifies all means. Secrecy tends to be a permanent condition in public affairs and when there is some flash of transparency one simply realizes the magnitude of the existing structural violence, anomie, and institutionalized impunity imposed by the cruellest version of the reason of state.

In this context, it is no exaggeration to conclude that the developing international criminal policy is moving steadily toward the creation of a global security law, constituent elements of which are an international criminal law deprived of the basic principles of (national) criminal law, extraordinarily strict police measures, military interventions, and intelligence agency actions. Although traditionally law and war represent two mutually exclusive extremes, today they are forced to coexist in harmony. The fight against crime is conducted more and more in terms of war (war on crime, drugs, terror), whereas wars, through a carefully applied phraseology ('police action', 'humanitarian intervention', 'proactive' and 'pre-emptive', consequently 'just'), are presented as justified/legitimized penal sanctions in periods where international humanitarian law is normatively impossible to be respected.

Institutional anomie leading to torture and killings, even when 'justified' as a means to a legitimized end – security – is still, and should remain, a state crime. Critical criminology has rejected an instrumental approach based on the principle that 'the end justifies the means' and has opted for an evaluative approach where 'the means determine the end', urging for the respect of the rule of law and accountability. Criminal policies based on the rigid version of the reason of state lead almost inevitably to state crime. The curtailment of civil liberties entails in the long run the resurrection of a police state. In this line, it is indispensable to rearticulate the issue of security in new terms: connected primarily with the protection of human rights and not exclusively with the preservation of the existing *status quo* (Baratta 2001). And critical criminology provides a sophisticated framework for this discussion.

Notes

1 In general terms, criminologists are totally conscious that 'the study of state criminality is by definition a political enterprise' (Barak 1991: 5). See also Ross (2003: 78ff.).

2 The use of political philosophy is a common practice in European criminology. See for example Melossi (1990), Swaaningen (1997).

3   For the definition of genealogy as anti-science, see Foucault (1997: 21ff.).

4   The term 'discipline' was applied in order to capture a different technology of power that includes the form-prison (Foucault 1975). 'Sovereignty' is the other idea recruited with the view to elaborate on a diverse technology of power that incorporates the form-law (Foucault 1997). These three technologies of power are not developing in a relation of substitution but they coexist, a fact that is proved by the development of a complex system of correlations among the juridical, disciplinary and security mechanisms (Foucault 2004a: 7–11).

5   Power is not a substance that derives from somewhere, but 'a set of mechanisms and procedures having the role or function and subject, even if they don't achieve it, to ensure exactly the power' (Foucault 2004a: 4). Concerning the methodology of Foucault in the study of government, see also the remarks of Séglard (1992: 117–25).

6   It is obvious that by government Foucault refers not so much to the political or administrative structures of the modern state as to the way in which the conduct of individuals or of groups might be directed (Foucault 2004a: 133).

7   These factors include the scientific revolution (Copernicus, Kepler, Galileo, Bacon, Descartes, Newton, etc.), the Reformation and the Counter-Reformation (Foucault 2004a: 233ff.; see also Pasquino 1992).

8   For an informative account on the role of social statistics in the new art of government, see Reynié (1992).

9   See also Foucault (1997), which examines the emergence of a critical, historical and political analysis of state, its institutions and mechanisms of power.

10 Generally, a secret is admissible only when it guarantees an interest protected by the Constitution without affecting other equally guaranteed interests (Bobbio 1999a: 368).

11 As Bobbio points out, since there is not only one morality, the political philosophy is developed with reference to the problem of the relation between good governance and bad governance, from which also arises the distinction between the king and the tyrant (Bobbio 1999c: 125; 1999d: 148ff.).

12 'And you have to understand this, that a prince, especially a new one, cannot observe all those things for which men are esteemed, being often forced, in order to maintain the state, to act contrary to faith, friendship, humanity, and religion. Therefore it is necessary for him to have a mind ready to turn itself accordingly as the winds and variations of fortune force it, yet, as I have said above, not to diverge from the good if he can avoid doing so, but, if compelled, then to know how to set about it' (Machiavelli 1505: 85).

13 This is the case of Guichardin (Lazzeri 1992: 109–11).

14 This is the case of Botero (utilitarian model), of the Spanish theologians (theological model), and Charron (innovative model) (Lazzeri 1992: 111ff.).

15 Bobbio begins his inquiry by defining civil society as 'the sphere of social relations not regulated by the State, which is conceived strictly and almost always in polemical terms, as the sum of apparatuses that exercise the coactive power in an organized social system' (Bobbio 1989: 39).

16 Assuming a retroactive approach, this revolutionary process can be perceived as the continuation of the effort of jurists to limit the reason of state during the sixteenth and seventeenth centuries (Foucault 2004b: 40–1).

17 The US prison at Guantánamo Bay is the perfect example (Agamben 2005b: 3–4).

Chapter 16

Epilogue: toward a public criminology of state crime

Ronald C. Kramer, Raymond Michalowski and William J. Chambliss

> The intellectual responsibility of the writer . . . as a moral agent is to . . . find out and tell the truth as best one can, about . . . matters of human significance to an audience that can do something about them.
>
> Noam Chomsky, *Powers and Prospects*

The chapters written for this volume have documented that state crimes are, by far, the most destructive of all crimes. War, the terror bombing of civilians, genocide, torture, imperial domination, structural violence, wrongful convictions and judicial errors, along with myriad other crimes of political power, fill the world daily with death and devastation, misery and want, far beyond the harms caused by common criminals who remain, to this day, the primary topic of inquiry among most criminologists. These chapters also document that the social control efforts by international legal bodies, bystander states or governments of offending states have been dismayingly inadequate when it comes to preventing or halting state crimes. In the Introduction we analyzed some of the reasons why the discipline of criminology has traditionally failed to address the issue of state crime and its control. In this concluding chapter we offer some reflections on the role that criminologists could play in preventing and controlling this destructive form of criminality and argue for what Bourdieu (2003) calls 'scholarship with commitment' that we hope can produce a *public criminology* of state crime.

For public criminology

In his impassioned plea for public sociology, Michael Burawoy (2007) argues that the discipline faces two fundamental questions: sociology for whom?, and: sociology for what? The field of criminology in general, and the criminology of state crime in particular, must answer the same two questions. Do we talk only to ourselves or do we reach out to address extra-academic audiences as well? Additionally, should we be concerned with the ends of society (reflexive knowledge), or only with the means to reach pre-given ends that are established by others (instrumental knowledge)?

Burawoy's call for public sociology proceeds from a fourfold conceptualization of the division of sociological labor. Professional sociology, the dominant form, consists of various research programs and theoretical frameworks that lead to accumulated bodies of knowledge. Critical sociology critiques the foundations of professional sociology while policy sociology works to service goals defined by specific clients. 'Public sociology', however, according to Burawoy (2007: 28), 'brings sociology into a conversation with publics, understood as people who are themselves involved in a conversation'. Following this conceptualization then, a public criminology of state crime must also engage audiences beyond small communities of academic scholars, and enter into dialectical conversations with public bodies such as the victims of state crimes (along with their supporters and allies), the international political community, including officials in international legal institutions (such as the International Criminal Court) as well as non-governmental organizations (NGOs), national social movements seeking to control the criminality of their own governments, state agents and their affiliates, and finally, broad public audiences through linkages with mass media organizations. The content of the conversations with these publics will be quite varied but should in some form be a dialogue about the moral and political implications of the findings and theoretical implications of state crime research developed by both critical and orthodox criminology. As Burawoy (2007: 34) notes, this 'reflexive knowledge . . . is concerned with a dialogue about ends' and should interrogate 'the value premises of society as well as our profession'. As we noted in the Introduction, interrogating these value premises transgresses the widely held illusion that genuine social science can only take place in a value-neutral environment. It is, however, a transgression that is long overdue, because without it state crime studies remain locked in, to use Jameson's (1975) term, a 'prison-house of language' constructed by the dominant legal order.

A public criminology of state crime can take several different forms. Again, following Burawoy's (2007: 28) analysis of public sociology, we can distinguish between *traditional* public criminology and *organic* public criminology. Traditional public criminology would seek to initiate a conversation, instigate a debate, or provoke a critical questioning within or between publics through the publication of books addressed to audiences outside the academy or opinion pieces in local and national newspapers that comment on important public issues. Traditional public criminology can work with or through various forms of media, involving what Barak (1995) calls 'newsmaking criminology', to 'expose' the underlying nature of crime problems and 'draw' connections between criminological analyses and public policies to control various forms of crime, especially state criminality. As Burawoy (2007: 28) points out concerning this type of public sociology (criminology), 'the publics being addressed are generally invisible in that they cannot be seen, thin in that they do not generate much internal interaction, and passive in that they do not constitute a movement or organization, and they are generally mainstream'. Most of the conversations that we who study state crime have with various publics can be characterized as traditional public criminology.

The other type of public criminology of state crime is what Burawoy (2007) calls organic public sociology. Criminologists who participate in organic public criminology work directly with specific groups, organizations, movements or state officials, engaging in a dialogue or a process of mutual education that may or may not lead to specific actions related to the prevention or control of state crime. Organic public criminology involves working in close connection with what Burawoy (2009: 28) describes as 'a visible, thick, active, local, and often counterpublic'. As noted above, these publics or counterpublics may include the victims of state crimes (along with their supporters and allies), members of the international political community, including officials in specific international legal institutions (such as the International Criminal Court), as well as non-governmental organizations (NGOs like Human Rights Watch or Amnesty International), social movements (for example for peace and social justice) and even state agents and their affiliates. Working directly with such publics, criminologists can share their research findings and theoretical analyses concerning state crime, help draw out the moral implications of their 'reflexive knowledge', participate in the crafting of political actions or policy choices and engage in further research on state crime by evaluating particular control policies or gathering additional evidence concerning specific criminal acts. Burawoy (2007: 28–9) argues that:

> The recognition of public sociology must extend to the organic kind, which often remains invisible and private and is often considered to be apart from our professional lives. The project of such public sociologies is to make visible the invisible, to make the private public, to validate these organic connections as part of our sociological life.

Given its track record with regard to the crimes of the powerful more generally, it is fair to ask whether the discipline of criminology is capable of developing a public criminology of state crime. In Chapter 1 and elsewhere we have analyzed why criminologists have generally failed to subject the moral and legal violations of states and corporations to the same level of critical scrutiny they give to other forms of criminal behavior (Michalowski and Kramer 2006, 2007; also see Tombs and Whyte 2003). Formal legalism, methodological individualism, an emphasis on ameliorating private crimes, the cultural dynamics of mass communication and the pro-systemic character of the criminological profession all combine to limit the attention of criminologists to state crimes (Michalowski 2009). Even when criminologists do focus on these crimes, they are still often guilty of what Cohen (2001) terms 'implicatory denial'. That is, despite their awareness of and even in some cases knowledge about atrocities such as aggressive war, genocide and torture, criminologists tend to ignore or evade their moral and political responsibility to engage in conversations with publics about these crimes and the suffering they induce. As Cohen (2001: 9) points out, 'knowledge itself is not an issue. The genuine challenge is doing the "right" thing with this knowledge.'

Doing the 'right' thing, however we define that, is really what a public criminology is all about. There is a rich history of intellectual resources and inspirations that criminology can call on in pursuit of this project. Criminology is closely related to the sociological tradition, a tradition characterized by repeated calls for the development of some form of 'emancipatory' project or public sociology. Marx's concept of praxis, understood as 'the synthesis of theory and practice' or 'theoretically informed action' (Appelbaum 1988: 43) provides one historic starting point. For the Frankfurt School 'critical theorists' the task of theory was practical, not just interpretive; that is, 'it should aim not just to bring about correct understanding, but to create social and political conditions more conducive to human flourishing than the present ones' (Finlayson 2005: 4). Feagin (2001: 8) has asserted that 'from the beginning there has been a robust "countersystem" tradition within US sociology – a tradition whose participants have intentionally undertaken research aimed at significantly reducing or eliminating social injustices'. In *The Sociological Imagination*, C. Wright Mills (1959: 187) famously called for the restoration of public sociology, stating: 'It is the political task of the social scientist ... continually to translate personal troubles into public issues, and public issues into the terms of their human meaning for a variety of individuals.' In the 1960s, 1970s and 1980s a variety of sociological approaches emerged to 'engage the world as a medium of critical analysis and change' (Seidman 2008: ix). More recently, Agger (2000: 259) has issued a call for the development of a *public sociology*, arguing that 'sociological writing must address major public issues, attempting to influence the public and policy'. And in his presidential address to the American Sociological Association in 2000, Feagin called for a critical public sociology that is committed to social justice (Feagin 2001; Feagin et al. 2009). Feagin and Vera (2001) have also championed the concept of a *liberation sociology* that is concerned with alleviating social oppressions and creating more just and equal societies. As they proclaim: 'The point of liberation sociology is not just to research the social world but to change it in the direction of democracy and social justice' (Feagin and Vera 2001: 1). Our point of departure in this chapter, Burawoy's call 'for a public sociology', was originally presented as his presidential address to the American Sociological Association in 2004, and it has touched off what he calls 'the public sociology wars' (Burawoy 2009). In the rest of this Epilogue we draw on various elements of this historical counter-system trend in sociology (Feagin *et al.* 2009) to encourage the development of a critical public criminology that is morally and politically engaged in public discussions and debates concerning the prevention and control of state crime.

In some limited ways, criminology has always been if not a public social science, at least a policy science (to use two of Burawoy's types). Criminological research is ameliorative in nature. That is, either explicitly or implicitly, most research in criminology is aimed not only at understanding crime as a behavioral phenomenon but toward helping to formulate policies to reduce crime as a social problem. Reflecting this goal, the American Society of Criminology recently created a new journal, *Criminology and Public Policy*, devoted specifically to inserting criminology in public policy debates. However, as we noted in the Introduction, most criminological policy work focuses only on conventional street crimes that tend to be socially constructed as 'crime problems' by moral entrepreneurs, politicians and the mass media (also see Beckett and Sasson 2004). And many of the policies generated by this work tend toward minor reforms in social institutions or, in the worst case, punitive sentencing and mass incarceration (Abramsky 2007; Gottschalk 2006). Since criminology tends to be individualistic in focus, the policy implications of orthodox criminological theory and research rarely concern eliminating social oppressions or creating more egalitarian societies, as does the work of liberation or public sociologists. Furthermore, as we have already pointed out, the illegal and socially harmful acts of economic and political elites are rarely analyzed or considered in any policy debates within orthodox criminology.

Some criminological perspectives and traditions do practice a form of public criminology and contribute to the development of an emancipatory project. The radical or critical criminology perspective in general constitutes one such effort (Lynch and Michalowski 2005; Michalowski 1985; Pfohl 1994). Particular mention should be made of Chambliss' (2000) sweeping indictment of conventional crime policy, Quinney's (2000) effort to 'bear witness to crime and social justice' and Currie's (1998) attempt to promote alternative social policies to deal with crime. Pepinsky and Quinney's (1991) 'criminology as peacemaking' perspective also deserves special mention, as does the work of Braithwaite (2002) and Sullivan and Tifft (2006) on restorative justice practices. Criminologists who do research

251

on state crime also need to take seriously the idea of a public criminology and attempt to develop the broader implications of their work in an effort to change social structures and reduce human suffering. As Michalowski and Kramer (2006: ix) have pointed out:

> But whenever we turn grave wrongs such as the Nazi Holocaust, the death and destruction of the Iraq war, or the loss of loved ones due to preventable occupational or consumer hazards into scholarly narratives, we risk rendering bloody events bloodless, transforming tears and anguish into sterile words, turning painful events into detached prose. So at the outset we want to remember that this book is about suffering, about those who suffered, and those who wronged them in their quest for political dominance or economic gain. It is our hope that by remembering and writing about these events we can contribute in some small way to a rethinking and restructuring of legal systems that presently devote far more effort to punishing the petty crimes of the poor than to the great crimes of the powerful and to transforming social systems that are presently all too willing to sacrifice the well-being of many for the private profit and political advantage of the few.

How, specifically, then should we proceed? How can the outstanding theory and research on state crime exemplified in this book and in the work of other scholars on the topic, and the awareness of and knowledge about atrocities and suffering we gain from this scholarship, be translated into conversations with publics that can assist in the prevention and social control of these destructive crimes and reduce the amount of human suffering they cause? We discuss two broad approaches. One concerns disrupting the denial and negating the normalization of state crimes. The other approach focuses on the interrelated issues of individual accountability, transitional/restorative justice and primary prevention.

Disrupting denial and negating normalization

In *States of Denial* (2001), Stanley Cohen demonstrates how individuals, organizations, publics, political cultures and governments, whether victims, perpetrators or observers, frequently incorporate statements of denial into their social definitions, beliefs, knowledge and practices in such a way that atrocities and suffering, such as those related to state crimes, are not acknowledged or acted upon. According to Cohen (2001: 51), denial 'refers to the maintenance of social worlds in which an undesirable situation (event, condition, phenomenon) is unrecognized, ignored or made to seem normal'. He identifies three categories of denials: literal, interpretive and implicatory. A literal denial is: 'the assertion that something did not happen or is not true'. With an interpretive denial, the basic facts are not denied; however, 'they are given a different meaning from what seems apparent to others'. As part of his analysis of interpretive denial Cohen draws on the important work of criminologists Sykes and Matza (1957) and their delineation of 'techniques of neutraliz-ation'. Finally, the notion of implicatory denial 'covers the multitude of vocabularies – justifications, rationalizations, evasions – that we use to deal with our awareness of so many images of unmitigated suffering'. Here, as we noted above, 'knowledge itself is not an issue. The genuine challenge is doing the "right" thing with this knowledge' (Cohen 2001: 7–9).

There are many examples of literal denial with regard to state crimes. Cohen (2001) frequently cites the historical denials of successive Turkish governments concerning the genocidal massacres of Armenian civilians at the hands of the Turkish army between 1915 and 1917. It is well documented that at least a million Armenians were killed directly or through starvation and deportation in these years. But Turkish govern-ments have for 80 years denied that these events took place (Cohen 2001). Another example of literal denial concerning a state crime can be found in the statements of the American government following the dropping of atomic bombs on Japan in 1945. As Lifton and Mitchell point out in *Hiroshima in America: Fifty Years of Denial* (1995), President Truman called Hiroshima, a city of 350,000 people, an 'important Japanese Army base' in his initial statement concerning the bombing, falsely implying that it was a legal military target during a time of war. US officials also later repeatedly denied and censured reports that Japanese citizens in Hiroshima and Nagasaki were getting sick and dying from exposure to radiation from the atomic bombs (Lifton and Mitchell 1995). More contemporary instances of literal denial related to state crimes are former President George W. Bush's insistence that the United States 'does not torture' (Welch 2009), and claims by supporters of the Sudanese govern-ment that the number of deaths in the Darfur region of Sudan did not rise to the level of the crime of genocide (Hagan *et al.* 2005; McCarthy and Hagan 2009).

Interpretive denial probably occurs more often than literal denial. State agents and their supporters admit that something happened, perhaps some harm occurred, but the event or the harm is socially and morally framed in such a way as to deny the state's responsibility or culpability. A narrative emerges that justifies the event and the harm that may have occurred, shifting the blame to the victims themselves or to some other party. Kramer analyzes a classic case of interpretive denial in Chapter 8 by showing how the official narrative of the atomic bombings of Japan justified the attacks on Hiroshima and Nagasaki by falsely claiming it was a military necessity that saved more lives than it killed and by shifting the responsibility for the devastation that occurred to the Japanese themselves. And as Iadicola points out in Chapter 3, crimes of empire are usually justified through some form of interpretive denial that works to make deliberate, wrongful state actions appear acceptable or unavoidable.

Cohen also observes that denial, in all its forms, is closely linked to the phenomenon of normalization. State atrocities and other deviant acts can, over time, come to be socially defined as normal and acceptable to individuals and societies. Normalization, he notes (2001: 188):

> ... suggests that facts and images once seen as unusual, unpleasant, or even intolerable eventually become accepted as normal. The sheer accretion of images leads not to a shutter mechanism, but to a change in beliefs, emotions and perceptions. What was once seen as disturbing and anomalous – a sense that things are not as they should be – now becomes normal, and even tolerable.

Many of the chapters in this book, and the more general literature on state crime, suggest that literal denial, interpretive denial and normalization are pervasive features of this form of criminality.

Criminologists and other scholars who present research evidence to document the state crimes in question and dispute literal denials, or who challenge the narratives of interpretive denial and the often-resulting normalization of deviance with empirically grounded theoretical counter-narratives, are engaging in a form of public criminology. They are entering into a conversation with various publics that may impact whether or not these acts will be socially defined as crimes and become suitable targets for prevention and control efforts. And, when they disrupt denials or negate normalization in their role as public criminologists they are participating as 'claims-makers' in the aforementioned process of the social construction of crime as a social problem to be addressed by society.

All social problems begin first as social constructions, and second as social movements that seek to resolve the problems that have been socially constructed (Best 2008; Blumer 1971; Spector and Kitsuse 1977). A critical first step in constructing social harms as either acceptable costs of doing business or as social problems that can and should be controlled by law is the creation of a conceptual framework, an image, of the harm (Best 1989; Pfohl 1994). In the arena of state crimes a number of social actors play important roles in the struggle over whether harms caused by state power exist at all (literal denial), and if they do exist can be interpreted as laudable (as in the case of wartime victories over the bodies and geography of the enemy), sad but tolerable or normal and acceptable (as in the imprisonment of hundreds of thousands for their crimes or the waging of imperial wars), or wrongful and intolerable (the Holocaust, and the genocidal programs in Rwanda and the former Yugoslavia). Thus, the effort to define the nature of state harms as social problems often involves disrupting the states of denial and normalization of deviance sought by the state.

Currently, the actors involved in these definitional struggles consist of four sometimes overlapping groups. First are state agents and affiliated opinion-makers that enjoy the highest political platforms when it comes to establishing the meaning of state action. This is particularly true not only because the statements of state agents and affiliates usually enjoy a degree of pre-established legitimacy in most states, but because they also exert the greatest control over and/or access to the technological means of communication. Therefore, when the Turkish government denies the genocide of the Armenians, Sudanese officials dispute the number of or responsibility for those killed in Darfur, American leaders justify the atomic bombings of Japan, the Bush administration denies torture in Iraq or at Guantánamo, or state agents in any imperial power create myths of morality to cover the crimes of empire, these communicative acts carry great weight in the claims-making process and significantly shape the social construction of the social problem of state crime.

The second group involved in this definitional struggle consists of the victims of these crimes and their supporters and allies. Victims' voices, if and when they can be heard, often carry their own legitimacy as embodied manifestations of the pain inflicted by states. But the voices of the Armenians, the Darfurians, the Japanese, the Iraqis, the Islamic terror suspects, and all those who are victimized by the crimes of states and empires are often suppressed or drowned out by official government narratives, and their claims and suffering are left unacknowledged. Even if heard, victims are often reduced to abstractions and statistics that do little to motivate sympathy or action.

The third important claims-making group, particularly under the human rights regime that emerged after World War Two (Glendon 2002), is the international political community comprising international justice organizations such as the United Nations and the International Criminal Court, and the many non-governmental organizations (NGOs) seeking to limit specific forms of state crimes. From the Nuremberg trials to the Geneva Conventions to the International Court of Justice at the Hague; from the involvement of concerned bystander states and the declarations of Human Rights Watch and Amnesty International, the loosely coupled international political community has played an important role in giving voice to victims, documenting the nature of state crimes, and creating a demand, and at times a legal process, for accountability. Throughout the post-World War Two era, the amorphous international political community has become ever more distinct, and has come to play an ever more important role in the definitional struggle over the social problem of state criminality.

Finally, we have criminologists, political scientists and other academic scholars and public intellectuals, whose voices can in some cases help legitimize state harms, and in other cases contribute to problematizing and controlling these harms. Our view of a public criminology of state crime obviously favors the latter role. When acting as public criminologists, scholars and intellectuals should enter into conversations with various publics, drawing out the moral and political implications of our theory, research and critiques. We can disrupt denial by challenging and documenting genocide, torture and other war crimes that states attempt to justify or excuse as analysts such as Cohen (2001), Hagan *et al.* (2005), Kramer and Michalowski (2005), Mullins and Rothe (2008) and Welch (2009) have done. We can negate normalization by offering counternarratives through our analytical and theoretical work as Lifton and Mitchell (1995), Vaughan (1996), Iadicola (this volume) and Kramer (this volume) have attempted to do. We must recognize and squarely face the implications of the fact that by entering into these conversations we become claims-makers ourselves and thus participants in the definitional struggle over the social construction of state crimes as social problems. There are problems and pitfalls to this form of engagement that arise from the elusiveness of consensus among scholars, the power of the state to attack and dismiss our work, the uncertainty of fair and balanced coverage by the mainstream media of the positions we advocate (McCarthy and Hagan 2009), and the professional risks for scholars who depend on university employment for their own financial well-being.

Despite these difficulties, we nevertheless encourage our colleagues to take on the role of a public criminologist. Whether we act as traditional public criminologists and seek to influence publics through our books, newspaper op-ed columns and media appearances, or we work directly with victims, social movement groups, international justice organizations, NGOs or government agencies as organic public criminologists, we can use our criminological knowledge and intellectual skills to disrupt denial, negate normalization, and help define certain harms as state crimes and legitimate targets for social control efforts.

Accountability, transitional justice, and prevention

The second broad approach we can take as public criminologists of state crime is to enter into conversations with the right audiences concerning specific social control or prevention efforts. In these conversations we can offer to share our research findings and theoretical narratives, our methodological and interpretive skills, with others who are struggling to react to or reduce the harms that flow from state criminality. We may be able to use our criminological knowledge and intellectual tools to advocate for or help construct policies related to individual accountability for state crimes, transitional justice responses to such crimes, or broad-based structural efforts to prevent these acts, the most destructive of all forms of crime, from occurring in the first place.

State officials, acting on behalf of the state, have generally been free to engage in illegal and socially harmful behavior throughout history due to political impunity and legal immunity. In contrast to ordinary powerless street criminals, powerful state and corporate offenders have mostly been immune to criminal prosecution and penalties. As Welch (2009: 4) observes: 'It is because of these states of impunity that crimes of power appear to have few bounds.' Not only are state officials covered by 'states of impunity', they have, until relatively recently, also been covered by a specific legal immunity from prosecution, particularly if they acted as heads of state. Prior to the twentieth century, a number of legal precedents in domestic courts, as well as specific legislative acts in various countries, granted absolute immunity for the official acts of sovereign foreign states. As Sands (2005: 27) points out, it was widely believed at the time that 'Immunity was necessary "to preserve the peace and harmony of nations", and that objective trumped all other values.'

Throughout the twentieth century, however, due to developments in public international law, particularly after World War Two, both political impunity and legal immunity for the criminal acts of state officials began to erode. The first significant move toward accountability for state crimes came with the creation of the international military tribunals at Nuremberg and Tokyo and the subsequent trials of German and Japanese war criminals. The prosecution and punishment of these state officials, even though tainted to some degree by the charge of victor's justice, established an important precedent for holding future political and military leaders accountable for crimes against peace, crimes against humanity and war crimes.

It is important to note that a well-known American criminologist, Sheldon Glueck, acted as a public criminologist concerning the issue of war crimes and the prosecution of Nazi war criminals at Nuremberg. Glueck was a criminologist and professor of law at Harvard University before and after World War Two. He is best known among criminologists for the pioneering work on the causes of juvenile delinquency done by him and his wife, Eleanor, that served as the foundation of what is today known as developmental criminology. What has been lost to criminological consciousness is that in the 1940s Sheldon Glueck, in the role of a traditional public criminologist, taught a graduate seminar and published a number of books and articles on war criminals, aggressive war and the Nuremberg trials (see Glueck 1943a, 1943b, 1944, 1946). In addition, Hagan and Greer (2002: 234–5) have recently restored Glueck's work as an organic public criminologist to criminological memory, noting that he 'also played a major public and private role in establishing the legal foundations for the Nuremberg trials'. For contemporary public criminologists who analyze state crime in the hope of reducing its occurrence, it is important to remember that our concern reaches back to one of the founders of modern criminology who played a central role in developing the legal strategy for the prosecution of Nazi war criminals and implementing that strategy during the Nuremberg trials (Jackson 1946).

Another significant event after World War Two that would eventually contribute to the erosion of political impunity and legal immunity for state crimes was the creation of the United Nations. The UN Charter, which would codify important aspects of international law, the creation of the Security Council, and the development of the International Court of Justice (World Court), imperfect as they were and distorted often by Cold War politics, all represented a step in the direction of greater accountability for states and their leaders with regard to violations of international law. At the very least, when combined with the four Geneva Conventions of 1949 and other post-war legal efforts, a vision of a new liberal, rules-based international system was placed before the international political community (Sands 2005). Despite Sheldon Glueck's contributions in this area, however, few criminologists followed his lead at that time, although other scholars and public intellectuals did occasionally focus on the issue of state crime and its control.

As Friedrichs points out in Chapter 5, following Chambliss' presidential address on state-organized crime to the American Society of Criminology in 1988 criminological interest in state criminality began to build. At the same time, following the end of the Cold War, the international political community began to make new efforts to hold state officials accountable for their crimes. International military tribunals for Rwanda and the former Yugoslavia were created and the momentum for a new International Criminal Court began to build (Rothe 2009; Rothe and Mullins 2006; Sands 2005). As Sands (2005: 13) points out, these new efforts toward accountability for state criminals were only possible because the new post-World War Two international legal rules 'provided a framework for judging individual behavior and government acts and, in theory at least, an end to impunity. It could no longer be said that international law allowed such atrocities.'

In 1998 Augusto Pinochet, the former Chilean dictator, was arrested in London on charges of genocide and torture issued by a Spanish magistrate. After a series of legal maneuvers and hearings, the Judicial Committee of the House of Lords, Britain's highest court, decided that while there was precedent for legal immunity for acts committed as a head of state, the 1984 Torture Convention and other significant changes in the international legal system since World War Two warranted a denial of Pinochet's claim of immunity for violations of international law. The court ruled that the former dictator could be turned over to Spain to stand trial for the crimes he committed while in office. Although British political authorities would eventually allow Pinochet to go back to Chile due to poor health, the House of Lords ruling confirmed the importance of the new international legal order. Sands (2005: 43) has spelled out the implications of the decision:

Internationally, every head of state now knows that he or she may be accountable for the consequences of acts which massively and systematically violate fundamental human rights laws and international criminal laws. Despots and dictators, indeed anyone who might be accused of committing international crimes, will now travel abroad with a great deal more trepidation.

The creation of a permanent International Criminal Court also provides a new opening for holding state officials accountable for their crimes. It is an important effort to end political impunity and legal immunity for powerful state actors. The court has the potential to provide genuine accountability for state criminals. In early 2009, the ICC issued a warrant for the arrest of Sudanese President Omar Hassan al-Bashir on charges of war crimes and crimes against humanity in connection with the situation in Darfur.

Yet, as Rothe and Mullins (2006) point out, the most powerful nation in the world, the United States, has not joined the court and in fact vigorously opposes the ICC. They also note (2006: 115) that 'As currently structured and empowered, the ICC cannot fulfill its potentials or stated mission.' In addition to the US rejection of the ICC, another serious flaw is that this court operates as a subsidiary of the UN Security Council. This means that any effort targeting state crimes by one of the permanent Security Council members or their allies can be vetoed by that member.

Some Marxist scholars dispute the notion, advanced by Sands (2005), that any progress toward greater accountability for the state officials of capitalist societies has actually occurred, arguing that international legal norms have always been complicit with the violence of empires (Mieville 2006). It is, to say the least, a great challenge for a public criminology of state crime to find ways to be effectively involved, as Sheldon Glueck was, in the struggle to provide justice and accountability for state officials who have violated international law.

While holding powerful state officials accountable for their crimes is an important moral and legal principle, there are also reasons to doubt the effectiveness of individual criminal punishment in preventing future state crimes. Criminologist Donald Taft raised this issue concerning the punishment of war criminals as far back as 1946, at the time of the Nuremberg trials. Reviewing what criminologists knew about the deleterious effects of criminal punishment at the time, Taft argued that punishing war criminals would be even less effective than punishing other types of offenders and would even increase the probability of World War Three since those punished would end up bitter, angry and resentful. Furthermore, he argued (1946: 444): 'To center attention on the punishment of war criminals as individuals, detracts attention from the ... need ... to understand and attack the war system – the social process by which aggressive war is produced.'

More recently, in a similar vein, John Braithwaite (2005: 283) has argued: 'The ideal of punishment proportionate to wrongdoing creates a criminal justice system that deters prevention.' Punishment deters prevention, particularly in organizational settings, he asserts, because it induces cover-ups and creates a 'blame culture' as opposed to a 'learning culture'. Citing Stanley Cohen, Braithwaite (2005: 285) observes: 'The trouble with criminal justice on this analysis is that it encourages cultures of denial.' Rather than punishing organizational offenders, he argues, we should attempt to implement restorative justice processes that help reveal truths and foster a learning culture that prevents harms from occurring in the first place. Speaking specifically about war criminals, Braithwaite (2005: 299), like Taft, concludes that:

> Like common criminals, war criminals accurately perceive that what they confront is a system that arbitrarily veers between impunity and vigorous proportionality (and that is 'victor's justice'). Such a dispensation leaves little hope for truth and collective memory. The alternative path advanced for critical examination and empirical testing is that more crime prevention is achieved by always confronting crime, but doing so with a presumption of mercy. Offenders who know that they will benefit from mercy so long as they participate in a high-integrity process of truth-seeking and take active responsibility for the hurts they have caused can help us to learn from the truth they tell.

In his advocacy for post-conflict restorative justice practices, which have been widely implemented in a number of countries, Braithwaite offers one model for the role of a public criminologist.

The restorative justice model overlaps with the transitional justice processes, examined by Stanley in Chapter 14. Much like restorative justice, transitional justice seeks to highlight truth, encourage reconciliation, build peace, and relieve trauma, while at the same time establishing the accountability of individuals for past harms. As Stanley notes, however, the 'internationals', that is, workers representing the UN, other international organizations, and western state actors, operating from a western mindset, often apply transitional justice practices in ways that can limit or exclude victims and local populations. She suggests: 'If powerful states and mainstream international institutions wish to create a global human rights culture they cannot continue to renege on the issue of preventing state crimes from occurring in the first instance and nor should they take transitional justice as an opportunity to embed their own values or to pursue their own victories.'

This brings us to the biggest challenge facing a public criminology of state crime. Can we, as Stanley asks, prevent such crimes from occurring in the first place? Can a public criminology realistically play a role in the project of preventing such harms as wars of aggression, the terror bombing of civilians, genocide, torture and the myriad other forms of harm that states can inflict? Can the knowledge, insights, skills and abilities of criminology contribute to rethinking and restructuring a global social order that currently perpetuates widespread economic inequality, misery and massive political and social violence? Can a public criminology contribute to a rethinking and restructuring of an international legal system that still maintains states of impunity for crimes of power? Can it enter into conversations with various publics that will contribute to a rethinking and restructuring of cultures of denial that refuse to acknowledge and act upon atrocities and suffering? And finally, can a public criminology of state crime help the discipline to overcome the implicatory denial of the crimes of the powerful that sits at the very heart of orthodox criminology?

Unfortunately these questions cannot be answered here. Much work must still be done if a public criminology of state crime is to be fully developed. But we fervently hope that the criminological work contained in this volume on state crime in the global age provides a sense of the challenges remaining for both criminologists and the multitude of humanity that seek a world where states, however constructed, serve the common good and desist from both extraordinary and everyday misuses of power in harmful ways.

References

AAP Newsfeed (2000) 'WA: AMA Supports Injecting Rooms and Prescribed Heroin', *AAP Newsfeed*, 21 July.

American Bar Association (1993) *ABA Standards for Criminal Justice: Prosecution Function and Defense Function*. Washington DC: American Bar Association.

ABC News (2007) '"High-Value Targets" Imprisoned by High-Level "Cover-up"', 8 June. Available at: blogs.abcnews.com/theblotter/2007/06/.investigator_hi. html [accessed 2 October 2009].

Abramsky, S. (2007) *American Furies: Crime, Punishment, and Vengeance in the Age of Mass Imprisonment*. Boston: Beacon Press.

Agamben, G. (2000) 'Sovereign Police', in V. Binetti and C. Casarino (eds) *Means Without End: Notes on Politics*. Minneapolis: University of Minnesota Press (pp. 103–9).

Agamben, G. (2005a) *Homo Sacer – Il Potere Sovrano e la Nuda Vita* (trans. P. Tsiamouras). Athens: Scripta.

Agamben, G. (2005b) *State of Exception* (trans. K. Attel). Chicago: University of Chicago Press.

Agger, B. (2000) *Public Sociology: From Social Facts to Literary Acts*. Lanham, MD: Rowman and Littlefield.

Ainsley, H. and Israel, M. (2004) *The Killing of the Fly: State-Corporate Victimization*. Papua New Guinea: Australian National University.

Ali, T. (2003) *Bush in Babylon: The Recolonisation of Iraq*. New York: Verso.

Alperovitz, G. (1965) *Atomic Diplomacy: Hiroshima and Potsdam: The Use of the Atomic Bomb and the American Confrontation with Soviet Power*. New York: Simon and Schuster.

Alperovitz, G. (1995) *The Decision to Use the Atomic Bomb and the Architecture of an American Myth*. New York: Alfred A. Knopf.

Althusser, L. (1971) *Lenin and Philosophy and Other Essays*. London: New Left Books.

Altman, L. (2000) 'Company Developing Marijuana for Medical Uses', *New York Times*, 10 April, p. A16.

Alvarez, A. (2001) *Governments, Citizens, and Genocide: A Comparative and Interdisciplinary Approach*. Bloomington: Indiana University Press.

American Civil Liberties Union (ACLU) (2005) 'Records Released under FOIA Request'. Available at: www.aclu.org/torturefoia/released/fbi.html [accessed 6 October 2009].

American Civil Liberties Union (ACLU) (2007) 'ACLU Sues Boeing Subsidiary for Participation in CIA Kidnapping and Torture Flights', 30 May. Available at:

www.aclu.org/safefree/torture/29920prs20070530.html [accessed 6 October 2009].

Americas Watch (2005) 'Getting away with Torture? Command Responsibility for the U.S. Abuse of Detainees', 17(1). Washington, DC: Americas Watch.

Amnesty International (2006a) 'Below the Radar: Secret Flights to Torture and "Disappearance"'. Available at: www.amnesty.org/en/library/info/AMR51/051/2006 [accessed 6 October 2009].

Amnesty International (2006b) 'Partners in Crime: Europe's Role in US Renditions'. Available at: www.amnesty.org/en/library/info/EUR01/008/2006 [accessed 6 October 2009].

Amnesty International (2006c) 'Outsourcing Facilitating Human Rights Violations'. Available at: www.amnestyusa.org/annualreport/2006/overview.html [accessed 6 October 2009].

Amnesty International (2008) 'States of Denial: Europe's Role in Rendition and Secret Detention'. Available at: www.amnesty.org/en/library/info/EUR01/003/2008/en [accessed 6 October 2009].

Amnesty International (2009) 'Accountability for US Counter-terrorism Human Rights Violations'. Available at: www.amnesty.org/en/appeals-for-action/accountability-for-US-counter-terrorism-human-rights-violations [accessed 12 July 2009].

An-Na'im, A. (2003) 'Introduction: Expanding Legal Protection of Human Rights in African Contexts', in A. An-Na'im (ed.) *Human Rights Under African Constitutions: Realizing the Promise for Ourselves*. Philadelphia: University of Pennsylvania Press (pp. 1–28).

Anderson, F. and Cayton, A. (2005) *The Dominion of War: Empire and Liberty in North America, 1500–2000*. New York: Penguin.

Andersson, N., Iagoinitzer, D. and Collier, D. (2008) *International Justice and Impunity: The Case of the United States*. Atlanta: Clarity Press.

Appelbaum, R. (1988) *Karl Marx*. Newbury Park, CA: Sage.

Aradau, C. (2007) 'Law Transformed: The Other Exception and the 'War on Terror',' *Third World Quarterly*, 28(3): 83–106.

Arendt, H. (1965/1977) *Eichmann in Jerusalem: A Report on the Banality of Evil*. London: Penguin.

Audi, A. (2004–05) 'Iraq's New Investment Laws and the Standard of Civilization: A Case Study on the Limits of International Law', *Georgetown Law Journal*, 93: 335–64.

Austin, J. and Irwin, J. (2001) *It's About Time: America's Imprisonment Binge*, 3rd edn. Belmont, CA: Wadsworth.

Badiou, A. (2001) *Ethics*. London: Verso.

Balakrishnan, G. (2005) 'States of War', *New Left Review*, 36: 5–32.

Bales, K. (2000) *Disposable People: New Slavery in the Global Economy*. Berkeley: University of California Press.

Bank Information Center (2007) 'World Bank and China Exim Bank Team up on Lending to Africa', 4 June. Available at: www.bicusa.org/en/Article.3386.aspx [accessed 6 October 2009].

Barak, G. (1991) 'Toward a Criminology of State Crime', in G. Barak (ed.) *Crimes by the Capitalist State: An Introduction to State Criminality*. Albany: State University of New York Press (pp. 3–16).

Barak, G. (ed.) (1991) *Crimes by the Capitalist State*. Albany: SUNY Press.

Barak, G. (ed.) (1995) *Media, Process, and the Social Construction of Crime: Studies in Newsmaking Criminology*. New York: Routledge.

Barak, G. (2000) 'Foreword', in J. Ross (ed.) *Varieties of State Crime and Its Control*. Monsey, NY: Criminal Justice Press (pp. i–ix).

Baratta, A. (2001) 'Diritto a la Sicurezza o Sicurezza Dei Diritti?', in S. Anastasia and M. Palma (eds) *Democrazia e Diritto, La Bilancia e la Misura: Guistizia, Sicurezza, Riforme*, No. 307.6. Rome: Franco Angeli (pp. 19–35).

Barrow, C. (1993) *Critical Theories of the State: Marxist, Neo-Marxist, Post-Marxist*. Madison, WI: University of Wisconsin Press.

Bartels, K. (2001) 'How IMF, World Bank failed Africa', *New African*, p. 1. Reprinted 2007. Available at: http://goliath.ecnext.com/coms2/gi_0199_6161944/How-IMF-World-Bank-failed.html [accessed 15 January 2008].

Bartholomew, A. (2006) 'Empire's Law and the Contradictory Politics of Human Rights', in A. Bartholomew (ed.) *Empire's Law*. London: Pluto (pp. 161–92).

Beard, C. and Beard, M. (1930) *The Rise of American Civilization*. New York: Macmillan.

Becker, H. (1963) *Outsiders: Studies in the Sociology of Deviance*. New York: Free Press.

Beckett, K. and Sasson, T. (2004) *The Politics of Injustice: Crime and Punishment in America*, 2nd edn. Thousand Oaks, CA: Sage.

Behn, S. (2005) 'Security Companies Lobby for Heavy Arms', *Washington Times*, 6 June. Available at: www.washingtontimes.com/news/2005/jun/06/20050606-122644-8009r/ [accessed 6 October 2009].

Beijing Summit (2006a) 'Plan Outlines Aims for Collaboration: Summary of the Beijing Action Plan', *China Daily*, 6 November, p. 2.

Beijing Summit (2006b) 'Full Text of the Declaration of the Beijing Summit of the Forum on China–Africa Co-operation (FOCAC)'. Available at: bbs.chinadaily.com.cn/viewthread.php?gid=2&tid [accessed 12 August 2007].

Beijing Summit (2006c) 'The Beijing Summit of the Forum on China–Africa Cooperation, November 5, 2006', *China Daily*, 6 November, p. 3. Available at: english.focacsummit.org/2006-11/05/content_5166.htm [accessed 4 October 2009].

Beirne, P. (2006) 'Preface', in P. Beirne (ed.) *The Chicago School of Criminology, Vol. 1, The Unadjusted Girl*. Chicago: University of Chicago Press.

Bell, C. and O'Rourke, C. (2007) 'Does Feminism Need a Theory of Transitional Justice? An Introductory Essay', *International Journal of Transitional Justice*, 1(1): 23–44.

Bell, C., Campbell, C. and Ní Aoláin, F. (2007) 'The Battle for Transitional Justice: Hegemony, Iraq, and International Law', in J. Morison, K. McEvoy and G. Anthony (eds) *Judges, Transition, and Human Rights*. Oxford: Oxford University Press (pp. 147–65).

Bello, W. (2009) *The Food Wars*. London: Verso.

Benjamin, W. (1978) 'Critique of Violence', in P. Demetz (ed.) *Reflections: Essays, Aphorisms, Autobiographical Writings*. New York: Schoken Books (pp. 277–300).

Bentham, J. (1780/1973) *An Introduction to the Principles of Morals and Legislation*. New York: Hafner Press.

Bentham, J. (1812) *Pauper Management Improved; Particularly by Means of an Application of the Panopticon Principle of Construction*. London: Baldwin and Ridgway.

Berdan, F. F. (2004) 'The Provinces of the Aztec Empire', in F. Solis, *The Aztec Empire*. New York: Guggenheim Museum.

Bergen, P. (2008) 'Exclusive: I was kidnapped by the CIA', *Mother Jones*, March/April. Available at: www.motherjones.com/politics/2008/03/exclusive-i-was-kidnapped-cia [accessed 6 October 2009].

Bess, M. (2006) *Choices Under Fire: Moral Dimensions of World War II*. New York: Alfred A. Knopf.

Best, J. (ed.) (1989) *Images of Issues: Typifying Contemporary Social Problems*. New York: Aldine de Gruyter.

Best, J. (1993) *Threatened Children: Rhetoric and Concern about Child-Victims*. Chicago: University of Chicago Press.

Best, J. (2008) *Social Problems*. New York: W. W. Norton.

Biddle, T. D. (2002) *Rhetoric and Reality in Air Warfare: The Evolution of British and American Ideas About Strategic Bombing, 1914–1945*. Princeton: Princeton University Press.

Blau, P. M. and Scott, W. R. (1963) *Formal Organizations: A Comparative Approach*. London: Routledge and Kegan Paul.

Bloche, M. G. and Marks, J. H. (2005) 'Doctors and Interrogators at Guantanamo Bay', *New England Journal of Medicine*, 335: 1–8.

Block, F. (1977) 'The Ruling Class Does Not Rule: Notes on the Marxist Theory of the State', *Socialist Revolution*, 7(33): 6–28.

Blom, P. (2008) *The Vertigo Years: Europe 1900–1914*. New York: Basic Books.

Blum, W. (1995) *Killing Hope: U.S. Military and CIA Interventions Since World War II*. Monroe: Common Courage Press.

Blum, W. (2000) *Rogue State*. Monroe: Common Courage Press.

Blumer, H. (1971) 'Social Problems as Collective Behavior', *Social Problems*, 18 (Winter): 298–306.

Bobbio, N. (1985) 'La Democracia y el Poder Invisible', in N. Bobbio (ed.) *El Futuro de la Democracia* (trans. J. Moreno). España: Plaza & Janes Editores (pp. 105–34).

Bobbio, N. (1989) 'La Sociedad Civil', in N. Bobbio (ed.) *Estado, Gobierno y Sociedad. Por una Teoría General de la Política* (trans. J. F. Fernández Santillán). México: Fondo de Cultura Económica (pp. 39–67).

Bobbio, N. (1999a) 'Democrazia e Secreto', in N. Bobbio (a cura di M. Bovero) *Teoria Generale della Politica*. Torino: Einaudi (pp. 352–69).

Bobbio, N. (1999b) 'Democrazia e Conoscenza', in N. Bobbio (a cura di M. Bovero), *Teoria Generale della Politica*. Torino: Einaudi (pp. 339–51).

Bobbio, N. (1999c) 'Etica e Politica', in N. Bobbio (a cura di M. Bovero), *Teoria Generale della Politica*. Torino: Einaudi (pp. 120–47).

Bobbio, N. (1999d) 'Il Duongoverno', in N. Bobbio (a cura di M. Bovero), *Teoria Generale della Politica*. Torino: Einaudi (pp. 148–60).

Bohm, R. (1993) 'Social Relationships that Arguably Should Be Criminal Although They Are Not: On the Political Economy of Crime', in K. Tunnell (ed.) *Political Crime in Contemporary America: A Critical Approach*. New York: Garland (pp. 3–29).

Boller, B. (1998) *The Medical Prescription of Opiates and the Swiss Press*. Fribourg, Switzerland: Institute of Journalism and Communications Research.

Bonger, W. A. (1936) *An Introduction to Criminology*. London: Methuen.

Boraine, A. (2006) 'Transitional Justice: A Holistic Interpretation', *Journal of International Affairs*, 60(1): 17–27.

Bourdieu, P. (2003) *Firing Back: Against the Tyranny of the Market 2*. New York: New Press.

Boyer, G. (1990) *Economic History of the English Poor Law, 1750–1850*. New York: Cambridge University Press.

Boyle, F. (2002) *The Criminality of Nuclear Deterrence: Could the U.S. War on Terrorism Go Nuclear?* Atlanta: Clarity Press.

Bracking, S. (2009) *Money and Power*. New York: Pluto Press.

Braithwaite, J. (2002) *Restorative Justice and Responsible Regulation*. New York: Oxford University Press.

Braithwaite, J. (2005) 'Between Proportionality and Impunity: Confrontation > Truth > Prevention', *Criminology*, 43: 283–305.

Brittain, V. (1944) *Seed of Chaos*. London: New Vision Press.

Brody, D. (2006) *The Halliburton Agenda: The Politics of Oil and Money*. London/ New York: Wiley.

Brody, R. (2004) 'The Road to Abu Ghraib', Washington, DC: *Human Rights Watch*, 1 June. Available at: hrw.org/reports/2004/usa0604/usa0604.pdf [accessed 6 October 2009].

Brody, R. (2005) 'Getting Away with Torture? Command Responsibility for the U.S. Abuse of Detainees', Washington, DC: *Human Rights Watch*, 24 April. Available at: www.hrw.org/reports/2005/us0405/us0405.pdf [accessed 6 October 2009].

Brown, D. (2001) *Bury My Heart At Wounded Knee*. New York: Holt.

Browning, C. (1992) *Ordinary Men: Reserve Police Battalion 101 and the Final Solution in Poland*. New York: Harper Collins.

Bruce, A. and Becker, P. (2006) 'State-Corporate Crime and the Paducah Gaseous Diffusion Plant', *Western Criminology Review*, 8(2): 29–43.

Burawoy, M. (2007) 'For Public Sociology', in D. Clawson, R. Zussman, J. Misra, N. Gerstel, R. Stokes, D. Anderton and M. Burawoy (eds) *Public Sociology: Fifteen Eminent Sociologists Debate Politics and the Profession in the Twenty-first Century*. Berkeley, CA: University of California Press (pp. 23–64).

Burawoy, M. (2009) 'The Public Sociology Wars', in V. Jeffries (ed.) *Handbook of Public Sociology*. Lanham, MD: Rowman and Littlefield (pp. 449–73).

Burns, R. and Lynch, M. (2004) *Environmental Crime: A Sourcebook*. New York: LFB Scholarly Publishing LLC.

Bush, G. H. W. (1990) 'State of the Union Address', 31 January. Available at: www2.hn.psu.edu/faculty/jmanis/poldocs/uspressu/SUaddressGHW Bush.pdf [accessed 6 October 2009].

Bush, G. H. W. (1991) 'Address to the Nation Announcing Allied Military Action in the Persian Gulf', 16 January 1991. Available at www.georgebushfoundation.org/articles/gulf_war [accessed 6 October 2009].

Bush, G. W. (2001) 'Address to Prayer Service in Washington National Cathedral', 13 September. Available at: www.allacademic.com/meta/p_mla_apa_research_ citation /1/1/2/2/0/p112200_index.html [accessed 6 October 2009].

Business Week (2002) 'Out in Front: Information Technology', 25 November. Available at: www.businessweek.com/magazine/content/02_47/b3809094 .htm [accessed 27 September 2009].

Calavita, K., Pontell, H. and Tillman, R. (1997) *Big Money Crime: Fraud and Politics in the Savings and Loan Crisis*. Berkeley, CA: University of California Press.

Campbell, D. and Norton-Taylor, R. (2008) 'Prison Ships, Torture Claims, and Missing Detainees: America May Have Held Terror Suspects in British Territory, Despite UK Denials', *The Guardian*, 2 June. Available at: www.guardian.co.uk/ world/2008/jun/02/terrorism.terrorism [accessed 14 November 2009].

Campbell, H. (2008) 'China in Africa: challenging US global hegemony. *Third World Quarterly*, Volume 29, Issue 1, February 2008, pp. 89–105.

Canadian Centre on Substance Abuse (CCSA) (1996) *Harm Reduction: Concepts and Practice: A Policy Discussion Pape*r. Canadian Centre on Substance Abuse (CCSA) National Working Group on Policy. Available at: www.csa.ca/wgharm.htm [accessed 6 October 2009].

Carrasco, D. (1999) *City of Sacrifice: The Aztec Empire and the Role of Violence in Civilization*. Boston, MA: Beacon Press.

Carroll, J. (2004) *Crusade: Chronicles of an Unjust War*. New York: Metropolitan Books.

Cassel, D. W. (1995) 'International Truth Commissions and Justice', in N. J. Kritz (ed.) *Transitional Justice: How Emerging Democracies Reckon with Former Regimes, Vol 1: General Considerations*. Washington, DC: United States Institute of Peace (pp. 326–33).

Castelle, G. (1999) 'Lessons Learned from the "Fred Zain Affair"', *The Champion*, 23: 12–16, 52–7.

CBS (2004) 'Photographs of Abu Ghraib Abuse', *60 Minutes II*, 28 April.

Center for Cooperative Research (2005) 'Prisoner Abuse in Iraq, Afghanistan and Elsewhere.' Available at: www.cooperativeresearch.org/project.jsp?project=us _torture_abuse [accessed October 2005].

Center for International Finance and Development (2006) 'Zimbabwe Budget and the Economic Crisis', University of Iowa, College of Law, 29 November. Available at: uicifd.blogspot.com/2006_11_01_archive.html [accessed 10 June 2007].

Chambliss, W. (1964) 'A Sociological Analysis of the Law of Vagrancy', *Social Problems*, 12: 67–77.

Chambliss, W. (ed.) (1969) *Crime and the Legal Process*. New York: McGraw-Hill.

Chambliss, W. (1974) 'The State, the Law, and the Definition of Behavior as Criminal or Delinquent', in D. Glaser (ed.) *Handbook of Criminology*. Chicago: Rand McNally (pp. 7–43).

Chambliss, W. (ed.) (1984) *Criminal Law in Action*. New York: John Wiley and Sons.

Chambliss, W. (1988a) *Exploring Criminology*. New York: Macmillan.

Chambliss, W. (1988b) *On the Take: From Petty Crooks to Presidents*, revised edn. Bloomington, IN: Indiana University Press.

Chambliss, W. (1989) 'State-Organized Crime', *Criminology*, 27(2): 183–208.

Chambliss, W. (2000) *Power, Politics and Crime*. Boulder, CO: Westview Press.

Chambliss, W. and Seidman, R. (1971) *Law, Order, Power*. Boston: Addison-Wesley.

Chambliss, W. and Zatz, M. S. (1993) *Making Law: The State, the Law, and Structural Contradictions*. Bloomington, IN: Indiana University Press.

Chandler, D. (1997) *Voices from S-21: Terror and History in Pol Pot's Secret Prison*. Berkeley, CA: University of California Press.

Chatterjee, P. (2004) *Iraq, Inc.: A Profitable Occupation*. New York: Seven Stories Press.

Chomsky, N. (1996) *Power and Prospects: Reflections on Human Nature and the Social Order*. Boston: South End Press.

Chrétien-Goni, J.-P. (1992) 'Institutio Arcanae: Théorie de l'Institution du Secret et Fondement de la Politique', in C. Lazzeri and D. Reynié (eds) *Le Pouvoir de la Raison d'état*. Paris: PUF (pp. 135–90).

Churchill, W. (1997) *A Little Matter of Genocide*. San Francisco: City Lights.

von Clausewitz, C. (1873) *On War* (trans. J. J. Graham). Available at: www.clausewitz.com/readings/OnWar1873/TOC.htm [accessed 15 March 2009].

Clendinnen, I. (1993) *Aztecs: An Interpretation*. Cambridge: Cambridge University Press.

Clinard, M. B. and Quinney, R. (1967) *Criminal Behavior Systems: A Typology*. New York: Holt, Rinehart and Winston.

Cloud, D. (2005) 'Private Found Guilty in Abu Ghraib Abuse', *New York Times*, 27

September. Available at: www.nytimes.com/2005/09/27/national/27england. html [accessed 7 October 2009].

CNN (2002) 'U.S. Policy on Assassination.' Available at: archives.cnn.com/2002/ LAW/11/04/us.assassination.policy/ [accessed 12 October 2005].

Cockburn, A. and St Clair, J. (1998) *Whiteout*. London: Verso.

Cohen, S. (1985) *Visions of Social Control: Crime, Punishment and Classification*. Cambridge: Polity Press.

Cohen, S. (1988) *Against Criminology*. New Brunswick, NJ: Transaction.

Cohen, S. (2001) *States of Denial: Knowing About Atrocities and Suffering*. Cambridge: Polity Press.

Coleman, J. S. (1982) *The Asymmetric Society*. Syracuse: Syracuse University Press.

Coleman, R., Sim, J., Tombs, S. and Whyte, D. (2010) 'Introduction', in R. Coleman, J. Sim, S. Tombs and D. Whyte (eds) *State, Power, Crime*. London: Sage (pp. 1–14).

Concerned Psychologists (2006) 'Letter to APA on Psychologist Involvement in Torture', Concerned Psychologists to APA President Sharon Brehm, PhD, 6 June. Available at: www.scoop.co.nz/stories/WO0706/S00113.htm [accessed 6 October 2009].

Conot, R. E. (1993) *Justice at Nuremburg*. New York: Basic Books.

Conrad, G. W. and Demarest, A. A. (1984) *Religion and Empire: The Dynamics of Aztec and Inca Expansion*. Cambridge: Cambridge University Press.

Conway-Lanz, S. (2006) *Collateral Damage: Americans, Noncombatant Immunity, and Atrocity after World War II*. New York: Routledge.

Cooper-Mahkorn, D. (1998) 'German Doctors Vote to Prescribe Heroin to Misusers', *British Medical Journal*. Available at: www.bmj.com/cgi/content/ full/316/7137/1037/c [accessed 20 March 2007].

Cornwell, R. (2005) 'Halliburton Given $30m to Expand Guantanamo Bay', *The Independent*, 18 June. Available at: www.commondreams.org/headlines05/0618-06.htm [accessed 7 October 2009].

Crelinsten, R. and Schmidt, A. (1995) *The Politics of Pain: Torturers and their Masters*. Boulder, CO: Westview Press.

Croall, H. (1992) *White Collar Crime*. Buckingham: Open University Press.

Cryer, R. (2005a) 'Post-conflict Accountability: A Matter of Judgment, Practice or Principle?', in N. W. White and D. Klaasen (eds) *The UN, Human Rights and Post-Conflict Situations*. Manchester: Manchester University Press (pp. 267–89).

Cryer, R. (2005b) *Prosecuting International Crimes: Selectivity and the International Criminal Law Regime*. Cambridge: Cambridge University Press.

Cunneen, C. (2008) 'Understanding Restorative Justice through the Lens of Critical Criminology', in T. Anthony and C. Cunneen (eds) *The Critical Criminology Companion*. Sydney: Hawkins Press (pp. 290–302).

Currie, E. (1998) *Crime and Punishment in America: Why the Solutions to America's Most Stubborn Social Crisis Have Not Worked – and What Will*. New York: Metropolitan Books.

Davies, C. A. (2007) *Reflexive Ethnography: A Guide to Researching Selves and Others*. New York: Routledge.

Davies, N. (1981) *Human Sacrifice*. New York: Morrow.

Dayan, C. (2007) *The Story of Cruel and Unusual*. Cambridge, MA: MIT Press.

Deleuze, G. (2005) *L'abécédaire de Gilles Deleuze*. Paris: Editions de Minuit.

Derrida, J. (2003) *Forza di Legge: Il Fondamento Mistico dell'autorità*. Torino: Bollati Boringhieri.

Dershowitz, A. (2002) 'Want to Torture? Get a Warrant', *San Francisco Chronicle*, 22

January. Available at: www.sfgate.com/cgi-bin/article.cgi?file=/chronicle/archive/2002/01/22/ED5329.DTL [accessed 7 October 2009].

Diamond, S. (1974) *In Search of the Primitive*. New Brunswick, NJ: Transaction.

Diamond, S. (1979) *Toward a Marxist Anthropology*. New York: Mouton.

Downes, D., Rock, P., Chinkin, C. and Gearty, C. (eds) (2007) *Crime, Social Control and Human Rights: From Moral Panics to States of Denial*. Portland, OR: Willan Publishing.

Drucker, E. and Vlahov, D. (1999) 'Controlled Clinical Evaluation of Diacetyl Morphine for Treatment of Intractable Opiate Dependence; Commentary', *Lancet*, 353 (8 May): p. 1543.

Drug Enforcement Administration (2004) 'Australia Country Brief 2003: Drug Intelligence Brief'. US Department of Justice, DEA-04009. Available at: www.hawaii.edu/hivandaids/australia_country_brief_drug_situation_report.pdf [accessed 6 October 2009].

Drumbl, M. (2007) *Atrocity, Punishment and International Law*. Cambridge: Cambridge University Press.

Duran, D. (1994) *The History of the Indies of New Spain*. Norman, OK: Oklahoma University Press.

Durkheim, E. (1883–84/2004) *Durkheim's Philosophy Lectures: Notes from the Lycée de Sens Course, 1883–1884*. Cambridge: Cambridge University Press.

Durkheim, E. (1893/1984) *The Division of Labor in Society*. London and Basingstoke: Macmillan.

Durkheim, E. (1897/1951) *Suicide*. New York: Free Press.

Durkheim, E. (1898/1994) 'Individualism and the Intellectuals', in W. S. F. Pickering (ed.) *Durkheim on Religion*. New York: American Academy of Religion.

Durkheim, E. (1899/1994) 'Concerning the Definition of Religious Phenomena', in W. S. F. Pickering (ed.) *Durkheim on Religion*. New York: American Academy of Religion.

Durkheim, E. (1912/1995) *The Elementary Forms of Religious Life*. New York: Free Press.

Durkheim, E. (1914/1960) 'The Dualism of Human Nature', in K. H. Wolf (ed.) *E. Durkheim et al., Essays on Sociology and Philosophy*. New York: Harper Torchbooks.

Durkheim, E. (1915) *Germany Above All: German Mentality and the War*. Paris: Colon.

Durkheim, E. (1925/1961) *Moral Education: A Study in the Theory and the Application of Sociology to Education*. New York: Free Press.

Durkheim, E. (1950/1957) *Professional Ethics and Civic Morals*. London: Routledge and Kegan Paul.

Duster, T. (1970) *The Legislation of Morality*. New York: Free Press.

Earthtimes.org (2005) 'Abu Ghraib Scandal: Army Gives Clean Chit to Senior Officers', 23 April. Available at: www.earthtimes.org/articles/show/2538.html [accessed 7 October 2009].

Earthtimes.org (2007) 'US Officer in Abu Ghraib Trial has Charges Reduced', 20 August. Available at: www.earthtimes.org/articles/show/95798.html [accessed 7 October 2009].

Economist (2000) 'Britain: Drugs – Good for You', *The Economist*, 19 February, p. 56.

Eisenman, J. (2005) 'Zimbabwe: China's African Ally', *China Brief, The Jamestown Foundation*, 5(15): 9–11.

Eisenman, J. and Kurlantzick, J. (2006) 'China's Africa Strategy', in G. Hastedt (ed.) *American Foreign Policy: Annual Editions*, 13. Dubuque, IA. McGraw Hill (pp. 69–73).

Englehardt, T. (2008a) 'Bombs Away Over Iraq.' Available at: www.tomdispatch, com/post/print/174887/Tomgram [accessed 29 January 2008].

Englehardt, T. (2008b) *The World According to TomDispatch: America in the New Age of Empire.* London: Verso.

Esping-Andersen, G. (1990) *The Three Worlds of Welfare Capitalism.* London: Polity Press.

European Parliament (2007) Press Release: 'CIA activities in Europe: European Parliament adopts final report deploring passivity from some Member States'. Giovanni Claudio Fava, Rapporteur on report into CIA renditions. Available at: www.europarl.europa.eu/sides/getDoc.do?type=IM-PRESS&reference =20070209IPR02947&language=EN [accessed 14 November 2009].

Evans, T. (1998) 'Introduction: Power, Hegemony and the Universalization of Human Rights', in T. Evans (ed.) *Human Rights Fifty Years On: A Reappraisal.* Manchester: Manchester University Press (pp. 1–23).

Ezeonu, I. and Koku, E. (2008) 'Crimes of Globalization: The Feminization of HIV Pandemic in Sub-Saharan Africa', *The Global South* 2(2): 112–29.

Fagan, B. and Beck, C. (1996) *The Oxford Companion to Archaeology.* Oxford: Oxford University Press.

Falk, R. (1993) *Global Visions: Beyond the New World Order.* Boston: South End Press.

Falk, R. (1999) *Predatory Globalization: A Critique.* Cambridge: Polity Press.

Falk, R. (2000) *Human Rights Horizons.* London: Taylor and Francis.

Falk, R. (2004a) 'State Terror versus Humanitarian Law', in M. Selden and A. So (eds) *War and State Terrorism: The United States, Japan, and the Asia-Pacific in the Long Twentieth Century.* Lanham, MD: Rowman and Littlefield (pp. 41– 61).

Falk, R. (2004b) *The Declining World Order: America's Imperial Geopolitics.* New York: Routledge.

Falk, R. (2008) 'Nuclear Weapons, War, and the Discipline of International Law', in R. Falk and D. Krieger (eds) *At the Nuclear Precipice: Catastrophe or Transformation?* New York: Palgrave Macmillan (pp. 225–33).

Farmer, P. (2005) *Pathologies of Power: Health, Human Rights and the New War on the Poor.* Berkeley, CA: University of California Press.

Fay, G. (2004) 'Executive Summary: Investigation of Intelligence Activities at Abu Ghraib', 25 August. Available at: fl1.findlaw.com/news.findlaw.com/hdocs/docs/dod/fay82504rpt.pdf [accessed 6 October 2009].

Feagin, J. (2001) 'Social Justice and Sociology: Agendas for the Twenty-First Century', *American Sociological Review*, 66: 1–22.

Feagin, J. and Vera, H. (2001) *Liberation Sociology.* Boulder, CO: Westview Press.

Feagin, J., Elias, S. and Mueller, J. (2009) 'Social Justice and Critical Public Sociology', in V. Jeffries (ed.) *Handbook of Public Sociology.* Lanham, MD: Rowman and Littlefield (pp. 71–88).

Federal Department of Home Affairs (FDHA) (2008) 'Heroin-assisted Treatment/ Treatment with Diacetylmorphine (HAT) 2007'. Available at: www.bag.ad-min.ch/themen/drogen/00042/00629/00798/01191/index.html?lang=en [accessed 8 May 2008].

Feeley, M. and Simon, J. (1992) 'The New Penology: Notes on the Emerging Strategy of Corrections and its Implications', *Criminology*, 30(4): 449–74.

Feeley, M. and Simon, J. (1994) 'Actuarial Justice: The Emerging Criminal Law', in D. Nelken (ed.) *The Futures of Criminology.* London: Sage (pp. 173–201).

Feldman, A. (1994) 'On Cultural Anesthesia: From Desert Storm to Rodney King', *American Ethnologist*, 21: 404–18.

Ferguson, N. (2004) *Colossus: The Price of America's Empire*. New York: Penguin.

Ferrajoli, L. (1984) 'Emergenza Penale e Crisi della Giurisdizione', *Dei delitti e delle pene*, 2: 271–92.

Ferrajoli, L. (1995) *Derecho y razón. Teoría del galantismo penal* (trans. P. Andrés Imbañez *et al.*). Madrid: Trotta.

Ferrajoli, L. (2004a) 'Guerra, Terrorismo y Derecho: Sobre el ataque a Afganistán', in L. Ferrajoli (ed.) *Razones Jurídicas del Pacifism* (trans. G. Pisarello). Madrid: Trotta (pp. 51–64).

Ferrajoli, L. (2004b) 'La "Guerra Infinita" y el Orden Internacional: A Propósito de la Invasión de Irak', in L. Ferrajoli (ed.) *Razones Jurídicas del Pacifismo* (trans. G. Pisarello). Madrid: Trotta (pp. 65–77).

Fiala, A. (2008) *The Just War Myth: The Moral Illusions of War*. Lanham, MD: Rowman and Littlefield.

Fidler, D. (2001) 'The Return of the Standard of Civilization', *Chicago Journal of International Law*, 2(1): 137–57.

Finlayson, J. (2005) *Habermas: A Very Short Introduction*. New York: Oxford University Press.

Fisher, S. (1993) '"Just the Facts, Ma'am": Lying and the Omission of Exculpatory Evidence in Police Reports', *New England Law Review*, 28: 1–62.

Fishman, M. (1978) 'Crime Waves as Ideology', *Social Problems*, 25(4): 531–43.

Fletcher, G. (2004) 'Black Hole in Guantánamo Bay', *Journal of International Criminal Justice*, 2(1): 121–32.

Flora, P. and Heidenheimer, A. (1982) *The Development of Welfare States in Europe and America*. New Brunswick, NJ: Transaction.

Foucault, M. (1975) *Surveiller et Punir: Naissance de la Prison*. Paris: Gallimard.

Foucault, M. (1977) *Discipline and Punish: The Birth of the Prison* (trans. A. Sheridan). New York: Vintage.

Foucault, M. (1981) *The History of Sexuality, Vol. 1*. London: Penguin.

Foucault, M. (1991) 'Questions of Method', in C. Gordon and P. H. Miller (eds) *The Foucault Effect: Studies in Governmentality*. Hemel Hempstead: Harvester Wheatsheaf (pp. 73–86).

Foucault, M. (1997) *Il Faut Défendre la Société: Cours au Collège de France, 1975–1976*. Paris: Gallimard/Seuil.

Foucault, M. (1998) *The History of Sexuality, Vol. 1: The Will to Knowledge*. London: Penguin.

Foucault, M. (2003) *Society Must Be Defended: Lectures at the Collège de France, 1975–1976* (trans. D. Macey). New York: Picador.

Foucault, M. (2004a) *Sécurité, Territoire, Population: Cours au Collège de France, 1977–1978*. Paris: Gallimard/Seuil.

Foucault, M. (2004b) *Naissance de la Biopolitique: Cours au Collège de France, 1978–1979*. Paris: Gallimard/Seuil.

Foucault. M. (2007) *Security, Territory, Population: Lectures at the Collège de France, 1977–1978*. New York: Palgrave.

Frank, R. (1999) *Downfall: The End of the Imperial Japanese Empire*. New York: Random House.

Frank, T. (2000) *One Market Under God: Extreme Capitalism, Market Populism, and the End of Economic Democracy*. New York: Doubleday.

Franke, K. M. (2006) 'Gendered Subjects of Transitional Justice', *Columbia Journal of Gender and Law*, 15(3): 813–28.

Frappier, J. (1985) 'Above the Law: Violations of International Law by the U.S. Government from Truman to Reagan', *Crime and Social Justice*, 21–22: 1–36.

French, H. (2006) 'Commentary: China and Africa', *African Affairs*, 106(422): 127–32.

Friedrich, C. J. (1957) *Constitutional Reason of State*. Brown University Press.

Friedrichs, D. (ed.) (1998) *State Crime*, Vols I and II. Aldershot: Ashgate.

Friedrichs, D. (2000) 'The Crime of the Century? The Case for the Holocaust', *Crime, Law and Social Change*, 34: 21–41.

Friedrichs, D. (2004) 'White-Collar Crime in a Globalized World', presentation at Western Michigan University, 15 March.

Friedrichs, D. (2007) 'White-Collar Crime in a Postmodern, Globalized World', in H. Pontell and G. Geis (eds) *International Handbook of White-Collar and Corporate Crime*. New York: Springer (pp. 163–84).

Friedrichs, D. (2010) *Trusted Criminals: White Collar Crime in Contemporary Society*, 4th edn. Belmont, CA: Wadsworth.

Friedrichs, D. and Friedrichs, J. (2002) 'The World Bank and Crimes of Globalization: A Case Study', *Social Justice*, 29: 13–36.

Friedrichs, D. and Schwartz, M. D. (2007) 'Editors' Introduction: On Social Harm and a Twenty-first Century Criminology', *Crime, Law and Social Change*, 48: 1–7.

Friedrichs, N. H. (1980) *Erinnerungen aus Meinem Leben in Braunschweig, 1912–1937*. Braunschweig: Stadtarchiv und Statsbibliotek.

Galliher, J. and Guess, T. (2009) 'Two Generations of Sutherland's White-collar Crime Data and Beyond', *Crime, Law and Social Change*, 51: 163–174.

Gardner, D. (2000) 'The Failed War on Drugs: US Bullies World into Waging Futile Drug War', *Chicago Sun Times*, 7 January, p. 12.

Garland, D. (1990) *Punishment and Modern Society: A Study of Social Theory*. Chicago: University of Chicago Press.

Garrison, J. (2004) *America as Empire: Global Leader or Rogue Power?* San Francisco: Berrett-Koehler.

Gartry, C., Oviedo-Joekes, E., Laliberté, N. and Schechter, M. (2009) 'NAOMI: The Trials and Tribulations of Implementing a Heroin Assisted Treatment Study in North America', *Harm Reduction Journal*, 6: 1–14.

Geis, G. (1967) 'White Collar Crime: The Heavy Electrical Equipment Antitrust Case of 1961', in M. B. Clinard and R. Quinney (eds) *Criminal Behavior Systems: A Typology*. New York: Holt, Rinehart and Winston (pp. 139–50).

Geis, G. (ed.) 1968) *White-Collar Criminal*. New York: Atherton.

Gershman, B. (1986) 'Why Prosecutors Misbehave', *Criminal Law Bulletin*, 22(2): 131–43.

Gerson, J. (2007) *Empire and the Bomb: How the U.S. Uses Nuclear Weapons to Dominate the World*. London: Pluto Press.

Gessner, V. (1998) 'Globalisation and Legal Certainty', in V. Gessner and A. Budak (eds) *Emerging Legal Certainty: Empirical Studies on the Globalisation of Law*. Aldershot: Dartmouth (pp. 1–16).

Gibson, C. (1964) *The Aztecs Under Spanish Rule*. Stanford: Stanford University Press.

Givelber, D. (2002) 'The Adversary System and Historical Accuracy: Can We Do Better?', in S. Westervelt and J. Humphrey (eds) *Wrongly Convicted: Perspectives on Failed Justice*. Newark: Rutgers University Press (pp. 253–68).

Glauner, L. (2001) 'The Need for Accountability and Reparation: 1830–1976: The United States Government's Role in the Promotion, Implementation, and Execution of the Crime of Genocide Against Native Americans', *DePaul Law Review*, 51: 911–62.

Glendon, R. (2002) *A World Made New: Eleanor Roosevelt and the Universal Declaration of Human Rights*. New York: Random House.

Global Security (2006) 'Alleged Secret Detentions and Unlawful Inter-state Transfers involving Council of Europe Member States, Parliamentary Assembly Committee on Legal Affairs and Human Rights Draft report – Part II. Explanatory memorandum.' Available at: www.globalsecurity.org/intell/library/reports/2006/secret-detentions_pace_060607-01.htm [accessed 6 October 2009].

Glueck, S. (1943a) 'Punishing the War Criminals', *The New Republic*, 109: 706–9.

Glueck, S. (1943b) 'By What Courts Shall War Offenders be Tried?', *Harvard Law Review*, 66: 1059.

Glueck, S. (1944) *War Criminals: Their Prosecution and Punishment*. New York: Alfred A. Knopf.

Glueck, S. (1946) *The Nuremberg Trial and Aggressive War*. New York: Alfred A. Knopf.

Goff, S. (2004) *Full Spectrum Disorder: The Military in the New American Century*. Brooklyn: Soft Skull Press.

Gold, H. (1996) *Unit 731 Testimony*. Singapore: Yen Books.

Goodman, D. (2008) 'The Enablers: The Psychology Industry's Long and Shameful History with Torture', *Mother Jones*, 1 March. Available at: www.motherjones.com/politics/2008/03/enablers [accessed 10 April 2008].

Gosch, E. and Busch, M. (1999) 'We Could Do With a Drug "Failure" Like This', *Canberra Times*, 6 July, p. A8.

Gottschalk, M. (2006) *The Prison and the Gallows: The Politics of Mass Incarceration in America*. New York: Cambridge University Press.

Graham, H. (2005) *The Spanish Civil War: A Very Short Introduction*. Oxford: Oxford University Press.

Gramsci, A. (1935/1971) *Selections from the Prison Notebooks* (trans. Hoare and Nowell-Smith). Moscow/New York: International Publishers.

Graulich, M. (2005) *Le Sacrifices Humain chez les Azteques*. Paris: Fayard.

Gray, P. (1996) *The Enlightenment: The Science of Freedom*. New York: Alfred A. Knopf.

Grayling, A. C. (2006) *Among the Dead Cities: The History and Moral Legacy of the WWII Bombing of Civilians in Germany and Japan*. New York: Walker & Company.

Green, P. (2005) 'Disaster by Design: Corruption, Construction and Catastrophe', *British Journal of Criminology*, 45(4): 528–46.

Green, P. and Ward, T. (2000) 'State Crime, Human Rights: The Limits of Criminology', *Social Justice*, 27(1): 101–15.

Green, P. and Ward, T. (2004) *State Crime: Governments, Violence and Corruption*. London: Pluto Press.

Greenwald, G. (2008) 'John Yoo's War Crimes', *Salon*, 2 April. Available at: www.salon.com/opinion/greenwald/2008/04/02/yoo/index.html [accessed 6 October 2009].

Greenwald, G. (2009a) 'The Washington Post Endorses Abu Ghraib Scapegoating for Torture'. Available at: www.salon.com/opinion/greenwald/2009/07/27/washington_justice/ [accessed 6 October 2009].

Greenwald, G. (2009b) 'Obama Contemplates Executive Order for Detention without Charges'. Available at: www.salon.com/opinion/greenwald/2009/06/27/preventive_detention/ [accessed 2 September 2009].

Greenwald, G. (2009c) *Drug Decriminalization in Portugal*. Washington, DC: Cato Institute.

Grey, S. (2007) *Ghost Plane: The True Story of the CIA Rendition and Torture Program.* New York: St Martins.

Grinde, D. A. and Johansen, B. (1998) *Ecocide of Native America: Environmental Destruction of Indian Lands and People.* Sante Fe: Clear Light.

Gurr, T. (1979) 'On the History of Violent Crime in Europe and America', in E. Bitner and S. Messenger (eds) *Criminology Review Yearbook.* Beverly Hills, CA: Sage (pp. 411–32).

Gurr, T. (1990) 'Historical Trends in Violent Crime: A Critical Review of the Evidence', in N. A. Weiner and M. A. Zahn (eds) *Violence, Patterns, Causes, and Public Policy.* New York: Harcourt Brace Jovanovich (pp. 15–24).

GW Pharmaceuticals (2009) 'Frequently Asked Questions.' Available at: www.gwpharm.co.uk/faqs.asp [accessed 19 March 2009].

Hagan, J. (2001) *Northern Passage: American Vietnam War Resisters in Canada.* Cambridge, MA: Harvard University Press.

Hagan, J. (2003) *Justice in the Balkans: Prosecuting War Crimes in the Hague Tribunal.* Chicago: University of Chicago Press.

Hagan, J. and Greer, S. (2002) 'Making War Criminal', *Criminology*, 40: 231–64.

Hagan, J., Rymond-Richmond, W. and Parker, P. (2005) 'The Criminology of Genocide: The Death and Rape of Darfur', *Criminology*, 43: 525–61.

Hall, J. (1952) *Theft, Law and Society*, 2nd edn. Indianapolis: Bobbs-Merrill.

Hall, S., Critcher, C., Jefferson, T., Clarke, J. and Roberts, B. (1978) *Policing the Crisis.* Basingstoke: Macmillan.

Hamber, B. (2006) '"Nunca Más" and the Politics of Person: Can Truth Telling Prevent the Recurrence of Violence', in T. Borer (ed.) *Telling the Truths: Truth Telling and Peace Building in Post-Conflict Societies.* Indiana: Notre Dame Press (pp. 207–30).

Haney, C, and Zimbardo, P. G. (1977) 'The Socialization into Criminality: On Becoming a Prisoner and a Guard', in J. Tapp and F. Levine (eds) *Law, Justice and the Individual in Society: Psychological and Legal Issues.* New York: Holt, Rinehart and Winston (pp. 198–223).

Harbury, J. (2005) *Truth, Torture, and the American Way: The History and Consequences of U.S. Involvement in Torture.* Boston, MA: Beacon.

Harding, R. (1983) 'Nuclear Energy and the Destiny of Mankind – Some Criminological Perspectives', *Australian and New Zealand Journal of Criminology*, 16: 81–92.

Harner, M. (1977) 'The Ecological Basis for Aztec Sacrifice', *American Ethnologist*, 4: 117–35.

Harriman, E. (2005) 'So, Mr Bremer, Where Did All the Money Go?', *The Guardian*, G2, 7 July, pp. 2–3.

Harriman, E. (2006a) 'The Least Accountable Regime in the Middle East', *London Review of Books*, 2 November. Available at: www.lrb.co.uk/v28/n21/harr04_.htmlpp [accessed 10 August 2008].

Harriman, E. (2006b) 'Cronyism and Kickbacks', *London Review of Books*, 26 January, pp. 14–16.

Harvey, D. (2003) *The New Imperialism.* New York: Oxford University Press.

Hasegawa, T. (2005) *Racing the Enemy: Stalin, Truman, and the Surrender of Japan.* Cambridge, MA: Belknap Press.

Hassig, R. (1988) *Aztec Warfare: Imperial Expansion and Political Control.* Norman, OK: University of Oklahoma Press.

Hayner, P. (2001) *Unspeakable Truths: Confronting State Terror and Atrocity.* London: Routledge.

Hazan, P. (2004) *Justice in a Time of War: The True Story Behind the International Criminal Tribunal for the Former Yugoslavia* (trans. J. T. Snyder). College Station, TX: Texas A&M University Press.

Headrick, A. (2007) *The Teotihuacan Trilogy: The Sociopolitical Structure of an Ancient Mesoamerican City*. Austin: University of Texas Press.

Health Canada (2009) 'Fact Sheet – Medical Access to Marihuana'. Available at: www.HC-SC.GC.CA/DMP-MPS/Marihuana/Law-La/Fact_sheet-Fofiche-Eng.Php [accessed 19 March 2009].

Hedges, C. (2009) 'America is in Need of a Moral Bailout'. Available at: www.truthdig.com/report/item/20090323_america_is_in_need_of_a_moral_bailout [accessed 6 October 2009].

Heilbroner, R. (1974) *An Inquiry into the Human Prospect*. New York: W. W. Norton.

Henry, V. (2004) *Death Work: Police Trauma and the Psychology of Survival*. New York: Oxford University Press.

Herde, C. (2000) 'Injecting Rooms not Guaranteed to Succeed', *AAP Newsfeed*, 11 March. Available at: www.homeoffice.gov.uk [accessed 6 October 2009].

Herrenschmidt, O. (1982) 'Sacrifice: Symbolic or Effective', in M. Izard and P. Smith (eds) *Between Belief and Transgression: Structuralist Essays in Religion, History and Myth*. Chicago: Chicago University Press.

Herring, E. and Ragwala, G. (2006) *Iraq in Fragments: The Occupation and its Legacy*. New York: Cornell University Press.

Heydebrand, W. (2001) 'From Globalisation of Law to Law under Globalisation', in D. Nelken and J. Feest (eds) *Adapting Legal Cultures*. Oxford: Hart.

Hillyard, P. (1993) *Suspect Community*. London: Pluto Press.

Hillyard, P., Pantazis, C., Tombs, S. and Gordon, D. (eds) (2004) *Beyond Criminology: Taking Harm Seriously*. London: Pluto Press.

Hindess, B. and Hirst, P. Q. (1975) *Pre-Capitalist Modes of Production*. London: Routledge and Kegan Paul.

Hirsch, S. (2004a) *Chain of Command: The Road from 9/11 to Abu Ghraib*. New York: Harper Collins.

Hirsch, S. (2004b) 'Torture at Abu Ghraib', 10 May. Available at: www.newyorker.com/archive/2004/05/10/040510fa_fact [accessed 6 October 2009].

Hirsch, S. (2007) 'The General's Report: How Antonio Taguba, who Investigated the Abu Ghraib Scandal, became one of its Casualties', 20 June. Available at: www.newyorker.com/reporting/2007/06/25/070625fa_fact_hersh [accessed 6 October 2009].

Hirsh, M. and Barry, J. (2005) 'The Salvador Option: The Pentagon may put Special-Forces-led Assassination or Kidnapping Teams in Iraq.' Available at: *www.msnbc.msn.com/id/6802629/site/newsweek/print/1/di splaymode/1098/* [accessed 12 October 2005].

Hochschild, A. (1998) *King Leopold's Ghost: A Story of Greed, Terror and Heroism in Colonial Africa*. London: Macmillan.

Hodgson, G. (2009) *The Myth of American Exceptionalism*. New Haven: Yale University Press.

Home Office (2009) 'Cannabis is a Class B drug.' Available at: www.home office.gov.uk/drugs/drugs-law/cannabis-reclassification [accessed 19 March 2009].

Horton, S. (2008) 'The Torture Team', 28 March. Available at: www.harpers.org/archive/2008/03/hbc-90002745 [accessed 6 October 2009].

Hubert, H. and Mauss, M. (1898/1964) *Sacrifice*. Chicago: University of Chicago Press.

Huggins, M. K. (1987) 'U.S. Supported State Terror: A History of Police Training in Latin America', *Crime and Social Justice*, 27–28: 149–71.

Huggins, M. K. (1998) *Political Policing: The United States and Latin America*. Durham, NC: Duke University Press.

Huggins, M. K. (2002) 'Treat Prisoners like Human Beings', *Albany Times Union*, 26 March, p. A-11.

Huggins, M. K. (2003) 'Moral Universes of Torturers and Murderers', *Albany Law Review*, 67(2): 527–35.

Huggins, M. K., Haritos-Fatouros, M. and Zimbardo, P. G. (2002) *Violence Workers: Police Torturers and Murderers Reconstruct Brazilian Atrocities*. San Francisco: University of California Press.

Human Rights Watch (2004a) 'The United States' "Disappeared": The CIA's Long-Term "Ghost Detainees"'. Available at: www.hrw.org/en/reports/2004/ 10/12/united-states-disappeared-cias-long-term-ghost [accessed 2 October 2009].

Human Rights Watch (2004b) '"Enduring Freedom": Abuses by U.S. Forces in Afghanistan'. Available at: thinkweb.hrw.org/en/reports/2004/03/07/endur ing-freedom [accessed 9 February 2006].

Human Rights Watch (2004c) 'The Road to Abu Ghraib'. Available at: thinkweb. hrw.org/en/reports/2004/06/08/road-abu-ghraib [accessed 9 February 2006].

Human Rights Watch (2007) 'Council of Europe: Secret CIA Prisons Confirmed', 7 June. Available at: www.hrw.org/en/news/2007/06/07/council-europe-secret-cia-prisons-confirmed [accessed 6 October 2009].

Iadicola, P. and Shupe, A. (2003) *Violence, Inequality, and Human Freedom*. Boulder, CO: Rowman and Littlefield.

International Advisory and Monitoring Board (IAMB) (2005a) 'Statement by the International Advisory and Monitoring Board on the Development Fund for Iraq', 23 May. Available at: www.iamb.info/pr/pr052308.htm [accessed 7 October 2009].

International Advisory and Monitoring Board (IAMB) (2005b) 'Statement by the International Advisory and Monitoring Board on the Development Fund for Iraq', 4 November. Available at: www.iamb.info/pr/pr011408.htm [accessed 7 October 2009].

International Narcotics Control Board (INCB) (1999) *Report of the International Narcotics Control Board for 1999*. International Narcotics Control Board, E/INCB/ 1999/1.

International Committee of the Red Cross (ICRC) (2007) 'ICRC Report on the Treatment of Fourteen "high value" detainees in CIA Custody', 14 February. Available at: www.iran-daily.com/1385/2580/html/index.htm [accessed 6 October 2009].

International Court of Justice (ICJ) (1986) 'Military and Paramilitary Activities in and against Nicaragua (Nicaragua v. United States of America)', *Archives of International Court of Justice*. Peace Palace: The Hague. Available at: www.icj-cij.org/docket/files/70/9973.pdf?PHPSESSID=dc54883eaf [accessed 18 May 2008].

International Monetary Fund (IMF) (2006) 'Transcript of a Teleconference Call on IMF/World Bank Report on Applying the Debt Sustainability Framework for Low-Income Countries Post-Debt Relief', 7 December. Available at: www.imf.org/external/np/tr/2006/tr061207.htm [accessed 6 October 2009].

International Monetary Fund (IMF) (1999) 'The IMF's Enhanced Structural

Adjustment Facility (ESAF): Is it Working?' Available at: www.imf.org/external/pubs/ft/esaf/exr/index.htm [accessed 28 March 2008].

Iran Daily (2006) 'Europe Colluded in CIA Prisoner Scam', 8 June. Available at www.iran-daily.com/1385/2580/html/index.htm [accessed 14 November 2009].

Iraq Occupation Focus (2005) 'Operation Steel Curtain'. Available at: www.iraqoccupationfocus.org.uk [accessed 10 February 2006].

Iraq Revenue Watch (2003) *Iraq Keeping Secrets: America and Iraq's Public Finances*, Report no. 3. New York: Open Society Institute.

Isenberg, D. (2004) 'A Fistful of Contractors: The Case for a Pragmatic Assessment of Private Military Companies in Iraq', *British-American Security Information Council Basic Report*, Appendix A. Available at: www.basicint.org/pubs/Research/2004PMCapp3.pdf [accessed 6 October 2009].

Jackall, R. (1980) 'Crime in the Suites', *Contemporary Sociology*, 9 (May): 354–8.

Jackson, R. H. (1946) 'Foreword', in S. Glueck, *The Nuremberg Trial and Aggressive War*. New York: Alfred A. Knopf (pp. vii–xii).

Jakobs, G. (2003) 'Derecho Penal del Ciudadano y Derecho Penal del Enemigo', in G. Jakobs and C. Meliá (eds) *Derecho Penal del Enemigo*. Madrid: Civitas (pp. 21–56).

Jameson, F. (1975) *The Prison-House of Language: A Critical Account of Structuralism*. Princeton: Princeton University Press.

Jamieson, R. (1998) 'Towards a Criminology of War in Europe', in V. Ruggiero, N. South and I. Taylor (eds) *The New European Criminology*. London: Routledge (pp. 480–95).

Jamieson, R. and McEvoy, K. (2005) 'State Crime by Proxy and Juridical Othering', *The British Journal of Criminology*, 45(4): 504–27.

Jenkins, B. M. (2000) 'Elite Units Troublesome but Useful', *Los Angeles Times*, 27 March. Available at: articles.latimes.com/2000/mar/27/local/me-1305 [accessed 6 October 2009].

Jenkins, S. (2006) 'Him and Us', *Times Literary Supplement*, 24 February, p. 11.

Jessop, B. (1979) 'Capitalism and Democracy: The Best Possible Political Shell?', in G. LittleJohn, B. Smart, J. Wakeford and N. Yual-Davis (eds) *Power and the State*. London: Billing and Sons (pp. 10–51).

Jessop, B. (1982) *The Capitalist State*. London: Oxford University Press.

Jessop, B. (1991) *State Theory: Putting the Capitalist State in Its Place*. State College, PA: Pennsylvania State University Press.

Jochnick, C. (1995) 'Amazon Oil Offensive', *Multinational Monitor*, January: 12–15.

Jochnick, C. and Normand, R. (1994) 'The Legitimation of Violence: A Critical History of the Laws of War', *Harvard International Law Journal*, 35(1): 49–95.

Johnson, C. (2004) *The Sorrows of Empire: Militarism, Secrecy, and the End of the Republic*. New York: Metropolitan Books.

Johnson, C. (2006) *Nemesis: The Last Days of the American Republic*. New York: Metropolitan Books.

Johnson, C. (2009) 'Prosecutor to Probe CIA Interrogations', *Washington Post*, 25 August, p. 1.

Johnson, R. (1997) *Death Work: A Study of the Modern Execution Process*. Belmont, CA: Wadsworth.

Kampfner, J. (2003) 'Blair was Told it Would be Illegal to Occupy Iraq', *New Statesman*, 26 May. Available at: www.informationclearinghouse.info/article 3505.htm [accessed 8 October 2009].

Kater, M. (1989) *Doctors Under Hitler*. Chapel Hill, NC: University of North Carolina.

Kauzlarich, D. and Kramer, R. (1998) *Crimes of the American Nuclear State: At Home and Abroad*. Boston, MA: Northeastern University Press.

Kauzlarich, D., Matthews, R. and Miller, W. (2001) 'Toward a Victimology of State Crime', *Critical Criminology*, 10(3): 173–94.

Kauzlarich, D., Mullins, C. and Matthews, R. (2003) 'A Complicity Continuum of State Crime', *Contemporary Justice Review*, 6(3): 241–54.

Kelly, C. (2004) 'The War on Jurisdiction: Troubling Questions about Executive Order 13303', *Arizona Law Review*, 46(483): 484–516.

Kelman, H. and Hamilton, V. L. (1989) *Crimes of Obedience: Towards a Social Psychology of Authority and Responsibility*. London, CT: Yale University Press.

Kemmesies, U. E. (1999) *The Open Drug Scene and the Safe Injection Room Offers in Frankfurt am Main 1995: Final Report*. A survey conducted on behalf of the City of Frankfurt/Municipal Department Women and Health. Frankfurt am Main: Drug Policy Coordination Office.

Kershaw, I. (2000) *Hitler: 1889–1936, Hubris*. New York: W. W. Norton.

Kiernan, B. (2007) *Blood and Soil*. New Haven: Yale University Press.

Killias, M. and Rbasa, J. (1998) 'Does Heroin Prescription Reduce Crime', *Studies on Crime and Crime Prevention*, 7: 127–33.

Kinzer, S. (2006) *Overthrow*. New York: Henry Holt.

Klein, N. (2007) *The Shock Doctrine: The Rise of Disaster Capitalism*. New York: Metropolitan Books.

Knight, A. (2002) *Mexico: From the Beginning to the Spanish Conquest*. Cambridge: Cambridge University Press.

Knox, O. (2009) 'Former Bush Aide says Politics Colored U.S. Terror Alert', *Yahoo News*, 20 August. Available at: news.yahoo.com/s/afp/20090820/pl_afp/usat tackspoliticsridge [accessed 6 October 2009].

Kolko, G. (1984) *Main Currents in Modern American History*. New York: Pantheon Books.

Kornblut, A. E. (2009) 'New Unit to Question Key Terror Suspects: Move Shifts Interrogation Oversight From the CIA to the White House', *Washington Post*, 24 August. Available at: www.washingtonpost.com/wp-dyn/content/article/2009/08/23/AR2009082302598.html?hpid=topnews [accessed 6 October 2009].

Kort, M. (2007) *The Columbia Guide to Hiroshima and the Bomb*. New York: Columbia University Press.

KPMG Bahrain (2004) *Development Fund for Iraq: Report of Factual Findings in Connection with Disbursements for the Period from 1 January 2004 to 28 June 2004*. Baghdad: International Advisory and Monitoring Board of the Development Fund for Iraq and the Project and Contracting Office.

Kramer, R. (1982) 'The Debate Over the Definition of Crime: Paradigms, Values, and Criminological Work', in F. Elliston and N. Bowie (eds) *Ethics, Public Policy, and Criminal Justice*. Cambridge, MA: Oelgeschlager, Gunn, and Hain (pp. 33–58).

Kramer, R. and Kauzlarich, D. (2010) 'Nuclear Weapons, International Law and the Normalization of State Crime', in D. L. Rothe and C. Mullins (eds) *State Crime: Current Perspectives*. New Brunswick, NJ: Rutgers University Press.

Kramer, R. and Michalowski, R. (1990) 'Toward an Integrated Theory of State and Corporate Crime', paper presented at the 42nd Annual Meeting of the American Society of Criminology, 9 November, Baltimore, Maryland.

Kramer, R. and Michalowski, R. (2005) 'War, Aggression and State Crime: A

Criminological Analysis of the Invasion and Occupation of Iraq', *British Journal of Criminology*, 45: 446–9.

Kramer, R. and Michalowski, R. (2006) 'The Original Formulation', in R. Michalowski and R. Kramer (eds) *State-Corporate Crime: Wrongdoing at the Intersection of Business and Government*. New Brunswick, NJ: Rutgers University Press (pp. 18–26).

Kramer, R., Michalowski, R. and Rothe, D. (2005) '"The Supreme International Crime": How the U.S. War in Iraq Threatens the Rule of Law', *Critical Criminology*, 32(2): 52–81.

Krasmann, S. (2007) 'The Enemy on the Border: Critique of a Programme in Favour of a Preventive State', *Punishment and Society*, 9(3): 301–18.

Kurlansky, M. (1999) *The Basque History of the World*. New York: Penguin.

Langguth, J. (1979) *Hidden Terrors: The Truth about Police Operations in Latin America*. New York: Pantheon.

Lawson, A. and Halford, S. (2004) *Fuelling Suspicion: The Coalition and Iraq's Oil Billions*. London: Christian Aid.

Lazzeri, C. (1992) 'Le Gouvernement de la Raison d'État', in C. Lazzeri and D. Reynié (eds) *Le Pouvoir de la Raison d'État*. Paris: PUF (pp. 91–134).

Lazzeri, C. and Reynié, D. (1992) 'Introduction', in C. Lazzeri and D. Reynié (eds) *Le Pouvoir de la Raison d'État*. Paris: PUF (pp. 9–12).

Lee-Shanok, P. and Gamble, D. (2001) 'Looser Pot Laws to Aid the Sick, but Critics Say Changes Flawed', *Toronto Sun*, 7 April, p. 24.

Leebaw, B. A. (2008) 'The Irreconcilable Goals of Transitional Justice', *Human Rights Quarterly*, 30: 95–118.

Leinwand, D. (2009) 'More States Move Toward Allowing Medical Marijuana Use', *USA Today*, 26 March. Available at: www.usatoday.com/news/nation/2009-03-25-pot_N.htm [accessed 26 March 2009].

Lemert, E. (1972) *Human Deviance, Social Problems and Social Control*. Englewood Cliffs, NJ: Prentice-Hall.

Lemke, T. (2005) 'A Zone of Indistinction – A Critique of Giorgio Agamben's Concept of Biopolitics', *Critical Social Studies*, 7(1): 3–13.

Lenning, E. (2007) 'Execution for Body Parts: A Case of State Crime', *Contemporary Justice Review*, 10(2): 173–91.

Lens, S. (1971/2003) *The Forging of the American Empire*. London: Pluto Press.

Leo, R. (2008) *Police Interrogation and American Justice*. Cambridge, MA: Harvard University Press.

Lesley, G. (2004) *The School of the Americas: Military Training and Political Violence in the Americas*. Durham, NC: Duke University Press.

Lewis, N. (2008) 'Alaska Senator is Guilty Over his Failures to Disclose Gifts', *New York Times*, 27 October, p. A1.

Lifton, R. J. (1986) *The Nazi Doctors: Medical Killing and the Psychology of Genocide*. New York: Basic Books.

Lifton, R. J. and Mitchell, G. (1995) *Hiroshima in America: Fifty Years of Denial*. New York: Grosset/Putnam.

Lindesmith Center (1999) 'Safer Injection Rooms.' Available at: www.lindesmith.org/library/safe_injection.html [accessed 10 April 2008].

Lofquist, W. (2002) 'Whodunit? An Examination of the Production of Wrongful Convictions', in S. Westervelt and J. Humphrey (eds) *Wrongly Convicted: Perspectives on Failed Justice*. Newark, NJ: Rutgers University Press (pp. 174–96).

Longman, T. (2006) 'Justice at the Grassroots? Gacaca Trials in Rwanda', in N.

Roht-Arriaza and J. Mariezcurrena (eds) *Transitional Justice in the Twenty-First Century: Beyond Truth versus Justice*. Cambridge: Cambridge University Press (pp. 206–28).

Luhmann, N. (1998) *Sistemas Sociales: Lineamientos para una Teoría General* (trans. S. Pappe and B. Erker). Mexico: Anthropos.

Lukes, S. (1975) *E. Durkheim: His Life and Work: A Historical and Critical Study*. Harmondsworth, Penguin.

Lundy, P. and McGovern, M. (2008) 'Whose Justice? Rethinking Transitional Justice from the Bottom Up', *Journal of Law and Society*, 35(2): 265–92.

Luscombe, B. (2001) 'When the Evidence Lies', *Time*, 13 May. Available at: www.time.com/time/nation/article/0,8599,109568,00.htm [accessed 5 May 2008].

Lutz, E. (2006) 'Transitional Justice: Lessons Learned and the Road Ahead', in N. Roht-Arriaza and J. Mariezcurrena (eds) *Transitional Justice in the Twenty-First Century: Beyond Truth versus Justice*. Cambridge: Cambridge University Press (pp. 325–41).

Lynch, M. and Michalowski, R. (2005) *Crime, Power and Identity: The New Primer in Radical Criminology*, 4th edn. Washington, DC: Criminal Justice Press.

Lynch, M. and Stretesky, P. (2001) 'Toxic Crimes: Examining Corporate Victimization of the General Public Employing Medical and Epidemiological Evidence', *Critical Criminology*, 10(3): 153–72.

Lyons M. and Mayall, J. (2003) *International Human Rights in the 21st Century: Protecting the Rights of Groups*. New York: Rowman and Littlefield.

MacCoun, R. and Reuter, P. (1997) 'Interpreting Dutch Cannabis Policy: Reasoning by Analogy in the Legalization Debate', *Science*, 278: 48, 50–1.

MacCoun, R. and Reuter, P. (1999) 'Does Europe do it Better? Lessons from Holland, Britain and Switzerland: Approaches to Drug Trafficking and Drug Addiction', *The Nation*, 269: 28.

MacCoun, R., Model, K., Philips-Shockley, H. and Reuter, P. (1995) 'Comparing Drug Policies in North America and Western Europe', in G. Estievenart (ed.) *Policies and Strategies to Combat Drugs in Europe*. Dordrecht: Martinus Nijhoff (pp. 197–220).

Machiavelli, N. (1505) *The Prince* (trans. W. K. Marriott). Available at: www.the-prince-by-machiavelli.com/ [accessed 1 October 2009].

Mack, J. E. (1988) 'The Enemy System', *Lancet*, 2(8607): 385–7.

Mackenzie, S. (2006) 'Systemic Crimes of the Powerful: Criminal Aspects of the Global Economy', *Social Justice*, 33(1): 162–82.

Mackenzie, S. and Green, P. (2008) 'Performative Regulation: A Case Study in How Powerful People Avoid Criminal Labels', *British Journal of Criminology*, 48: 138–53.

Macrae, C. and Fadhil, A. (2006) 'Iraq Awash in Cash', *The Guardian*, 20 March. Available at: www.springerlink.com/index/R3773J4076724X68.pd [accessed 4 April 2008].

Maffie, J. (2002) '"We Eat of the Earth then the Earth Eats Us": The Concept of Nature in Pre-Hispanic Nahua Thought', *Ludis Vitalis*, X(17): 5–20.

Maier, C. (2005) 'An American Empire?: The Problems of Frontiers and Peace in Twenty-First Century Politics', in L. Gardner and M. Young (eds) *The New American Empire: A 21st Century Teach-In on U.S. Foreign Policy*. New York: New Press (pp. xi–xix).

Maltz, M. (1995) 'On Defining Organized Crime', in N. Passas (ed.) *Organized Crime*. Boston, MA: Dartmouth (pp. 338–46).

Mamdani, M. (2008) 'The New Humanitarian Order', *The Nation*, 29 September, pp. 17–22.

Mani, R. (2002) *Beyond Retribution: Seeking Justice in the Shadows of War*. Cambridge: Polity Press.

Mann, S. (1999) 'UN Drugs Agency Threatens Ban on $160m Poppy Trade', *Sydney Morning Herald*, 18 December, p. A4.

Markusen, E. and Kopf, D. (1995) *The Holocaust and Strategic Bombing: Genocide and Total War in the Twentieth Century*. Boulder, CO: Westview Press.

Martin, D. (2002) 'The Police Role in Wrongful Convictions: An International Comparative Study', in S. Westervelt and J. Humphrey (eds) *Wrongly Convicted: Perspectives on Failed Justice*. New Brunswick, NJ: Rutgers University Press (pp. 77–95).

Marvin, C. and Ingle, D. W. (1999) *Blood Sacrifice and the Nation: Totem Rituals and the America Flag*. Cambridge: Cambridge University Press.

Marx, K. and Engels, F. (1848/1969) 'Manifesto of the Communist Party', in *Marx and Engels: Selected Works*, Vol. I. Moscow: Progress Publishers.

Mathiesen, T. (2004) *Silently Silenced: Essays on the Creation of Acquiescence in Modern Society*. Winchester: Waterside Press.

Mattei, U. (2003) 'A Theory of Imperial Law: A Study on U.S. Hegemony and the Latin Resistance', *Global Jurist Frontiers*, 3(2): 383–448.

Matthews, R. and Kauzlarich, D. (2000) 'The Crash of ValuJet Flight 592: A Case Study in State-Corporate Crime', *Sociological Focus*, 3(3): 281–98.

Matthews, R. and Kauzlarich, D. (2007) 'State Crime and State Harms: A Tale of Two Definitional Frameworks', *Crime, Law and Social Change*, 48(1–2): 43–55.

Maxwell, M. and Watts, S. (2007) '"Unlawful Enemy Combatant": Status, Theory of Culpability, or Neither?', *Journal of International Criminal Justice*, 5: 19–25.

Mbembe, A. (2003) 'Necropolitics', *Public Culture*, 15(1): 11–40.

McCafferty, G. (2000) 'Tollan Cholollan and the Legacy of Legitimacy During the Classic-Postclassic Transition', in D. Carrasco, L. Jones and S. Sessions (eds) *Mesoamerica's Classic Heritage: From Teotihuacan to the Aztecs*. Boulder, CO: University of Colorado Press.

McCarthy, B. and Hagan, J. (2009) 'Counting the Deaths in Darfur: Pitfalls on the Pathway to a Public Sociology', in V. Jeffries (ed.) *Handbook of Public Sociology*. Lanham, MD: Rowman and Littlefield (pp. 319–37).

McCoy, A. (1972) *The Politics of Heroin in Southeast Asia*. New York: Harper and Row.

McCoy, A. (2006) *A Question of Torture: CIA Interrogation, From the Cold War to the War on Terror*. New York: Henry Holt.

McEvoy, K. (2008) 'Letting Go of Legalism: Developing a "Thicker" Version of Transitional Justice', in K. McEvoy and L. McGregor (eds) *Transitional Justice from Below*. Oxford: Hart (pp. 15–45).

McLeary, P. (2007) 'A Different Kind of Great Game', *Foreign Policy*. Available at: www.foreignpolicy.com/story/cms.php?story_id=3744 [accessed 6 October 2009].

McMahon, P. (1999) 'Medical Marijuana Nears Mainstream', *USA Today*, 15 March, p. A1.

Medical Industry Today (2000) 'Medical Marijuana Trials to Begin in UK', 10 April, p. 10.

Meiksins-Wood, E. (2003) *Empire of Capital*. London: Verso.

Meinecke, F. (1983) *La idea de la razón de Estado en la edad moderna* (trans. F. González Vicen). Madrid: Centro de Estudios Constitucionales.

Melossi, D. (1990) *The State of Social Control: A Sociological Study of Concepts of State and Social Control in the Making of Democracy.* Cambridge: Polity Press.

Merle, R. (2006) 'Census Counts 100,000 Contractors in Iraq', *Washington Post,* 5 December, p. A4.

Michalowski, R. (1985) *Order, Law and Crime.* New York: Random House.

Michalowski, R. (2009) 'Power, Crime and Criminology in the New Imperial Age', *Crime, Law and Social Change,* 51(3–4): 303–26.

Michalowski, R. and Bohlander, E. (1976) 'Repression and Criminal Justice in Capitalist America', *Sociological Inquiry,* 46: 95–106.

Michalowski, R. and Kramer, R. (1987) 'The Space Between Laws: The Problem of Corporate Crime in a Transnational Context', *Social Problems,* 34(1): 34–53.

Michalowski, R. and Kramer, R. (2006) *State-Corporate Crime: Wrongdoing at the Intersection of Business and Government.* New Brunswick, NJ: Rutgers University Press.

Michalowski, R. and Kramer, R. (2007) 'State-Corporate Crime and Criminological Inquiry', in H. Pontell and G. Geis (eds) *International Handbook of White-Collar and Corporate Crime.* New York: Springer (pp. 200–19).

Mickleburgh, R. (2000) 'Safe Drug-injection Site Sought: B.C. Facing Worst Hepatitis C Epidemic in the Western World.' Available at: www.lindesmith.org [accessed 1 December 2008].

Mieville, C. (2006) *Between Equal Rights: A Marxist Theory of International Law.* Chicago: Haymarket.

Miles, S. (2004) 'Abu Ghraib: Its Legacy for Military Medicine', *Lancet.* Available at: www.globalresearch.ca/articles/MIL408A.html [accessed 1 October 2009].

Miller, A. S. (1975) *The Modern Corporate State: Private Governments and the American Constitution.* Westport, CT: Greenwood Press.

Miller, C. (2005) 'Private Security Guards in Iraq Operate with Little Supervision', *Los Angeles Times,* 4 December, p. A2.

Mills, C. W. (1959) *The Sociological Imagination.* New York: Oxford University Press.

Moccia, S. (1997) *La Perenne Emergenza: Tendenze Autoritarie nel Sistema Penale,* 2nd edn. Napoli: Edizioni Scientifiche Italiane.

Montefiore, S. S. (2007) *Young Stalin.* New York: Alfred A. Knopf.

Moore, R. I. (2001) *The Formation of a Persecuting Society.* New York: John Wiley.

Morales, F. (1999) 'The Militarization of the Police', *Covert Action Quarterly,* 67 (Spring–Summer): 67.

Morrison, R. (1995) *Theoretical Criminology: From Modernity to Post-Modernism.* London: Routledge Cavendish.

Mother Jones (2008a) 'Exclusive: Who's Behind Abu Ghraib?', 20 March. Available at: www.motherjones.com/politics/2008/03/exclusive-whos-behind-abu-ghraib [accessed 6 October 2009].

Mother Jones (2008b) 'The Final Act of Abu Ghraib', March/April. Available at www.motherjones.com/politics/2008/03/final-act-abu-ghraib [accessed 6 October 2009].

Mullins, C. and Rothe, D. (2008) *Power, Bedlam, and Bloodshed: State Crime in Post-colonial Africa.* New York: Peter Lang.

Mustill, L. J. (1988) 'The New Lex Mercatoria: The First Twenty Five Years', *Arbitration International,* 4: 86–119.

Nader, L. (2005) 'The Americanisation of International Law', in F. von Benda-Beckman, K. von Benda-Beckman and A. Griffiths (eds) *Mobile People, Mobile Law: Expanding Legal Relations in a Contracting World.* Aldershot: Ashgate (pp. 199–213).

Nader, R. (2002) 'A Corporate (Crime) State', *Counterpunch*. Available at: www.counterpunch.org/nader0615.html [accessed 6 October 2009].

Nagy, R. (2008) 'Transitional Justice as Global Project: Critical Reflections', *Third World Quarterly*, 29(2): 275–89.

NAOMI (2008) *Status Report*. Available at: www.naomistudy.ca [accessed 10 January 2009].

National Security Archive (NSA) (n.d.) 'Prisoner Abuse: Patterns From the Past', National Security Archive Electronic Briefing Book No. 122. Available at: www.gwu.edu/~nsarchiv/NSAEBB/NSAEBB122/ [accessed 5 January 2009].

Nelken, D. (ed.) (1994) *White Collar Crime*. Dartmouth: Ashgate.

New York Times (2004a) 'Photos of Dead Show the Horrors of Abuse', 7 May, p. A11.

New York Times (2004b) '"My Deepest Apology" from Rumsfeld; "Nothing Less than Tragic", says top General', 8 May, p. A6.

New York Times (2005) 'CIA Empowered to Send Suspects Abroad to Jails.' Available at: www.drudgereportarchives.com/.../20050305_232600.htm [accessed 12 May 2008].

Newman, R. (1995) *Truman and the Hiroshima Cult*. East Lansing, MI: Michigan State University Press.

Nugent, W. (2008) *Habits of Empire: A History of American Expansion*. New York: Alfred A. Knopf.

O'Connor, J. (1973) *Fiscal Crisis of the State*. New York: St Martin's Press.

Offe, K. and Ronge, V. (1982) 'Theses on the Theory of the State', in A. Giddens and D. Held (eds) *Classes, Power and Conflict: Classical and Contemporary Debates*. London: Macmillan (pp. 249–56).

Okonta, I. and Douglas, O. (2001) *Where Vultures Feast: Shell, Human Rights and Oil in the Niger Delta*. San Francisco: Sierra Club Books.

Orentlicher, D. F. (2007) '"Settling Accounts" Revisited: Reconciling Global Norms with Local Agency', *International Journal of Transitional Justice*, 1: 10–22.

Orford, A. (2006) 'Commissioning the Truth', *Columbia Journal of Gender and Law*, 15(3): 851–83.

Padden, R. C. (1962) *The Hummingbird and the Hawk: Conquest and Sovereignty in the Valley of Mexico, 1503–1541*. New York: Harper Torchbooks.

Panezi, M. (2007) 'Source of Law in Transition: Re-visiting General Principles of International Law', unpublished paper presented at the annual meeting of the Law and Society Association, Montreal, Quebec, 27 May.

Panitch, L. and Gindin S. (2006) 'Theorizing American Empire', in A. Bartholomew (ed.) *Empire's Law*. London: Pluto Press (pp. 21–43).

Pape, R. (1996) *Bombing to Win: Air Power and Coercion in War*. Ithaca, NY: Cornell University Press.

Parenti, C. (2005) *The Freedom: Shadows and Hallucinations in Occupied Iraq*. New York: New Press.

Pasquino, P. (1992) 'Police Spirituelle et Police Terrienne', in C. Lazzeri and D. Reynié (eds) *La Raison d'État: Politique et Rationalité*. Paris: PUF (pp. 83–115).

Pasztory, E. (1997) *Teotihuacan: An Experiment in Living*. London: University of Oklahoma Press.

Paternoster, R., Braeme, R. and Bacon, S. (2008) *The Death Penalty: America's Experience with Capital Punishment*. New York: Oxford University Press.

Patrick, I. (2001) 'East Timor Emerging from Conflict: The Role of Local NGOs and International Assistance', *Disasters*, 25(1): 48–66.

Patterson, I. (2007) *Guernica and Total War*. Cambridge: Harvard University Press.

Patterson, O. (1982) *Slavery and Social Death: A Comparative Study*. Harvard: Harvard University Press.

Payne, L. (2003) 'Confessions of Torturers: Reflections on Cases from Argentina', in S. E. Eckstein and T. P. Wickham-Crowley (eds) *What Justice? Whose Justice? Fighting for Fairness in Latin America*. Berkeley, CA: University of California Press.

Pearce, F. (1976) *Crimes of the Powerful*. London: Pluto Press.

Pearce, F. (2001) *The Radical Durkheim*, 2nd edn. Toronto: Canadian Scholars Press.

Pearce, F. (2007) 'An Age of Miracles?', in H. Pontell and G. Geis (eds) *International Handbook of White Collar and Corporate Crime*. Springer: New York (pp. 148–162).

Pearce, F. and Tombs, S. (1998) *Toxic Capitalism: Corporate Crime and the Chemical Industry*. Aldershot: Ashgate.

Pearce, J. (1981) *Under the Eagle*. Boston, MA: South End Press.

Pearce, K. C. and Fadely, D. (1992) 'Justice, Sacrifice and the Universal Audience: George Bush's Address to the Nation Announcing the Allied Military Action in the Persian Gulf', *Rhetoric Society Quarterly*, 22(2): 39–40.

Pemberton, S. (2004) 'A Theory of Moral Indifference: Understanding the Production of Harm by Capitalist Societies', in P. Hillyard, C. Pazantis, D. Gordon and S. Tombs (eds) *Beyond Criminology: Taking Harm Seriously*. London: Pluto Press (pp. 67–83).

Pepinsky, H. and Quinney, R. (eds) (1991) *Criminology as Peacemaking*. Bloomington, IN: Indiana University Press.

Perkins, J. (2004) *Confessions of an Economic Hit Man*. New York: Plume.

Perrow, C. (1986) *Normal Accidents: Living with High-Risk Technologies*. Princeton, NJ: Princeton University Press.

Petras, J. (2007) *Rulers and Ruled in the US Empire*. Atlanta: Clarity Press.

Pfohl, S. (1994) *Images of Deviance and Social Control: A Sociological History*. New York: McGraw-Hill.

Phillips, K. (2004) *American Dynasty: Aristocracy, Fortune and the Politics of Deceit in the House of Bush*. New York: Viking Penguin.

Platform (2005) *Crude Designs: The Rip-Off of Iraq's Oil Wealth*. London: Platform.

Platt, A. (1969) *The Child Savers*. Chicago: University of Chicago Press.

Platt, A. (1978) 'Street Crime – A View from the Left', *Crime and Social Justice*, 9: 26–34.

Pogge, T. (2002) *World Poverty and Human Rights*. Cambridge: Polity Press.

Polanyi, K. (1944/2001) *The Great Transformation: The Political and Economic Origins of Our Time*. Boston, MA: Beacon Press.

Poulantzas, N. (1968) *Political Power and Social Classes*. London: New Left Books.

Pouligny, B. (2006) *Peace Operations Seen from Below: UN Missions and Local People*. Bloomfield: Kumarian Press.

Powell, E. H. (1988) *The Design of Discord: Studies of Anomie*. New York: Oxford University Press.

Presser, L. (2008) 'Power, Safety, and Ethics in Cross-Gendered Research with Violent Men', in M. Huggins and M. Glebbeek (eds) *Women Fielding Danger: Negotiating Ethnographic Identities in Field Research*. Lanham, MD.: Rowman and Littelfield.

Preuss, U. (2006) 'The Iraq War: Critical Reflections from "Old Europe"', in A. Bartholomew (ed.) *Empire's Law*. London: Pluto Press (pp. 52–70).

Priest, D. (2005) 'CIA Holds Terror Suspects in Secret Prisons: Debate is Growing Within Agency about Legality and Morality of Overseas System Set Up After 9/11', *Washington Post*, 2 November, p. A01.

Protess, D. and Warden, R. (1998) *A Promise of Justice*. New York: Hyperion.

Punch, M. (1996) *Dirty Business*. London: Sage.

Purvis, T. (2006) 'Looking for Life Signs in an International Rule of Law', in A. Bartholomew (ed.) *Empire's Law*. London: Pluto Press (pp. 110–36).

Quinney, R. (1962) 'Retail Pharmacy as a Marginal Occupation: A Study of Prescription Violation', unpublished PhD dissertation, University of Wisconsin.

Quinney, R. (1970) *The Social Reality of Crime*. Boston, MA: Little, Brown.

Quinney, R. (1974) *Critique of Legal Order: Crime Control in Capitalist Society*. Boston, MA: Little, Brown.

Quinney, R. (1977) *Class, State and Crime: On the Theory and Practice of Criminal Justice*. New York: David McKay.

Quinney, R. (2000) *Bearing Witness to Crime and Social Justice*. Albany, NY: SUNY Press.

Radelet, M., Bedau, H. and Putnam, C. (1992) *In Spite of Innocence*. Boston, MA: Northeastern University Press.

Rajagopal, B. (2008) 'Counter-hegemonic International Law: Rethinking Human Rights and Development as a Third World Strategy', in R. Falk, B. Rajagopal and J. Stevens (eds) *International Law and the Third World: Reshaping Justice*. London: Routledge-Cavendish (pp. 63–79).

Rall, T. (2009) 'Barack Obama, Torture Enabler', 10 April. Available at: www.commondreams.org/view/2009/04/10-6 [accessed 6 October 2009].

Reid, T. R. (2000) 'Campaign to Legalize Marijuana Use in Britain Picks up Steam', *Washington Post*, 10 October, p. A26.

Reifert, S. and Carlson, S. M. (2007) 'Police Departments as Victims of State-Corporate Crime', paper presented at the annual meeting of the American Society of Criminology, Atlanta, Georgia.

Renee, Y. (1978) *The Search for Criminal Man: A Conceptual History of the Dangerous Offender*. Lexington, MA: Lexington Books.

Retort (2005) *Afflicted Powers: Capital and Spectacle in a New Age of War*. London: Verso.

Reuters (2000) 'Germany Passes Law Allowing Drug Injection Rooms', Reuters Ltd, 25 February. Available at: www.aidsinfobbs.org/library/cdcsums/2000/002.feb/1791 [accessed 10 January 2008].

Reynié, D. (1992) 'Le Regard Souverain: Statistique Social et Raison d'État du XVIe au XVIIIe Siècle', in C. Lazzeri and D. Reynié (eds) *La Raison d'État: Politique et Rationalité*. Paris: PUF (pp. 43–82).

Rogers, L. (2000) 'NHS Supplies Addicts with 11m of Heroin Pounds', *Sunday Times*, 16 July, p. C6.

Roht-Arriaza, N. (2006) 'The New Landscape of Transitional Justice', in N. Roht-Arriaza and J. Mariezcurrena (eds) *Transitional Justice in the Twenty-First Century: Beyond Truth versus Justice*. Cambridge: Cambridge University Press (pp. 1–16).

Rosen, R. (1987) 'Disciplinary Sanctions Against Prosecutors for *Brady* Violations: A Paper Tiger', *North Carolina Law Review*, 65: 693–744.

Ross, J. I. (1995) *Controlling State Crime: An Introduction*. New York: Garland.

Ross, J. I. (2000) 'Introduction: Protecting Democracy by Controlling State Crime in Advanced Industrialized Countries', in J. I. Ross (ed.) *Varieties of State Crime and Its Control*. Monsey, NY: Criminal Justice Press (pp. 1–10).

Ross, J. I. (2003) *The Dynamics of Political Crime*. Thousand Oaks, CA: Sage.

Ross, J. I. (2006) *Political Terrorism: An Interdisciplinary Approach*. New York: Peter Lang.

Ross, J. I. (2009) *Cutting the Edge: Current Perspectives in Radical/Critical Criminology and Criminal Justice*. New Brunswick, NJ: Transaction.

Rossi, G. (2006) *Il Gioco delle Regole*. Milan: Adelphi.

Roszak, T. (1969) *The Making of a Counterculture*. Garden City, NY: Doubleday.

Rothe, D. (2009) *State Criminality: The Crime of All Crimes*. Lanham, MD: Lexington Books.

Rothe, D. and Friedrichs, D. (2006) 'The State of the Criminology of Crimes of the State', *Social Justice*, 33(1): 147–61.

Rothe, D. and Mullins, C. (2006) *Symbolic Gestures and the Generation of Social Control: The International Criminal Court*. Lanham, MD: Lexington Books.

Rothe, D. and Muzzatti, S. (2004) 'Enemies Everywhere: Terrorism, Moral Panic, and US Civil Society', *Critical Criminology*, 12: 327–50.

Rothe, D. and Ross, J. I. (2008) 'The Marginalization of State Crime', *Critical Sociology*, 34(5): 741–2.

Rothe, D., Mullins, C. and Sandstrom, K. (2009) 'The Rwandan Genocide: International Finance Policies and Human Rights', *Social Justice*, 35(3): 66–86.

Rothe, D., Muzzatti, S. and Mullins, C. (2006) 'Crime on the High Seas: Crimes of Globalization and the Sinking of the Senegalese Ferry Le Joola', *Critical Criminology*, 14(2): 159–80.

Ruggiero, V. (1996) *Organized and Corporate Crime in Europe: Offers That Can't Be Refused*. Aldershot: Dartmouth.

Ruggiero, V. (2006) *Understanding Political Violence*. London: Open University Press.

Rusche, S. and Caltrider, W. (1999) 'Prescribing Heroin: Response and Rebuttal to Heroin Study Findings', *Science*, 23 July, pp. 285, 532.

Ruttan, V. W. (2005) *Is War Necessary for Economic Growth? Military Procurement and Technology Development*. Oxford: Oxford University Press.

Ryan, D. (2007) *Frustrated Empire: U.S. Foreign Policy, 9/11 to Iraq*. London: Pluto Press.

Sadat, L. N. (2005) 'Ghost Prisoners and Black Sites: Extraordinary Rendition under International Law', *Case Western Reserve Journal of International Law*, 37: 309–42.

Sahagun, B. de (1981) *Florentine Codex: General History of the Things of New Spain: Book 2: The Ceremonies* (translated from the Nahuatl with notes by Arthur J. O. Anderson and Charles E. Dibble). Salt Lake City: University of Utah Press.

Sands, P. (2005) *Lawless World*. New York: Penguin.

Santiago, C. (2006) 'From Insular Cases to Camp X-Ray: Agamben's State of Exception and United States Territorial Law', *Studies in Law, Politics and Society*, 39: 15–55.

Schabas, W. A. (2006) 'The Sierra Leone Truth and Reconciliation Commission', in N. Roht-Arriaza and J. Mariezcurrena (eds) *Transitional Justice in the Twenty-First Century: Beyond Truth versus Justice*. Cambridge: Cambridge University Press (pp. 21–42).

Schaffer, R. (1985) *Wings of Judgment: American Bombing in World War II*. New York: Oxford University Press.

Scheck, B., Neufeld, P. and Dwyer, J. (2000) *Actual Innocence*. New York: Doubleday.

Schell, J. (1982) *The Fate of the Earth*. New York: Avon.

Scheper-Hughes, N. and Bourgois, P. (2004) *Violence in War and Peace: An Anthology*. Oxford: Blackwell.

Scherer, M. and Ghosh, B. (2009) 'How Waterboarding Got Out of Control', *Time Magazine*, 20 April. Available at: www.time.com/time/nation/article/0,8599,1892708,00.html [accessed 15 June 2009].

Schmalleger, F. (2008) *Criminology Today: An Integrative Introduction*, 5th edn. Englewood Cliffs, NJ: Prentice Hall.

Schmidt, C. (1922/1985) *Political Theology: Four Chapters on the Concept of Sovereignty* (trans. G. D. Schwab). Amherst, MA: MIT Press.

Schmitt, C. (1950/2003) *The Nomos of the Earth: In the International Law of the Jus Publicum Europaeum*. New York: Telos.

Schmitt, C. (2005) *Political Theology. Four Chapters on the Concept of Sovereignty* (trans. G. Schwab). Chicago: University of Chicago Press.

Schons, G. W., Coleman, J. P., Summerhays, D. L., Sinunu, K. and Michaels, B. E. (2001) *Professionalism: A Sourcebook of Ethics and Civil Liability Principles for Prosecutors*. California: District Attorney's Association.

Schur, E. (1971) *Labeling Deviant Behavior*. New York: Harper and Row.

Schwartz, M. (2007) 'Neo-liberalism on Crack: Cities under Siege in Iraq', *City*, 11: 21–69.

Schwendinger, H. and Schwendinger, J. (1970) 'Defenders of Order or Guardians of Human Rights?', *Issues in Criminology*, 5: 123–57.

Scraton, P. (ed.) (1987) *Law, Order and the Authoritarian State: Readings in Critical Criminology*. Philadelphia: Open University Press.

Scully, D. and Marolla, J. (1985) '"Riding the Bull at Gilley's": Convicted Rapists Describe the Rewards of Rape', *Social Problems*, 32(3): 251–63.

Séglard, D. (1992) 'Foucault et le Problème du Gouvernement', in C. Lazzeri and D. Reynié (eds) *La Raison d'État: Politique et Rationalité*. Paris: PUF (pp. 117–40).

Seidman, S. (2008) *Contested Knowledge: Social Theory Today*, 4th edn. Malden, MA: Blackwell.

Selden, M. (2009) 'A Forgotten Holocaust: U.S. Bombing Strategy, the Destruction of Japanese Cities and the American Way of War from the Pacific War to Iraq', in Y. Tanaka and M. Young (eds) *Bombing Civilians: A Twentieth-Century History*. New York: New Press (pp. 77–96).

Selden, M. and So, A. (2004) *War and State Terrorism: The United States, Japan, and the Asia-Pacific in the Long Twentieth Century*. Lanham, MD: Rowman and Littlefield.

Sellin, T. (1938) *Culture, Conflict and Crime*. New York: Social Science Research Council.

Senellart, M. (1992) 'La Raison d'État Antimachiavélienne', in C. Lazzeri and D. Reynié (eds) *La Raison d'État: Politique et Rationalité*. Paris: PUF (pp. 15–42).

Sengupta, K. (2006) 'Blair Accused of Trying to Privatise War in Iraq', *The Independent*, 30 October, p. A1.

Serrano, R. A. (2005) 'Civil-Liberties Report Spotlights U.S. Use of Rendition', *Los Angeles Times*, 25 April, p. A3.

Sevastopulo, D. (2005) 'Activists Condemn Abu Ghraib Verdict', *Financial Times*, 25 April. Available at: www.uslaboragainstwar.org/article.php?id = 8094 [accessed 1 October 2009].

Sewall, J. (1905/1995) *The Log Book of the Captain's Clerk*. Chicago: R. R. Donnelly and Sons.

Sharpe, K. (2006) 'Realpolitik or Imperial Hubris: The Latin American Drug War and U.S. Foreign Policy in Iraq', *Orbis*, 50(3): 481–99.

Shayne, S. and Mazzetti, M. (2009) 'In Adopting Harsh Tactics, No Look at Past Use', *New York Times*, 21 April. Available at: www.nytimes.com/2009/04/22/us/politics/22detain.html [accessed 20 May 2009].

Sherry, M. (1987) *The Rise of American Air Power: The Creation of Armageddon.* New Haven: Yale University Press.

Sherry, M. (1995) *In the Shadow of War: The United States since the 1930s.* New Haven: Yale University Press.

Sherry, M. (2009) 'The United States and Strategic Bombing: From Prophecy to Memory', in Y. Tanaka and M. Young (eds) *Bombing Civilians: A Twentieth-Century History.* New York: New Press (pp. 175–90).

Siegel, L. (2005) *Criminology,* 9th edn. Belmont, CA: Wadsworth.

Sikkink, K. and Walling, C. B. (2006) 'Argentina's Contribution to Global Trends in Transitional Justice', in N. Roht-Arriaza and J. Mariezcurrena (eds) *Transitional Justice in the Twenty-First Century: Beyond Truth versus Justice.* Cambridge: Cambridge University Press (pp. 301–24).

Sikkink, K. and Walling, C. B. (2007) 'The Impact of Human Rights Trials in Latin America', *Journal of Peace Research,* 44(4): 427–45.

Silvis, J. (1996) 'Enforcing Drug Laws in the Netherlands', in E. Leuw and I. Haen Marshall (eds) *Between Prohibition and Legalization: The Dutch Experiment in Drug Policy.* Amsterdam: Kugler (pp. 41–58).

Single, E. (1989) 'The Impact of Marijuana Decriminalization: An Update', *Journal of Public Health Policy,* 10: 456–66.

Skocpol, T. (1985) 'Bringing the State Back In: Strategies for Analysis in Current Research', in P. Evans, D. Rueschemeyer and T. Skocpol (eds) *Bringing the State Back In.* New York: Cambridge University Press (pp. 3–43).

Skolnick, J. (1966) *Justice Without Trial.* New York: John Wiley.

Skolnick, J. and Fyfe, J. (1993) *Above the Law: Police and the Excessive Use of Force.* New York: Free Press.

Slapper, G. and Tombs, S. (1999) *Corporate Crime.* Harlow: Longman.

Smeulers, A. and Haveman, R. (eds) (2008) *Supranational Criminology: Toward Criminology of International Crimes.* Portland, OR: Intersentia.

Smeulers, A. and Van Niekerk, S. (2009) 'Abu Ghraib and the War on Terror – A Case Against Donald Rumsfeld?', *Crime, Law and Social Change,* 51: 327–49.

de Sousa Santos, B. (1995) *Towards a New Common Sense: Law, Science and Politics in the Paradigmatic Transition.* London: Routledge.

Soustelle, J. (1955/1970) *Daily Life of the Aztecs on the Eve of the Spanish Conquest.* Stanford: Stanford University Press.

Spector, M. and Kitsuse, J. (1977) *Constructing Social Problems.* Menlo Park, CA: Cummings.

Sriram, C. (2004) *Confronting Past Human Rights Violations: Justice vs. Peace in Times of Transition.* London: Frank Cass.

Sriram, C. (2005) *Globalizing Justice for Mass Atrocities: A Revolution in Accountability.* New York: Routledge.

Stanley, E. (2001) 'Evaluating the Truth and Reconciliation Commission', *Journal of Modern African Studies,* 39(3): 525–46.

Stanley, E. (2008) 'The Political Economy of Transitional Justice in Timor-Leste', in K. McEvoy and L. McGregor (eds) *Transitional Justice from Below.* Oxford: Hart Publishing (pp. 167–87).

Stanley, E. (2009a) *Torture, Truth and Justice: The Case of Timor-Leste.* London: Routledge.

Stanley, E. (2009b) 'Transitional Justice: From the Local to the International', in P. Hayden (ed.) *The Ashgate Research Companion to Ethics and International Relations.* London: Ashgate (pp. 275–92).

Stiglitz, J. (2003) *Globalization and Its Discontents.* New York: W. W. Norton.

Stover, E. and Nightingale, E. (1985) *The Breaking of Bodies and Minds: Torture,*

Psychiatric Abuse, and the Health Professions. Washington, DC: AAAS Science and Human Rights Program.

Stover E., Megally, H. and Mufti, H. (2006) 'Bremer's 'Gordian Knot': Transitional Justice and the US Occupation of Iraq', in N. Roht-Arriaza and J. Mariezcurrena (eds) *Transitional Justice in the Twenty-First Century: Beyond Truth versus Justice.* Cambridge: Cambridge University Press (pp. 229–54).

Sugiyama, S. (2005) *Human Sacrifice, Militarism and Rulership: Materialization of State Ideology at the Feathered Serpent Pyramid, Teotihuacan.* Cambridge: Cambridge University Press.

Sullivan, D. and Tifft, L. (eds) (2006) *Handbook of Restorative Justice: A Global Perspective.* New York: Routledge.

Surette, R. (1992) *Media, Crime and Criminal Justice.* Belmont, CA: Wadsworth.

Sutherland, E. (1940) 'White Collar Criminality', *American Sociological Review*, 5: 1–12.

Sutherland, E. (1943) 'War and Crime', in W. F. Ogburn (ed.) *American Society in Wartime.* Chicago: University of Chicago Press (pp. 185–206).

Sutherland, E. (1949) *White Collar Crime.* New York: Dryden Press.

Sutherland, E. (1951) 'Critique of Sheldon's *Varieties of Delinquent Youth*', *American Sociological Review*, 16: 10–13.

Sutherland, E. (1983) *White Collar Crime: The Uncut Version.* New Haven: Yale University Press.

Swaaningen, R. V. (1997) *Critical Criminology: Visions from Europe.* Thousand Oaks, CA: Sage.

Swan, P. (2006) 'American Empire or Empires? Alternative Juridifications of the New World Order', in A. Bartholomew (ed.) *Empire's Law.* London: Pluto Press (pp. 137–60).

Swiss Federal Office of Public Health (2007) 'Heroin Assisted Treatment: Trials with the Medical Prescription of Narcotics in Switzerland'. Available at: www.admin.ch/bag/sucht/therp-hr/e/hegebee.htm [accessed 4 June 2009].

Sykes, G. and Matza, D. (1957) 'Techniques of Neutralization: A Theory of Delinquency', *American Sociological Review*, 22(6): 664–70.

Taft, D. (1946) 'Punishment of War Criminals', *American Sociological Review*, 11: 439–44.

Taguba, A. (2004) *The Taguba Report on Treatment of Abu Ghraib Prisoners in Iraq.* New York: Cosimo Reports. Available at: news.findlaw.com/cnn/docs/iraq/tagubarpt.html [accessed 27 September 2009].

Takagi, P. (1981) 'Race, Crime and Social Policy', *Crime and Delinquency*, 27: 48–63.

Taussig, M. (2003) *Law in a Lawless Land: Diary of a Limpieza in Colombia.* Chicago: University of Chicago Press.

Taylor, C. (2004) *Modern Social Imaginaries.* Durham, NC: Duke University Press.

Taylor, I., Walton, P. and Young, J. (1974) *The New Criminology: For a Social Theory of Deviance.* New York: Harper Torchbooks.

Teitel, R. G. (2000) *Transitional Justice.* Oxford: Oxford University Press.

Terkel, S. (1984) *The 'Good War': An Oral History of World War II.* New York: Ballantine.

Teubner, G. (2002) 'Breaking Frames: Economic Globalisation and the Emergence of *Lex Mercatoria*', *European Journal of Social Theory*, 5(2): 199–217.

Thieren, M. (2007) 'Medicine and Public Health in "Dark Times"', OpenDemocracy.net, 26 April. Available at: www.isn.ethz.ch/news/sw/details.cfm?ID= 17544 [accessed 2 March 2007].

Thompson, H. (2006) 'Iraq Occupation makes Possible Record profits for British

Private Military Contractor.' Available at: www.uruknet.info [accessed 2 September 2009].

Thomson, G. (2007) 'How IMF, World Bank failed Africa', *New African*, 458: p. 12.

Tifft, L. and Sullivan, D. (1980) *The Struggle to be Human: Crime, Criminology, and Anarchism*. Orkney, UK: Cienfuegos Press.

Toch, H. (1996) 'The Violence-prone Police Officer', in W. Geller and H. Toch (eds) *Police Violence: Understanding and Controlling Police Abuse of Force*. New Haven, CT: Yale University Press (pp. 94–112).

Tombs, S. and Whyte, D. (eds) (2003) *Unmasking the Crimes of the Powerful: Scrutinizing States and Corporations*. New York: Peter Lang.

Tomlinson, C. (2007) 'U.S. Hires Contractor to Back Somalis', *Washington Post*, 7 March. Available at: www.washingtonpost.com/wp-dyn/content/article/2007/03/07/AR2007030701304.html [accessed 10 September 2009].

Toscano, A. (2008) 'Sovereign Impunity', *New Left Review*, 50: 128–35.

Toussaint, E. (1999) *Your Money or Your Life! Tyranny of Global Finance*. London: Pluto Press.

Toussaint, E. (2004) 'Rwanda 10 years On: Uncovering the Financiers of the Genocide.' Available at: www.redpepper.org.uk/May2004/x-May2004-Toussaint.html.

Tunell, K. (ed.) (1993) *Political Crime in Contemporary America*. New York: Garland.

Tyler, T. (2000) 'Patient Asking Ottawa for Pot', *The Toronto Star*, 21 January. Available at: https://hemp.net/news/index.php?article=949248314 [accessed 1 October 2009].

Uchtenhagen, A., Gutzwiller, F. and Dobler-Mikola, A. (eds) (1997) *Programme for Medical Prescription of Narcotics: Final Report of the Research Representatives*. Zurich: University of Zurich.

United Nations High Commissioner for Refugees (UNHCR) (2008) *Rule of Law Tools for Post-Conflict States: Maximising the Legacy of Hybrid Courts*. HR/PUB/08/2. New York: United Nations.

United Nations (1948) *Convention on the Prevention and Punishment of the Crime of Genocide*, opened for signature 9 December 1948. New York: United Nations.

United Nations (1961a) *Single Convention on Narcotic Drugs*, United Nations Economic and Social Council res. I, U.N. Sales No. E.62.XI.1. 1973, art. 44, pp. 34–5.

United Nations (1961b) *Conference to Consider Amendments to the Single Convention on Narcotic Drugs, Final Act and Protocol Amending the Single Convention of Narcotic Drugs*, United Nations Economic and Social Council, 25 March, 1972, UN Doc. E/CONF.63/9. New York: United Nations.

United Nations (1988a) *Committee I, Summary Record of the 24th Meeting*, 15 December. UN Doc. E/CONF.82/C.1/SR.24: 4. New York: United Nations.

United Nations (1988b) *Committee I, Summary Record of the 2nd Meeting*. UN Doc. E/CONF.82/C.1/SR.2: 2. New York: United Nations.

United Nations (1988c) *Conference for the Adoption of a Convention Against Illicit Traffic in Narcotic Drugs and Psychotropic Substances, Summary Record of the 3rd Meeting*, 5 December. UN Doc. E/CONF.82/SR.3: 4. New York: United Nations.

United Nations (2001) *Civil and Political Rights, Including the Questions of Torture and Detention*. Report of the Special Rapporteur, Sir Nigel Rodley, submitted pursuant to Commission on Human Rights resolution 2000/43, 30 March. Available at: www.unhchr.ch/Huridocda/Huridoca.nsf/TestFrame/b573b69cf6c3da28c1256a2b00498ded?Opendocument [accessed 29 September 2009].

United Nations (2004) *The Rule of Law and Transitional Justice in Conflict and Post-Conflict Societies: Report of the Secretary-General*. UN doc. S/2004/616, 3. New York: United Nations.

United Nations Office on Drugs and Crime (UNODC) (2008) 'Drug Policy and Results in Australia'. Available at: www.unodc.org/documents/data-ananaly sis/studies/drug_policy_australia_oct2008.pdf [accessed 27 September 2009].

United States (1975) *Alleged Assassination Plots Involving Foreign Leaders: An Interim Report of the Select Committee to Study Governmental Operations with Respect to Intelligence Activities*. Washington, DC: United States Goverment Printing Office.

United States (2005) 'National Defense Strategy of the United States of America.' Available at: www.defenselink.mil/news/Mar2005/d20050318nds2.pdf [accessed 14 September 2009].

US Department of Defense (n.d.) 'Military Code of Conduct'. Available at: www.au.af.mil/au/awc/awcgate/readings/code_of_conduct.htm [accessed 20 September 2009].

Vaughan, D. (1983) *Controlling Unlawful Organizational Behavior: Social Structure and Corporate Misconduct*. Chicago: University of Chicago Press.

Vaughan, D. (1996) *The Challenger Launch Decision: Risky Technology, Culture, and Deviance at NASA*. Chicago: University of Chicago Press.

Vaughan, D. (2007) 'Beyond Macro- and Micro-Levels of Analysis, Organizations, and the Cultural Fix', in H. Pontell and G. Geis (eds) *International Handbook of White-Collar and Corporate Crime*. New York: Springer (pp. 3–24).

Vittala, K. (1999) 'Heroin as Treatment [for Opiate Addiction] Group to Propose Clinical Trials', *Journal of Addiction and Mental Health*, April: 9–29.

de Vries, P. (1992) 'A Research Journey: On Actors, Contexts and Texts', in N. Long and A. Long (eds) *Battlefields of Knowledge: The Interlocking of Theory and Practice in Social Research*. New York: Routledge (pp. 47–84).

Waldorf, L. (2006) 'Rwanda's Failing Experiment in Restorative Justice', in D. Sullivan and L. Tifft (eds) *Handbook of Restorative Justice*. London: Routledge (pp. 422–34).

Walker, J. S. (2004) *Prompt and Utter Destruction: Truman and the Use of Atomic Bombs Against Japan*. Chapel Hill: University of North Carolina Press.

Walker, S. (1999) *The Police in America*. Boston, MA: McGraw-Hill.

Walker, S. (2005) *Sense and Nonsense About Crime and Drugs*. New York: Wadsworth.

Ward, T. (2005) 'State Crime in the Heart of Darkness', *British Journal of Criminology*, 45(4): 434–45.

Warden, E. (1996) 'The Causes of Police Brutality: Theory and Evidence on Police Use of Force', in W. Geller and H. Toch (eds) *Police Violence: Understanding and Controlling Police Abuse of Force*. New Haven, CT: Yale University Press (pp. 31–60).

Washington Post (2004) 'Bush Administration Documents on Interrogation', 23 June. Available at: www.washingtonpost.com/wp-dyn/articles/A62516-2004 Jun22.html [accessed 27 September 2009].

Washington Technology (WT) (2004) 'Top 100 Federal Prime Contractors: Companies by Ranking', 2 May. Available at: www.wwt.com/news_events/docu ments/WashTech_5-10-04 [accessed 29 September 2009].

Watson, J. (1973) 'Deindividuation and Changing Appearance Before Battle', *Journal of Abnormal and Social Psychology*, 25: 342–5.

Weber, M. (1958) *From Max Weber: Essays in Sociology* (trans. H. H. Gerth and C. W. Mills). New York: Oxford University Press.

Weber, M. (2002) *Economía y Sociedad* (trans. J. Echavarría). España: Fondo de Cultura Económica.

Weinberg, S., Gordon, N. and Williams, B. (2006) *Harmful Error: Investigating America's Local Prosecutors*. Washington, DC: Center for Public Integrity.

Weisbrot, M. (2007) 'The World Bank After Wolfowitz: Harm Reduction', *ZMag*, 30(1), May. Available at: www.zmag.org/content/showarticle.cfm?ItemID= 12936 [accessed 15 January 2008].

Welch, M. (2006) *Scapegoats of September 11th: Hate Crimes and State Crimes in the War on Terror*. New Brunswick, NJ: Rutgers University Press.

Welch, M. (2009) *Crimes of Power and States of Impunity: The U.S. Response to Terror*. New Brunswick, NJ: Rutgers University Press.

Welle, D. (2008) 'Amid Debate, Germany's Heroin Injection Clinics Fight to Survive'. Available at: www.dw-world.de [accessed 9 September 2009].

Westermeyer, R. (2008) 'Reducing Harm: A Very Good Idea'. Available at: www.cts.com/crash/habtsmrt.harm.html [accessed 7 May 2009].

Westervelt, S. and Cook, K. (2007) 'Feminist Research Methods in Theory and Action: Learning from Death Row Exonerees', in S. Miller (ed.) *Criminal Justice Research and Practice: Diverse Voices from the Field*. Boston, MA: University Press of New England (pp. 21–38).

Westervelt, S. and Cook, K. (2008) 'Coping with Innocence after Death Row', *Contexts*, 7(4): 32–37.

Westervelt, S. and Humphrey, J. (eds) (2002) *Wrongly Convicted: Perspectives on Failed Justice*. New Brunswick, NJ: Rutgers University Press.

Westley, W. (1970) *Violence and the Police*. Cambridge, MA: MIT Press.

Wetzell, R. F. (2000) *Inventing the Criminal: A History of German Criminology, 1880–1945*. Chapel Hill, NC: University of North Carolina Press.

White, R. (2008) 'Depleted Uranium, State Crime and the Politics of Knowing', *Theoretical Criminology*, 12: 31–54.

Whyte, D. (2003) 'Lethal Regulation: State-Corporate Crime and the United Kingdom Government's New Mercenaries', *Journal of Law and Society*, 30(4): 575–600.

Whyte, D. (2007a) 'The Crimes of Neo-Liberal Rule in Occupied Iraq', *British Journal of Criminology*, 47: 177–95.

Whyte, D. (2007b) 'Hire an American! Tyranny and Corruption in Occupied Iraq', *Social Justice*, 35(3): 153–68.

Whyte, D. (2007c) 'Market Patriotism and the War on Terror', *Social Justice*, 35(2–3): 111–31.

Wilensky, H. (1975) *The Welfare State and Equality*. Berkeley, CA: University of California Press.

Williams, W. A. (1969) *The Roots of the Modern American Empire: A Study of the Growth and Shaping of Social Consciousness in a Marketplace Society*. New York: Random House.

Williams, W. A. (1959/1988) *The Tragedy of American Diplomacy*. New York: Norton.

Wolf, E. (1999) *Envisioning Power: Ideologies of Dominance and Crisis*. Berkeley, CA: University of California Press.

Wonders, N. and Solop, F. (1993) 'Understanding the Emergence of Law and Public Policy: Toward a Relational Model of the State', in W. Chambliss and M. Zatz (eds) *Making Law: The State, the Law, and Structural Contradictions*. Bloomington, IL: Indiana University Press (pp. 204–25).

Wood, E. W., Jr (2006) *Worshipping the Myths of World War II: Reflections on America's Dedication to War*. Washington, DC: Potomac Books.

Woods, N. (2000) 'The Challenge to International Institutions', in N. Woods (ed.) *The Political Economy of Globalization*. New York: St Martin's Press (pp. 202–23).

World Bank (2004) Multilateral Investment Guarantee Agency. News AR2004. Available at: www.miga.org/documents/04arappendices.pdf [accessed 13 November 2009].

Wright, R. (2008) *What is America? A Short History of the New World Order*. Philadelphia: Da Capo Press.

Wroughton, L. (2007) 'China's Exim-bank, World Bank to Cooperate on Africa', 22 May. Available at: africa.reuters.com/wire/news/usnN21367006.html [accessed 26 November 2007].

Young, M. (2009) 'Bombing Civilians from the Twentieth to the Twenty-first Centuries', in Y. Tanaka and M. Young (eds) *Bombing Civilians: A Twentieth-Century History*. New York: New Press (pp. 154–74).

Youngers, C. and Rosin, E. (2005) *Drugs and Democracy in Latin America: The Impact of U.S. Policy*. Boulder, CO: Lynne Rienner.

Zaffaroni, E. R. (2006) *El Enemigo en el Derecho Penal*. Madrid: Dykinson.

Zimbardo, P. (1970) 'The Human Choice: Individuation, Reason, and Order Versus Deindividuation, Impulse, and Chaos', in W. J. Arnold and D. Levine (eds) *1969 Nebraska Symposium on Motivation*. Lincoln, NE: University of Nebraska Press (pp. 237–307).

Zimbardo, P. (2007) *The Lucifer Effect: Understanding How Good People Turn Evil*. Random House.

Zimbardo, P., Haney, C., Banks, W. C. and Jaffe, D. (1973) 'The Mind is a Formidable Jailer: A Pirandellian Prison', *New York Times Magazine*, 8 April, p. 38.

Zimbardo, P., Maslach, C. and C. Haney (2000) 'Reflections on the Stanford Prison Experiment: Genesis, Transformations, Consequences', in T. Blass (ed.) *Obedience to Authority: Current Perspectives on the Milgram Paradigm*. Hillsdale, NJ: Lawrence Erlbaum (pp. 1–35).

Zimmerman, C. (2002) 'From the Jailhouse to the Courthouse: The Role of Informants in Wrongful Convictions', in S. Westervelt and J. Humphrey (eds) *Wrongly Convicted: Perspectives on Failed Justice*. New Brunswick, NJ: Rutgers University Press (pp. 55–76).

Zinn, H. (1980) *A People's History of the United States: 1492–Present*. New York: HarperCollins.

Zolo, G. (2006) *La Giustizia dei Vincitori: da Norimberga a Baghdad*. Rome: Editori Laterza.

Index

Added to the page number 'f' denotes a figure, 'n' denotes a footnote and 't' denotes a table.

9/11 38, 51–2, 145, 243
1908, year of 67–8

absolutist state, dividing line between
    constitutional and 239–40
Abu Ghraib prison
    and the state of exception 136
    torture 18, 83, 87–8, 90–1, 92, 94, 95, 97,
        98–9, 114
accountability
    respect for 245
    for state crimes and human rights
        violations 229, 257–9
    for wrongful convictions 172–3, 185–6
accumulation, relations between
    governance and 13, 26–7
ad hoc legalism, and state torture 84, 87–8,
    90, 95
Aegis Defence Services 112–13
Afghanistan 8, 32, 114
    competition between and within US
        intelligence organizations 93–4
    prisoner abuse 97
Africa
    aid for health and education 165–6
    China's economic and political influence
        162–4, 166–7, 168
    reliance on IFIs 161
    see also Congo; Darfur; Ghana; Rwanda;
        Senegal; South Africa; Uganda,
        Somalia
Agamben, Georgio 135–6, 141–2, 148,
    244
aggression, wars of see war
al-Bashir, Omar Hassan 259
Allied terror bombing campaigns 119–20,
    121, 130
altruistic suicide 47
Amazon region
    and international loans 108
    see also Brazil
America see US
American empire see US empire
American exceptionalism 125–6, 132
'American Taliban' 97
Americas

colonization 143
    see also US
anomie
    zone 244
    see also institutional anomie
'anti-criminologies' 6
arcana imperii, institution 239
area bombing 119–20, 121, 130
    see also terror bombing
Argentina
    and structural adjustment policies (SAPs)
        157–8
    withdrawal from IMF program 167
Armenian massacres 253
armies, permanent 236
art of government
    and the principles of liberalism 241
    reason of state (raison d'état) as 233–7
assassinations 35–7, 44
atomic attacks on Japan 74, 119, 123, 130
    interpretive denial 121–2, 132–3, 253–4
    literal denial 253
    political factors 124–5
Atzcapotzalco 60–1
Australia, harm reduction policies 205–7
Aztec societies 52, 54
    sacrifice in see sacrifice in Aztec societies

Baan Committee 211
Beijing Declaration 162, 165–6, 167
Belmarsh 141
bio-power 3, 26, 29
biopolitical model, intersection between the
    juridical definitional model and 244
Bloodsworth, Kirk 178, 181, 182, 185–6
Bloom, Philip 110
Bobbio, N. 239–40
Bolivia, and US drug policy 200
bombing of civilians see terror bombing
Bordenkircher v. Hayes (1978, 434 US 357)
    189–90
Braunschweig 69–70
Brazil, state torture 86, 91, 92, 93, 95, 96, 100
Bremer, Paul 109, 137
Brown, Shabaka 176–7, 178
Burawoy, Michael 247–9, 251

bureaucratic organization
  and state torture 84, 89–91
    division and specialization of labour 91
    hierarchy 90–1
  and terror bombing 126
Bush Doctrine 38
Bush, George H. W. 34, 50–1, 62
Bush, George W. 51–2, 62
business, links with violence 107–8
Butler, Sabrina 177–8, 180, 182

CACI International 94, 102n, 114
Canada
  harm reduction policies 207
    medical marijuana 210
cannabis
  reclassification 209–10
  see also marijuana
'cannabis-based' medicine 209
capital accumulation, governance and 13,
    26–7
CAVR (Commission for Reception, Truth
    and Reconciliation) 222
censorship, and state torture 85, 96–7
Central America
  death squads 35, 36, 42
  see also Panama
Chalco 60–1
Chambliss, William J. 70
  definition of state crime 183
  presidential address (1988) 7, 32, 69, 72–3,
    75–6, 77, 258
children, and sacrifice 46
China
  economy 147
  foreign policy 9, 153–4
    as a constraint against IFI policies
      166–9
    domestic and foreign policy
      recognition 164–6
    role in African economic structures
      162–4
  Opium Wars 42
China-Africa Business Council 163
Cholula 60
civil liberties, curtailment 245
civil society 104
  concept 241–2
civilians, normalization of terror bombing
    see normalization of terror bombing
civilization, standard of 144–6
civilizing mission, colonization as 143–4
claims-makers
  groups 255–6

public criminologists as 16, 254
claims-making 18–20
classification of trauma and suffering 221–2
Cobb, Perry 181–2
cocaine, influence of US drug policy 200
Code of Conduct for Members of the
    Armed Forces of the United States
    63–4
Cohen, Stanley 70, 252–4
'The Cold War' 124
collateral damage 36, 127, 133
collective imaginary 116
colonization, relationship between a legal
    civilizing mission and 143–4
Commission for Reception, Truth and
    Reconciliation (CAVR) 222
conduct norms, Sellin's theory 15
conflict
  constructing political myths about 224–6
  see also violence; war
Congo 67–8
  crime and IFI policies 161
constitutional state, dividing line between
    the absolutist and 239–40
corporate crime
  concept 103–4
  distinctions between social, political and
    legal definitions 104–6
  in Iraq 134, 140
  war as see war as corporate crime
coup d'état, theory 236–7, 239
CPA 109–11
  as an example of the state of exception
    137–41
  external auditing procedures 140–1
  transitional justice measures 223
CPA Order 17 140
Creative Associates International 111
crime
  against the state 1
  concept 15–23
  definitions xiii, 13, 14
    challenging the state-centric paradigm
      5–6
  relationship between war and 115
  state wrongs as 17–19
  see also corporate crime; environmental
    crimes; 'governmental crime';
    nuclear-related crimes; organized
    crime; 'political crime'; state crime;
    war crimes; white collar crime
'crimes against humanity' 128
'crimes against peace' 128
Crimes of the American Nuclear State 77

crimes of empire 31
  distinguishing empire's crimes from 33–4
  interpretive denial 254
crimes of globalization
  examples 153
  IFIs and 152–4, 157–61
    interrelationship between globalization 153
  links with state crimes 153, 159
  as mass social harms 153
crimes of power 149, 257
Criminal Behaviour Systems: A Typology 71
criminal state 7
criminalization of drug policies 202–3, 213–14
  see also decriminalization of drugs
criminological inquiry 1–5
criminological knowledge 1, 80
criminological research 21, 27, 29, 251
criminology
  as an extension of state power 1
  countercultures within 6
  and the development of public criminology 249–50
  'paradigm revolution' xiii
  as a policy science 251
  and the study of state crime 2, 5–6, 71–2
  retrospective 77–8
  see also empire's criminology; prospective criminology; public criminology; radical criminology
criminology of empire 43–4
  distinguishing between empire's criminology and 40–3
Criminology and Public Policy 251
criminology of war 115
critical criminology 6–7, 13, 14, 232, 243, 245, 251
critical penal theory 243
critical public sociology 250
critical sociology 248
cultures of denial
  punishment as an encouragement 260
  and terror bombing 123, 125, 127, 132

Darfur 68, 78, 259
  humanitarian aid 163
  literal denial 253
Darwin, Charles 4
de-Ba'athification 223
death row exonerees 170
  denial of innocence 173
  and exoneration 176–82
    feelings of grief and loss 179–81

the possibility of death by court order 176–8
  problems of everyday living 178–9
  stigma and reintegration 181–2
  as victims of state harms 171–5
    blaming 173
    the harmfulness of institutional policies 172–3
    as the least socially powerful actors 171–2
    redress 173–4
    repeated victimization 174–5
    role of the state 182–3
death squads 35, 36, 42
debt restructuring 155–6
Declaration of the Beijing Summit of the Forum on China-Africa Co-operation (FOCAC) 162, 165–6, 167
The Declining World Order: America's Imperial Geopolitics 79
decriminalization of drugs, in Portugal 208
Della Ragione di Stato 234
democracy 240
Democratic Republic of Congo (DRC) *see* Congo
denial
  categories 252–4
  cultures *see* cultures of denial
  disrupting 252–6
  of innocence 173
  links with normalization 254
  and state torture 85, 96–7
deviance model of crime *see* organizational deviance model
differential impunity, and state torture 85, 97–8
diplomacy, systematic development 236
domestic state crimes 9
dominant consciousness, reproduction 2–3
drug policies 2–3
  criminalization 202–3, 213–14
  decriminalization 208
  harm reduction *see* harm reduction policies
  US *see* US drug policy
drugs
  criminological inquiry into use 2, 4–5
  role in imperial expansion 42
Duke Lacrosse Rape Case 187
Durkheim, Emile 45–9
Dyncorp 113

economic sphere, and the development of society 105–6

economic violence, crimes of 42–3
Ecuador, and international loans 108
education, aid for 165–6
Eisenhower, Dwight D. 49–50
emergency criminal law, to a permanent
    state of exception from 243–5
empire
    centrality 31–44
    defining 32
    and international legal norms 259
    return of 7
    'empire in denial' 31–2
    Empires of Capital 143
empire's crimes, distinguishing crimes of
    empire from 33–4
empire's criminology 43–4
    distinguishing between the criminology
        of empire and 40–3
Empire's law 37–40, 43
England
    harm reduction policies 207–8
        medical marijuana 209–10
    Poor Laws 9n
enhanced structural adjustment facility
    (ESAF) 164–5
the Enlightenment 3–4
entrepreneurs 105–6
environmental crimes 41–2
'escape lines' 117
'essentials course', International Center for
    Transitional Justice (ICTJ) 216–17
ethics, relation between politics and 240–1
ethnic cleansing 35
exception, relationship between the norm
    and 149–50
exceptionalism 38
executions 175
Executive Order 13303 138–40, 142
Exploring Criminology 73
'extra-judicial executions' 35
'extraordinary rendition' 37, 96

Foucault, M. 233–7, 241, 242
    perspective on 'power-knowledge' 15
'founding force', violations as 117
free-market states 26
freedom, concepts 242
'frugal government' 242

gacaca 219
Gauger, Gary 180–1, 182
Gell, Alan 174, 178–9
genocide 2, 35, 44, 78, 226
    Allied terror bombing campaigns as 119
    in Armenia 253
    in Darfur 68, 253, 259
    in Rwanda *see* Rwanda, genocide
    see also Holocaust
Genocide Convention 35
Germany
    Allied terror bombing 119–20, 130, 132
    safer injection rooms 201, 203, 205
Ghana
    fees for health services 165
    interference by IFIs 165
    and structural adjustment policies (SAPs)
        159
'ghost prisoners' 96
global economic restructuring 144
global governance 80
global security law, creation 245
global trends 79
globalization 79
    crimes *see* crimes of globalization
    interrelationship between IFIs, crimes of
        globalization and 153
    'top-down' 153, 158
    see also neo-liberal globalization
globalization of transitional justice 215–31
    devaluation 227–8
    employment opportunities 217–18
    formalization 217–18
    funding 215, 217
    route to dominance 223–7
        appropriation of transitional justice
            223–4
        as a legitimizing discourse 226–7
        political myths about conflict and
            violence 224–6
    transfer of knowledge and practice
        216–18
    and western norms *see* western norms
Glueck, Sheldon 257–8
'Good War', World War Two as 122, 125–6,
    132
government
    and the law 239
    liberal art 243
    state as 14
    see also art of government; 'frugal
        government'
'governmental crime' 72
governmental institutions, the state as 24–5
governmentality
    concept 233
    dynamics 25
    see also transnational governmentality
Guantánamo 18, 83, 87, 98–9, 114

and the state of exception 136, 137, 141, 147
Guernica (painting) 119
Guernica (town) 118, 119

Hagan, John 70–1
Halliburton 111
Hariri, Rafiq 37
harm reduction policies 9, 199–214
in Australia 205–7
in Canada 207
in Europe 203
England 207–8
Germany 201, 203, 205
Netherlands *see* Netherlands
Portugal 208
Switzerland *see* Switzerland
heroin maintenance *see* heroin maintenance programs
medical marijuana *see* medical marijuana
safer injection rooms *see* safer injection rooms
harms *see* social injury/harm model; state harms
heads of state, political impunity and legal immunity 258–9
healing-killing paradox 122, 126, 132
health, aid for 165–6
Heilbroner, Robert 4
heroin maintenance programs 201
in Australia 206
in Canada 207
in England 207–8
International Narcotics Board policy 202
in Switzerland 201, 203–5
US response 202
high-altitude bombings 36
High-Value Detainee Interrogation Group (HIG) 101
Hiroshima 74, 119, 123
interpretive denial 121–2, 253–4
literal denial 253
Holocaust 73, 77–8
Hulsman Committee 211
human rights 79
and the doctrine of reason of state (*raison d'état*) 232
see also international human rights
Human Rights Data Analysis Group (HRDAG) 221
human rights violations 17–19
accountability 229
and corporate actions 225
involvement of external states 224–5

measurement and classification 221–2
human sacrifice 45
by the Tenochca 55–6
festival of Tlacaxipehualitzli 56–8
schema 50t
humanitarian law 18, 118
see also laws of war

IAMB (International Advisory and Monitoring Board) 140
ICC 35, 41, 152, 225
and accountability 258, 259
as a claims-maker 255
and the US 38, 39, 41
ICTJ (International Center for Transitional Justice), 'essentials course' 216–17
ideology, and state torture 84, 85–6
IFIs 107–8, 152, 155–7, 227
as controls over state crime 153, 154–5
and crimes of globalization 152–4, 157–61
domestic and foreign policy recognition 164–6
external monitoring system 166
interrelationship between globalization, crimes of globalization and 153
role of China as a constraint 166–9
IMF 152, 156–7
as a control on criminal states 154
crisis of confidence and legitimacy 167
enhanced structural adjustment facility (ESAF) 165
voting structure 157, 158t
'implicatory denial' 250
imprisonment 37
impunity *see* differential impunity; political impunity
In Spite of Innocence 170
indifference, zone 244
individualism, in western legal norms 220
Indonesia
withdrawal from IMF program 167
see also Timor-Leste
innocence, denial of 173
institutional anomie 245
institutions of governance, the state as 24–5
instrumentalist state theory 28t
intellectuals, as claims-makers 255–6
International Advisory and Monitoring Board (IAMB) 140
International Center for Transitional Justice (ICTJ), 'essentials course' 216–17
international controls of state agencies 154–5
International Court of Justice (World Court) 35, 39, 258

International Criminal Court *see* ICC
International Criminal Tribunal for Rwanda
   219
international criminal tribunals 152
international development agencies 107–8
international financial institutions *see* IFIs
international human rights, growth 7
international humanitarian law 18, 118
   see also laws of war
international humanitarian order 38–9
international law
   and accountability 258, 259
   controlling state crime through 17
   and defining state crime 72
   effect of 9/11 38
   enforcement mechanism 128
   status 151n
   and transitional justice 218–20
   and universal civilization 145
   universalism 39
   violations 17–19
      and harm reduction strategies 199, 213
international loans 108
international military tribunals 152, 257,
   258
   see also Nuremberg trials; Tokyo military
   tribunals
International Narcotics Control Board 200
   policy on medical marijuana 209
   policy on safer injection rooms and
      heroin maintenance 201–2, 203, 206
international political community, as a
   claim-maker 255
interpretive denial 253–4
   of atomic attacks on Japan 121–2, 132–3,
      253–4
   of crimes of empire 254
interrogation
   use of private military services 114
   see also state torture
Iran 68
Iraq
   invasion (1991) 51, 62
   invasion and occupation *see* US-UK
      invasion and occupation of Iraq
Iraqi Special Tribunal 224–5

James, Gary 180
Janusian Security Risk Management 112
Japan
   Allied terror bombing 119–20, 130, 132
   atomic attacks *see* atomic attacks on Japan
juridical definitional model 15, 16–19, 33
   breaching 244–5

intersection between the biopolitical
   model and 244
strengths and weaknesses 20t
and wrongful conviction 171, 184
juridical reason 237, 241
just retribution, concept 122

kidnapping 37, 44
Korean War, use of terror bombing 133
Krone, Ray 180, 185
Kuhn, T. S. xiii

Latin America, death squads 35, 36, 42
law
   coexistence with war 245
   concepts 242
   effect of war and crimes of the powerful
      117
   humanistic or moralistic conception 72
   and the limitation of governmental
      rationality 242
   link between power and 14
   in post-invasion Iraq 137–41
   relationship of the state of exception to
      135
   and state crime 72
      as a violation *see* juridical definitional
         model
   and transitional justice 229
   universalism 44
   see also ad hoc legalism; emergency
      criminal law; Empire's law; global
      security law; humanitarian law;
      international law; natural law; rule
      of law; state law
law-making violence, in Iraq 141–3
law's empire 39–40, 44
laws of war 18
   and terror bombing 118, 127–9
   enforcement mechanism 128
   the legitimation of violence 128–9
Le Joola ferry, sinking 159
legal exceptionalism 38
legal immunity, erosion 257–9
legalistic definitions of crime *see* juridical
   definitional model
legitimacy 79
legitimation of violence 128–9
lex mercatoria 144–9
   challenging 146–8
liberal art of government 243
liberal states 26
liberation, act of 32
liberation sociology 250–1

Lindh, John Walker 97
literal denial 252–3, 254
　examples 253

Machiavelli, N. 237–8, 240, 241
MacMillan, Walter 176
Manifest Destiny, doctrine 63
marijuana
　policy of 'de jure prohibition and de facto
　　legalization' 211–13
　see also cannabis; medical marijuana
market economy, and the development of
　society 105
'market patriotism', in the US 144
Marx, K.
　concept of praxis 250
　sense of state 24
mechanical solidarity 46
media accounts of criminal investigations
　172
medical marijuana 208–11
　in Canada 210
　in England 209–10
　International Narcotics Control Board
　　policy 209
　in the US 210–11
Melendez, Juan 176, 179
Members of the Armed Forces of the United
　States, Code of Conduct 63–4
military industry, private security and
　111–14
'military necessity', definition 129
military neo-liberalism 108
　and Iraq 108–15
military planning, technological fanaticism
　and 126–7
mislabeling, and state torture 84, 86, 95
moral judgements, social inquiry and 4–5
morality, of political action 240–1
morality of war goals, social construction
　121–6
Multilateral Investment Guarantee
　Agency(MIGA) 155

Nagasaki 74, 119, 123
　interpretive denial 121–2, 253–4
NAOMI (North American Opiate
　Maintenance Initiative) 207
National Defense Strategy Doctrine, US 39
National Drug Strategy for Prevention of Drug
　Abuse and Drug Trafficking 200
national security 245
　and state torture 98, 99–100
national security states 99

nationalism 79
Native Americans 35, 143, 144
natural law, theory 237
natural rights, theory 237
'naturality of society' 241–2
Nazis 73
　personal story of refugees 69–70
　see also Third Reich
necrotist state theory 26, 27, 28t
neo-liberal globalization 7, 27
neo-liberal standard of civilization 145
neo-liberalism 7–8, 26
　imposition on Iraq 142, 144
　promotion by IFIs 157
　see also military neo-liberalism
Netherlands
　harm reduction policies 211–13
　heroin maintenance programs 201
　safer injection rooms 201
'the New World order' 34
'newsmaking criminology' 249
Nicaragua 34–5
noncombatant immunity 118, 122, 127
norm
　relationship between the exception and
　　149–50
　relationship between the state and 149
normalization of deviance 120, 121
　links with denial 254
　negating 254–6
normalization of terror bombing 118–33
　erosion of constraints 129–31
　and laws of war see laws of war, and
　　terror bombing
　social construction of the morality of war
　　goals 121–6
　weapons technology, military planning
　　and technological fanaticism 126–7
North American Opiate Maintenance
　Initiative (NAOMI) 207
nuclear weapons
　proliferation 40
　use in Japan see atomic attacks on Japan
nuclear-related crimes 77
Nuremberg trials 16, 34, 73, 74, 128, 225,
　257–8

Obama, Barack 65–6
On the Origin of Species 4
Opium Wars 42
organic public criminology 249
organic solidarity 46–7
organizational deviance model 15, 16, 17t,
　19–21, 33

integrated model 120
and research 21
strengths and weaknesses 20t
organizational problem, state crime as 14
organized crime, state torture as 98–100
'othering' 52, 85, 143
overcharging, prosecutorial *see*
    prosecutorial overcharging

Panama 51
'paradigm revolution' in criminology xiii
parrot's perch torture 101n
'pathologies of power' 9
Pearl Harbor 122, 123–4
permanent armies 236
Pinochet, Augusto 258
police
    accountability 172
    and wrongful convictions 184
police state 236, 241, 245
Policing the Crisis 150
policy science, criminology as 251
policy sociology 248
political action, morality 240–1
'political crime' 71
political economy, and government 241
political impunity, erosion 257–9
political perspective, as a feature of state
    crime 232
political white collar crime 13, 72
politics
    Machiavellian interpretation 237–8, 240,
        241
    and necessity 239
    purpose 242–3
    relation between ethics and 240–1
Poor Laws in England 9n
Portugal, harm reduction policies 208
post-conflict restorative justice 260
'post-Westphalian' developments 79
power 5
    and the line between the constitutional
        and absolutist state 239–40
    link between law and 14
    see also bio-power; crimes of power;
        'pathologies of power'; state power
'power-knowledge', Foucault's perspective 15
praxis, concept 250
precision bombing 121, 126–7, 130
presidents of the US, speeches 49–52, 65–6
prevention
    and public criminology 260–1
    punishment as a deterrent 260
Prince 240

private sector development (PSD) 156
private security and military industry 103,
    111–14, 115–16
    outsourcing interrogation and guard
        work to 93–4
privatization 107
production sharing agreements (PSAs) 110
professional sociology 248
prosecutorial overcharging 9, 187–95
    confronting and reducing 191
    data 189, 193–5
        pattern 191
    definition 188
    methodology of study 188
prosecutors
    accountability 173
    duties 189–90
    organizational context 175
    power differentials between defendants
        and 172
    and wrongful convictions 184
prospective criminology, towards 43, 67–80
PSAs (production sharing agreements) 110
public criminology 9, 16, 29, 247–61
    accountability, transitional justice, and
        prevention 256–61
    and disrupting denial and negating
        normalization 252–6
    and doing the 'right' thing 250–1
    engaging audiences 249
    forms 248–9
    and prevention of crime 260–1
public intellectuals, as claims-makers 255–6
public sociology 247–8, 250, 251
'the public sociology wars' 251
public sphere, and the development of
    society 105
punishment, effectiveness 259–60

radical criminology 14, 251
reason of state (*raison d'état*)
    as an art of government 233–7
    basic precepts 237–40
        concept of necessity 142–3, 237–8
        concept of secret 239–40
        potential violation of moral and legal
            norms 238–9
        predominance of state interest 238
    externally, governance according to 235–6
    and human rights 232
    internally, governance according to 236
    purpose 234
    and the relation between ethics and
        politics 240–1

and the state of exception 136, 142–3
from emergency criminal law 243–5
reconstruction of Iraq 109–12, 134–5
regime change 34, 38
in Syria 37
'religion of air power', terror bombing as 132
religious and ritual sacrifice 48–9
Rendering Program 37, 96
repeated victimization, and state crime victims 174–5
research see criminological research; state crime research
resources, exploitation 108
restorative justice 260
overlap with transitional justice 260
retrospective criminology of state crime 77–8
Revised Opium Act (1976) 211, 212
risk, as a trait of war and corporate crime 106
ritual sacrifice, religious and 48–9
Ross, Jeffrey Ian 71
routinization of torture 84–5, 94, 95
rule of law
doctrine 241–3
respect for 245
suspending 137
in post-invasion Iraq 137–44
Rule of Law Tools for Post-Conflict States 217
Rwanda
gacaca 219
genocide
role of IFI policies 160
trials 219, 258
and structural adjustment policies (SAPs) 158

sacrifice
terms and categories 49
theorizing 25, 45–9
sacrifice in Aztec societies 52, 55–62
discourse and practices of the Tenochca 58–62
of humans see human sacrifice
sacrifice in the US 49–52, 62–4, 65f
dominant discourses 53t
safer injection rooms 201
in Australia 206–7
in Canada 207
in Germany 201, 205
International Narcotics Board policy 201–2, 206
in Switzerland 201, 203

US response 202
'Salvador Option' 36
SAPs (structural adjustment policies) 157–9
scholars, as claims-makers 254, 255–6
'scholarship with commitment' 247
Second World War see World War Two
secrecy
and the reason of state (raison d'état) 239–40, 245
and state torture 85, 95–6
security 21, 245
Security Council 38, 258
security imperative 243
Sellin's theory of conduct norms 15
Senegal
sinking of Le Joola ferry 159
and structural adjustment policies (SAPs) 157–8
Serbia, withdrawal from IMF program 167
'shooting galleries' see safer injection rooms
SIGIR (Special Inspector General for Iraq Reconstruction) 140
Slavic nations 68
see also Yugoslavia
social construction of the morality of war goals 121–6
social contract, theory 237
social imaginary 116
social injury/harm model xiii–xiv, 15–16, 17t, 21–2, 33, 72, 75, 171
and crimes of globalization 153
and empire 41
and prosecutorial overcharging 191
and wrongful conviction 171, 184
social inquiry 4
and moral judgements 4–5
social problems, state harms as 254–5
'social science', concept 3–4
society
development 105
naturality 241–2
socio-economic reordering in Iraq 141–3, 148–9
The Sociological Imagination 250
sociological labor, division 248
Somalia 34
South Africa, Truth and Reconciliation Commission 222, 225
sovereignty 79
Soviet Union, contest between the US and 34, 124–5
Special Inspector General for Iraq Reconstruction (SIGIR) 140
Special Panels for Serious Crimes 223–4

standard of civilization 144–6
state
  crimes against 1
  and criminological practices 2
  as government 14
  meaning 23–7
    and state crime research 27, 29
  policing 236
  and the regulation and generation of
      crime 232
  relationship between the norm and 149
  rights of 3
  role in the harms exonerees face 182–3
  types 28t
  see also absolutist state; constitutional
      state; criminal state; heads of state;
      national security states; police state;
      reason of state (raison d'état)
state agencies, controls of 154–5
state agents
  as claims-makers 255
  and death row exonerees 182–3
    denial of innocence 173
  see also police; prosecutors; state officials
state crime
  control mechanisms 152
    IFIs 153, 154–5
  criminalization 2
  defining 1–2, 13, 32–3, 170–1, 183–4
  growth in interest 7–8
  historical perspective 67–9
  key features 232
  legitimation 76
  links with crimes of globalization 153, 159
  the meaning of 'state' and 'crime' in
      13–30
  pathways to interest 70–1
  relationship between the norm and the
      state 149
  terror bombing of civilians as 118–19,
      131–2
  understanding 137
State Crime (2000) (Friedrichs, D. (ed.)) 76–7
State Crime (2004) (Green, P and Ward, T.)
      24, 77
state crime research 252
  and the meaning of state and crime 27, 29
state crime victims see victims
state crime wedding cake 22–3, 43
state of exception 21
State of Exception 135
state of exception 135–7
  and an understanding of necessity 144
  from emergency criminal law to 243–5

functions 150
historical analysis 135
in Iraq 137–43, 148–50
legitimating narrative 136
and state power 135–6, 141–2, 150
state harms 171
  death row exonerees as victims see death
      row exonerees, as victims of state
      harms
  as social problems 254–5
state interest 245
  predominance 238
state law 4
The State Must be Defended 26
state officials
  accountability 172–3, 257–9
  and wrongful convictions 183–4
  see also prosecutors; state agents
state power 5
  assumptions underlying 3
  core 137
  criminology as an extension 1
  and the state of exception 135–6, 141–2,
      150
state practices, critique 6
state terrorism, bombing of civilians as 118,
      120
state torture 8–9, 37, 44, 83–102
  dismantling systems 100–1
  as organized crime 98–100
  torture essentials model 83–5, 99
    ad hoc legalism 84, 87–8, 95
    bureaucratic organization see
        bureaucratic organization, and state
        torture
    censorship and denial 85, 96–7
    competition 84, 93–4
    differential impunity 85, 97–8
    ideology 84, 85–6
    insularity and secrecy 85, 95–6
    mislabeling 84, 86, 95
    multiple actors 84, 91–3
    routinization 84–5, 94, 95
    US policy see US torture policy
    see also interrogation
state victimization 183
state wrongs 29
  as crimes 17–19
state-building measures 227
state-corporate crime model 25–6, 116
'State-Organized Crime' presidential
      address (1988) 7, 32, 69, 72–3, 75–6,
      77, 258
States of Denial 252

Stein, Robert 110–11
Stevens, Ted 16
strategic bombing
    in World War Two 121, 122–3
    see also area bombing; terror bombing
structural adjustment policies (SAPs) 157–9
structural violence 41
structuralist state theory 28t
Sudan
    economic aid from China 163
    see also Darfur
suffering, classification 221–2
Suspect Community 150
Sutherland, Edwin H. 73–4, 103–4
Sweden 27
Switzerland
    heroin maintenance programs 201, 203–5
    safer injection rooms 201, 203
Syria, regime change 37

technological fanaticism, and terror
        bombing 126–7
Tenochca 54
    human sacrifice by 55–6
        festival of Tlacaxipehualitzli 56–8
    sacrificial discourse and practices 58–62
Teotihuacan 60
terror bombing
    normalization see normalization of terror
        bombing
    as a state crime 118, 131–2
terrorists
    assassination of 36
    defining 33
    see also 'war on terror'
theft 4
Third Reich
    suspension of the law 136
    see also Nazis
'three strikes and you're out' 190, 191, 192n
Timor-Leste, transitional justice 219, 222,
        223–4, 225, 230n
Titan 94, 102n
Tlacaxipehualitzli 56–8
Tokyo military tribunals 128, 257
'tolerance areas' see safer injection rooms
'top-down' globalization 153, 158
torture see state torture
torture perpetrators 84, 91–3
traditional public criminology 248–9
transitional justice
    globalization see globalization of
        transitional justice
    growth 215

local endeavours 228–9
overlap with restorative justice 260
transitional justice bodies
    devaluation 227
    legitimacy 229
    see also tribunals; truth commissions
translation, use of private military services
        114
transnational governmentality 27
trauma, classification 221–2
Treaty of Westphalia 236
    see also 'post-Westphalian' developments
tribunals 39–40
    see also international criminal tribunals;
        international military tribunals; war
        crimes tribunals
truth commissions 218
    exclusions and inclusions 225
Turkey, and the Armenian massacres 253

UDHR (Universal Declaration of Human
        Rights) 7, 18, 19
Uganda, crime and IFI policies 158, 161
UN Convention Against Torture 87
'uni-polar' new world order 7
Uniform Code of Military Justice (UCMJ) 64
United Nations 80, 133, 152
    and accountability 258
    as a claims-maker 255
    and harm reduction drug policies 203
    and transitional justice measures 215
    and US drug policies 199–200
        safer injection rooms and heroin
            maintenance 201
United Nations Charter 7, 258
    and genocide 35
    and wars of aggression 34
Universal Declaration of Human Rights
        (UDHR) 7, 18, 19
universalism of law 44
US 27
    contest between the Soviet Union and 34,
        124–5
    differential impunity 97–8
    influence on the World Bank Group (WB)
        156
    'market patriotism' 144
    National Defense Strategy Doctrine 39
    'national security' ideologies 85–6
    presidential speeches 49–52, 65–6
    sacrifice in see sacrifice in the US
    see also American exceptionalism
US drug policy 2, 199–200, 202, 213–14
    and marijuana usage rates 213

medical marijuana 210–11
US empire 31–2, 43, 44, 123, 145–6
  and assassinations 35–7
  civilising mission 143
  and Empire's law 37–9
  and genocide and ethnic cleansing 35
  the 'myth of morality' 133
  and torture, kidnapping and
      imprisonment 37, 44
  and wars of aggression 34–5
  and World War Two 123–5
US torture policy 2, 9, 37, 62, 86, 90–1, 92–3,
      98–9
  dismantling 100–1
  literal denial 253
  see also Abu Ghraib prison; Guantánamo
US-UK invasion and occupation of Iraq 5, 7,
      8, 32, 68
  as a civilizing mission 144
  competition between and within US
      intelligence organizations 93–4
  death squads 42
  law-making violence 141–3
  legitimating narrative 136, 148, 226
  lex mercatoria in 144, 146, 147–8
  military neo-liberalism 108–15
  private security contractors 111–14
  reconstruction 109–12, 134–5
  socio-economic reordering 141–3, 148–9
  and the state of exception 137–43, 148–50
  suspending the normal rule of law 137–44
  transitional justice 223, 224–5, 226
  violations of human rights and
      international law 18
  see also Abu Ghraib prison
utilitarianism, emergence 3, 4

victims 21–2
  as claims-makers 255
  death row exonerees see death row
      exonerees, as victims of state harms
  definition 171
Vietnam War 63
  use of terror bombing 133
violence
  collation and analysis of hard data 222
  constructing political myths 224–6
  legitimation 128–9
  links with business 107–8
  see also economic violence; law-making
      violence; structural violence

war 34–5, 236
  coexistence with law 245

complicity in 34
criminology of 115
effect on the legal and political spheres 117
rationalization of 116
relationship between crime and 115
social construction of the morality of
      goals 121–6
and suicide and self-sacrifice 47
see also conflict; Korean War; US-UK
      invasion and occupation of Iraq;
      Vietnam war; World War Two
war as corporate crime 103–17
  the bellicose corporation 107–12
  'experimental logic' 117
  harm and benefit 103–7
  private security and military industry
      103, 111–14, 115–16
war crimes 2, 8, 73–4, 115
war crimes tribunals 128
  see also Nuremberg trials; Tokyo military
      tribunals
war criminals, punishing 74, 259–60
'war on drugs', US see US drug policy
'war on terror' 68
  use of assassinations 35
  use of 'extraordinary rendition' 37, 96
  see also terrorists; US torture policy
waterboarding 89
wealth redistribution 47
western legal norms
  critique 220
  normalizing international 218–20
western norms
  classifying trauma and suffering 221–2
  dominance and consolidation 218–22, 260
white collar crime 70, 73
White Collar Crime 73
white collar crime 74–5
  concept 103–4
  distinctions between social, political and
      legal definitions 104–6
  in Iraq 140
White-Collar Criminal 74
WHO
  stance on heroin maintenance programs
      205
  substance abuse program 200
World Bank Group (WB) 107, 152, 155–6
  as a control on criminal states 154
  and debt restructuring 155–6
  private sector development (PSD) 156
  user fees for health and education 165
World Court (International Court of Justice)
      35, 39, 258

world financial organizations *see* IFIs
World Health Organization *see* WHO
World Trade Organization (WTO), as a
    control on criminal states 154
World War Two
    and the expansion of the US Empire
        123–5
    as the 'Good War' 122, 125–6, 132
    social construction of the morality of war
        goals 121–6
    terror bombing of civilians 119–20, 122–3
        absence of enforcement and
            legitimation of violence 127–9
        erosion of constraints 130–1

Worshipping the Myths of World War II 125–6
wrongful conviction 9, 170–86
    accountability 172–3, 185–6
    of death row exonerees *see* death row
        exonerees
    organizational context conducive to 175

Yugoslavia, international military tribunal
    16, 258

Zambia, user fees for health and education
    165
Zimbabwe, economic aid from China 162–3